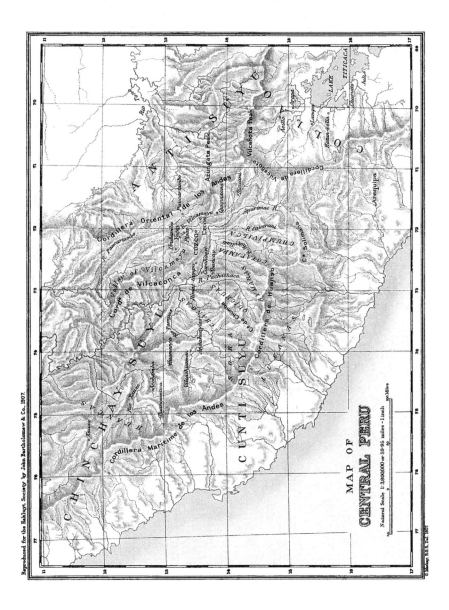

MAP OF
CENTRAL PERU

Natural Scale 1:3,800,000 or 59·95 miles = 1 inch

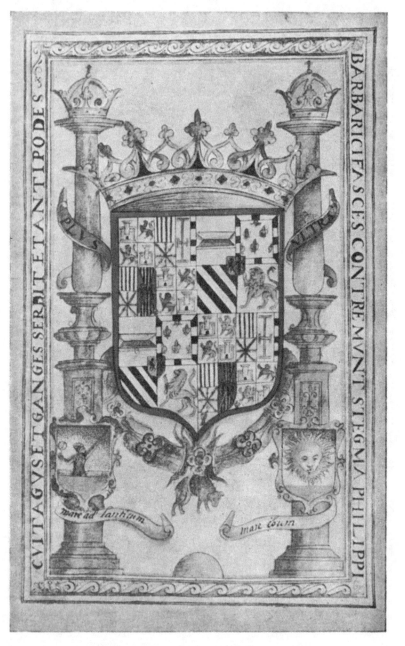

Facsimile (reduced) of the
COAT OF ARMS OF KING PHILIP II.,
From the Sarmiento MS., 1572, Göttingen University Library.

Reproduced and printed for the Hakluyt Society by Donald Macbeth.

HISTORY OF THE INCAS

PEDRO SARMIENTO DE GAMBOA

DOVER PUBLICATIONS, INC.
Mineola, New York

Published in Canada by General Publishing Company, Ltd., 30 Lesmill Road, Don Mills, Toronto, Ontario.
Published in the United Kingdom by Constable and Company, Ltd., 3 The Lanchesters, 162–164 Fulham Palace Road, London W6 9ER.

Bibliographical Note

This Dover edition, first published in 1999, is an unabridged republication of *History of the Incas by Pedro Sarmiento de Gamboa and The Execution of the Inca Tupac Amaru by Captain Baltasar de Ocampo*, translated and edited with notes and an introduction by Sir Clements Markham, which was originally published by The Hakluyt Society and printed at The University Press, Cambridge, England, in 1907.

Library of Congress Cataloging-in-Publication Data

Sarmiento de Gamboa, Pedro, 1532?–1608?
   [Historia de los Incas. English]
   History of the Incas / Pedro Sarmiento de Gamboa.
      p.   cm.
   English translation originally published: Cambridge : Printed for the Hakluyt Society, 1907. (Works issued by the Hakluyt Society, 2nd ser., no. 22)
   Includes The execution of the Inca Tupac Amaru by Baltasar de Ocampo.
   Translated and edited with notes and an introduction by Sir Clements Markham.
   Includes bibliographical references and index.
   ISBN 0-486-40441-2 (pbk.)
   1. Peru—History—To 1548. 2. Indians of South America—Peru—History. 3.   Incas—History. 4. Tupac Amaru, Inca, d. 1571. 5. Peru—History—Bibliography. I. Ocampo, Baltasar de, fl. 1610. Descripcion de la provincia de Sant Francisco de la Vitoria de Villcapampa. English. 1999. II. Markham, Clements R. (Clements Robert), Sir, 1830–1916. III. Title.
G161.H23 2d ser., no. 22, 1999
[F3429]
985'.01—dc21   98-38954
                                                    CIP

Manufactured in the United States of America
Dover Publications, Inc., 31 East 2nd Street, Mineola, N.Y. 11501

TABLE OF CONTENTS.

PAGE

LIST OF ILLUSTRATIONS.

Plates 2—7 have been reproduced from the negatives, kindly lent for the purpose by Professor Dr Richard Pietschmann, Director of the Göttingen University Library.

PORTRAITS OF THE INCAS.

INTRODUCTION.

THE publication of the text of the Sarmiento manuscript in the Library of Göttingen University, has enabled the Council to present the members of the Hakluyt Society with the most authentic narrative of events connected with the history of the Incas of Peru.

The history of this manuscript, and of the documents which accompanied it, is very interesting. The Viceroy, Don Francisco de Toledo, who governed Peru from 1569 to 1581, caused them to be prepared for the information of Philip II. Four cloths were sent to the King from Cuzco, and a history of the Incas written by Captain Pedro Sarmiento de Gamboa. On three cloths were figures of the Incas with their wives, on medallions, with their *Ayllus* and a genealogical tree. Historical events in each reign were depicted on the borders. The fable of Tampu-tocco was shown on the first cloth, and also the fables touching the creations of Viracocha, which formed the foundation for the whole history. On the fourth cloth there was a map of Peru, the compass lines for the positions of towns being drawn by Sarmiento.

The Viceroy also caused reports to be made to him, to prove that the Incas were usurpers. There were thirteen reports from Cuzco, Guamanga, Xauxa, Yucay, and other places, forming a folio of 213 leaves, preserved in the *Archivo de Indias*[1]. At Cuzco all the Inca descendants

---

[1] Printed in the same volume with Montesinos, and edited by Jimenes de la Espada, *Informaciones acerca del señorio y gobierno de los Ingas hechas por mandado de Don Francisco de Toledo*, 1570—72.

were called upon to give evidence respecting the history of Peru under their ancestors. They all swore that they would give truthful testimony. The compilation of the history was then entrusted to Captain Pedro Sarmiento de Gamboa, the cosmographer of Peru. When it was completed the book was read to the Inca witnesses, chapter by chapter, in their own language. They discussed each chapter, and suggested some corrections and alterations which were adopted. It was then submitted to the Viceroy, who caused the documents to be attested by the principal Spaniards settled at Cuzco, who had been present at the conquest, or had taken a leading part in the subsequent administration. These were Dr Loarte, the licentiate Polo de Ondegardo[1], Alonso de Mena[2], Mancio Sierra de Leguisano[3], Pedro Alonso Carrasco, and Juan de Pancorvo[4], in whose house the Viceroy resided while he was at Cuzco. Mancio Sierra de Leguisano married Beatriz Ñusta, an Inca princess, daughter of Huayna Ccapac. The Viceroy then made some final interpolations to vilify the Incas, which would not have been approved by some of those who had attested, certainly not by Polo de Ondegardo or Leguisano.

Sarmiento mentions in his history of the Incas that it was intended to be the Second Part of his work. There were to be three Parts. The First, on the geography of Peru, was not sent because it was not finished. The Third Part was to have been a narrative of the conquest.

The four cloths, and the other documents, were taken to Spain, for presentation to the King, by a servant of the

---

[1] The accomplished lawyer, author, and statesman.

[2] One of the first conquerors. His house at Cuzco was in the square of our Lady, near that of Garcilasso de la Vega.

[3] A generous defender of the cause of the Indians.

[4] One of the first conquerors. He occupied a house near the square, with his friend and comrade Alonso de Marchena.

Viceroy named Geronimo Pacheco, with a covering letter dated at Yucay on March 1st, 1572.

Of all these precious documents the most important was the history of the Incas by Sarmiento, and it has fortunately been preserved. The King's copy found its way into the famous library of Abraham Gronovius, which was sold in 1785, and thence into the library of the University of Göttingen, where it remained, unprinted and unedited, for 120 years. But in August, 1906, the learned librarian, Dr Richard Pietschmann published the text at Berlin, very carefully edited and annotated with a valuable introduction. The Council of the Hakluyt Society is thus enabled to present an English translation to its members very soon after the first publication of the text. It is a complement of the other writings of the great navigator, which were translated and edited for the Hakluyt Society in 1895.

The manuscript consists of eight leaves of introduction and 138 of text. The dedicatory letter to the King is signed by Sarmiento on March 4th, 1572. The binding was of red silk, under which there is another binding of green leather. The first page is occupied by a coloured shield of the royal arms, with a signature *el Capitã Sarmi de Gãboa*. On the second page is the title, surrounded by an ornamental border. The manuscript is in a very clear hand, and at the end are the arms of Toledo (*chequy azure and argent*) with the date Cuzco, 29 Feb., 1572. There is also the signature of the Secretary, Alvaro Ruiz de Navamuel[1].

---

[1] Alvaro Ruiz and his brother Captain Francisco Ruiz were the sons of Francisco Santiago Rodriguez de los Rios by Inez de Navamuel. Both used their mother's name of Navamuel as their surname; and both were born at Aquilar del Campo. Alvaro Ruiz de Navamuel was Secretary to the governments of five successive Viceroys. He wrote a *Relacion de las cosas mas notables que hiza en el Peru, siendo Virev Don Francisco de Toledo*, 20 Dec. 1578. He

The history of the Incas by Sarmiento is, without any doubt, the most authentic and reliable that has yet appeared. For it was compiled from the carefully attested evidence of the Incas themselves, taken under official sanction. Each sovereign Inca formed an *ayllu* or "gens" of his descendants, who preserved the memory of his deeds in *quipus*, songs, and traditions handed down and learnt by heart. There were many descendants of each of these *ayllus* living near Cuzco in 1572, and the leading members were examined on oath; so that Sarmiento had opportunities of obtaining accurate information which no other writer possessed. For the correct versions of the early traditions, and for historical facts and the chronological order of events, Sarmiento is the best authority.

But no one can supersede the honest and impartial old soldier, Pedro de Cieza de Leon, as regards the charm of his style and the confidence to be placed in his opinions; nor the Inca Garcilasso de la Vega as regards his reminiscences and his fascinating love for his people. Molina and Yamqui Pachacuti give much fuller details respecting the ceremonial festivals and religious beliefs. Polo de Ondegardo and Santillana supply much fuller and more reliable information respecting the laws and administration of the Incas. It is in the historical narrative and the correct order of events that Sarmiento, owing to his exceptional means of collecting accurate information, excels all other writers.

---

died in the year 1613. The descendants of his son Juan de los Rios formed the *mayorazgos* of Rios and Cavallero.

By his wife Angela Ortiz de Arbildo y Berriz, a Biscayan, he had a daughter Inez married to her cousin Geronimo Aliaga, a son of the Secretary's brother Captain Francisco Ruiz de Navamuel, the *encomendero* of Caracoto in the Collao, by Juana, daughter of Captain Geronimo de Aliaga. His marriage, at which the Viceroy Toledo was present, took place on November 23rd, 1578. From the marriage of the younger Geronimo de Aliaga with Inez Navamuel, descend the Aliagas, Counts of Luringancho in Peru.

There is one serious blemish. Sarmiento's book was written, not only or mainly to supply interesting information, but with an object. Bishop Las Casas had made Europe ring with the cruelties of the Spaniards in the Indies, and with the injustice and iniquity of their conquests. Don Francisco de Toledo used this narrative for the purpose of making a feeble reply to the good bishop. Under his instructions Sarmiento stated the Viceroy's argument, which was that the King of Spain was the rightful sovereign of Peru because the Incas had usurped their power by conquest and had been guilty of acts of cruelty. Hence the constant repetition of such phrases as "cruel tyranny" and "usurping tyrant"; and the numerous interpolations of the Viceroy himself are so obvious that I have put them in italics within brackets. He goes back as far as the first Inca to make out the usurpation, and he is always harping on illegitimacy. If we go back as far as Sancho IV the title of Philip II to Spain was voided by the grossest usurpation, while we need only go back to Henry II to see how Philip's title was vitiated by illegitimacy. As for cruelty, it would be a strange plea from the sovereign by whose orders the Netherlands were devastated, the Moors of Granada almost annihilated, and under whose rule the Inquisition was in full swing. It is the old story of preaching without practice, as Dr Newman once observed in quoting what James I said to George Heriot:

"O Geordie, jingling Geordie, it was grand to hear Baby Charles laying down the guilt of dissimulation, and Steenie lecturing on the turpitude of incontinence."

It is right to say that Philip never seems to have endorsed the argument of his Viceroy, while his father prohibited the circulation of a book by Dr Sepulveda which contained a similar argument; nor was the work of Sarmiento published.

Barring this blemish, the history of the Incas, written by order of the Viceroy Toledo, is a most valuable addition to the authorities who have given us authentic accounts of Andean civilization; for we may have every confidence in the care and accuracy of Sarmiento as regards his collection and statement of historical facts, provided that we always keep in mind the bias, and the orders he was under, to seek support for the Viceroy's untenable argument.

I have given all I have been able to find respecting the life of Sarmiento in the introduction to my edition of the voyages of that celebrated navigator.

But the administration of the Viceroy Don Francisco de Toledo, from 1569 to 1581, forms a landmark in the history of Peru, and seems to call for some notice in this place. He found the country in an unsettled state, with the administrative system entirely out of gear. Though no longer young he entered upon the gigantic task of establishing an orderly government, and resolved to visit personally every part of the vast territory under his rule. This stupendous undertaking occupied him for five years. He was accompanied by ecclesiastics, by men well versed in the language of the Incas and in their administrative policy, and by his secretary and aide-de-camp. These were the Bishop of Popayan, Augustin de la Coruña, the Augustine friars Juan Vivero and Francisco del Corral, the Jesuit and well-known author, Joseph de Acosta, the Inquisitor Pedro Ordoñez Flores, his brother, the Viceroy's chaplain and confessor, the learned lawyer Juan Matienzo, whose work is frequently quoted by Solorzano[1], the licentiate Polo de Ondegardo, who had been some years in the country and had acquired an intimate knowledge of the laws of the Incas, the secretary Alvaro Ruiz de Navamuel, and as aide-de-camp his young nephew, Geronimo de

---

[1] In his *Politica Indiana*. There are two manuscripts of Juan Matienzo de Peralta at the British Museum, *Govierno del Peru* and *Relacion del libro intitulado Govierno del Peru*, apparently one work in two parts. *Add. MSS.* 5469, in Gayangos Catalogue, vol. II. p. 470.

Figueroa, son of his brother Juan, the Ambassador at Rome[1].

Toledo was endowed with indefatigable zeal for the public service, great energy, and extraordinary powers of application. He took the opinions of others, weighed them carefully, and considered long before he adopted any course. But he was narrow-minded and obstinate, and when he had once determined on a measure nothing could alter him. His ability is undoubted, and his appointment, at this particular juncture, is a proof of Philip's sagacity.

The Viceroy's intercourse with Polo de Ondegardo informed him respecting the administrative system of the Incas, so admirably adapted to the genius of the people, and he had the wisdom to see that there was much to learn from it. His policy was to collect the people, who, to a great extent, were scattered over the country and hiding from the Spaniards, in villages placed near the centres of their cultivated or pasture lands. He fixed the numbers in each village at 400 to 500, with a priest and Alcalde. He also ordered the boundaries of all the parishes to be settled. Spanish Corregidors were to take the places of the *Tucuyricoc* or governors of Inca times, and each village had an elected Alcalde approved by the Corregidor. Under him there were to be two overseers, a *Pichca pachaca* over 500, and a *Pachaca* as assistant. Another important measure was the settlement of the tribute. The name "tribute" was unfortunate. The system was that of the Incas, and the same which prevailed throughout the east. The government was the landlord, and the so-called "tribute" was rent. The Incas took two-thirds for the

---

[1] Some sons took the father's surname, others that of the mother. The Viceroy had the name of his father, Francisco Alvarez de Toledo, the third Count of Oropesa, while his brother Juan had the surname of Figueroa, being that of his mother.

state and for religion, and set apart one-third for the
cultivators. Toledo did much the same, assessing, according to the nature of the soil, the crops, and other local
circumstances. For the formation of villages and the
assessment of the tribute he promulgated a whole code
of ordinances, many of them intended to prevent local
oppression in various forms.

The Viceroy next took up the questions of the position
of *yanacunas* or domestic servants, and of forced service.
Both these institutions existed in Incarial times. All that
was needed were moderate laws for the protection of servants
and conscripts, and the enforcement of such laws. Toledo
allowed a seventh of the adult male population in each
village to be made liable for service in mines or factories,
fixed the distance they could be taken from their homes,
and made rules for their proper treatment. It is true that
the *mita*, as it was called, was afterwards an instrument of
cruel oppression, that rules were disregarded, and that it
depopulated the country. But this was not the fault of
Toledo.

The Viceroy gave much attention to the mining industry, promoted the introduction of the use of mercury
in the extraction of silver, and founded the town of
Huancavelica near the quick-silver mine. His personality
pervaded every department of the state, and his *tasas* or
ordinances fill a large volume. He was a prolific legislator
and a great statesman.

His worst mistake was the policy he adopted with
regard to the family of the Incas. He desired to establish
the position of the King of Spain without a rival. He,
therefore, sought to malign the preceding dynasty, perse-
cuted the descendants of the Incas, and committed one act
of cruel injustice.

When Atahualpa put his half-brother Huascar, the last
reigning Inca, to death, there remained three surviving sons

of their father the great Inca Huayna Ccapac, named Manco, Paullu, and Titu Atauchi, and several daughters. After his occupation of Cuzco, Pizarro acknowledged Manco Inca as the legitimate successor of his brother Huascar, and he was publicly crowned, receiving all the insignia on March 24th, 1534. He escaped from the Spaniards and besieged them in Cuzco at the head of a large army. Forced to raise the siege he established his headquarters at Ollantay-tampu, where he repulsed an attack led by Hernando Pizarro. He was, however, defeated by Orgoñez, the lieutenant of Almagro, and took refuge in the mountainous province of Vilcapampa on the left bank of the Vilcamayu. From thence he made constant attacks on the Spaniards, maintaining his independence in this small remnant of his dominions. Some of the partisans of Almagro took refuge with him, and he was accidentally killed by one of them in 1544, after a not inglorious reign of ten years.

He left two legitimate sons, named Sayri Tupac and Tupac Amaru, by his wife and niece the Princess Ataria Cusi Huarcay, daughter of his ill-fated brother Huascar. This marriage was legalized by a bull of Pope Paul III in the time of the Viceroy Marquis of Cañete, 1555—1561. He had also an illegitimate son named Cusi Titu Yupanqui, and a daughter named Maria Tupac Usca, married to Don Pedro Ortiz de Orue, one of the first conquerors[1].

---

[1] Pedro Ortiz de Orue was born in the village of Getafe, near Madrid. He went out to Peru in 1559, and at once began to study the Quichua language. He was *encomendero* of Maras, a village overlooking the valley of Yucay. By the Inca princess he had a daughter named Catalina married to Don Luis Justiniani of Seville, descended from the Genoese family. Their son Luis was the grandfather of Dr Justo Pastor Justiniani who married Manuela Cataño, descended from Tupac Inca Yupanqui. Their son Don Pablo Justiniani was Cura of Laris until his death in 1858, and was a great depository of Inca lore. He had a very early copy of the Inca drama of Ollanta.

Sayri Tupac succeeded as fourteenth Inca of Peru. On the arrival of the Marquis of Cañete as Viceroy in 1555, he caused overtures to be made to Sayri Tupac through his aunts, who were living at Cuzco with their Spanish husbands, Juan Sierra de Leguisano and Diego Hernandez. It was finally arranged that the Inca should receive 17000 *castellanos* of rent and the valley of Yucay. On October 7th, 1557, Sayri Tupac left Vilcapampa with 300 followers, reaching Andahuaylas on November 5th. He entered Lima on January 6th, 1558, was cordially greeted by the Viceroy and received investiture, assuming the names of Manco Ccapac Pachacuti Yupanqui. He went to live in the lovely vale of Yucay. He had been baptized with the name of Diego, but he did not long survive, dying at Yucay in 1560. His daughter Clara Beatriz married Don Martin Garcia Loyola. Their daughter Lorenza was created Marchioness of Oropesa and Yucay, with remainder to descendants of her great uncle Tupac Amaru. She was the wife of Juan Henriquez de Borja, grandson of the Duke of Gandia.

On the death of Sayri Tupac, his illegitimate brother, Cusi Titu Yupanqui assumed sovereignty, owing to the youth of the legitimate brother Tupac Amaru, both remaining in Vilcapampa.

Paullu Tupac Yupanqui, the next brother of Manco Inca, was baptized with the name of Cristóval. He accompanied Almagro in his expedition to Chile, and was with young Almagro at the battle of Chupas. Eventually he was allowed to fix his residence on the Colcampata of Cuzco, at the foot of the fortress, and by the side of the church of San Cristóval. From the terrace of the Colcampata there is a glorious view with the snowy peak of Vilcañota in the far distance. Paullu died in May, 1549, and was succeeded on the Colcampata by his son Carlos Inca. He had two other sons named Felipe and Bartolomé.

From the latter was descended the late Archdeacon of Cuzco, Dr Justo Salmaraura Inca.

Titu Atauchi, the youngest son of Huayna Ccapac, had a son Alonso.

The princesses, daughters of Huayna Ccapac and sisters of Manco and Paullu, were Beatriz Ñusta, married first to Martin de Mustincia, and secondly to Diego Hernandez of Talavera; Leonor Ñusta, the wife of Juan de Balsa, who was killed at the battle of Chupas on the side of young Almagro, secondly of Francisco de Villacastin : Francisca Ñusta, niece of Huayna Ccapac, married to Juan de Collantes, and was great-grandmother of Bishop Piedrahita, the historian of Nueva Granada : another Beatriz Ñusta married Mancio Sierra de Leguisano, the generous defender of the natives; and Inez Ñusta married first Francisco Pizarro and had a daughter Francisca, who has descendants, and secondly to Francisco Ampuero. Angelina, daughter of Atahualpa, was married to Juan de Betanzos, the author and Quichua scholar. The brother of Huayna Ccapac, named Hualpa Tupac Yupanqui, had a daughter, Isabel Ñusta Yupanqui, the wife of Garcilasso de la Vega, and mother of the Inca Garcilasso de la Vega[1], the historian, author of the *Comentarios Reales.*

This then was the position of the Inca family when the Viceroy, Francisco de Toledo, came to Cuzco in 1571. Cusi Titu Yupanqui and Tupac Amaru, sons of the Inca Manco were in the mountains of Vilcapampa, the former maintaining his independence. Carlos Inca, son of Paullu, was baptized, and living on the Colcampata at Cuzco with his wife Maria de Esquivel. Seven Inca princesses had married Spaniards, most of them living at Cuzco with their husbands and children.

---

[1] The Inca Garcilasso was a third cousin of the regicide Viceroy Toledo. Their great grandfathers were brothers.

The events, connected with the Inca family, which followed on the arrival of the Viceroy Toledo at Cuzco, will be found fully described in this volume. It need only be stated here that the inexorable tyrant, having got the innocent young prince Tupac Amaru into his power, resolved to put him to death. The native population was overwhelmed with grief. The Spaniards were horrified. They entreated that the lad might be sent to Spain to be judged by the King. The heads of religious orders and other ecclesiastics went down on their knees. Nothing could move the obstinate narrow-minded Viceroy. The deed was done.

When too late Toledo seems to have had some misgivings. The judicial murder took place in December, 1571. The history of the Incas was finished in March, 1572. Yet there is no mention of the death of Tupac Amaru. For all that appears he might have been still in Vilcapampa. Nevertheless the tidings reached Philip II, and the Viceroy's conduct was not approved.

There was astonishing audacity on the part of Toledo, in basing arguments on the alleged cruelty and tyranny of the Incas, when the man was actually red-handed with the blood of an innocent youth, and engaged in the tyrannical persecution of his relations and the hideous torture of his followers. His arguments made no impression on the mind of Philip II. The King even showed some favour to the children of Tupac Amaru by putting them in the succession to the Marquisate of Oropesa. In the Inca pedigrees Toledo is called "el execrable regicidio." When he presented himself on his return from Peru the King angrily exclaimed: "Go away to your house; for I sent you to serve kings; and you went to kill kings[1]."

---

[1] "Idos a vuestra casa, que yo os envie a servir reyes; y vos fuiste a matar reyes."

All his faithful services as a legislator and a statesman could not atone for this cruel judicial murder in the eyes of his sovereign. He went back to his house a disgraced and broken-hearted man, and died soon afterwards.

The history of the Incas by Sarmiento is followed, in this volume, by a narrative of the execution of Tupac Amaru and of the events leading to it, by an eye-witness, the Captain Baltasar de Ocampo. It has been translated from a manuscript in the British Museum.

The narrative of Ocampo, written many years after the event, is addressed to the Viceroy Marquis of Montes Claros. Its main object was to give an account of the province of Vilcapampa, and to obtain some favours for the Spanish settlers there.

Vilcapampa is a region of very special historical and geographical interest, and it is one of which very little is known. It is a mountainous tract of country, containing the lofty range of Vilcacunca and several fertile valleys, between the rivers Apurimac and Vilcamayu, to the north of Cuzco. The mountains rise abruptly from the valley of the Vilcamayu below Ollantay-tampu, where the bridge of Chuqui-chaca opened upon paths leading up into a land of enchantment. No more lovely mountain scenery can be found on this earth. When Manco Inca escaped from the Spaniards he took refuge in Vilcapampa, and established his court and government there. The Sun temple, the convent of virgins, and the other institutions of the Incas at Cuzco, were transferred to this mountain fastness. Even handsome edifices were erected. Here the Incas continued to maintain their independence for 35 years.

Ocampo opens his story with a very interesting account of the baptism of Melchior Carlos, son of Carlos Inca, who had become a Christian, and lived in the palace on the Colcampata at Cuzco. He then describes the events which culminated in the capture of the Inca Tupac Amaru, and gives a pathetic and touching account of the judicial murder of that ill-fated young prince. Ocampo was an actor in these events and an eye-witness. The rest of his narrative consists of reminiscences of occurrences in Vilcapampa after it was occupied by the Spaniards. He owned property there, and was a settler holding official posts. He tells of the wealth and munificence of a neighbour. He gives the history of an expedition into the forests to the northward, which will form material for the history of these expeditions when it is written. He tells the story of an insurrection among the negro labourers, and complains of the spiritual destitution of his adopted land. He finally returns to Cuzco and gives an account of a very magnificent pageant and tilting match. But this story should have preceded the mournful narrative of the fate of Tupac Amaru; for the event took place at the time of the baptism of Melchior Carlos, and before the Viceroy Toledo became a regicide. Ocampo's story is that of an honest old soldier, inclined to be garrulous, but an eye-witness of some most interesting events in the history of Peru.

I think it is an appropriate sequel to the history by Sarmiento, because it supplies material for judging whether the usurpation and tyranny were on the side of the Incas or of their accuser.

THE

SECOND PART

OF THE

GENERAL HISTORY

CALLED

"INDICA"

WHICH WAS COMPOSED

BY

THE CAPTAIN PEDRO SARMIENTO DE GAMBOA

BY ORDER OF

THE MOST EXCELLENT
LORD DON FRANCISCO DE TOLEDO

VICEROY GOVERNOR AND CAPTAIN-GENERAL

OF THE

KINGDOMS OF PERU
AND MAYOR-DOMO OF THE ROYAL HOUSEHOLD
OF CASTILLE

1572

BARBARICIFA&CE&
CONTREMVNT&TEGM
PHILIPPI: CVITAGVS
ETGANGES SERVITET
AN TIPODES&

PLVS   VLTRA

Facsimile (reduced) of
PAGE 1 OF THE SARMIENTO MS. 1572.
From the original, Göttingen University Library.
Reproduced and printed for the Hakluyt Society by Donald Macbeth.

Facsimile (reduced) of
PAGE II OF THE SARMIENTO MS. 1572.
From the original, Göttingen University Library.

Reproduced and printed for the Hakluyt Society by Donald Macbeth.

TO HIS SACRED CÆSARIAN MAJESTY THE KING, DON FELIPE, OUR LORD.

Among the excellencies, O sovereign and catholic Philip, that are the glorious decorations of princes, placing them on the highest pinnacle of estimation, are, according to the father of Latin eloquence, generosity, kindness, and liberality. And as the Roman Consuls held this to be the principal praise of their glory, they had this title curiously sculptured in marble on the Quirinal and in the forum of Trajan—" Most powerful gift in a Prince is liberality[1]." For this kings who desired much to be held dear by their own people and to be feared by strangers, were incited to acquire the name of liberal. Hence that royal sentence became immortal " It is right for kings to give." As this was a quality much valued among the Greeks, the wise Ulysses, conversing with Antinous[2], King of the Phæacians, said—" You are something like a king, for you know how to give, better than others." Hence it is certain that liberality is a good and necessary quality of kings.

I do not pretend on this ground, most liberal monarch, to insinuate to your Majesty the most open frankness, for it would be very culpable on my part to venture to suggest a thing which, to your Majesty, is so natural that you would be unable to live without it. Nor will it happen to so high minded and liberal a lord and king, what befell the Emperor Titus who, remembering once, during supper

---

[1] " Primum signum nobilitatis est liberalitas."

[2] Alcinous.

time, that he had allowed one day to pass without doing some good, gave utterance to this laudable animadversion of himself. "O friends! I have lost a day[1]." For not only does your Majesty not miss a day, but not even an hour, without obliging all kinds of people with benefits and most gracious liberality. The whole people, with one voice, says to your Majesty what Virgil sang to Octavianus Augustus:

> "Nocte pluit tota, redeunt spectacula mane,
> Divisum imperium cum Jove Cæsar habet."

But what I desire to say is that for a king who complies so well with the obligation of liberality, and who gives so much, it is necessary that he should possess much; for nothing is so suitable for a prince as possessions and riches for his gifts and liberalities, as Tully says, as well as to acquire glory. For it is certain, as we read in Sallust that "in a vast empire there is great glory[2]"; and in how much it is greater, in so much it treats of great things. Hence the glory of a king consists in his possessing many vassals, and the abatement of his glory is caused by the diminution of the number of his subjects.

Of this glory, most Christian king, God Almighty gives you so large a share in this life that all the enemies of the holy catholic church of Christ our Lord tremble at your exalted name; whence you most justly deserve to be named the strength of the church. As the treasure which God granted that your ancestors should spend, with such holy magnanimity, on worthy and holy deeds, in the extirpation of heretics, in driving the accursed Saracens out of Spain, in building churches, hospitals and monasteries, and in an infinite number of other works of charity and justice, with the zeal of zealous fathers of their country,

---

[1] "Amici! diem perdidi." Suetonius.
[2] Proem of Catiline.

not only entitled them to the most holy title of catholics, but the most merciful and almighty God, whom they served with all their hearts, saw fit to commence repayment with temporal goods, in the present age. It is certain that "He who grants celestial rewards does not take away temporal blessings[1]," so that they earned more than the mercies they received. This was the grant to them of the evangelical office, choosing them from among all the kings of this world as the evangelizers of his divine word in the most remote and unknown lands of those blind and barbarous gentiles. We now call those lands the Indies of Castille, because through the ministry of that kingdom they will be put in the way of salvation, God himself being the true pilot. He made clear and easy the dark and fearful Atlantic sea which had been an awful portent to the most ancient Argives, Athenians, Egyptians, and Phœnicians, and what is more to the proud Hercules, who, having come to Cadiz from the east, and seen the wide Atlantic sea, he thought this was the end of the world and that there was no more land. So he set up his columns with this inscription "Ultra Gades nil" or "Beyond Cadiz there is nothing." But as human knowledge is ignorance in the sight of God, and the force of the world but weakness in his presence, it was very easy, with the power of the Almighty and of your grandparents, to break and scatter the mists and difficulties of the enchanted ocean. Laughing with good reason at Alcides and his inscription, they discovered the Indies which were very populous in souls to whom the road to heaven could be shown. The Indies are also most abundant in all kinds of inestimable treasures, with which the heavy expenses were repaid to them, and

---

[1] From the poem of Cœlius Sedulius, a Christian poet who flourished about A.D. 450. The passage is—"Hostis Herodes impie Christum venire quod timeo? Non eripit mortalia qui regna dat cœlestia." (Note by Dr Peitschmann.)

yet remained the richest princes in the world, and thus continued to exercise their holy and Christian liberality until death. By reason of this most famous navigation, and new and marvellous discovery, they amended the inscription on the columns of Hercules, substituting " Plus ultra " for " Ultra Gades nil "; the meaning was, and with much truth, that further on there are many lands. So this inscription, " Plus ultra," remained on the blazon of the arms and insignia of the Indies of Castille.

As there are few who are not afflicted by the accursed hunger for gold, and as good successes are food for an enemy, the devil moved the bosoms of some powerful princes with the desire to take part in this great business. Alexander VI, the Vicar of Jesus Christ, considering that this might give rise to impediments in preaching the holy evangel to the barbarous idolaters, besides other evils which might be caused, desired of his own proper motion, without any petition from the catholic kings, by authority of Almighty God, to give, and he gave and conceded for ever, the islands and main lands which were then discovered and which might hereafter be discovered within the limits and demarcation of 180° of longitude, which is half the world, with all the dominions, rights, jurisdictions and belongings, prohibiting the navigation and trading in those lands from whatever cause, to the other princes, kings, and emperors from the year 1493, to prevent many inconveniences.

But as the devil saw that this door was shut, which he had begun to open to introduce by it dissensions and disturbances, he tried to make war by means of the very soldiers who resisted him, who were the same preachers. They began to make a difficulty about the right and title which the kings of Castille had over these lands. As your invincible father was very jealous in matters touching his conscience, he ordered this point to be examined, as closely as possible, by very learned doctors who, according to the report which was given out, were indirect and doubtful in their conclusions. They gave it as their opinion that these Incas, who ruled in these kingdoms of Peru, were and are the true and natural lords of that land. This gave a handle to foreigners, as well catholics as heretics and other infidels, for throwing doubt on the right which the kings of Spain claim and have claimed to the Indies. Owing to this the Emperor Don Carlos of glorious memory was on the point of abandoning them, which was what the enemy of the faith of Christ wanted, that he might regain the possession of the souls which he had kept in blindness for so many ages.

All this arose owing to want of curiosity on the part of the governors in those lands, at that time, who did not use the diligence necessary for ascertaining the truth, and also owing to certain reports of the Bishop of Chiapa who was moved to passion against certain conquerors in his bishoprick with whom he had persistent disputes, as I knew when I passed through Chiapa and Guatemala[1]. Though his zeal appears holy and estimable, he said things on the right to this country gained by the conquerors of it, which differ from the evidence and judicial proofs which have been seen and taken down by us, and from what we who have travelled over the Indies enquiring about these things, leisurely and without war, know to be the facts[2].

---

[1] See the introduction to my *Voyages of Sarmiento*, p. x.

[2] Sarmiento here refers to the efforts of Las Casas to protect the natives from the tyranny and cruelties of the Spanish settlers. He appears to have been in Guatemala when Las Casas arrived to take up his appointment as Bishop of Chiapas, and encountered hostility and obstruction from certain "conquistadores de su obispado," as Sarmiento calls them. On his return to Spain, the good Las Casas found that a certain Dr Sepulveda had written a treatise maintaining the right of Spain to subdue the natives by war. Las Casas put forward his *Historia Apologetica* in reply. A Junta of theologians was convoked at Valladolid in 1550, before which Sepulveda attacked and Las Casas defended the cause of the natives. Mr Helps (*Spanish conquest in America*, vol. IV. Book xx. ch. 2) has given a lucid account of the controversy. Sarmiento is quite wrong in saying that

This chaos and confusion of ignorance on the subject being so spread over the world and rooted in the opinions of the best informed literary men in Christendom, God put it into the heart of your Majesty to send Don Francisco de Toledo, Mayor-domo of your royal household, as Viceroy of these kingdoms[1]. When he arrived, he found many things to do, and many things to amend. Without resting after the dangers and long voyages in two seas which he had suffered, he put the needful order into all the things

---

Las Casas was ignorant of the history of Peru. The portion of his *Historia Apologetica* relating to Peru, entitled *De las antiguas gentes del Peru*, has been edited and published by Don Marcos Jimenez de la Espada in the "Coleccion de libros Españoles raros ó curiosos" (1892). It shows that Las Casas knew the works of Xeres, Astete, Cieza de Leon, Molina, and probably others ; and that he had a remarkably accurate knowledge of Peruvian history.

[1] Don Francisco de Toledo was Viceroy of Peru, from Nov. 16th, 1569, to Sept. 28th, 1581, and in some respects a remarkable man. He was a younger son of the third Count of Oropesa who had a common ancestor with the Dukes of Alva. His mother was Maria de Figueroa daughter of the Count of Feria. Through her he was directly descended from the first Duke of Alva. He was a first cousin of that Duke of Feria who made a love match with Jane Dormer, the friend and playmate of our Edward VI. Moreover Don Francisco was a third cousin of Charles V. Their great grandmothers were sisters, daughters of Fadrique Henriquez, the Admiral of Castille.

This Viceroy was advanced in years. He held the appointment of a Mayor-domo at the court of Philip II, and another brother Juan was Ambassador at Rome. The Viceroy Toledo came to Peru with the Inquisition, which proved as great a nuisance to him as it was a paralyzing source of terror to his people. He was a man of extraordinary energy and resolution, and was devoted heart and soul to the public service. Sarmiento does not speak too highly of his devotion to duty in undertaking a personal visit to every part of his government. He was a most prolific legislator, founding his rules, to some extent, on the laws of the Incas. He was shrewd but narrow minded and heartless ; and his judicial murder of the young Inca, Tupac Amaru, has cast an indelible stain on his memory.

Such a man could have no chance in an attack on the sound arguments of Las Casas.

There is a picture which depicts the outward appearance of the Viceroy Toledo. A tall man with round stooping shoulders, in a suit of black velvet with the green cross of Alcantara embroidered on his cloak. A gloomy sallow face, with aquiline nose, high forehead and piercing black eyes too close together. The face is shaded by a high beaver hat, while one hand holds a scroll, and the other rests on a table.

SVPERBOSGLADIO: FIDLESPREMIO

Maxima Tolleti Proreges glória creuit,
Dum regni tenebras, lucida cura, fugat
Ite Procul scioli, uobis non locus in istis,
Rex indos noster, nam tenet in nocue.

Facsimile (reduced) of the
COAT OF ARMS OF DON FRANCISCO DE TOLEDO,
VICEROY OF PERU, 1569—1581.
From the Sarmiento MS. 1572, Göttingen University Library.
Reproduced and printed for the Hakluyt Society by Donald Macbeth.

that were necessary. He amended the errors of former times, and laid a sure foundation for the future in such a way that the fruits of his measures will be lasting, because they rest on solid and reasoned foundations. He provided not only for what was his more direct duty, but also for the needs of contiguous governments. Especially he succoured the rich kingdom of Chile with troops and munitions of war, supplying a complete remedy for that land, which was on the point of being lost if help had not promptly come. He provided for the province of Esmeraldas, which would have been entirely neglected if he had not supplied its needs. The government of Yagualsongo and Cumdinama, in Santiago de los Montañas, of which Juan de Salinas had charge, would certainly have been abandoned owing to differences among the Spaniards if his good ruling had not made them listen to reason and respect justice. Besides this it was an object that, in the same government, a very good and rich piece of land should be occupied by Spaniards. When his measures became known throughout this new world, applications for help came from the remotest parts of it. This he gave, both as regards their spiritual and their temporal affairs, to the provinces of Tucuman, Juries, and Diaguitas, giving safety to them which it previously seemed impossible that they could ever secure. In the same way he helped and provided for the government of Santa Cruz de la Sierra, to enable it to check and punish the Chirihuanas, eaters of human flesh who infested this your kingdom of Peru in the direction of Charcas. Thanks to Don Francisco de Toledo are due for his measures to help these provinces and secure their future welfare ; thus giving occupation to all sorts of idle people. This was all done with the utmost diligence. For he did not care to enjoy the pleasures and ease of Lima, where his predecessors lived a life of enchantment. But with that lively and untiring zeal which he has to serve your Majesty, he undertook new and greater labours, such as no former viceroys or governors had undertaken or even thought of. His determination was to travel over this most rugged country himself, to make a general visitation of it, during which, though it is not finished, it is certain that he has remedied many and very great faults and abuses in the teaching and ministry of the Christian doctrine, giving holy and wise advice to its ministers that they should perform their offices as becomes the service of God, and the discharge of your royal conscience, reducing the people to congregations of villages formed on suitable and healthy sites which had formerly been on crags and rocks where they were neither taught nor received spiritual instruction. In such places they lived and died like wild savages, worshipping idols as in the time of their Inca tyrants and of their blind heathenism. Orders were given to stop their public drinking bouts, their concubinage and worship of their idols and devils, emancipating and freeing them from the tyrannies of their *curacas*, and finally giving them a rational life, which was before that of brutes in their manner of loading them as such.

The work done by your Viceroy is such that the Indians are regenerated, and they call him loudly their protector and guardian, and your Majesty who sent him, they call their father. So widely has the news spread of the benefits he has conferred and is still conferring, that the wild warlike Indians in many contiguous provinces, holding themselves to be secure under his word and safe conduct, have come to see and communicate with him, and have promised obedience spontaneously to your Majesty. This has happened in the Andes of Xauxa, near Pilcocanti, and among the Mañaries and Chunchos to the east of Cuzco. These were sent back to their homes, grateful and attached to your royal service, with the presents he gave them and the memory of their reception.

Among Christians, it is not right to take anything

DON FRANCISCO DE TOLEDO,
Viceroy of Peru, A.D. 1569—1581.
After the portrait at Lima, from a sketch by Sir Clements Markham, 1853.

Reproduced for the Hakluyt Society by John Clay.

without a good title, yet that which your Majesty has to these parts, though more holy and more honourable than that which any other kings in the world have for any of their possessions, has suffered detriment, as I said before, in the consciences of many learned men and others, for want of correct information. The Viceroy proposes to do your Majesty a most signal service in this matter, besides the performance of all the other duties of which he has charge. This is to give a secure and quiet harbour to your royal conscience against the tempests raised even by your own natural subjects, theologians and other literary men, who have expressed serious opinions on the subject, based on incorrect information. Accordingly, in his general visitation, which he is making personally throughout the kingdom, he has verified from the root and established by a host of witnesses examined with the greatest diligence and care, taken from among the principal old men of the greatest ability and authority in the kingdom, and even those who pretend to have an interest in it from being relations and descendants of the Incas, the terrible, inveterate and horrible tyranny of the Incas, being the tyrants who ruled in these kingdoms of Peru, and the *curacas* who governed the districts. This will undeceive all those in the world who think that the Incas were legitimate sovereigns, and that the *curacas* were natural lords of the land. In order that your Majesty may, with the least trouble and the most pleasure, be informed, and the rest, who are of a contrary opinion, be undeceived, I was ordered by the Viceroy Don Francisco de Toledo, whom I follow and serve in this general visitation, to take this business in hand, and write a history of the deeds of the twelve Incas of this land, and of the origin of the people, continuing the narrative to the end. This I have done with all the research and diligence that was required, as your Majesty will see in the course of the perusal and by

the ratification of witnesses. It will certify to the truth of
the worst and most inhuman tyranny of these Incas and of
their *curacas* who are not and never were original lords of
the soil, but were placed there by Tupac Inca Yupanqui,
[*the greatest, the most atrocious and harmful tyrant of them
all*]. The *curacas* were and still are great tyrants appointed
by other great and violent tyrants, as will clearly and
certainly appear in the history; so that the tyranny is
proved, as well as that the Incas were strangers in Cuzco,
and that they had seized the valley of Cuzco, and all the
rest of their territory from Quito to Chile by force of arms,
making themselves Incas without the consent or election of
the natives.

Besides this, there are their tyrannical laws and customs.
[*It will be understood that your Majesty has a specially true
and holy title to these kingdoms of Peru, because your
Majesty and your most sacred ancestors stopped the sacrifices
of innocent men, the eating of human flesh, the accursed sin,
the promiscuous concubinage with sisters and mothers, the
abominable use of beasts, and their wicked and accursed
customs[1].*] For from each one God demands an account of
his neighbour, and this duty specially appertains to princes,
and above all to your Majesty. Only for this may war
be made and prosecuted by the right to put a stop to the
deeds of tyrants. Even if they had been true and natural
lords of the soil, it would be lawful to remove them and
introduce a new government, because man may rightly be
punished for these sins against nature, though the native
community has not been opposed to such practices nor
desires to be avenged, as innocent, by the Spaniards. For
in this case they have no right to deliver themselves and
their children over to death, and they should be forced
to observe natural laws, as we are taught by the Archbishop

---

[1] For a contradiction of these slanders by an impartial witness see
Cieza de Leon, ii. p. 78.

of Florence, Innocent, supported by Fray, Francisco de
Victoria in his work on the title to the Indies. So that by
this title alone, without counting many others, your Majesty
has the most sufficient and legitimate right to the Indies,
better than any other prince in the world has to any
lordship whatever. For, whether more or less concealed
or made known, in all the lands that have been discovered
in the two seas of your Majesty, north and south, this
general breaking of the law of nature has been found.

By this same title your Majesty may also, without
scruple, order the conquest of those islands of the archipelago of " Nombre de Jesus," vulgarly but incorrectly
called the Solomon Isles, of which I gave notice and
personally discovered in the year 1567 ; although it was
for the General Alvaro de Mendaña ; and many others
which are in the same South Sea[1]. I offer myself to your
Majesty to discover and settle these islands, which will
make known and facilitate all the commercial navigation,
with the favour of God, by shorter routes. I offer much,
well do I see it, but I trust in almighty God with whose
favour, I believe I can do what I say in your royal service.
The talent which God has given me leads me to aspire to
the accomplishment of these achievements, and does not
demand of me a strict account, and I believe that I shall
comply with what will be required, for never did I so wish
to achieve anything. Your Majesty sees and does not lose
what other kings desire and hold by good fortune. This
makes me speak so freely of my desire to die in your
service in which I have laboured since my childhood, and
under what circumstances others may say.

Believing that, in writing this present history, I have
not done a less but a greater service than all the rest,
I obeyed your Viceroy who made me undertake it. Your

---

[1] See my introduction to the *Voyages of Sarmiento*, pp. xiii—xvii.

Majesty will read it many times because, besides that the reading of it is pleasant, your Majesty will take a great interest in the matters of conscience and of administration of which it treats.   I call this the Second Part, because it is to be preceded by the geographical description of all these lands, which will form the First Part.   This will result in great clearness for the comprehension of the establishment of governments, bishopricks, new settlements, and of discoveries, and will obviate the inconveniences formerly caused by the want of such knowledge.   Although the First Part ought to precede this one in time, it is not sent to your Majesty because it is not finished, a great part of it being derived from information collected during the general visitation.   Suffice that it will be best in quality, though not in time.   After this Second Part will be sent a Third Part on the times of the evangel.   All this I have to finish by order of the Viceroy Don Francisco de Toledo. May your Majesty receive my work with the greatest and most favourable attention, as treating of things that will be of service to God and to your Majesty and of great profit to my nation ; and may our Lord preserve the sacred catholic and royal person of your Majesty, for the repair and increase of the catholic Church of Jesus Christ.

From CUZCO.   *The 4th of March,* 1572.

Your catholic royal Majesty
from the least vassal of your Majesty
The Captain
Pedro Sarmiento de Gamboa.

I.

DIVISION OF THE HISTORY.

This general history of which I took charge by order of Don Francisco de Toledo, Viceroy of these kingdoms of Peru, will be divided into three Parts. The First will be the natural history of these lands, being a particular description of them. It will contain accounts of the marvellous works of nature, and other things of great profit and interest. I am now finishing it, that it may be sent to your Majesty after this, though it ought to have come before it. The Second and Third Parts treat of the people of these kingdoms and of their deeds in the following order. In the Second Part, which is the present one, the most ancient and first peoplers of this land will be discussed in general, and then, descending to particulars, I shall describe [*the terrible and inveterate tyranny of*] the Ccapac Incas of these kingdoms, down to the end and death of Huascar, the last of the Incas. The Third and Last Part will treat of the times of the Spaniards, and of their notable deeds in the discovery and settlement of this kingdom and others adjoining it, with the captains, governors, and viceroys who have ruled here, down to the present year 1572.

II.

THE ANCIENT DIVISION OF THE LAND.

When historians wish to write, in an orderly way, of the world or some part of it, they generally first describe the situation containing it, which is the land, before they deal with what it contains, which is the population, to avoid the former in the historical part. If this is so in ancient and well known works, it is still more desirable that in treating of new and strange lands, like these, of such vast extent, a task which I have undertaken, the same order should be preserved. This will not only supply interesting information but also, which is more to be desired, it will be useful for navigation and new discoveries, by which God our Lord may be served, the territories of the crown of Spain extended, and Spaniards enriched and respected. As I have not yet finished the particular description of this land, which will contain everything relating to geography and the works of nature minutely dealt with, in this volume I shall only offer a general summary, following the most ancient authors, to recall the remains of those lands which are now held to be new and previously unknown, and of their inhabitants.

The land, which we read of as having existed in the first and second age of the world, was divided into five parts. The three continents, of which geographers usually write, Asia, Africa, and Europe, are divided by the river Tanais, the river Nile, and the Mediterranean Sea, which Pomponius calls "our" sea. Asia is divided from Europe by the river Tanais[1], now called Silin, and from Africa by the Nile, though Ptolemy divides it by the Red Sea and isthmus of the desert of Arabia Deserta. Africa is divided from Europe by "our" sea, commencing at the strait of Gibraltar and ending with the Lake of Meotis. The other two parts are thus divided. One was called, and still ought to be called, Catigara[2] in the Indian Sea, a very extensive land now distinct from Asia. Ptolemy describes it as being, in

---

[1] The Don.

[2] Marinus of Tyre, quoted by Ptolemy, gave an enormous extension to eastern Asia, and placed the region he called Catigara far to the S.E. of it. Catigara was described by Marinus of Tyre as an emporium and important place of trade. It is not mentioned in the Periplus of the Erythræan Sea.

his time and in the time of Alexander the Great, joined on
to Asia in the direction of Malacca.   I shall treat of this in
its place, for it contains many and very precious secrets,
and an infinity of souls, to whom the King our Lord may
announce the holy catholic faith that they may be saved,
for this is the object of his Majesty in these new lands of
barbarous idolatry.   The fifth part is or was called the
Atlantic Island, as famous as extensive, and which exceeded
all the others, each one by itself, and even some joined
together.   The inhabitants of it and their description will
be treated of, because this is the land, or at least part of it,
of these western Indies of Castille.

III.

DESCRIPTION OF THE ANCIENT ATLANTIC ISLAND.

The cosmographers do not write of this ancient Atlantic
Island because there was no memory, when they wrote, of
its very rich commercial prosperity in the second, and
perhaps in the first age.   But from what the divine Plato
tells us and from the vestiges we see which agree with what
we read, we can not only say where it was and where parts
of it were, as seen in our time, but we can describe it
almost exactly, its grandeur and position.   This is the
truth, and the same Plato affirms it as true, in the Timæus,
where he gives its truthful and marvellous history.

We will speak first of its situation, and then of its
inhabitants.   It is desirable that the reader should give his
attention because, although it is very ancient history, it is
so new to the ordinary teaching of cosmography that it
may cause such surprise as to raise doubts of the story,
whence may arise a want of appreciation.

From the words which Plato refers to Solon, the

wisest of the seven of Greece, and which Solon had heard with attention from the most learned Egyptian priest in the city called Delta, we learn that this Atlantic Island was larger than Asia and Africa together, and that the eastern end of this immense island was near the strait which we now call of Gibraltar. In front of the mouth of the said strait, the island had a port with a narrow entrance ; and Plato says that the island was truly continental. From it there was a passage by the sea, which surrounded it, to many other neighbouring islands, and to the main land of Europe and Africa. In this island there were kings of great and admirable power who ruled over that and many adjacent islands as well as the greater part of Europe and Africa, up to the confines of Egypt, of which I shall treat presently. The extent of the island was from the south, where were the highest mountains, to the north. The mountains exceeded in extent any that now exist, as well in their forests, as in height, and in beauty. These are the words of Plato in describing the situation of this most richly endowed and delightful Atlantic Island. It now remains for me to do my duty, which is to explain what has been said more clearly and from it to deduce the situation of the island.

From what Plato says that this island had a port near the mouth of the strait of the pillars of Hercules, that it was larger than Asia and Africa together, and that it extended to the south, I gather three things clearly towards the understanding of all that invites attention. The first is that the Atlantic Island began less than two leagues from the mouth of the strait, if more it was only a little more. The coast of the island then turned north close to that of Spain, and was joined to the island of Cadiz or Gadiz, or Caliz, as it is now called. I affirm this for two reasons, one by authority and the other by conjectural demonstration.

The authority is that Plato in his Critias, telling how Neptune distributed the sovereignty of the island among his ten sons, said that the second son was called in the mother tongue " Gadirum," which in Greek we call " Eumelo." To this son he gave the extreme parts of the island near the columns of Hercules, and from his name the place was called Gadiricum which is Caliz. By demonstration we see, and I have seen with my own eyes, more than a league out at sea and in the neighbourhood of the island of Caliz, under the water, the remains of very large edifices of a cement which is almost imperishable[1], an evident sign that this island was once much larger, which corroborates the narrative of Critias in Plato. The second point is that the Atlantic Island was larger than Asia and Africa. From this I deduce its size, which is incredible or at least immense. It would give the island 2300 leagues of longitude, that is from east to west. For Asia has 1500 leagues in a straight line from Malacca which is on its eastern front, to the boundary of Egypt ; and Africa has 800 leagues from Egypt to the end of the Atlantic mountains or " Montes Claros " facing the Canary Islands; which together make 2300 leagues of longitude. If the island was larger it would be more in circuit. Round the coast it would have 7100 leagues, for Asia is 5300 and Africa 2700 leagues in circuit, a little more or less, which together makes 7100 leagues, and it is even said that it was more.

Having considered the measurement of its great size we come to the third point, which is the true position over

---

[1] Dr Peitschmann quotes from Juan Bautista Suarez de Salazar, *Grandezas y antigüedades de la isla y ciudad de Cadiz* (Cadiz, 1610)— "That which all those who traverse the sea affirm was that to the south, the water being clear, there is seen beneath it at a distance of a league, ruins of edifices which are good evidence that the ocean has gained upon the land in this part." He refers also to a more recent history of Cadiz and its province by Adolfo de Castro (1858), and to the five first books of the *General Chronicle of Spain* of Florian de Ocampo, 1552 (lib. ii. cap. 11).

which this great island extended. Plato says that the position of the island extended to the south; opposite to the north. From this we should understand that, the front conterminous with Spain from the strait of Gibraltar to Cadiz thence extended westward, making a curve along the coast of Barbary or Africa, but very close to it, between west and south, which is what sailors call south-west. For if it was opposite to north, which is between east and north, called north-east, it must necessarily have its direction in the said south-west, west-south-west, or south south-west. It would include and incorporate the Canary Islands which, according to this calculation, would be part of it, and from thence the land trended south-west. As regards the south, it would extend rather more to the south and south-south-west, finally following the route by which we go when we sail from Spain to the Indies, forming a continent or main land with these western Indies of Castille, joining on to them by the parts stretching south-west, and west-south-west, a little more or less from the Canaries. Thus there was sea on one side and on the other of this land, that is on the north and south, and the Indies united with it, and they were all one. The proof of this is that if the Atlantic Island had 2300 leagues of longitude, and the distance of Cadiz to the mouth of the river Marañon or Orellana and Trinidad, on the coast of Brazil, is not more than 1000, 900, or 1100 leagues, being the part where this land joined to America, it clearly appears that, to complete the complement of 2300 leagues, we have to include in the computation all the rest of the land from the mouth of the Marañon and Brazil to the South Sea, which is what they now call America. Following this course it would come to Coquimbo. Counting what is still wanting, this would be much less than 2300 leagues. Measuring the circumference, the island was more than 7100 leagues round, because that is about the circumference of Asia and Africa by their coasts. If this land is joined to the other, which in fact it was in conformity with the description, it would have a much greater circuit, for even now these parts of the western Indies, measured by compass, and latitude, have more than 7100 leagues.

From all this it may be inferred that the Indies of Castille formed a continent with the Atlantic Island, and consequently that the same Atlantic Island, which extended from Cadiz over the sea we traverse to the Indies, and which all cosmographers call the Atlantic Ocean because the Atlantic Island was in it, over which we now navigate, was land in ancient times. Finally we shall relate the sequel, first giving an account of the sphere at that time and of the inhabitants.

IV.

FIRST INHABITANTS OF THE WORLD AND PRINCIPALLY OF THE ATLANTIC ISLAND.

Having described the four parts of the world, for of Catigara, which is the fifth, we shall not speak except in its place which the ancients assigned to it, it will be right to come to the races which peopled them. All of which I have to treat has to be personal and heathen history. The chief value and perfection of history consists in its accuracy, thoroughly sifting each event, verifying the times and periods of what happened so that no doubt may remain of what passed. It is in this way that I desire to write the truth in so far as my ability enables me to do so respecting a thing so ancient as the first peopling of these new lands. I wish, for the better illustration of the present history, to precede it with the foundations that cannot be denied, counting the time in conformity with the chronology of the Hebrews in the days before our Saviour Jesus Christ, and the times after his most holy nativity according to the counting used by our mother the holy church, not making account of the calculations of Chaldean or Egyptian interpreters.

Thus, passing over the first age from Adam to the Deluge, which covers 1656 years, we will begin from the second age, which is that of the patriarch Noah, second universal father of mortals. The divine scriptures show us that eight persons were saved from the flood, in the ark. Noah and his wife Terra or Vesta, named from the first fire lighted by crystal for the first sacrifice as Berosus would have: and his three sons to wit, Cam and his wife Cataflua, Sem and his wife Prusia or Persia, Japhet and his wife Funda, as we read in the register of the chronicles. The names of some of these people remain, and to this day we can see clearly whence they were derived, as the Hebrews from Heber, the Assyrians from Asur, but most of them have been so changed that human intelligence is insufficient to investigate by this way. Besides the three sons, Noah had others after the flood.

The descendants of these men having multiplied and become very numerous, Noah divided the world among his first sons that they might people it, and then embarked on the Euxine Sea as we gather from Xenophon. The giant Noah then navigated along the Mediterranean Sea, as Filon says and Annius repeats, dividing the whole land among his sons. He gave it in charge to Sem to people Asia from the Nile to the eastern Indies, with some of the sons he got after the flood. To Cam he gave Africa from the Rinocoruras to the straits of Gibraltar with some more of the sons. Europe was chosen for Japhet to people with the rest of the sons begotten after the flood, who were all the sons of Tuscan, whence descend the Tadescos, Alemanes, and the nations adjacent to them.

In this voyage Noah founded some towns and colonies on the shores of the Mediterranean Sea, and remained in them for ten years, until 112 years after the universal deluge. He ordered his daughter Araxa to remain in Armenia where the ark rested, with her husband and children, to people that country. Then he, with the rest of his companions, went to Mesopotamia and settled. There Nembrot was raised up for king, of the descendants of Cam. This Nembrot, says Berosus, built Babylon 130 years after the flood. The sons of Sem elected for their king, Jektan, son of Heber. Those of Japhet chose Fenec for their king, called Assenes by Moses. There were 300,000 men under him only 310 years after the deluge. Each king, with his companions, set out to people the part of the world chosen for them by the patriarch Noah. It is to be noted that, although Noah divided the parts of the world among his three sons and their descendants, many of them did not keep to the boundaries. For some of one lineage settled on the lands of another brother. Nembrot, being of the line of Cam, remained in the parts of Sem, and many others were mixed together in the same way.

Thus the three parts of the world were peopled by these and their descendants, of whom I do not propose to treat in detail, for our plan is to proceed in our narrative until we come to the inhabitants of the Atlantic Island, the subject of this history. This was so near Spain that, according to the common fame, Caliz used to be so close to the main land in the direction of the port of Santa Maria, that a plank would serve as a bridge to pass from the island to Spain. So that no one can doubt that the inhabitants of Spain, Jubal and his descendants, peopled that land, as well as the inhabitants of Africa which was also near. Hence it was called the Atlantic Island from having been peopled by Atlas, the giant and very wise astrologer who first settled Mauritania now called Barbary, as Godefridus and all the chronicles teach us. This Atlas was the son of Japhet by the nymph Asia, and grandson of Noah. For this there is no authority except the above, corroborated by the divine Plato as I began by explaining, and it will be necessary to seek his help to give the reader such evidence as merits belief respecting the inhabitants of this Atlantic Island.

V.

INHABITANTS OF THE ATLANTIC ISLAND.

We have indicated the situation of the Atlantic Island and those who, in conformity with the general peopling of the world, were probably its first inhabitants, namely the early Spaniards and the first Mauritanian vassals of the King Atlas. This wonderful history was almost forgotten in ancient times, Plato alone having preserved it, as has already been related in its place, and which should again be consulted for what remains. Plato, in Critias, says that to Neptune's share came the Atlantic Island, and that he had ten sons. He divided the whole island amongst them, which before and in his time was called the empire of the floating islands, as Volaterranius tells us. It was divided by Neptune into ten regions or kingdoms. The chief one, called Venus, he gave to his eldest son named Atlantis, and appointed him sovereign of the whole island ; which consequently took the name of Atlantica, and the sea Atlantic, a name which it retains to this day. The second son, named Gadirun, received the part which lies nearest to Spain and which is now Caliz. To the third son Neptune gave a share. His name was Amferes, the fourth's Eutoctenes, the seventh's Alusipo, the eighth's Mestores, the ninth's Azaen, the tenth's Diaprepem.

These and their descendants reigned for many ages, holding the lordships, by the sea, of many other islands, which could not have been other than Hayti, which we call Santo Domingo, Cuba and others, also peopled by emigrants from the Atlantic Island. They also held sway over Africa as far as Egypt, and over Europe to Tirrenia and Italy.

The lineage of Atlas extended in a grand succession of generations, and his kingdom was ruled in succession by the firstborns. They possessed such a copious supply of riches that none of the natives had seen it all, and that no new comers could realise it. This land abounded in all that is necessary for sustaining human life, pasture, timber, drugs, metals, wild beasts and birds, domestic animals including a great number of elephants, most fragrant perfumes, liquors, flowers, fruits, wine, and all the vegetables used for food, many dates, and other things for presents. That island produced all things in great profusion. In ancient times it was sacred, beautiful, admirable and fertile, as well as of vast extent. In it were extensive kingdoms, sumptuous temples, palaces calling forth great admiration, as is seen from the relation of Plato respecting the metropolis of the island which exceeded Babylon, Troy, or Rome, with all their rich buildings, curious and well-constructed forts, and even the seven wonders of the world concerning which the ancients sing so much. In the chief city of this empire there was a port to which so many ships and merchants resorted from all parts, that owing to the vast concourse a great and continual noise caused the residents to be thunderstruck. The number of these Atlantics ready for war was so great that in the capital city alone they had an ordinary garrison of 60,000 soldiers, always distributed among farms, each farm measuring 100 furlongs. The rest inhabited the woods and other places, and were innumerable. They took to war 10,000 two-horse chariots each containing eight armed men, with six slingers and stone throwers on either side. For the sea they had 200,000 boats with four men in each, making 800,000 men for the sea-service alone. This was quite necessary owing to the great number of subject nations which had to be governed and kept in obedience.

The rest which Plato relates on this subject will be discussed in the sequel, for I now proceed to our principal point, which is to establish the conclusion that as these people carried their banners and trophies into Europe and Africa which are not contiguous, they must have overrun the Indies of Castille and peopled them, being part of the same main land. They used much policy in their rule. But at the end of many ages, by divine permission, and perhaps owing to their sins, it happened that a great and continuous earthquake, with an unceasing deluge, perpetual by day and night, opened the earth and swallowed up those warlike and ambitious Atlantic men. The Atlantic Island remained absorbed beneath that great sea, which from that cause continued to be unnavigable owing to the mud of the absorbed island in solution, a wonderful thing.

This special flood may be added to the five floods recorded by the ancients. These are the general one of Moses, the second in Egypt of which Xenophon makes mention, the third flood in Achaia of Greece in the time of Ogyges Atticus, described by Isidore as happening in the days of Jacob, the fourth in Thessaly in the time of Deucalion and Pyrrha, in the days of Moses according to Isidore, in 782 as given by Juan Annius. The fifth flood is mentioned by Xenophon as happening in Egypt in the time of Proteus. The sixth was this which destroyed so great a part of the Atlantic Island and sufficed so to separate the part that was left unsubmerged, that all mortals in Asia, Africa and Europe believed that all were drowned. Thus was lost the intercourse and commerce of the people of these parts with those of Europe and Africa, in such sort that all memory of them would have been lost, if it had not been for the Egyptians, preservers of the most ancient deeds of men and of nature. The destruction of the Atlantic Island, over at least 1000 leagues of longitude, was in the time when Aod[1] governed the people of Israel, 1320 years before Christ and 2162 years after the Creation, according to the Hebrews. I deduce this calculation from what Plato relates of the conversation between Solon and the Egyptian priest. For, according to all the chronicles, Solon lived in the time of Tarquinius Priscus the King of Rome, Josiah being King of Israel at Jerusalem, before Christ 610 years. From this period until the time when the Atlantics had put a blockade over the Athenians 9000 lunar years had passed which, referred to solar years, make 869. All added together make the total given above. Very soon afterwards the deluge must have come, as it is said to have been in the time of Aod[1] or 748 years after the general deluge of Noah. This being so it is to be noted that the isle of Caliz, the Canaries, the Salvages, and Trinidad must have been parts of the absorbed land.

It may be assumed that these very numerous nations of Atlantis were sufficient to people those other lands of the Western Indies of Castille. Other nations also came to them, and peopled some provinces after the above destruction. Strabo and Solinus say that Ulysses, after the fall of Troy, navigated westward to Lusitania, founded Lisbon, and, after it had been built, desired to try his fortune on the Atlantic Ocean by the way we now go to the Indies. He disappeared, and it was never afterwards known what had become of him. This is stated by Pedro Anton Beuter, a noble Valencian historian and, as he

---

[1] Ehud.

mentions, this was the opinion of Dante Alighieri, the illustrious Florentine poet. Assuming this to be correct we may follow Ulysses from island to island until he came to Yucatan and Campeachy, part of the territory of New Spain. For those of that land have the Grecian bearing and dress of the nation of Ulysses, they have many Grecian words, and use Grecian letters. Of this I have myself seen many signs and proofs. Their name for God is "Teos" which is Greek, and even throughout New Spain they use the word "Teos" for God. I have also to say that in passing that way, I found that they anciently preserved an anchor of a ship, venerating it as an idol, and had a certain genesis in Greek, which should not be dismissed as absurd at first sight. Indeed there are a sufficient number of indications to support my conjecture concerning Ulysses. From thence all those provinces of Mexico, Tabasco, Xalisco, and to the north the Capotecas, Chiapas, Guatemalas, Honduras, Lasandones, Nicaraguas, Tlaguzgalpas, as far as Nicoya, Costa Rica, and Veragua.

Moreover Esdras recounts that those nations which went from Persia by the river Euphrates came to a land never before inhabited by the human race. Going down this river there was no way but by the Indian Sea to reach a land where there was no habitation. This could only have been Catigara, placed in 9° S. by Ptolemy, and according to the navigators sent by Alexander the Great, 40 days of navigation from Asia. This is the land which the describers of maps call the unknown land of the south, whence it is possible to go on settling people as far as the Strait of Magellan to the west of Catigara, and the Javas, New Guinea, and the islands of the archipelago of Nombre de Jesus which I, our Lord permitting, discovered in the South Sea in the year 1568, the unconquered Felipe II reigning as King of Spain and its dependencies by the demarcation of 180° of longitude.

It may thus be deduced that New Spain and its provinces were peopled by the Greeks, those of Catigara by the Jews, and those of the rich and most powerful kingdoms of Peru and adjacent provinces by the Atlantics who were descended from the primeval Mesopotamians and Chaldæans, peoplers of the world.

These, and other points with them, which cannot be discussed with brevity, are true historical reasons, of a quality worthy of belief, such as men of reason and letters may adopt respecting the peopling of these lands. When we come to consider attentively what these barbarians of Peru relate of their origin and of the tyrannical rule of the Incas Ccapacs, and the fables and extravagances they recount, the truth may be distinguished from what is false, and how in some of their fables they allude to true facts which are admitted and held by us as such. Therefore the reader should peruse with attention and read the most strange and racy history of barbarians that has, until now, been read of any political nation in the world.

VI.

THE FABLE OF THE ORIGIN OF THESE BARBAROUS INDIANS OF PERU, ACCORDING TO THEIR BLIND OPINIONS.

As these barbarous nations of Indians were always without letters, they had not the means of preserving the monuments and memorials of their times, and those of their predecessors with accuracy and method. As the devil, who is always striving to injure the human race, found these unfortunates to be easy of belief and timid in obedience, he introduced many illusions, lies and frauds, giving them to understand that he had created them from the first, and afterwards, owing to their sins and evil deeds, he had destroyed them with a flood, again creating them and giving them food and the way to preserve it. By chance they formerly had some notice, passed down to them from mouth to mouth, which had reached them from their ancestors, respecting the truth of what happened in former times. Mixing this with the stories told them by the devil, and with other things which they changed, invented, or added, which may happen in all nations, they made up a pleasing salad, and in some things worthy of the attention of the curious who are accustomed to consider and discuss human ideas.

One thing must be noted among many others. It is that the stories which are here treated as fables, which they are, are held by the natives to be as true as we hold the articles of our faith, and as such they affirm and confirm them with unanimity, and swear by them. There are a few, however, who by the mercy of God are opening their eyes and beginning to see what is true and what is false respecting those things. But we have to write down what they say and not what we think about it in this part. We shall hear what they hold respecting their first age, [*and afterwards we shall come to the inveterate and cruel tyranny of the Inca tyrants who oppressed these kingdoms of Peru for so long. All this is done by order of the most excellent Don Francisco de Toledo, Viceroy of these kingdoms*]. I have collected the information with much diligence so that this history can rest on attested proofs from the general testimony of the whole kingdom, old and young, Incas and tributary Indians.

The natives of this land affirm that in the beginning, and before this world was created, there was a being called Viracocha. He created a dark world without sun, moon or stars. Owing to this creation he was named Viracocha Pachayachachi, which means "Creator of all things[1]." And

---

[1] Uiracocha (Viracocha) was the Creator. Garcilasso de la Vega pointed out the mistake of supposing that the word signified "foam of the sea" (ii. p. 16). He believed it to be a name, the derivation of which he did not attempt to explain. Blas Valera (i. p. 243) said the

when he had created the world he formed a race of giants of disproportioned greatness painted and sculptured, to see whether it would be well to make real men of that size. He then created men in his likeness as they are now ; and they lived in darkness.

Viracocha ordered these people that they should live without quarrelling, and that they should know and serve him. He gave them a certain precept which they were to observe on pain of being confounded if they should break it. They kept this precept for some time, but it is not mentioned what it was. But as there arose among them the vices of pride and covetousness, they transgressed the precept of Viracocha Pachayachachi and falling, through this sin, under his indignation, he confounded and cursed them. Then some were turned into stones, others into other things, some were swallowed up by the earth, others by the sea, and over all there came a general flood which they call *uñu pachacuti*, which means " water that overturns the land." They say that it rained 60 days and nights,

---

meaning was the "will and power of God"; not that this is the signification of the word, but by reason of the godlike qualities attributed to Him who was known by it. Cieza de Leon says that Tici-Uiracocha was God, Creator of heaven and earth : Acosta that to Ticci-Uiracocha they assigned the chief power and command over all things ; Montesinos that Illa-tici-Uiracocha was the name of the creator of the world ; Molina that Tecsi-Uiracocha was the Creator and incomprehensible God ; the anonymous Jesuit that Uiracocha meant the great God of " Pirua " ; Betanzos that the Creator was Con-Tici-Uiracocha.

According to Montesinos and the anonymous Jesuit *Uira* or *Vira* is a corruption of *Pirua* meaning a depository. The first meaning of *Cocha* is a lake, but here it is held to signify profundity, abyss, space. The " Dweller in Space." *Ticci* or *Tici* is base or foundation, hence the founder. *Illa* means light. The anonymous Jesuit gives the meaning " Eternal Light " to *Illa-Ticci*. The word *Con*, given by Betanzos and Garcia, has no known meaning.

Pachacamac and Pachayachachi are attributes of the deity. *Pacha* means time or place, also the universe. *Camac* is the Ruler, *Yachachi* the Teacher. " The Ruler and Teacher of the Universe."

The meaning and significance of the word *Uiracocha* has been very fully discussed by Señor Don Leonardo Villar of Cuzco in a paper entitled *Lexicologia Keshua Uiracocha* (Lima, 1887).

that it drowned all created things, and that there alone remained some vestiges of those who were turned into stones, as a memorial of the event, and as an example to posterity, in the edifices of Pucara, which are 60 leagues from Cuzco.

Some of the nations, besides the Cuzcos, also say that a few were saved from this flood to leave descendants for a future age. Each nation has its special fable which is told by its people, of how their first ancestors were saved from the waters of the deluge. That the ideas they had in their blindness may be understood, I will insert only one, told by the nation of the Cañaris, a land of Quito and Tumibamba, 400 leagues from Cuzco and more.

They say that in the time of the deluge called *uñu pachacuti* there was a mountain named Guasano in the province of Quito and near a town called Tumipampa. The natives still point it out. Up this mountain went two of the Cañaris named Ataorupagui and Cusicayo. As the waters increased the mountain kept rising and keeping above them in such a way that it was never covered by the waters of the flood. In this way the two Cañaris escaped. These two, who were brothers, when the waters abated after the flood, began to sow. One day when they had been at work, on returning to their hut, they found in it some small loaves of bread, and a jar of chicha, which is the beverage used in this country in place of wine, made of boiled maize. They did not know who had brought it, but they gave thanks to the Creator, eating and drinking of that provision. Next day the same thing happened. As they marvelled at this mystery, they were anxious to find out who brought the meals. So one day they hid themselves, to spy out the bringers of their food. While they were watching they saw two Cañari women preparing the victuals and putting them in the accustomed place. When about to depart the men tried to seize them, but they evaded their would-be captors and escaped. The Cañaris, seeing the mistake they had made in molesting those who had done them so much good, became sad and prayed to Viracocha for pardon for their sins, entreating him to let the women come back and give them the accustomed meals. The Creator granted their petition. The women came back and said to the Cañaris—"The Creator has thought it well that we should return to you, lest you should die of hunger." They brought them food. Then there was friendship between the women and the Cañari brothers, and one of the Cañari brothers had connexion with one of the women. Then, as the elder brother was drowned in a lake which was near, the survivor married one of the women, and had the other as a concubine. By them he had ten sons who formed two lineages of five each, and increasing in numbers they called one Hanansaya which is the same as to say the upper party, and the other Hurinsaya, or the lower party. From these all the Cañaris that now exist are descended[1].

In the same way the other nations have fables of how some of their people were saved from whom they trace their origin and descent. But the Incas and most of those of Cuzco, those among them who are believed to know most, do not say that anyone escaped from the flood, but that Viracocha began to create men afresh, as will be related further on. One thing is believed among all the nations of these parts, for they all speak generally and as well known of the general flood which they call *uñu pachacuti*. From this we may clearly understand that if, in these parts they have a tradition of the great flood, this great mass of the floating islands which they afterwards

---

[1] The same story of the origin of the Cañaris is told by Molina, p. 8. But the mountain is called Huaca-yuan ; and instead of women the beings who brought the food were macaws. Molina tells another story received from the people of Ancas-mayu. Both seem to have been obtained by asking leading questions about a deluge.

called the Atlanticas, and now the Indies of Castille or America must have begun to receive a population immediately after the flood, although, by their account, the details are different from those which the true Scriptures teach us. This must have been done by divine Providence, through the first people coming over the land of the Atlantic Island, which was joined to this, as has been already said. For as the natives, though barbarous, give reasons for their very ancient settlement, by recording the flood, there is no necessity for setting aside the Scriptures by quoting authorities to establish this origin. We now come to those who relate the events of the second age after the flood, which is the subject of the next chapter.

VII.

FABLE OF THE SECOND AGE, AND CREATION OF THE BARBAROUS INDIANS ACCORDING TO THEIR ACCOUNT.

It is related that everything was destroyed in the flood called *uñu pachacuti*[1]. It must now be known that Viracocha Pachayachachi, when he destroyed that land as has been already recounted, preserved three men, one of them named Taguapaca, that they might serve and help him in the creation of new people who had to be made in the second age after the deluge, which was done in this manner. The flood being passed and the land dry, Viracocha determined to people it a second time, and, to make it more perfect, he decided upon creating luminaries to give it light. With this object he went, with his servants, to a great lake in the Collao, in which there is an island called Titicaca, the

---

[1] *Uñu pachacuti* would mean the world (*pacha*) overturned (*cuti*) by water (*uñu*). Probably a word coined by the priests, after putting leading questions about a universal deluge.

meaning being "the rock of lead," of which we shall treat in the first part. Viracocha went to this island, and presently ordered that the sun, moon, and stars should come forth, and be set in the heavens to give light to the world, and it was so. They say that the moon was created brighter than the sun, which made the sun jealous at the time when they rose into the sky. So the sun threw over the moon's face a handful of ashes, which gave it the shaded colour it now presents. This frontier lake of Chucuito, in the territory of the Collao, is 57 leagues to the south of Cuzco. Viracocha gave various orders to his servants, but Taguapaca disobeyed the commands of Viracocha. So Viracocha was enraged against Taguapaca, and ordered the other two servants to take him, tie him hands and feet, and launch him in a *balsa* on the lake. This was done. Taguapaca was blaspheming against Viracocha for the way he was treated, and threatening that he would return and take vengeance, when he was carried by the water down the drain of the same lake, and was not seen again for a long time. This done, Viracocha made a sacred idol in that place, as a place for worship and as a sign of what he had there created[1].

Leaving the island, he passed by the lake to the main land, taking with him the two servants who survived.

[1] This servant of Uiracocha is also mentioned by Cieza de Leon and Yamqui Pachacuti. Cieza appears to consider that Tuapaca was merely the name of Uiracocha in the Collao. Yamqui Pachacuti gives the names Tarapaca and Tonapa and connects them with Uiracocha. But he also uses the word Pachacca, a servant. These names are clearly the same as the Tahuapaca of Sarmiento. *Tahua* means four, but Sarmiento gives three as the number of these servants of Uiracocha. The meaning of *paca* is anything secret or mysterious, from *pacani* to hide. The names represent an ancient myth of some kind, but it is not possible, at this distance of time, to ascertain more than the names. Tonapa looks like a slip of the pen, and is probably Tarapa for Tarapaca. Don Samuel A. Lapone Quevedo published a mythological essay entitled *El Culto de Tonapa* with reference to the notice in the work of Yamqui Pachacuti ; but he is given to speculations about phallic and solar worship, and to the arbitrary alteration of letters to fit into his theories.

He went to a place now called Tiahuanacu in the province of Colla-suyu, and in this place he sculptured and designed on a great piece of stone, all the nations that he intended to create.   This done, he ordered his two servants to charge their memories with the names of all tribes that he had depicted, and of the valleys and provinces where they were to come forth, which were those of the whole land.   He ordered that each one should go by a different road, naming the tribes, and ordering them all to go forth and people the country.   His servants, obeying the command of Viracocha, set out on their journey and work.   One went by the mountain range or chain which they call the heights over the plains on the South Sea.   The other went by the heights which overlook the wonderful mountain ranges which we call the Andes, situated to the east of the said sea.   By these roads they went, saying with a loud voice "Oh you tribes and nations, hear and obey the order of Ticci Viracocha Pachayachachi, which commands you to go forth, and multiply and settle the land."   Viracocha himself did the same along the road between those taken by his two servants, naming all the tribes and places by which he passed.   At the sound of his voice every place obeyed, and people came forth, some from lakes, others from fountains, valleys, caves, trees, rocks and hills, spreading over the land and multiplying to form the nations which are to-day in Peru.

Others affirm that this creation of Viracocha was made from the Titicaca site where, having originally formed some shapes of large strong men[1] which seemed to him out of proportion, he made them again of his stature which was, as they say, the average height of men, and being made he gave them life.   Thence they set out to people the land.

---

[1] Jayaneo.   This was the name given to giants in the books of chivalry.   See *Don Quijote*, i. cap. 5, p. 43.

As they spoke one language previous to starting, they built those edifices, the ruins of which may still be seen, before they set out. This was for the residence of Viracocha, their maker. After departing they varied their languages, noting the cries of wild beasts, insomuch that, coming across each other afterwards, those could not understand who had before been relations and neighbours.

Whether it was in one way or the other, all agree that Viracocha was the creator of these people. They have the tradition that he was a man of medium height, white and dressed in a white robe like an alb secured round the waist, and that he carried a staff and a book in his hands.

Besides this they tell of a strange event; how that Viracocha, after he had created all people, went on his road and came to a place where many men of his creation had congregated. This place is now called Cacha. When Viracocha arrived there, the inhabitants were estranged owing to his dress and bearing. They murmured at it and proposed to kill him from a hill that was near. They took their weapons there, and gathered together with evil intentions against Viracocha. He, falling on his knees on some plain ground, with his hands clasped, fire from above came down upon those on the hill, and covered all the place, burning up the earth and stones like straw. Those bad men were terrified at the fearful fire. They came down from the hill, and sought pardon from Viracocha for their sin. Viracocha was moved by compassion. He went to the flames and put them out with his staff. But the hill remained quite parched up, the stones being rendered so light by the burning that a very large stone which could not have been carried on a cart, could be raised easily by one man. This may be seen at this day, and it is a wonderful sight to behold this hill, which is a quarter of a league in extent, all burnt up. It is in the Collao[1].

After this Viracocha continued his journey and arrived at a place called Urcos, 6 leagues to the south of Cuzco. Remaining there some days he was well served by the natives of that neighbourhood. At the time of his departure, he made them a celebrated *huaca* or statue, for them to offer gifts to and worship; to which statue the Incas, in after times, offered many rich gifts of gold and other metals, and above all a golden bench. When the Spaniards entered Cuzco they found it, and appropriated it to themselves. It was worth $17,000. The Marquis Don Francisco Pizarro took it himself, as the share of the General.

Returning to the subject of the fable, Viracocha continued his journey, working his miracles and instructing his created beings. In this way he reached the territory on the equinoctial line, where are now Puerto Viejo and Manta. Here he was joined by his servants. Intending to leave the land of Peru, he made a speech to those he had created, apprising them of the things that would happen. He told them that people would come, who would say that they were Viracocha their creator, and that they were not to believe them; but that in the time to come he would send his messengers who would protect and teach them. Having said this he went to sea with his two servants, and went travelling over the water as if it was land, without sinking. For they appeared like foam over the water and the people, therefore, gave them the name of Viracocha which is the same as to say the grease or foam of the sea[2]. At the end of some years

---

[1] Not in the Collao, but in the valley of the Vilcamayu. Afterwards a very remarkable temple was built there, described by Squier.

[2] A mistake. See Garcilasso de la Vega, ii. p. 66.

after Viracocha departed, they say that Taguapaca, who Viracocha ordered to be thrown into the lake of Titicaca in the Collao, as has already been related, came back and began, with others, to preach that he was Viracocha. Although at first the people were doubtful, they finally saw that it was false, and ridiculed them[1].

This absurd fable of their creation is held by these barbarians and they affirm and believe it as if they had really seen it to happen and come to pass[2].

VIII.

THE ANCIENT *BEHETRIAS*[3] OF THESE KINGDOMS OF PERU AND THEIR PROVINCES.

It is important to note that these barbarians could tell nothing more respecting what happened from the second creation by Viracocha down to the time of the Incas. But it may be assumed that, although the land was peopled and full of inhabitants before the Incas, it had no regular government, nor did it have natural lords elected by common consent to govern and rule, and who were respected by the people, so that they were obeyed and received tribute. On the contrary all the people were scattered and disorganized, living in complete liberty, and each man being sole lord of his house and estate. In each

---

[1] This story is told in a somewhat different form by Yamqui Pachacuti, p. 72.

[2] The tradition of the exercise of his creative powers by Viracocha at lake Titicaca, is derived from the more ancient people who were the builders of Tiahuanacu. Besides Sarmiento, the authors who give this Titicaca Myth are Garcilasso de la Vega, Cieza de Leon, Molina, Betanzos, Yamqui Pachacuti, Polo de Ondegardo, and the anonymous Jesuit. Acosta, Montesinos, Balboa and Santillana are silent respecting it.

[3] *Behetria.* A condition of perfect equality without any distinction of rank. Freedom from the subjection of any lord.

tribe there were two divisions. One was called Hanansaya, which means the upper division, and the other Hurinsaya, which is the lower division, a custom which continues to this day. These divisions do not mean anything more than a way to count each other, for their satisfaction, though afterwards it served a more useful purpose, as will be seen in its place.

As there were dissensions among them, a certain kind of militia was organized for defence, in the following way. When it became known to the people of one district that some from other parts were coming to make war, they chose one who was a native, or he might be a stranger, who was known to be a valiant warrior. Often such a man offered himself to aid and to fight for them against their enemies. Such a man was followed and his orders were obeyed during the war. When the war was over he became a private man as he had been before, like the rest of the people, nor did they pay him tribute either before or afterwards, nor any manner of tax whatever. To such a man they gave and still give the name of *Sinchi* which means valiant. They call such men "Sinchi-cuna" which means "valiant now" as who should say—"now during the time the war lasts you shall be our valiant man, and afterwards no": or another meaning would be simply "valiant men," for "cuna" is an adverb of time, and also denotes the plural[1]. In whichever meaning, it is very applicable to these temporary captains in the days of *behetrias* and general liberty. So that from the general flood of which they have a tradition to the time when the Incas began to reign, which was 3519 years, all the natives

---

[1] Cinchicona. *Sinchi* means strong. *Cuna* is the plural particle. *Sinchi* was the name for a chief or leader. I have not met with *cuna* as an adverb of time and meaning "now." No such meaning is given in the *Grammar* of Domingo de Santo Tomas, which was published in 1560, twelve years before Sarmiento wrote.

of these kingdoms lived on their properties without acknowledging either a natural or an elected lord. They succeeded in preserving, as it is said, a simple state of liberty, living in huts or caves or humble little houses. This name of "Sinchi" for those who held sway only during war, lasted throughout the land until the time of Tupac Inca Yupanqui, the tenth Inca, who instituted "Curacas" and other officials in the order which will be fully described in the life of that Inca. Even at the present time they continue this use and custom in the provinces of Chile and in other parts of the forests of Peru to the east of Quito and Chachapoyas, where they only obey a chief during war time, not any special one, but he who is known to be most valiant, enterprising and daring in the wars. The reader should note that all the land was private property with reference to any dominion of chiefs, yet they had natural chiefs with special rights in each province, as for instance among the natives of the valley of Cuzco and in other parts, as we shall relate of each part in its place.

IX.

THE FIRST SETTLERS IN THE VALLEY OF CUZCO.

I have explained how the people of these lands preserved their inheritances and lived on them in ancient times, and that their proper and natural countries were known. There were many of these which I shall notice in their places, treating specially at present of the original settlers of the valley where stands the present city of Cuzco. For from there we have to trace the origin of the tyranny of the Incas, who always had their chief seat in the valley of Cuzco.

Before all things it must be understood that the valley

of Cuzco is in 13° 15′ from the equator on the side of the
south pole[1]. In this valley, owing to its being fertile for
cultivation, there were three tribes settled from most ancient
times, the first called Sauaseras, the second Antasayas,
the third Huallas. They settled near each other, although
their lands for sowing were distinct, which is the property
they valued most in those days and even now. These
natives of the valley lived there in peace for many years,
cultivating their farms.

Some time before the arrival of the Incas, three Sinchis,
strangers to this valley, the first named Alcabisa[2], the second
Copalimayta, and the third Culunchima, collected certain
companies and came to the valley of Cuzco, where, by
consent of the natives, they settled and became brothers
and companions of the original inhabitants. So they lived
for a long time. There was concord between these six
tribes, three native and three immigrant. They relate that
the immigrants came out to where the Incas then resided,
as we shall relate presently, and called them relations.
This is an important point with reference to what happened
afterwards.

Before entering upon the history of the Incas I wish
to make known or, speaking more accurately, to answer
a difficulty which may occur to those who have not been
in these parts. Some may say that this history cannot
be accepted as authentic being taken from the narratives
of these barbarians, because, having no letters, they could
not preserve such details as they give from so remote an

---

[1] 13° 31′. He is 16 minutes out in his latitude.

[2] The Alcabisas, as original inhabitants of the Cuzco valley, are
mentioned by Cieza de Leon (ii. p. 105) who calls them Alcaviquiza.
Betanzos has Alcaviya, and Balboa Allcay-villcas. Cieza describes
the victory over them by Mayta Ccapac. Yamqui Pachacuti gives
Allcayviesas, Cullinchinas, and Cayancachis as the names of the tribes
who originally inhabited the Cuzco valley. Cayancachi is a southern
suburb of Cuzco outside the Huatanay river.

antiquity. The answer is that, to supply the want of letters, these barbarians had a curious invention which was very good and accurate. This was that from one to the other, from fathers to sons, they handed down past events, repeating the story of them many times, just as lessons are repeated from a professor's chair, making the hearers say these historical lessons over and over again until they were fixed in the memory. Thus each one of the descendants continued to communicate the annals in the order described with a view to preserve their histories and deeds, their ancient traditions, the numbers of their tribes, towns, provinces, their days, months and years, their battles, deaths, destructions, fortresses and "Sinchis." Finally they recorded, and they still record, the most notable things which consist in their numbers (or statistics), on certain cords called *quipu*, which is the same as to say reasoner or accountant. On these cords they make certain knots by which, and by differences of colour, they distinguish and record each thing as by letters. It is a thing to be admired to see what details may be recorded on these cords, for which there are masters like our writing masters[1].

Besides this they had, and still have, special historians in these nations, an hereditary office descending from father to son. The collection of these annals is due to the great diligence of Pachacuti Inca Yupanqui, the ninth Inca, who sent out a general summons to all the old historians in all the provinces he had subjugated, and even to many others throughout those kingdoms. He had them in Cuzco for

---

[1] The system of recording by *quipus* is described by Garcilasso de la Vega, i. pp. 150 and 191, also ii. p. 117 and more fully at ii. pp. 121—125. Cieza de Leon mentions the *quipu* system in his first part (see i. p. 291 and note) and in the second part (ii. pp. 33—35, 53, 57, 61, 165). At p. 32 the method of preserving the memory of former events is described very much as in the text. See also Molina, pp. 10, 169. Molina also describes the boards on which historical events were painted, p. 4. They were, he says, kept in a temple near Cuzco, called Poquen-cancha. See also Cieza de Leon (second part), p. 28.

a long time, examining them concerning their antiquities, origin, and the most notable events in their history. These were painted on great boards, and deposited in the temple of the Sun, in a great hall. There such boards, adorned with gold, were kept as in our libraries, and learned persons were appointed, who were well versed in the art of understanding and declaring their contents. No one was allowed to enter where these boards were kept, except the Inca and the historians, without a special order of the Inca.

In this way they took care to have all their past history investigated, and to have records respecting all kinds of people, so that at this day the Indians generally know and agree respecting details and important events, though, in some things, they hold different opinions on special points. By examining the oldest and most prudent among them, in all ranks of life, who had most credit, I collected and compiled the present history, referring the sayings and declarations of one party to their antagonists of another party, for they are divided into parties, and seeking from each one a memorial of its lineage and of that of the opposing party. These memorials, which are all in my possession, were compared and corrected, and ultimately verified in public, in presence of representatives of all the parties and lineages, under oaths in presence of a judge, and with expert and very faithful interpreters also on oath, and I thus finished what is now written. Such great diligence has been observed, because a thing which is the foundation of the true completion of such a great work as the establishment of the tyranny of the cruel Incas of this land will make all the nations of the world understand the judicial and more than legitimate right that the King of Castille has to these Indies and to other lands adjacent, especially to these kingdoms of Peru. As all the histories of past events have been verified by proof, which in this case has been done so carefully and faithfully by order and owing to the industry of the most excellent Viceroy Don Francisco de Toledo, no one can doubt that everything in this volume is most sufficiently established and verified without any room being left for reply or contradiction. I have been desirous of making this digression because, in writing the history, I have heard that many entertain the doubts I have above referred to, and it seemed well to satisfy them once for all.

X.

HOW THE INCAS BEGAN TO TYRANNIZE OVER THE LANDS AND INHERITANCES.

Having explained that, in ancient times, all this land was owned by the people, it is necessary to state how the Incas began their tyranny. Although the tribes all lived in simple liberty without recognising any lord, there were always some ambitious men among them, aspiring for mastery. They committed violence among their countrymen and among strangers to subject them and bring them to obedience under their command, so that they might serve them and pay tribute. Thus bands of men belonging to one region went to others to make war and to rob and kill, usurping the lands of others.

As these movements took place in many parts by many tribes, each one trying to subjugate his neighbour, it happened that 6 leagues from the valley of Cuzco, at a place called Paccari-tampu, there were four men with their four sisters, of fierce courage and evil intentions, although with lofty aims. These, being more able than the others, understood the pusillanimity of the natives of those districts and the ease with which they could be made to believe anything that was propounded with authority or with any force. So they conceived among themselves the idea of being able to subjugate many lands by force and deception. Thus all the eight brethren, four men and four women, consulted together how they could tyrannize over other tribes beyond the place where they lived, and they proposed to do this by violence. Considering that most of the natives were ignorant and could easily be made to believe what was said to them, particularly if they were addressed with some roughness, rigour and authority, against which they could make neither reply nor resistance, because they are timid by nature, they sent abroad certain fables respecting their origin, that they might be respected and feared. They said that they were the sons of Viracocha Pachayachachi, the Creator, and that they had come forth out of certain windows to rule the rest of the people. As they were fierce, they made the people believe and fear them, and hold them to be more than men, even worshipping them as gods. Thus they introduced the religion that suited them. The order of the fable they told of their origin was as follows.

XI.

THE FABLE OF THE ORIGIN OF THE INCAS OF CUZCO.

All the native Indians of this land relate and affirm that the Incas Ccapac originated in this way. Six leagues S.S.W. of Cuzco by the road which the Incas made, there is a place called Paccari-tampu, which means "the house of production[1]" at which there is a hill called Tampu-tocco, meaning "the house of windows." It is certain that in this hill there are three windows, one called " Maras-tocco," the other "Sutic-tocco," while that which is in the middle,

---

[1] Correctly "the tavern of the dawn."

between these two, was known as "Ccapac-tocco," which means "the rich window," because they say that it was ornamented with gold and other treasures. From the window called "Maras-tocco" came forth, without parentage, a tribe of Indians called Maras. There are still some of them in Cuzco. From the "Sutic-tocco" came Indians called Tampus, who settled round the same hill, and there are also men of this lineage still in Cuzco. From the chief window of "Ccapac-tocco," came four men and four women, called brethren. These knew no father nor mother, beyond the story they told that they were created and came out of the said window by order of Ticci Viracocha, and they declared that Viracocha created them to be lords. For this reason they took the name of Inca, which is the same as lord. They took "Ccapac" as an additional name because they came out of the window "Ccapac-tocco," which means "rich," although afterwards they used this term to denote the chief lord over many.

The names of the eight brethren were as follows: The eldest of the men, and the one with the most authority was named MANCO CCAPAC, the second AYAR AUCA, the third AYAR CACHI, the fourth AYAR UCHU. Of the women the eldest was called MAMA OCCLO, the second MAMA HUACO, the third MAMA IPACURA, or, as others say, MAMA CURA, the fourth MAMA RAUA.

The eight brethren, called Incas, said—"We are born strong and wise, and with the people who will here join us, we shall be powerful. We will go forth from this place to seek fertile lands and when we find them we will subjugate the people and take the lands, making war on all those who do not receive us as their lords." This, as they relate, was said by Mama Huaco, one of the women, who was fierce and cruel. Manco Ccapac, her brother, was also cruel and atrocious. This being agreed upon between the eight, they began to move the people who lived near the hill, putting it to them that their reward would be to become rich and to receive the lands and estates of those who were conquered and subjugated. For these objects they moved ten tribes or *ayllus*, which means among these barbarians "lineages" or "parties"; the names of which are as follows :

I. CHAUIN CUZCO AYLLU of the lineage of AYAR CACHI, of which there are still some in Cuzco, the chiefs being MARTIN CHUCUMBI, and DON DIEGO HUAMAN PAUCAR.

II. ARAYRACA AYLLU CUZCO-CALLAN. At present there are of this ayllu JUAN PIZARRO YUPANQUI, DON FRANCISCO QUISPI, ALONSO TARMA YUPANQUI of the lineage of AYAR UCHU.

III. TARPUNTAY AYLLU. Of this there are now some in Cuzco.

IV. HUACAYTAQUI AYLLU. Some still living in Cuzco.

V. SAÑOC AYLLU. Some still in Cuzco.
The above five lineages are HANAN-CUZCO, which means the party of Upper Cuzco.

VI. SUTIC-TOCCO AYLLU is the lineage which came out of one of the windows called "SUTIC-TOCCO," as has been before explained. Of these there are still some in Cuzco, the chiefs being DON FRANCISCO AVCA MICHO AVRI SUTIC, and DON ALONSO HUALPA.

VII. MARAS AYLLU. These are of the men who came forth from the window "MARAS-TOCCO." There are some of these now in Cuzco, the chiefs being DON ALONSO LLAMA OCA, and DON GONZALO AMPURA LLAMA OCA.

VIII. CUYCUSA AYLLU. Of these there are still some in Cuzco, the chief being CRISTOVAL ACLLARI.

IX. MASCA AYLLU. Of this there is in Cuzco—
JUAN QUISPI.

X. ORO AYLLU. Of this lineage is DON PEDRO
YUCAY.

I say that all these *ayllus* have preserved their records
in such a way that the memory of them has not been lost.
There are more of them than are given above, for I only
insert the chiefs who are the protectors and heads of the
lineages, under whose guidance they are preserved. Each
chief has the duty and obligation to protect the rest, and
to know the history of his ancestors. Although I say that
these live in Cuzco, the truth is that they are in a suburb
of the city which the Indians call Cayocache and which is
known to us as Belem, from the church of that parish
which is that of our Lady of Belem.

Returning to our subject, all these followers above
mentioned marched with Manco Ccapac and the other
brethren to seek for land [*and to tyrannize over those who
did no harm to them, nor gave them any excuse for war,
and without any right or title beyond what has been stated*].
To be prepared for war they chose for their leaders Manco
Ccapac and Mama Huaco, and with this arrangement
the companies of the hill of Tampu-tocco set out, to put
their design into execution.

XII.

THE ROAD WHICH THESE COMPANIES OF THE INCAS
TOOK TO THE VALLEY OF CUZCO, AND OF
THE FABLES WHICH ARE MIXED WITH THEIR
HISTORY.

The Incas and the rest of the companies or *ayllus*
set out from their homes at Tampu-tocco, taking with
them their property and arms, in sufficient numbers to

form a good squadron, having for their chiefs the said Manco Ccapac and Mama Huaco. Manco Ccapac took with him a bird like a falcon, called *indi*[1], which they all worshipped and feared as a sacred, or, as some say, an enchanted thing, for they thought that this bird made Manco Ccapac their lord and obliged the people to follow him. It was thus that Manco Ccapac gave them to understand, and it was carried in *vahidos*[2], always kept in a covered hamper of straw, like a box, with much care. He left it as an heirloom to his son, and the Incas had it down to the time of Inca Yupanqui. In his hand he carried with him a staff of gold, to test the lands which they would come to.

Marching together they came to a place called Huana-cancha, four leagues from the valley of Cuzco, where they remained for some time, sowing and seeking for fertile land. Here Manco Ccapac had connexion with his sister Mama Occlo, and she became pregnant by him. As this place did not appear able to sustain them, being barren, they advanced to another place called Tampu-quiro, where Mama Occlo begot a son named Sinchi Rocca. Having celebrated the natal feasts of the infant, they set out in search of fertile land, and came to another place called Pallata, which is almost contiguous to Tampu-quiro, and there they remained for some years.

Not content with this land, they came to another called Hays-quisro, a quarter of a league further on. Here they consulted together over what ought to be done respecting their journey, and over the best way of getting rid of Ayar Cachi, one of the four brothers. Ayar Cachi was fierce

---

[1] This bird called *indi*, the familiar spirit of Manco Ccapac, is not mentioned by any other author. There is more about it in the life of Mayta Ccapac, the great-grandson of Manco Ccapac. The word seems to be the same as *Ynti* the Sun-God.

[2] *Vahido* means giddiness, vertigo.

and strong, and very dexterous with the sling. He committed great cruelties and was oppressive both among the natives of the places they passed, and among his own people. The other brothers were afraid that the conduct of Ayar Cachi would cause their companies to disband and desert, and that they would be left alone. As Manco Ccapac was prudent, he concurred with the opinion of the others that they should secure their object by deceit. They called Ayar Cachi and said to him, "Brother! Know that in Ccapac-tocco we have forgotten the golden vases called *tupac-cusi* [1], and certain seeds, and the *napa* [2], which is our principal ensign of sovereignty." The *napa* is a sheep of the country, the colour white, with a red body cloth, on the top ear-rings of gold, and on the breast a plate with red badges such as was worn by rich Incas when they went abroad; carried in front of all on a pole with a cross of plumes of feathers. This was called *suntur-paucar* [3]. They said that it would be for the good of all, if he would go back and fetch them. When Ayar Cachi refused to return, his sister Mama Huaco, raising her foot, rebuked him with furious words, saying, "How is it that there should be such cowardice in so strong a youth as you are? Get ready for the journey, and do not fail to go to Tampu-tocco, and do what you are ordered." Ayar Cachi was shamed by these words. He obeyed and started to carry out his orders. They gave him, as a companion, one of those who had come with them, named Tampu-chacay, to whom they

---

[1] *Tupac-cusi*, meaning golden vases, does not occur elsewhere. It may be a mis-print for *tupac-ccuri*, *tupac* meaning anything royal and *ccuri* gold.

[2] *Napa* was the name of a sacred figure of a llama, one of the insignia of royalty. See Molina, pp. 19, 39, 47. The verb *napani* is to salute, *napay*, salutation. *Raymi-napa* was the flock dedicated for sacrifice.

[3] *Suntur-paucar* was the head-dress of the Inca. See Balboa, p. 20. Literally the "brilliant circle." See also Molina, pp. 6, 17, 39, 42, 44, and Yamqui Pachacuti, pp. 14, 106, 120.

gave secret orders to kill Ayar Cachi at Tampu-tocco, and not to return with him. With these orders they both arrived at Tampu-tocco. They had scarcely arrived when Ayar Cachi entered through the window Ccapac-tocco, to get the things for which he had been sent. He was no sooner inside than Tampu-chacay, with great celerity, put a rock against the opening of the window and sat upon it, that Ayar Cachi might remain inside and die there. When Ayar Cachi turned to the opening and found it closed he understood the treason of which the traitor Tampu-chacay had been guilty, and determined to get out if it was possible, to take vengeance. To force an opening he used such force and shouted so loud that he made the mountain tremble. With a loud voice he spoke these words to Tampu-chacay, "Thou traitor! thou who hast done me so much harm, thinkest thou to convey the news of my mortal imprisonment? That shall never happen. For thy treason thou shalt remain outside, turned into a stone." So it was done, and to this day they show the stone on one side of the window Ccapac-tocco. Turn we now to the seven brethren who had remained at Hays-quisro. The death of Ayar Cachi being known, they were very sorry for what they had done, for, as he was valiant, they regretted much to be without him when the time came to make war on any one. So they mourned for him. This Ayar Cachi was so dexterous with a sling and so strong that with each shot he pulled down a mountain and filled up a ravine. They say that the ravines, which we now see on their line of march, were made by Ayar Cachi in hurling stones.

The seven Incas and their companions left this place, and came to another called Quirirmanta at the foot of a hill which was afterwards called Huanacauri. In this place they consulted together how they should divide the duties of the enterprise amongst themselves, so that there should be distinctions between them. They agreed that as

Manco Ccapac had had a child by his sister, they should be married and have children to continue the lineage, and that he should be the leader. Ayar Uchu was to remain as a *huaca* for the sake of religion. Ayar Auca, from the position they should select, was to take possession of the land set apart for him to people.

Leaving this place they came to a hill at a distance of two leagues, a little more or less, from Cuzco. Ascending the hill they saw a rainbow, which the natives call *huanacauri*. Holding it to be a fortunate sign, Manco Ccapac said: " Take this for a sign that the world will not be destroyed by water. We shall arrive and from hence we shall select where we shall found our city." Then, first casting lots, they saw that the signs were good for doing so, and for exploring the land from that point and becoming lords of it. Before they got to the height where the rainbow was, they saw a *huaca* which was a place of worship in human shape, near the rainbow. They determined among themselves to seize it and take it away from there. Ayar Uchu offered himself to go to it, for they said that he was very like it. When Ayar Uchu came to the statue or *huaca*, with great courage he sat upon it, asking it what it did there. At these words the *huaca* turned its head to see who spoke, but, owing to the weight upon it, it could not see. Presently, when Ayar Uchu wanted to get off he was not able, for he found that the soles of his feet were fastened to the shoulders of the *huaca*. The six brethren, seeing that he was a prisoner, came to succour him. But Ayar Uchu, finding himself thus transformed, and that his brethren could not release him, said to them— " O Brothers, an evil work you have wrought for me. It was for your sakes that I came where I must remain for ever, apart from your company. Go! go! happy brethren, I announce to you that you will be great lords. I, therefore, pray that in recognition of the desire I have always

had to please you, you will honour and venerate me in all
your festivals and ceremonies, and that I shall be the first
to whom you make offerings. For I remain here for your
sakes. When you celebrate the *huarachico* (which is the
arming of the sons as knights) you shall adore me as their
father, for I shall remain here for ever." Manco Ccapac
answered that he would do so, for that it was his will and
that it should be so ordered. Ayar Uchu promised for the
youths that he would bestow on them the gifts of valour,
nobility, and knighthood, and with these last words he
remained, turned into stone. They constituted him the
huaca of the Incas, giving it the name of Ayar Uchu
Huanacauri[1]. And so it always was, until the arrival of
the Spaniards, the most venerated *huaca*, and the one that
received the most offerings of any in the kingdom. Here
the Incas went to arm the young knights until about
twenty years ago, when the Christians abolished this
ceremony. It was religiously done, because there were
many abuses and idolatrous practices, offensive and contrary to the ordinances of God our Lord.

---

[1] Huanacauri was a very sacred *huaca* of the Peruvians. Cieza de
Leon tells much the same story as Sarmiento, ii. pp. 17, 18, 19, 22, 89,
101, 107, 111. Garcilasso de la Vega mentions Huanacauri four times,
i. pp. 65, 66, and ii. pp. 169, 230, as a place held in great veneration. It
is frequently mentioned by Molina. The word is given by Yamqui
Pachacuti as Huayna-captiy. *Huayna* means a youth, *captiy* is the
subjunctive of the verb *cani*, I am. The word appears to have
reference to the arming of youths, and the ordeals they went through,
which took place annually at this place.

XIII.

ENTRY OF THE INCAS INTO THE VALLEY OF CUZCO, AND THE FABLES THEY RELATE CONCERNING IT.

The six brethren were sad at the loss of Ayar Uchu, and at the loss of Ayar Cachi; and, owing to the death of Ayar Cachi, those of the lineage of the Incas, from that time to this day, always fear to go to Tampu-tocco, lest they should have to remain there like Ayar Cachi.

They went down to the foot of the hill, whence they began their entry into the valley of Cuzco, arriving at a place called Matahua, where they stopped and built huts, intending to remain there some time. Here they armed as knight the son of Manco Ccapac and of Mama Occlo, named Sinchi Rocca, and they bored his ears, a ceremony which is called *huarachico*, being the insignia of his knighthood and nobility, like the custom known among ourselves. On this occasion they indulged in great rejoicings, drinking for many days, and at intervals mourning for the loss of their brother Ayar Uchu. It was here that they invented the mourning sound for the dead, like the cooing of a dove. Then they performed the dance called *Ccapac Raymi*, a ceremony of the royal or great lords. It is danced, in long purple robes, at the ceremonies they call *quicochico*[1], which is when girls come to maturity, and the *huarachico*[2], when

---

[1] Quicu-chicuy was the ceremony when girls attained puberty. The customs, on this occasion, are described by Molina, p. 53. See also Yamqui Pachacuti, p. 80, and the anonymous Jesuit, p. 181.

[2] Huarachicu was the great festival when the youths went through their ordeals, and were admitted to manhood and to bear arms. Garcilasso de la Vega gives the word as "Huaracu"; and fully describes the ordeals and the ceremonies, ii. pp. 161—178. See also Molina, pp. 34 and 41—46, and Yamqui Pachacuti, p. 80.

they bore the ears of the Incas, and the *rutuchico*[1], when the Inca's hair is cut the first time, and the *ayuscay*[2], which is when a child is born, and they drink continuously for four or five days.

After this they were in Matahua for two years, waiting to pass on to the upper valley to seek good and fertile land. Mama Huaco, who was very strong and dexterous, took two wands of gold and hurled them towards the north. One fell, at two shots of an arquebus, into a ploughed field called Colcapampa and did not drive in well, the soil being loose and not terraced. By this they knew that the soil was not fertile. The other went further, to near Cuzco, and fixed well in the territory called Huanay-pata, where they knew the land to be fertile. Others say that this proof was made by Manco Ccapac with the staff of gold which he carried himself, and that thus they knew of the fertility of the land, when the staff sunk in the land called Huanay-pata, two shots of an arquebus from Cuzco. They knew the crust of the soil to be rich and close, so that it could only be broken by using much force.

Let it be by one way or the other, for all agree that they went trying the land with a pole or staff until they arrived at this Huanay-pata, when they were satisfied. They were sure of its fertility, because after sowing per-petually, it always yielded abundantly, giving more the more it was sown. They determined to usurp that land by force, in spite of the natural owners, and to do with it as they chose. So they returned to Matahua.

From that place Manco Ccapac saw a heap of stones

---

[1] Rutuchicu is the ceremony when a child reaches the age of one year, from *rutuni*, to cut or shear. It receives the name which it retains until the Huarachicu if a boy, and until the Quicu-chicuy if a girl. They then receive the names they retain until death. At the Rutuchicu the child was shorn. Molina, p. 53.

[2] Molina says that Ayuscay was the ceremony when the woman conceives. Molina, p. 53.

near the site of the present monastery of Santo Domingo
at Cuzco. Pointing it out to his brother Ayar Auca, he
said, "Brother! you remember how it was arranged between
us, that you should go to take possession of the land where
we are to settle. Well! look at that stone." Pointing out
the stone he continued, "Go thither flying," for they say
that Ayar Auca had developed some wings, "and seating
yourself there, take possession of land seen from that heap
of stones. We will presently come to settle and reside."
When Ayar Auca heard the words of his brother, he
opened his wings and flew to that place which Manco
Ccapac had pointed out. Seating himself there, he was
presently turned into stone, and was made the stone of
possession. In the ancient language of this valley the heap
was called *cozco*, whence that site has had the name of
Cuzco to this day[1]. From this circumstance the Incas had
a proverb which said, "Ayar Auca cuzco huanca," or, "Ayar
Auca a heap of marble." Others say that Manco Ccapac
gave the name of Cuzco because he wept in that place where
he buried his brother Ayar Cachi. Owing to his sorrow
and to the fertility he gave that name which in the ancient
language of that time signified sad as well as fertile. The
first version must be the correct one because Ayar Cachi
was not buried at Cuzco, having died at Ccapac-tocco
as has been narrated before. And this is generally
affirmed by Incas and natives.

Five brethren only remaining, namely Manco Ccapac,
and the four sisters, and Manco Ccapac being the only
surviving brother out of four, they presently resolved to
advance to where Ayar Auca had taken possession. Manco
Ccapac first gave to his son Sinchi Rocca a wife named

---

[1] *Cuzco* means a clod, or hard unirrigated land. *Cuzquini* is to
break clods of earth, or to level. Montesinos derives the name of the
city from the verb "to level," or from the heaps of clods of earth called
cuzco. Cusquic-Raymi is the month of June.

Mama Cuca, of the lineage of Sañu, daughter of a Sinchi named Sitic-huaman, by whom he afterwards had a son named Sapaca. He also instituted the sacrifice called *capa cocha*[1], which is the immolation of two male and two female infants before the idol Huanacauri, at the time when the Incas were armed as knights. These things being arranged, he ordered the companies to follow him to the place where Ayar Auca was.

Arriving on the land of Huanay-pata, which is near where now stands the *Arco de la plata* leading to the Charcas road, he found settled there a nation of Indians named Huallas, already mentioned. Manco Ccapac and Mama Occlo began to settle and to take possession of the land and water, against the will of the Huallas. On this business they did many violent and unjust things. As the Huallas attempted to defend their lives and properties, many cruelties were committed by Manco Ccapac and Mama Occlo. They relate that Mama Occlo was so fierce that, having killed one of the Hualla Indians, she cut him up, took out the inside, carried the heart and lungs in her mouth, and with an *ayuinto*, which is a stone fastened to a rope, in her hand, she attacked the Huallas with diabolical resolution. When the Huallas beheld this horrible and inhuman spectacle, they feared that the same thing would be done to them, being simple and timid, and they fled and abandoned their rights. Mama Occlo reflecting on her cruelty, and fearing that for it they would be branded as tyrants, resolved not to spare any Huallas, believing that the affair would thus be forgotten. So they killed all they could lay their hands upon, dragging infants

---

[1] Ccapac-cocha. The weight of evidence is, on the whole, in favour of this sacrifice of two infants having taken place at the Huara-chicu. Cieza de Leon, in remarking that the Spaniards falsely imputed crimes to the Indians to justify their ill-treatment, says that the practice of human sacrifice was exaggerated, ii. pp. 79, 80. See also Molina, pp. 54, 57. Yamqui Pachacuti, p. 86.

from their mothers' wombs, that no memory might be left of these miserable Huallas.

Having done this Manco Ccapac advanced, and came within a mile of Cuzco to the S.E., where a Sinchi named Copalimayta came out to oppose him. We have mentioned this chief before and that, although he was a late comer, he settled with the consent of the natives of the valley, and had been incorporated in the nation of Sauaseray Panaca, natives of the site of Santo Domingo at Cuzco. Having seen the strangers invading their lands and tyrannizing over them, and knowing the cruelties inflicted on the Huallas, they had chosen Copalimayta as their Sinchi. He came forth to resist the invasion, saying that the strangers should not enter his lands or those of the natives. His resistance was such that Manco Ccapac and his companions were obliged to turn their backs. They returned to Huanay-pata, the land they had usurped from the Huallas. From the sowing they had made they derived a fine crop of maize, and for this reason they gave the place a name which means something precious[1].

After some months they returned to the attack on the natives of the valley, to tyrannize over them. They assaulted the settlement of the Sauaseras, and were so rapid in their attack that they captured Copalimayta,

---

[1] The origin of the Inca dynasty derived from Manco Ccapac and his brethren issuing from the window at Paccari-tampu may be called the Paccari-tampu myth. It was universally received and believed. Garcilasso de la Vega gives the meanings of the names of the brothers. Ayar Cachi means salt or instruction in rational life, Ayar Uchu is pepper, meaning the delight experienced from such teaching, and Ayar Sauca means pleasure, or the joy they afterwards experienced from it. Balboa gives an account of the death of Ayar Cachi, but calls him Ayar Auca. He also describes the turning into stone at Huanacauri. Betanzos tells much the same story as Sarmiento ; as do Cieza de Leon and Montesinos, with some slight differences. Yamqui Pachacuti gives the names of the brothers, but only relates the Huanacauri part of the story. Montesinos and Garcilasso de la Vega call one of the brothers Ayar Sauca. Sarmiento, Betanzos and Balboa call him Ayar Auca. All agree in the names of the other brothers.

slaughtering many of the Sauaseras with great cruelty. Copalimayta, finding himself a prisoner and fearing death, fled out of desperation, leaving his estates, and was never seen again after he escaped. Mama Huaco and Manco Ccapac usurped his houses, lands and people. In this way MANCO CCAPAC, MAMA HUACO, SINCHI ROCCA, and MANCO SAPACA settled on the site between the two rivers, and erected the House of the Sun, which they called YNTI-CANCHA. They divided all that position, from Santo Domingo to the junction of the rivers into four neighbourhoods or quarters which they call *cancha*. They called one QUINTI-CANCHA, the second CHUMPI-CANCHA, the third SAYRI-CANCHA, and the fourth YARAMPUY-CANCHA. They divided the sites among themselves, and thus the city was peopled, and, from the heap of stones of Ayar Auca it was called CUZCO[1].

XIV.

THE DIFFERENCE BETWEEN MANCO CCAPAC AND THE ALCABISAS, RESPECTING THE ARABLE LAND.

It has been said that one of the natural tribes of this valley of Cuzco was the Alcabisas. At the time when Manco Ccapac settled at Ynti-cancha and seized the goods of the Sauaseras and Huallas, the Alcabisas were settled half an arquebus shot from Ynti-canchi, towards the part where Santa Clara now stands. Manco Ccapac had a plan to spread out his forces that his tyrannical

---

[1] Garcilasso de la Vega gives the most detailed description of the city of Cuzco and its suburbs, ii. p. 235, but he does not mention these four divisions. The space from Santo Domingo to the junction of the rivers only covers a few acres ; and was devoted to the gardens of the Sun.

intentions might not be impeded, so he sent his people, as if loosely and idly, making free with the land. He took the lands without distinction, to support his companies. As he had taken those of the Huallas and Sauaseras, he wished also to take those of the Alcabisas. As these Alcabisas had given up some, Manco Ccapac wished and intended to take all or nearly all. When the Alcabisas saw that the new comers even entered their houses, they said : " These are men who are bellicose and unreasonable ! they take our lands ! Let us set up landmarks on the fields they have left to us." This they did, but Mama Huaco said to Manco Ccapac, " let us take all the water from the Alcabisas, and then they will be obliged to give us the rest of their land." This was done and they took away the water. Over this there were disputes ; but as the followers of Manco Ccapac were more and more masterful, they forced the Alcabisas to give up their lands which they wanted, and to serve them as their lords, although the Alcabisas never voluntarily served Manco Ccapac nor looked upon him as their lord. On the contrary they always went about saying with loud voices 'to those of Manco Ccapac—" Away ! away ! out of our territory." For this Manco Ccapac was more hard upon them, and oppressed them tyrannically.

Besides the Alcabisas there were other tribes, as we have mentioned before. These Manco Ccapac and Mama Huaco totally destroyed, and more especially one which lived near Ynti-cancha, in the nearest land, called Humana-mean, between Ynti-cancha and Cayocachi[1], where there also lived another native Sinchi named Culunchima. Manco Ccapac entered the houses and lands of all the

---

[1] Garcilasso de la Vega describes Cayau-cachi as a small village of about 300 inhabitants in his time. It was about 1000 paces west of the nearest house of the city in 1560 ; but he had been told that, at the time of his writing in 1602, the houses had been extended so as to include it.

natives, especially of the Alcabisas, condemned their Sinchi to perpetual imprisonment, sending the others to banishment in Cayocachi, and forcing them to pay tribute. But they were always trying to free themselves from the tyranny, as the Alcabisas did later[1].

Having completed the yoke over the natives, their goods and persons, Manco Ccapac was now very old. Feeling the approach of death, and fearing that in leaving the sovereignty to his son, Sinchi Rocca, he and his successors might not be able to retain it owing to the bad things he had done and to the tyranny he had established, he ordered that the ten lineages or companies that had come with him from Tampu-tocco should form themselves into a garrison or guard, to be always on the watch over the persons of his son and of his other descendants to keep them safe. They were to elect the successor when he had been nominated by his father, or succeeded on the death of his father. For he would not trust the natives to nominate or elect, knowing the evil he had done, and the force he had used towards them. Manco Ccapac being now on the point of death, he left the bird *indi* enclosed in its cage, the *tupac-yauri*[2] or sceptre, the *napa* and the *suntur-paucar*, the insignia of a prince, [*though tyrant,*] to his son Sinchi Rocca that he might take his place, [*and this without the consent or election of any of the natives*].

Thus died Manco Ccapac, according to the accounts of those of his *ayllu* or lineage, at the age of 144 years, which were divided in the following manner. When he set out from Paccari-tampu or Tampu-tocco he was 36 years of age. From that time until he arrived at the

---

[1] Cieza de Leon and Balboa corroborate the story of Sarmiento that the Alcabisas (Cieza calls them Alcaviquizas, Balboa has Allcayvillcas) were hostile to the Incas, Cieza, ii. p. 105, Balboa, p. 25. Yamqui Pachacuti mentions them as Allcayviesas, p. 76.

[2] *Tupac-yauri.* The sceptre of the sovereign. Molina, pp. 25, 40, 41. Yamqui Pachacuti, p. 92.

valley of Cuzco, during which interval he was seeking for fertile lands, there were eight years. For in one place he stayed one, in another two years, in others more or less until he reached Cuzco, where he lived all the rest of the time, which was 100 years, as *Ccapac* or supreme and rich sovereign.

They say that he was a man of good stature, thin, rustic, cruel though frank, and that in dying he was converted into a stone of a height of a vara and a half. The stone was preserved with much veneration in the Ynti-cancha until the year 1559 when, the licentiate Polo Ondegardo being Corregidor of Cuzco, found it and took it away from where it was adored and venerated by all the Incas, in the village of Bimbilla near Cuzco.

From this Manco Ccapac were originated the ten ayllus mentioned above. From his time began the idols *huauquis*, which was an idol or demon chosen by each Inca for his companion and oracle which gave him answers[1]. That of Manco Ccapac was the bird *indi* already mentioned. This Manco Ccapac ordered, for the preservation of his memory, the following: His eldest son by his legitimate wife, who was his sister, was to succeed to the sovereignty. If there was a second son his duty was to be to help all the other children and relations. They were to recognize him as the head in all their necessities, and he was to take charge of their interests, and for this duty estates were set aside. This party or lineage was called *ayllu*. If there was no second son, or if there was one who was incapable, the duty was to be passed on to the nearest and ablest relation. And that those to come might have a precedent or example, Manco Ccapac made the first *ayllu* and called

---

[1] Sarmiento says that every sovereign Inca had a familiar demon or idol which he called *guauqui*, and that the *guauqui* of Manco Ccapac was the *indi* or bird already mentioned. This is corroborated by Polo de Ondegardo. The word seems to be the same as *Hua-uqui*, a brother.

it *Chima Panaca Ayllu,* which means the lineage descending from Chima, because the first to whom he left his *ayllu*
or lineage in charge was named *Chima,* and *Panaca* means
"to descend." It is to be noted that the members of this
ayllu always adored the statue of Manco Ccapac, and not
those of the other Incas, but the *ayllus* of the other Incas
always worshipped that statue and the others also. It is
not known what was done with the body, for there was
only the statue. They carried it in their wars, thinking
that it secured the victories they won. They also took it
to Huanacauri, when they celebrated the *huarachicos* of the
Incas. Huayna Ccapac took it with him to Quito and
Cayambis, and afterwards it was brought back to Cuzco
with the dead body of that Inca. There are still those of
this *ayllu* in Cuzco who preserve the memory of the deeds
of Manco Ccapac. The principal heads of the *ayllu* are
now Don Diego Chaco, and Don Juan Huarhua Chima.
They are Hurin-cuzcos. Manco Ccapac died in the year
665 of the nativity of Christ our Lord, Loyba the Goth
reigning in Spain, Constantine IV being Emperor. He
lived in the Ynti-cancha, House of the Sun.

XV.

COMMENCES THE LIFE OF SINCHI ROCCA,
THE SECOND INCA.

It has been said that Manco Ccapac, the first Inca, who
tyrannized over the natives of the valley of Cuzco, only
subjugated the Huallas, Alcabisas, Sauaseras, Culunchima,
Copalimayta and the others mentioned above, who were
all within the circuit of what is now the city of Cuzco.

To this Manco Ccapac succeeded his son Sinchi Rocca,

son also of Mama Occlo, his mother and aunt[1]. He succeeded by nomination of his father, under the care of the *ayllus* who then all lived together, but not by election of the people, they were all either in flight, prisoners, wounded or banished, and were all his mortal enemies owing to the cruelties and robberies exercised upon them by his father Manco Ccapac. Sinchi Rocca was not a warlike person, and no feats of arms are recorded of him, nor did he sally forth from Cuzco, either himself or by his captains[2]. He added nothing to what his father had subjugated, only holding by his *ayllus* those whom his father had crushed. He had for a wife Mama Cuca of the town of Saño by whom he had a son named Lloqui Yupanqui. Lloqui means left-handed, because he was so. He left his *ayllu* called *Raura Panaca Ayllu* of the Hurin-cuzco side. There are some of this *ayllu* living, the chiefs being Don Alonso Puscon and Don Diego Quispi. These have the duty of knowing and maintaining the things and memories of Sinchi Rocca. He lived in Ynti-cancha, the House of the Sun, and all his years were 127. He succeeded when 108, and reigned 19 years. He died in the year of the nativity of our Lord Jesus Christ 675, Wamba being King of Spain, Leo IV Emperor, and Donus Pope. He left an idol of stone shaped like a fish called *Huanachiri Amaru*, which during life was his idol or *guauqui*. Polo, being Corregidor of Cuzco, found this idol, with the body of Sinchi Rocca, in the village of Bimbilla, among some bars of copper. The idol had attendants and cultivated lands for its service.

---

[1] All the authorities concur that Sinchi Rocca was the second sovereign of the Inca dynasty, except Montesinos, who makes him the first and calls him Inca Rocca. Acosta has Inguarroca, and Betanzos Chincheroca.

[2] Cieza de Leon and Garcilasso de la Vega also say that Sinchi Rocca waged no wars. The latter tells us that, by peaceful means, he extended his dominions over the Canchis, as far as Chuncara.

XVI.

THE LIFE OF LLOQUI YUPANQUI, THE THIRD INCA.

On the death of Sinchi Rocca the Incaship was occupied by Lloqui Yupanqui, son of Sinchi Rocca by Mama Cuca his wife. It is to be noted that, although Manco Ccapac had ordered that the eldest son should succeed, this Inca broke the rule of his grandfather, for he had an elder brother named Manco Sapaca[1], as it is said, who did not consent, and the Indians do not declare whether he was nominated by his father. From this I think that Lloqui Yupanqui was not nominated, but Manco Sapaca as the eldest, for so little regard for the natives or their approval was shown. This being so, it was tyranny against the natives and infidelity to relations with connivance of the *ayllus* legionaries; and with the Inca's favour they could do what they liked, by supporting him. So Lloqui Yupanqui lived in Ynti-cancha like his father[2]. He never left Cuzco on a warlike expedition nor performed any memorable deed, but merely lived like his father, having communication with some provinces and chiefs. These were Huaman Samo, chief of Huaro, Pachaculla Viracocha, the Ayamarcas of Tampu-cunca, and the Quilliscachis[3].

---

[1] Manco Sapaca, the eldest son of Sinchi Rocca, is also mentioned by Balboa, pp. 14, 20, 22.

[2] All the authorities concur in making Lloqui Yupanqui the third Inca, except Acosta, who has Iaguarhuaque. Herrera spells it Lloki Yupanqui, Fernandez has Lloccuco Panque, merely corrupt spellings. Cieza de Leon also represents this reign to have been peaceful, but Garcilasso de la Vega makes Lloqui Yupanqui conquer the Collao.

[3] Huaro or Guaro is a village south of Cuzco in the valley of the Vilcamayu (Balboa, p. 110). Huaman Samo was the chief of Huaro. Balboa mentions Pachachalla Viracocha as a chief of great prudence and ability who submitted to Lloqui Yupanqui, pp. 21, 22. The Ayamarcas formed a powerful tribe about 12 miles south of Cuzco. The Quilliscachis formed one of the original tribes in the valley of Cuzco (Yamqui Pachacuti, p. 110). Tampu-cunca only occurs here.

One day Lloqui Yupanqui being very sad and afflicted, the Sun appeared to him in the form of a person and consoled him by saying—"Do not be sorrowful, Lloqui Yupanqui, for from you shall descend great Lords," also, that he might hold it for certain that he would have male issue. For Lloqui Yupanqui was then very old, and neither had a son nor expected to have one. This having been made known, and what the Sun had announced to Lloqui Yupanqui having been published to the people, his relations determined to seek a wife for him. His brother Manco Sapaca, understanding the fraternal disposition, sought for a woman who was suitable for it. He found her in a town called Oma, two leagues from Cuzco, asked for her from her guardians, and, with their consent, brought her to Cuzco. She was then married to Lloqui Yupanqui. Her name was Mama Cava, and by her the Inca had a son named Mayta Ccapac.

This Lloqui did nothing worthy of remembrance. He carried with him an idol, which was his *guauqui* called *Apu Mayta*. His *ayllu* is *Avayni Panaca Ayllu*, because the first who had the charge of this *ayllu* was named Avayni. This Inca lived and died in Ynti-cancha. He was 132 years of age, having succeeded at the age of 21, so that he was sovereign or "ccapac" for 111 years. He died in 786, Alfonso el Casto being King of Spain and Leo IV Supreme Pontiff. Some of this *ayllu* still live at Cuzco. The chiefs are Putisuc Titu Avcaylli, Titu Rimachi, Don Felipe Titu Cunti Mayta, Don Agustin Cunti Mayta, Juan Bautista Quispi Cunti Mayta. They are Hurincuzcos. The Licentiate Polo found the body of this Inca with the rest.

XVII.

THE LIFE OF MAYTA CCAPAC, THE FOURTH INCA[1].

Mayta Ccapac, the fourth Inca, son of Lloqui Yupanqui and his wife Mama Cava, is to those Indians what Hercules is to us, as regards his birth and acts, for they relate strange things of him. At the very first the Indians of his lineage, and all the others in general, say that his father, when he was begotten, was so old and weak that every one believed he was useless, so that they thought the conception was a miracle. The second wonder was that his mother bore him three months after conception, and that he was born strong and with teeth. All affirm this, and that he grew at such a rate that in one year he had as much strength and was as big as a boy of eight years or more. At two years he fought with very big boys, knocked them about and hurt them seriously. This all looks as if it might be counted with the other fables, but I write what the natives believe respecting their ancestors, and they hold this to be so true that they would kill anyone who asserted the contrary.

They say of this Mayta that when he was of very tender years, he was playing with some boys of the Alcabisas and Culunchimas, natives of Cuzco, when he hurt many of them and killed some. And one day, drinking or taking water from a fountain, he broke the leg of the son of a Sinchi of the Alcabisas, and hunted the rest until they

---

[1] All authorities agree that Mayta Ccapac was the fourth Inca, except Acosta and Betanzos. Acosta has Viracocha. Betanzos places Mayta Ccapac after Ccapac Yupanqui, whom other authorities make his son. His reign was peaceful except that he encountered and finally vanquished the Alcabisas. But Garcilasso de la Vega makes him the conqueror of the region south of lake Titicaca, as well as provinces to the westward, including the settlement of Arequipa. All this is doubtless a mistake on the part of Garcilasso.

shut themselves up in their houses, where the Alcabisas lived without injuring the Incas.

But now the Alcabisas, unable to endure longer the naughtiness of Mayta Ccapac, which he practised under the protection of Lloqui Yupanqui, and the *ayllus* who watched over him, determined to regain their liberty and to venture their lives for it. So they selected ten resolute Indians to go to the House of the Sun where Lloqui Yupanqui and his son Mayta Ccapac lived, and enter it with the intention of killing them. At the time Mayta Ccapac was in the court yard of the house, playing at ball with some other boys. When he saw enemies entering the house with arms, he threw one of the balls he was playing with, and killed one. He did the same to another, and, attacking the rest, they all fled. Though the rest escaped, they had received many wounds, and in this state they went back to their Sinchis of Calunchima and Alcabasa.

The Chiefs, considering the harm Mayta Ccapac had done to the natives when a child, feared that when he was grown up he would destroy them all, and for this reason they resolved to die for their liberty. All the inhabitants of the valley of Cuzco, that had been spared by Manco Ccapac, united to make war on the Incas. This very seriously alarmed Lloqui Yupanqui. He thought he was lost, and reprehended his son Mayta Ccapac, saying, " Son ! why hast thou been so harmful to the natives of this valley, so that in my old age I shall die at the hands of our enemies?" As the *ayllus*, who were in garrison with the Incas, rejoiced more in rapine and disturbances than in quiet, they took the part of Mayta Ccapac and told the old Inca to hold his peace, leaving the matter to his son, so Lloqui Yupanqui took no further steps in reprehending Mayta Ccapac. The Alcabisas and Culunchimas assembled their forces and Mayta Ccapac marshalled his *ayllus*. There was a battle between the two armies and although it was doubtful for some time, both sides fighting desperately for victory, the Alcabisas and Calunchimas were finally defeated by the troops of Mayta Ccapac.

But not for this did the Alcabisas give up the attempt to free themselves and avenge their wrongs. Again they challenged Mayta Ccapac to battle, which he accepted. As they advanced they say that such a hail storm fell over the Alcabisas that they were defeated a third time, and entirely broken up. Mayta Ccapac imprisoned their Sinchi for the remainder of his life.

Mayta Ccapac married Mama Tacucaray, native of the town of Tacucaray, and by her he had a legitimate son named Ccapac Yupanqui, besides four others named Tarco Huaman, Apu Cunti Mayta, Queco Avcaylli, and Rocca Yupanqui.

This Mayta Ccapac was warlike, and the Inca who first distinguished himself in arms after the time of Mama Huaco and Manco Ccapac. They relate of him that he dared to open the hamper containing the bird *indi*. This bird, brought by Manco Ccapac from Tampu-tocco, had been inherited by his successors, the predecessors of Mayta Ccapac, who had always kept it shut up in a hamper or box of straw, such was the fear they had of it. But Mayta Ccapac was bolder than any of them. Desirous of seeing what his predecessors had guarded so carefully, he opened the hamper, saw the bird *indi* and had some conversation with it. They say that it gave him oracles, and that after the interview with the bird he was wiser, and knew better what he should do, and what would happen.

With all this he did not go forth from the valley of Cuzco, although chiefs from some distant nations came to visit him. He lived in Ynti-cancha, the House of the Sun. He left a lineage called *Usca Mayta Panaca Ayllu*, and some members of it are still living in Cuzco. The heads are named Don Juan Tambo Usca Mayta, and Don

Baltasar Quiso Mayta. They are Hurin-cuzcos. Mayta
Ccapac died at the age of 112 years, in the year 890 of the
nativity of our Lord Jesus Christ. The Licentiate Polo
found his body and idol *guauqui* with the rest.

XVIII.

THE LIFE OF CCAPAC YUPANQUI, THE FIFTH INCA[1].

At the time of his death, Mayta Ccapac named Ccapac
Yupanqui as his successor, his son by his wife Mama
Tacucaray. This Ccapac Yupanqui, as soon as he succeeded
to the Incaship, made his brothers swear allegiance to him,
and that they desired that he should be Ccapac. They
complied from fear, for he was proud and cruel. At first
he lived very quietly in the Ynti-cancha. It is to be noted
that although Ccapac Yupanqui succeeded his father, he
was not the eldest son. Cunti Mayta, who was older, had
an ugly face. His father had, therefore, disinherited him and
named Ccapac Yupanqui as successor to the sovereignty,
and Cunti Mayta as high priest. For this reason Ccapac
Yupanqui was not the legitimate heir, although he tyrannically forced his brothers to swear allegiance to him.

This Inca, it is said, was the first to make conquests
beyond the valley of Cuzco. He forcibly subjugated the
people of Cuyumarca and Ancasmarca, four leagues from
Cuzco. A wealthy Sinchi of Ayamarca, from fear,
presented his daughter, named Ccuri-hilpay to the Inca.
Others say that she was a native of Cuzco. The Inca
received her as his wife, and had a son by her named Inca
Rocca, besides five other sons by various women. These
sons were named Apu Calla, Humpi, Apu Saca, Apu

---

[1] All authorities are agreed that Ccapac Yupanqui was the fifth
Inca, except Betanzos, who puts him in his father's place. Garcilasso
attributes extensive conquests to him, both to south and west.

Chima-chaui, and Uchun-cuna-ascalla-rando[1]. Apu Saca had a son named Apu Mayta, a very valiant and famous captain, who greatly distinguished himself in the time of Inca Rocca and Viracocha Inca, in company with Vicaquirau, another esteemed captain. Besides these Ccapac Yupanqui had another son named Apu Urco Huaranca[2]. This Ccapac Yupanqui lived 104 years, and was Ccapac for 89 years. He succeeded at the age of 15, and died in the year 980 of the nativity of our redeemer Jesus Christ. His *ayllu* or lineage was and is called *Apu Mayta Panaca Ayllu*. Several of this lineage are now living, the principal heads being four in number, namely, Don Cristobal Cusi-hualpa, Don Antonio Piçuy, Don Francisco Cocasaca, and Don Alonso Rupaca. They are Hurin-cuzcos. The Licentiate Polo found the idol or *guaoqui* of this Inca with the body. They were hidden with the rest, to conceal the idolatrous ceremonies of heathen times.

XIX.

THE LIFE OF INCA ROCCA, THE SIXTH INCA[3].

When Ccapac Yupanqui died, Inca Rocca, his son by his wife Ccuri-hilpay, succeeded by nomination of his father and the guardian *ayllus*. This Inca Rocca showed force and valour at the beginning of his Incaship, for he con-

---

[1] *Calla* means a distaff. *Humpi* means perspiration. *Saca* is a game bird, also a comet. Chima-chaui is a proper name with no meaning. The name of the fifth son is rather unmanageable. Uchun-cuna-ascalla-rando. *Uchun-cuna* would mean the Peruvian pepper with the plural particle. *Ascalla* would be a small potato. *Rando* is a corrupt form of *runtu*, an egg. This little Inca seems to have done the marketing.

[2] *Urco*, the male gender. *Huaranca*, a thousand.

[3] All authorities are agreed respecting Inca Rocca as the sixth Inca. Garcilasso makes him extend the Inca dominion beyond the Apurimac, and into the country of the Chancos.

quered the territories of Muyna[1] and Pinahua with great violence and cruelty. They are rather more than four leagues to the south-south-east of Cuzco. He killed their Sinchis Muyna Pancu, and Huaman-tupac, though some say that Huaman-tupac fled and was never more seen. He did this by the help of Apu Mayta his nephew, and grandson of Ccapac Yupanqui. He also conquered Caytomarca, four leagues from Cuzco. He discovered the waters of Hurin-chacan and those of Hanan-chacan, which is as much as to say the upper and lower waters of Cuzco, and led them in conduits; so that to this day they irrigate fields; and his sons and descendants have benefited by them to this day.

Inca Rocca gave himself up to pleasures and banquets, preferring to live in idleness. He loved his children to that extent, that for them he forgot duties to his people and even to his own person. He married a great lady of the town of Pata-huayllacan, daughter of the Sinchi of that territory, named Soma Inca. Her name was Mama Micay. From this marriage came the wars between Tocay Ccapac and the Cuzcos as we shall presently relate. By this wife Inca Rocca had a son named Titu Cusi Hualpa[2], and by another name Yahuar-huaccac, and besides this eldest legitimate son he had four other famous sons named Inca Paucar, Huaman Taysi Inca, and Vicaquirau Inca[2]. The latter was a great warrior, companion in arms with Apu Mayta. These two captains won great victories and subdued many provinces for Viracocha Inca and Inca Yupanqui. They were the founders of the great power to which the Incas afterwards attained.

As the events which happened in the reign of Inca Rocca touching the Ayamarcas will be narrated in the

---

[1] Muyna is a district with a lake, 14 miles S.S.W. of Cuzco. Pinahua is mentioned by Garcilasso as a chief to the westward, i. p. 71.

[2] *Titu* means august or magnanimous. *Cusi* joyful. *Hualpa* a game bird. *Paucar* means beautiful or bright coloured. *Huaman* a falcon. *Vica* may be *uilca* sacred. *Quirau* a cradle.

life of his son, we will not say more of this Inca, except that, while his ancestors had always lived in the lower part of Cuzco, and were therefore called Hurin-cuzcos, he ordered that those who sprang from him should form another party, and be called Hanan-cuzcos, which means the Cuzcos of the upper part. So that from this Inca began the party of upper or Hanan-cuzcos, for presently he and his successors left their residence at the House of the Sun, and established themselves away from it, building palaces where they lived, in the upper part of the town. It is to be noted that each Inca had a special palace in which he lived, the son not wishing to reside in the palace where his father had lived. It was left in the same state as it was in when the father died, with servants, relations, *ayllus* or heirs that they might maintain it, and keep the edifices in repair. The Incas and their *ayllus* were, and still are Hanan-cuzco; although afterwards, in the time of Pachacuti, these *ayllus* were reformed by him. Some say that then were established the two parties which have been so celebrated in these parts.

Inca Rocca named his son Vicaquirao as the head of his lineage, and it is still called after him the *Vicaquirao Panaca Ayllu*. There are now some of this lineage living in Cuzco, the principal heads who protect and maintain it being the following: Don Francisco Huaman Rimachi Hachacoma, and Don Antonio Huaman Mayta. They are Hanan-cuzcos. Inca Rocca lived 103 years, and died in the year 1088 of the nativity of our Lord. The Licentiate Polo found his body in the town called Rarapa, kept there with much care and veneration according to their rites.

XX.

THE LIFE OF TITU CUSI HUALPA, VULGARLY
CALLED YAHUAR-HUACCAC.

Titu Cusi Hualpa Inca, eldest son of Inca Rocca and
his wife Mama Micay, had a strange adventure in his childhood[1]. These natives therefore relate his life from his
childhood, and in the course of it they tell some things
of his father, and of some who were strangers in Cuzco, as
follows. It has been related how the Inca Rocca married
Mama Micay by the rites of their religion. But it must be
understood that those of Huayllacan had already promised
to give Mama Micay, who was their countrywoman and very
beautiful, in marriage to Tocay Ccapac, Sinchi of the Ayamarcas their neighbours. When the Ayamarcas[2] saw that
the Huayllacans had broken their word, they were furious
and declared war, considering them as enemies. War was
carried on, the Huayllacans defending themselves and also
attacking the Ayamarcas, both sides committing cruelties,
inflicting deaths and losses, and causing great injury to each
other. While this war was being waged, Mama Micay gave
birth to her son Titu Cusi Hualpa. The war continued for
some years after his birth, when both sides saw that they
were destroying each other, and agreed to come to terms,
to avoid further injury. The Ayamarcas, who were the
most powerful, requested those of Huayllacan to deliver

[1] The very interesting story of the kidnapping of the heir of Inca
Rocca, is well told by Sarmiento.

[2] The Ayarmarcas seem to have occupied the country about 15
miles S.S.W. of Cuzco, near Muyna. The word Ayar is the same as
that in the names of the brethren of Manco Ccapac. But others
omit the r, and make it Ayamarca, Cieza de Leon, pp. 114, 115,
Garcilasso, i. p. 80, Yamqui Pachacuti, p. 90. The month of October
was called Ayamarca-Raymi. Molina says that it was because the
Ayamarca tribe celebrated the feast of Huarachicu in that month.

the child Titu Cusi Hualpa into their hands, to do what they liked with him.   On this condition they would desist from further hostilities, but if it was not complied with, they announced that they would continue a mortal war to the end.   The Huayllacans, fearing this, and knowing their inability for further resistance, accepted the condition, although they were uncles and relations of the child.   In order to comply it was necessary for them to deceive the Inca.   There was, in the town of Paulo, a brother of Inca Rocca and uncle of Titu Cusi Hualpa named Inca Paucar. He went or sent messengers to ask Inca Rocca to think well of sending his nephew Titu Cusi Hualpa to his town of Paulo in order that, while still a child, he might learn to know and care for his relations on his mother's side, while they wanted to make him the heir of their estates. Believing in these words the Inca Rocca consented that his son should be taken to Paulo, or the town of Micocancha. As soon as they had the child in their town the Huayllacans made great feasts in honour of Titu Cusi Hualpa, who was then eight years old, a little more or less.   His father had sent some Incas to guard him.   When the festivities were over, the Huayllacans sent to give notice to the Ayamarcas that, while they were occupied in ploughing certain lands which they call *chacaras*, they might come down on the town and carry off the child, doing with him what they chose, in accordance with the agreement.   The Ayamarcas, being informed, came at the time and to the place notified and, finding the child Titu Cusi Hualpa alone, they carried it off.

Others say that this treason was carried out in another way.   While the uncle was giving the child many presents, his cousins, the sons of Inca Paucar, became jealous and treated with Tocay Ccapac to deliver the child into his hands.   Owing to this notice Tocay Ccapac came.   Inca Paucar had gone out to deliver to his nephew a certain

estate and a flock of llamas. Tocay Ccapac, the enemy of
Inca Rocca was told by those who had charge of the boy.
He who carried him fled, and the boy was seized and carried
off by Tocay Ccapac.

Be it the one way or the other, the result was that the
Ayamarcas took Titu Cusi Hualpa from the custody of
Inca Paucar in the town of Paulo, while Inca Paucar and
the Huayllacans sent the news to Inca Rocca by one party,
and with another took up arms against the Ayamarcas.

XXI.

WHAT HAPPENED AFTER THE AYAMARCAS HAD STOLEN TITU CUSI HUALPA.

When the Ayamarcas and their Sinchi Tocay Ccapac
stole the son of Inca Rocca, they marched off with him.
The Huayllacans of Paulopampa, under their Sinchi Paucar
Inca, marched in pursuit, coming up to them at a place
called Amaro, on the territory of the Ayamarcas. There
was an encounter between them, one side to recover the
child, and the other to keep their capture. But Paucar was
only making a demonstration so as to have an excuse ready.
Consequently the Ayamarcas were victorious, while the
Huayllacans broke and fled. It is said that in this
encounter, and when the child was stolen, all the *orejones*
who had come as a guard from Cuzco, were slain. The
Ayamarcas then took the child to the chief place of their
province called Ahuayro-cancha.

Many say that Tocay Ccapac was not personally in this
raid but that he sent his Ayamarcas, who, when they
arrived at Ahuayro-cancha, presented the child Titu Cusi
Hualpa to him, saying, " Look here, Tocay Ccapac, at the
prisoner we have brought you." The Sinchi received his
prize with great satisfaction, asking in a loud voice if this

was the child of Mama Micay, who ought to have been his wife. Titu Cusi Hualpa, though but a child, replied boldly that he was the son of Mama Micay and of the Inca Rocca. Tocay was indignant when he had heard those words, and ordered those who brought the child as a prisoner to take him out and kill him. The boy, when he heard such a sentence passed upon him, was so filled with sadness and fright, that he began to weep from fear of death. He began to shed tears of blood and with indignation beyond his years, in the form of a malediction he said to Tocay and the Ayamarcas, " I tell you that as sure as you murder me there will come such a curse on you and your descendants that you will all come to an end, without any memory being left of your nation."

The Ayamarcas and Tocay attentively considered this curse of the child together with the tears of blood. They thought there was some great mystery that so young a child should utter such weighty words, and that the fear of death should make such an impression on him that he should shed tears of blood. They were in suspense divining what it portended, whether that the child would become a great man. They revoked the sentence of death, calling the child *Yahuar-huaccac*, which means " weeper of blood," in allusion to what had taken place.

But although they did not wish to kill him then and with their own hands, they ordered that he should lead such a life as that he would die of hunger. Before this they all said to the child that he should turn his face to Cuzco and weep over it, because those curses he had pronounced, would fall on the inhabitants of Cuzco, and so it happened.

This done they delivered him to the most valiant Indians, and ordered them to take him to certain farms where flocks were kept, giving him to eat by rule, and so sparingly that he would be consumed with hunger before he died. He was there for a year without leaving the place, so that they did not know at Cuzco, or anywhere else, whether he was dead or alive. During this time Inca Rocca, being without certain knowledge of his son, did not wish to make war on the Ayamarcas because, if he was alive, they might kill him. So he did no more than prepare his men of war and keep ready, while he enquired for his son in all the ways that were possible.

XXII.

HOW IT BECAME KNOWN THAT YAHUAR-HUACCAC WAS ALIVE.

As the child Yahuar-huaccac was a year among the shepherds without leaving their huts, which served as a prison, no one knew where he was, because he could not come forth, being well watched by the shepherds and other guards. But it so happened that there was a woman in the place called Chimpu Orma, native of the town of Anta, three leagues from Cuzco. She was a concubine of the Sinchi Tocay Ccapac, and for this reason she had leave to walk about and go into all parts as she pleased. She was the daughter of the Sinchi of Anta, and having given an account of the treatment of the child to her father, brothers, and relations, she persuaded them to help in his liberation. They came on a certain day and, with the pass given them by Chimpu Orma, the father and relations arranged the escape of Yahuar-huaccac. They stationed themselves behind a hill. Yahuar-huaccac was to run in a race with some other boys, to see which could get to the top of the hill first. When the prince reached the top, the men of Anta, who were hidden there, took him in their arms and ran swiftly with him to Anta. When the other boys saw this they quickly gave notice to the valiant guards, who ran after the men of Anta. They overtook them at the lake of

Huaypon, where there was a fierce battle. Finally the Ayamarcas got the worst of it, for they were nearly all killed or wounded. The men of Anta continued their journey to their town, where they gave many presents to Yahuar-huaccac and much service, having freed him from the mortal imprisonment in which Tocay Ccapac held him. In this town of Anta the boy remained a year, being served with much love, but so secretly that his father Inca Rocca did not know that he had escaped, during all that time. At the end of a year those of Anta agreed to send messengers to Inca Rocca to let him know of the safety of his son and heir, because they desired to know and serve him. The messengers went to Inca Rocca and, having delivered their message, received the reply that the Inca only knew that the Ayamarcas had stolen his son. They were asked about it again and again, and at last Inca Rocca came down from his throne and closely examined the messengers, that they might tell him more, for not without cause had he asked them so often. The messengers, being so persistently questioned by Inca Rocca, related what had passed, and that his son was free in Anta, served and regaled by the chief who had liberated him. Inca Rocca rejoiced, promised favours, and dismissed the messengers with thanks. Inca Rocca then celebrated the event with feasts and rejoicings.

But not feeling quite certain of the truth of what he had been told, he sent a poor man seeking charity to make enquiries at Anta, whether it was all true. The poor man went, ascertained that the child was certainly liberated, and returned with the news to Inca Rocca ; which gave rise to further rejoicings in Cuzco. Presently the Inca sent many principal people of Cuzco with presents of gold, silver, and cloth to the Antas, asking them to receive them and to send back his son. The Antas replied that they did not want his presents which they returned, that they cared more that Yahuar-huaccac should remain with them, that they might serve him and his father also, for they felt much love for the boy. Yet if Inca Rocca wanted his son, he should be returned on condition that, from that time forwards, the Antas should be called relations of the *orejones*. When Inca Rocca was made acquainted with the condition, he went to Anta and conceded what they asked for, to the Sinchi and his people. For this reason the Antas were called relations of the Cuzcos from that time.

Inca Rocca brought his son Yahuar-huaccac to Cuzco and nominated him successor to the Incaship, the *ayllus* and *orejones* receiving him as such. At the end of two years Inca Rocca died, and Yahuar-huaccac, whose former name was Titu Cusi Hualpa, remained sole Inca. Before Inca Rocca died he made friends with Tocay Ccapac, through the mediation of Mama Chicya, daughter of Tocay Ccapac, who married Yahuar-huaccac, and Inca Rocca gave his daughter Ccuri-Occllo in marriage to Tocay Ccapac.

XXIII.

YAHUAR-HUACCAC INCA YUPANQUI COMMENCES HIS REIGN ALONE, AFTER THE DEATH OF HIS FATHER[1].

When Yahuar-huaccac found himself in possession of the sole sovereignty, he remembered the treason with which he had been betrayed by the Huayllacans who sold him and delivered him up to his enemies the Ayamarcas;

---

[1] *Yahuar* means blood. *Huaccani* to weep. Yahuar-huaccac succeeded to Inca Rocca according to Garcilasso de la Vega, Montesinos, Betanzos, Balboa, Yamqui Pachacuti and Sarmiento. Cieza de Leon and Herrera have Inca Yupanqui. Garcilasso makes this Inca banish his son Viracocha, who returns in consequence of a dream, and defeats the Chancas. This all seems to be a mistake. It was Viracocha who fled, and his son Inca Yupanqui, surnamed Pachacuti, who defeated the Chancas and dethroned his father.

and he proposed to inflict an exemplary punishment on them. When the Huayllacans knew this, they humbled themselves before Yahuar-huaccac, entreating him to forgive the evil deeds they had committed against him. Yahuar-huaccac, taking into consideration that they were relations, forgave them. Then he sent a force, under the command of his brother Vicaquirau, against Mohina and Pinahua, four leagues from Cuzco, who subdued these places. He committed great cruelties, for no other reason than that they did not come to obey his will. This would be about 23 years after the time when he rested in Cuzco. Some years afterwards the town of Mollaca, near Cuzco, was conquered and subjugated by force of arms.

Yahuar-huaccac had, by his wife Mama Chicya, three legitimate sons. The eldest was Paucar Ayllu. The second, Pahuac Hualpa Mayta[1], was chosen to succeed his father, though he was not the eldest. The third was named Viracocha, who was afterwards Inca through the death of his brother. Besides these he had three other illegitimate sons named Vicchu Tupac because he subdued the town of Vicchu, Marca-yutu, and Rocca Inca. As the Huayllacans wanted Marca-yutu to succeed Yahuar-huaccac, because he was their relation, they determined to kill Pahuac Hualpa Mayta, who was nominated to succeed. With this object they asked his father to let him go to Paulo. Forgetting their former treason, he sent the child to its grandfather Soma Inca with forty *orejones* of the *ayllus* of Cuzco as his guard. When he came to their town they killed him, for which the Inca, his father, inflicted a great punishment on the Huayllacans, killing some and banishing others until very few were left.

The Inca then went to the conquest of Pillauya, three leagues from Cuzco in the valley of Pisac, and to Choyca,

---

[1] Or Pahuac Mayta Inca (Garcilasso de la Vega, i. p. 23) so named from his swiftness. *Pahuani*, to run.

an adjacent place, and to Yuco. After that he oppressed by force and with cruelties, the towns of Chillincay, Taocamarca, and the Caviñas, making them pay tribute. The Inca conquered ten places himself or through his son and captains. Some attribute all the conquests to his son Viracocha.

This Inca was a man of gentle disposition and very handsome face. He lived 115 years. He succeeded his father at the age of 19, and was sovereign for 96 years. He left an *ayllu* named *Aucaylli Panaca*, and some are still living at Cuzco. The principal chiefs who maintain it are Don Juan Concha Yupanqui, Don Martin Titu Yupanqui, and Don Gonzalo Paucar Aucaylli. They are Hanan-cuzcos. The body of this Inca has not been discovered[1]. It is believed that those of the town of Paulo have it, with the Inca's *guauqui*.

XXIV.

LIFE OF VIRACOCHA THE EIGHTH INCA[2].

As the Huayllacans murdered Pahuac Hualpa Mayta who should have succeeded his father Yahuar-huaccac, the second son Viracocha Inca was nominated for the succession, whose name when a child was Hatun Tupac Inca, younger legitimate son of Yahuar-huaccac and Mama Chicya. He was married to Mama Runtucaya, a native of Anta. Once when this Hatun Tupac Inca was in Urcos, a town which is a little more than five leagues S.S.E. of Cuzco, where there was a sumptuous *huaca* in honour of Ticci Viracocha, the deity appeared to him in the night. Next morning he assembled his *orejones*, among them his tutor Hualpa Rimachi, and told them how Viracocha had appeared to him that night, and had

---

[1] In the margin of the MS., "The witnesses said that they believed that the licentiate Polo found it." Navamuel.

[2] All authorities agree respecting Viracocha as the eighth Inca.

announced great good fortune to him and his descendants. In congratulating him Hualpa Rimachi saluted him, "O Viracocha Inca." The rest followed his example and celebrated this name, and the Inca retained it all the rest of his life. Others say that he took this name, because, when he was armed as a knight and had his ears bored, he took Ticci Viracocha as the godfather of his knighthood. Be it as it may, all that is certain is that when a child, before he succeeded his father, he was named Hatun Tupac Inca, and afterwards, for the rest of his life, Viracocha Inca.

After he saw the apparition in Urcos, the Inca came to Cuzco, and conceived the plan of conquering and tyrannizing over all the country that surrounds Cuzco. For it is to be understood that, although his father and grandfather had conquered and robbed in these directions, as their only object was rapine and bloodshed, they did not place garrisons in the places they subdued, so that when the Inca, who had conquered these people, died, they rose in arms and regained their liberty. This is the reason that we repeat several times that a place was conquered, for it was by different Incas. For instance Mohina and Pinahua, although first overrun by Inca Rocca, were also invaded by Yahuar-huaccac, and then by Viracocha and his son Inca Yupanqui. Each town fought so hard for its liberty, both under their Sinchis and without them, that one succeeded in subjugating one and another defeated another. This was especially the case in the time of the Incas. Even in Cuzco itself those of one suburb, called Carmenca, made war on another suburb called Cayocachi. So it is to be understood that, in the time of the seven Incas preceding Viracocha, although owing to the power they possessed in the *ayllus*, they terrorized those of Cuzco and the immediate neighbourhood, the subjection only lasted while the lance was over the vanquished, and that the moment they had a chance they took up arms for their liberty. They did this at great risk to themselves, and sustained much loss of life, even those in Cuzco itself, until the time of Viracocha Inca.

This Inca had resolved to subjugate all the tribes he possibly could by force and cruelty. He selected as his captains two valiant *orejones*, the one named Apu Mayta and the other Vicaquirau, of the lineage of Inca Rocca. With these captains, who were cruel and impious, he began to subjugate, before all things, the inhabitants of Cuzco who were not Incas *orejones*, practising on them great cruelties and putting many to death. At this time many towns and provinces were up in arms. Those in the neighbourhood of Cuzco had risen to defend themselves from the *orejones* Incas of Cuzco who had made war to tyrannize over them. Others were in arms with the same motives as the Incas, which was to subdue them if their forces would suffice. Thus it was that though many Sinchis were elected, their proceedings were confused and without concert, so that each force was small, and they were all weak and without help from each other. This being known to Viracocha, it encouraged him to commence his policy of conquest beyond Cuzco.

Before coming to treat of the nations which Viracocha Inca conquered, we will tell of the sons he had. By Mama Runtucaya, his legitimate wife, he had four sons, the first and eldest Inca Rocca, the second Tupac Yupanqui, the third Inca Yupanqui, and the fourth Ccapac Yupanqui. By another beautiful Indian named Ccuri-chulpa, of the Ayavilla nation in the valley of Cuzco he also had two sons, the one named Inca Urco, the other Inca Socso. The descendants of Inca Urco, however, say that he was legitimate, but all the rest say that he was a bastard[1].

---

[1] Urco is made by Cieza de Leon to succeed, and to have been dethroned by Inca Yupanqui owing to his flight from the Chancas. Yamqui Pachacuti records the death of Urco. Herrera, Fernandez, Yamqui Pachacuti also make Urco succeed Viracocha.

XXV.

THE PROVINCES AND TOWNS CONQUERED BY THE EIGHTH INCA VIRACOCHA.

Viracocha, having named Apu Mayta and Vicaquirau as his captains, and mustered his forces, gave orders that they should advance to make conquests beyond the valley of Cuzco. They went to Pacaycacha, in the valley of Pisac, three leagues and a half from Cuzco. And because the besieged did not submit at once they assaulted the town, killing the inhabitants and their Sinchi named Acamaqui. Next the Inca marched against the towns of Mohina, Pinahua, Casacancha, and Runtucancha, five short leagues from Cuzco. They had made themselves free, although Yahuar-huaccac had sacked their towns. The captains of Viracocha attacked and killed most of the natives, and their Sinchis named Muyna Pancu and Huaman Tupac. The people of Mohina and Pinahua suffered from this war and subsequent cruelties because they said that they were free, and would not serve nor be vassals to the Incas.

At this time the eldest son, Inca Rocca, was grown up and showed signs of being a courageous man. Viracocha, therefore, made him captain-general with Apu Mayta and Vicaquirau as his colleagues. They also took with them Inca Yupanqui, who also gave hopes owing to the valour he had shown in the flower of his youth. With these captains the conquests were continued. Huaypar-marca was taken, the Ayamarcas were subdued, and Tocay Ccapac and Chihuay Ccapac, who had their seats near Cuzco, were slain. The Incas next subjugated Mollaca and ruined the town of Cayto, four leagues from Cuzco, killing its Sinchi named Ccapac Chani. They assaulted the towns.

of Socma and Chiraques, killing their Sinchis named Puma Lloqui and Illacumbi, who were very warlike chiefs in that time, who had most valorously resisted the attacks of former Incas, that they might not come from Cuzco to subdue them. The Inca captains also conquered Calca and Caquia Xaquixahuana, three leagues from Cuzco, and the towns of Collocte and Camal. They subdued the people between Cuzco and Quiquisana with the surrounding country, the Papris and other neighbouring places; all within seven or eight leagues round Cuzco. [*In these conquests they committed very great cruelties, robberies, put many to death and destroyed towns, burning and desolating along the road without leaving memory of anything.*]

As Viracocha was now very old, he nominated as his successor his bastard son Inca Urco, without regard to the order of succession, because he was very fond of his mother. This Inca was bold, proud, and despised others, so that he aroused the indignation of the warriors, more especially of the legitimate sons, Inca Rocca, who was the eldest, and of the valiant captains Apu Mayta and Vicaquirau. These took order to prevent this succession to the Incaship, preferring one of the other brothers, the best conditioned, who would treat them well and honourably as they deserved. They secretly set their eyes on the third of the legitimate sons named Cusi, afterwards called Inca Yupanqui, because they believed that he was mild and affable, and, besides these qualities, he showed signs of high spirit and lofty ideas. Apu Mayta was more in favour of this plan than the others, as he desired to have some one to shield him from the fury of Viracocha Inca. Mayta thought that the Inca would kill him because he had seduced a woman named Cacchon Chicya, who was a wife of Viracocha. Apu Mayta had spoken of his plan and of his devotion to Cusi, to his colleague Vicaquirau. While they were consulting how it should be managed, the Chancas of Andahuaylas, thirty leagues from Cuzco, marched upon that city, as will be narrated in the life of Inca Yupanqui. Inca Viracocha, from fear of them, fled from Cuzco, and went to a place called Caquia Xaquixahuana, where he shut himself up, being afraid of the Chancas. Here he died after some years, deprived of Cuzco of which his son Cusi had possession for several years before his father's death. Viracocha Inca was he who had made the most extensive conquests beyond Cuzco and, as we may say, he tyrannized anew even as regards Cuzco, as has been said above.

Viracocha lived 119 years, succeeding at the age of 18. He was Ccapac 101 years. He named the *ayllu*, which he left for the continuance of his lineage, *Socso Panaca Ayllu*, and some are still living at Cuzco, the heads being Amaru Titu, Don Francisco Chalco Yupanqui, Don Francisco Anti Hualpa. They are Hanan-cuzcos.

This Inca was industrious, and inventor of cloths and embroidered work called in their language *Viracocha-tocapu*, and amongst us *brocade*. He was rich [*for hè robbed much*] and had vases of gold and silver. He was buried in Caquia Xaquixahuana and Gonzalo Pizarro, having heard that there was treasure with the body, discovered it and a large sum of gold. He burnt the body, and the natives collected the ashes and hid them in a vase. This, with the Inca's *guauqui*, called *Inca Amaru*, was found by the Licentiate Polo, when he was Corregidor of Cuzco.

XXVI.

THE LIFE OF INCA YUPANQUI OR PACHACUTI[1], THE NINTH INCA.

It is related, in the life of Inca Viracocha, that he had four legitimate sons. Of these the third named Cusi, and as surname Inca Yupanqui, was raised to the Incaship by the famous captains Apu Mayta and Vicaquirau, and by the rest of the legitimate sons, and against the will of his father. In the course of their intrigues to carry this into effect, the times gave them the opportunity which they could not otherwise have found, in the march of the Chancas upon Cuzco. It happened in this way.

Thirty leagues to the west of Cuzco there is a province called Andahuaylas, the names of the natives of it being Chancas. In this province there were two Sinchis, [*robbers and cruel tyrants*] named Uscovilca and Ancovilca who, coming on an expedition from near Huamanca with some companies of robbers, had settled in the valley of Andahuaylas, and had there formed a state. They were brothers. Uscovilca being the elder and principal one, instituted a tribe which he called Hanan-chancas or upper Chancas. Ancovilca formed another tribe called Hurin-chancas or lower Chancas. These chiefs, after death, were embalmed, and because they were feared for their cruelties in life, were kept by their people. The Hanan-chancas carried the statue of Uscovilca with them, in their raids and wars. Although they had other Sinchis, they always attributed their success to the statue of Uscovilca, which they called Ancoallo.

---

[1] Inca Yupanqui surnamed Pachacuti was the ninth Inca. All the authorities agree that he dethroned either his father Viracocha, or his half brother Urco, after his victory over the Chancas, and that he had a long and glorious reign.

The tribes and companies of Uscovilca had multiplied prodigiously in the time of Viracocha. It seemed to them that they were so powerful that no one could equal them, so they resolved to march from Andahuaylas and conquer Cuzco. With this object they elected two Sinchis, one named Asto-huaraca, and the other Tomay-huaraca, one of the tribe of Hanan-chanca, the other of Hurin-chanca. These were to lead them in their enterprise. The Chancas and their Sinchis were proud and insolent. Setting out from Andahuaylas they marched on the way to Cuzco until they reached a place called Ichu-pampa, five leagues west of that city, where they halted for some days, terrifying the neighbourhood and preparing for an advance.

The news spread terror among the *orejones* of Cuzco, for they doubted the powers of Inca Viracocha, who was now very old and weak. Thinking that the position of Cuzco was insecure, Viracocha called a Council of his sons and captains Apu Mayta and Vicaquirau. These captains said to him—"Inca Viracocha! we have understood what you have proposed to us touching this matter, and how you ought to meet the difficulty. After careful consideration it appears to us that as you are old and infirm owing to what you have undergone in former wars, it will not be well that you should attempt so great a business, dangerous and with victory doubtful, such as that which now presents itself before your eyes. The wisest counsel respecting the course you should adopt is that you should leave Cuzco, and proceed to the place of Chita, and thence to Caquia Xaquixahuana, which is a strong fort, whence you may treat for an agreement with the Chancas." They gave this advice to Viracocha to get him out of Cuzco and give them a good opportunity to put their designs into execution, which were to raise Cusi Inca Yupanqui to the throne. In whatever manner it was done, it is certain that this advice was taken by the Inca Viracocha. He determined to leave

Cuzco and proceed to Chita, in accordance with their proposal. But when Cusi Inca Yupanqui found that his father was determined to leave Cuzco, they say that he thus addressed him, " How father can it fit into your heart to accept such infamous advice as to leave Cuzco, city of the Sun and of Viracocha, whose name you have taken, whose promise you hold that you shall be a great lord, you and your descendants." Though a boy, he said this with the animated daring of a man high in honour. The father answered that he was a boy and that he spoke like one, in talking without consideration, and that such words were of no value. Inca Yupanqui replied that he would remain where they would be remembered, that he would not leave Cuzco nor abandon the House of the Sun. They say that all this was planned by the said captains of Viracocha, Apu Mayta and Vicaquirau, to throw those off their guard who might conceive suspicion respecting the remaining of Inca Yupanqui in Cuzco. So Viracocha left Cuzco and went to Chita, taking with him his two illegitimate sons Inca Urco and Inca Socso. His son Inca Yupanqui remained at Cuzco, resolved to defend the city or die in its defence. Seven chiefs remained with him ; Inca Rocca his elder and legitimate brother, Apu Mayta, Vicaquirau, Quillis-cacha, Urco Huaranca, Chima Chaui Pata Yupanqui, Viracocha Inca Paucar, and Mircoy-mana the tutor of Inca Yupanqui.

XXVII.

COMING OF THE CHANCAS AGAINST CUZCO.

At the time when Inca Viracocha left Cuzco, Asto-huaraca and Tomay-huaraca set out for Ichu-pampa, first making sacrifices and blowing out the lungs of an animal, which they call *calpa*. This they did not well understand, from what happened afterwards. Marching on towards Cuzco, they arrived at a place called Conchacalla, where they took a prisoner. From him they learnt what was happening at Cuzco, and he offered to guide them there secretly. Thus he conducted them half way. But then his conscience cried out to him touching the evil he was doing. So he fled to Cuzco, and gave the news that the Chancas were resolutely advancing. The news of this Indian, who was a Quillis-cachi of Cuzco, made Viracocha hasten his flight to Chita, whither the Chancas sent their messengers summoning him to surrender, and threatening war if he refused. Others say that these were not messengers but scouts and that Inca Viracocha, knowing this, told them that he knew they were spies of the Chancas, that he did not want to kill them, but that they might return and tell their people that if they wanted anything he was there. So they departed and at the mouth of a channel of water some of them fell and were killed. At this the Chancas were much annoyed. They said that the messengers had been ordered to go to Inca Viracocha, and that they were killed by his captain Quequo Mayta.

While this was proceeding with the messengers of the Chancas, the Chanca army was coming nearer to Cuzco. Inca Yupanqui made great praying to Viracocha and to the Sun to protect the city. One day he was at Susur-puquio in great affliction, thinking over the best plan for opposing his enemies, when there appeared a person in the air like the Sun, consoling him and animating him for the battle. This being held up to him a mirror in which the provinces he would subdue were shown, and told him that he would be greater than any of his ancestors: he was to have no doubt, but to return to the city, because he would conquer the Chancas who were marching on Cuzco. With these words the vision animated Inca Yupanqui. He took the mirror, which he carried with him ever afterwards, in peace or war, and returned to the city, where he began to encourage those he had left there, and some who came from afar[1]. The latter came to look on, not daring to declare for either party, fearing the rage of the conqueror if they should join the conquered side. Inca Yupanqui, though only a lad of 20 or 22 years, provided for everything as one who was about to fight for his life.

While the Inca Yupanqui was thus engaged the Chancas had been marching, and reached a place very near Cuzco called Cusi-pampa, there being nothing between it and Cuzco but a low hill. Here the Quillis-cachi was encountered again. He said that he had been to spy, and that he rejoiced to meet them. This deceiver went from one side to the other, always keeping friends with both, to secure the favour of the side which eventually conquered. The Chancas resumed the march, expecting that there would be no defence. But the Quillis-cachi, mourning over the destruction of his country, disappeared from among the Chancas and went to Cuzco to give the alarm. " To arms! to arms!" he shouted, " Inca Yupanqui. The Chancas are upon you."

At these words the Inca, who was not off his guard, mustered and got his troops in order, but he found very few willing to go forth with him to oppose the enemy, almost all took to the hills to watch the event. With those who were willing to follow, though few in number, chiefly the men of the seven Sinchis, brothers and captains, named above, he formed a small force and came forth to receive the enemy who advanced in fury and without order. The opposing forces advanced towards each other, the Chancas attacking the city in four directions. The

---

[1] Susurpuquio seems to have been a fountain or spring on the road to Xaquixahuana. Molina relates the story of the vision somewhat differently, p. 12. Mrs Zelia Nuttall thinks that the description of the vision bears such a very strong resemblance to a bas relief found in Guatemala that they must have a common origin.

Inca Yupanqui sent all the succour he could to the assailed points, while he and his friends advanced towards the statue and standard of Uscovilca, with Asto-huaraca and Tomay-huaraca defending them. Here there was a bloody and desperate battle, one side striving to enter the city, and the other opposing its advance. Those who entered by a suburb called Chocos-chacona were valiantly repulsed by the inhabitants. They say that a woman named Chañan-ccuri-coca here fought like a man, and so valiantly opposed the Chancas that they were obliged to retire. This was the cause that all the Chancas who saw it were dismayed. The Inca Yupanqui meanwhile was so quick and dexterous with his weapon, that those who carried the statue of Uscovilca became alarmed, and their fear was increased when they saw great numbers of men coming down from the hills. They say that these were sent by Viracocha, the creator, as succour for the Inca. The Chancas began to give way, leaving the statue of Uscovilca, and they say even that of Ancovilca. Attacking on two sides, Inca Rocca, Apu Mayta, and Vicaquirau made great havock among the Chancas. Seeing that their only safety was in flight, they turned their backs, and their quickness in running exceeded their fierceness in advancing. The men of Cuzco continued the pursuit, killing and wounding, for more than two leagues, when they desisted. The Chancas returned to Ichu-pampa, and the *orejones* to Cuzco, having won a great victory and taken a vast amount of plunder which remained in their hands. The Cuzcos rejoiced at this victory won with so little expectation or hope. They honoured Inca Yupanqui with many epithets, especially calling him PACHACUTI, which means "over-turner of the earth," alluding to the land and farms which they looked upon as lost by the coming of the Chancas. For he had made them free and safe again. From that time he was called Pachacuti Inca Yupanqui.

As soon as the victory was secure, Inca Yupanqui did not wish to enjoy the triumph although many tried to persuade him. He wished to give his father the glory of such a great victory. So he collected the most precious spoils, and took them to his father who was in Chita, with a principal *orejon* named Quillis-cachi Urco Huaranca. By him he sent to ask his father to enjoy that triumph and tread on those spoils of the enemy, a custom they have as a sign of victory. When Quillis-cachi Urco Huaranca arrived before Viracocha Inca, he placed those spoils of the Chancas at his feet with great reverence, saying, " Inca Viracocha! thy son Pachacuti Inca Yupanqui, to whom the Sun has given such a great victory, vanquishing the powerful Chancas, sends me to salute you, and says that, as a good and humble son he wishes you to triumph over your victory and to tread upon these spoils of your enemies, conquered by your hands." Inca Viracocha did not wish to tread on them, but said that his son Inca Urco should do so, as he was to succeed to the Incaship. Hearing this the messenger rose and gave utterance to furious words, saying that he did not come for cowards to triumph by the deeds of Pachacuti. He added that if Viracocha did not wish to receive this recognition from so valiant a son, it would be better that Pachachuti should enjoy the glory for which he had worked. With this he returned to Cuzco, and told Pachacuti what had happened with his father.

XXVIII.

THE SECOND VICTORY OF PACHACUTI INCA YUPANQUI OVER THE CHANCAS.

While Pachacuti Inca Yupanqui was sending the spoil to his father, the Chancas were recruiting and assembling more men at Ichu-pampa, whence they marched on Cuzco the first time. The Sinchis Tomay-huaraca and Astoy-huaraca began to boast, declaring that they would return to Cuzco and leave nothing undestroyed. This news came to Pachacuti Inca Yupanqui. He received it with courage and, assembling his men, he marched in search of the Chancas. When they heard that the Incas were coming, they resolved to march out and encounter them, but the advance of Pachacuti Inca Yupanqui was so rapid that he found the Chancas still at Ichu-pampa.

As soon as the two forces came in sight of each other, Asto-huaraca, full of arrogance, sent to Inca Yupanqui to tell him that he could see the power of the Chancas and the position they now held. They were not like him coming from the poverty stricken Cuzco, and if he did not repent the past and become a tributary and vassal to the Chancas, Asto-huaraca would dye his lance in an Inca's blood. But Inca Yupanqui was not terrified by the embassy. He answered in this way to the messenger. " Go back brother and say to Asto-huaraca, your Sinchi, that Inca Yupanqui is a child of the Sun and guardian of Cuzco, the city of Ticci Viracocha Pachayachachi, by whose order I am here guarding it. For this city is not mine but his ; and if your Sinchi should wish to own obedience to Ticci Viracocha, or to me in His name, he will be honourably received. If your Sinchi should see things in another light, show him that I am here with our friends, and if he should conquer us he can call himself Lord and Inca. But let him understand

that no more time can be wasted in demands and replies.
God (Ticci Viracocha) will give the victory to whom he
pleases."

With this reply the Chancas felt that they had profited
little by their boasting. They ran to their arms because
they saw Pachacuti closely following the bearer of his
reply. The two armies approached each other in Ichu-
pampa, encountered, and mixed together, the Chancas
thrusting with long lances, the Incas using slings, clubs, axes
and arrows, each one defending himself and attacking his
adversary. The battle raged for a long time, without
advantage on either side. At last Pachacuti made a way
to where Asto-huaraca was fighting, attacked him and
delivered a blow with his hatchet which cut off the Chanca's
head. Tomay-huaraca was already killed. The Inca caused
the heads of these two captains to be set on the points of
lances, and raised on high to be seen by their followers. The
Chancas, on seeing the heads, despaired of victory without
leaders. They gave up the contest and sought safety in
flight. Inca Yupanqui and his army followed in pursuit,
wounding and killing until there was nothing more to do.

This great victory yielded such rich and plentiful spoils,
that Pachacuti Inca Yupanqui proposed to go to where his
father was, report to him the story of the battle and the
victory, and to offer him obedience that he might triumph as
if the victory was his own. Loaded with spoil and Chanca
prisoners he went to visit his father. Some say that it was
at a place called Caquia Xaquixahuana, four leagues from
Cuzco, others that it was at Marco, three leagues from
Cuzco. Wherever it was, there was a great ceremony,
presents being given, called *muchanaco*[1]. When Pachacuti
had given his father a full report, he ordered the spoils of
the enemy to be placed at his feet, and asked his father to

---

[1] *Muchani*, I worship. *Nacu* is a particle giving a reciprocal or
mutual meaning, "joint worship."

tread on them and triumph over the victory. But Viracocha Inca, still intent upon having Inca Urco for his successor, desired that the honour offered to him should be enjoyed by his favourite son. He, therefore, did not wish to accept the honours for himself. Yet not wishing to offend the Inca Yupanqui Pachacuti on such a crucial point, he said that he would tread on the spoils and prisoners, and did so. He excused himself from going to triumph at Cuzco owing to his great age, which made him prefer to rest at Caquia Xaquixahuana.

With this reply Pachacuti departed for Cuzco with a great following of people and riches. The Inca Urco also came to accompany him, and on the road there was a quarrel in the rear guard between the men of Urco and those of Pachacuti. Others say that it was an ambush laid for his brother by Urco and that they fought. The Inca Pachacuti took no notice of it, and continued his journey to Cuzco, where he was received with much applause and in triumph. Soon afterwards, as one who thought of assuming authority over the whole land and taking away esteem from his father, as he presently did, he began to distribute the spoils, and confer many favours with gifts and speeches. With the fame of these grand doings, people came to Cuzco from all directions and many of those who were at Caquia Xaquixahuana left it and came to the new Inca at Cuzco.

XXIX.

THE INCA YUPANQUI ASSUMES THE SOVEREIGNTY AND TAKES THE FRINGE, WITHOUT THE CONSENT OF HIS FATHER.

When the Inca Yupanqui found himself so strong and that he had been joined by so many people, he determined not to wait for the nomination of his father, much less for his death, before he rose with the people of Cuzco with

GROUP OF INCAS, in ceremonial dresses, from the pictures in the Church of Santa Ana, Cuzco, A.D. 1570.
From a sketch by Sir Clements Markham, 1853.

Reproduced for the Hakluyt Society by John Clay.

the further intention of obtaining the assent of those without. With this object he caused a grand sacrifice to be offered to the Sun in the Inti-cancha or House of the Sun, and then went to ask the image of the Sun who should be Inca. The oracle of the devil, or perhaps some Indian who was behind to give the answer, replied that Inca Yupanqui Pachacuti was chosen and should be Inca. On this answer being given, all who were present at the sacrifice, prostrated themselves before Pachacuti, crying out " Ccapac Inca Intip Churin," which means " Sovereign Lord Child of the Sun."

Presently they prepared a very rich fringe of gold and emeralds wherewith to crown him. Next day they took Pachacuti Inca Yupanqui to the House of the Sun, and when they came to the image of the Sun, which was of gold and the size of a man, they found it with the fringe, as if offering it of its own will. First making his sacrifices, according to their custom, he came to the image, and the High Priest called out in his language " Intip Apu," which means " Governor of things pertaining to the Sun." With much ceremony and great reverence the fringe was taken from the image and placed, with much pomp, on the forehead of Pachacuti Inca Yupanqui. Then all called his name and hailed him " Intip Churin Inca Pachacuti," or " Child of the Sun Lord, overturner of the earth." From that time he was called Pachacuti besides his first name which was Inca Yupanqui. Then the Inca presented many gifts and celebrated the event with feasts. [*He was sovereign Inca without the consent of his father or of the people, but by those he had gained over to his side by gifts.*]

XXX.

PACHACUTI INCA YUPANQUI REBUILDS THE CITY OF CUZCO.

As soon as the festivities were over, the Inca laid out the city of Cuzco on a better plan ; and formed the principal streets as they were when the Spaniards came. He divided the land for communal, public, and private edifices, causing them to be built with very excellent masonry. It is such that we who have seen it, and know that they did not possess instruments of iron or steel to work with, are struck with admiration on beholding the equality and precision with which the stones are laid, as well as the closeness of the points of junction. With the rough stones it is even more interesting to examine the work and its composition. As the sight alone satisfies the curious, I will not waste time in a more detailed description.

Besides this, Pachacuti Inca Yupanqui, considering the small extent of land round Cuzco suited for cultivation, supplied by art what was wanting in nature. Along the skirts of the hills near villages, and also in other parts, he constructed very long terraces of 200 paces more or less, and 20 to 30 wide, faced with masonry, and filled with earth, much of it brought from a distance. We call these terraces *andenes*, the native name being *sucres*. He ordered that they should be sown, and in this way he made a vast increase in the cultivated land, and in provision for sustaining the companies and garrisons.

In order that the precise time of sowing and harvesting might be known, and that nothing might be lost, the Inca caused four poles to be set up on a high mountain to the east of Cuzco, about two *varas* apart, on the heads of which there were holes, by which the sun entered, in the manner of a watch or astrolabe.

Observing where the sun struck the ground through these holes, at the time of sowing and harvest, marks were made on the ground. Other poles were set up in the part corresponding to the west of Cuzco, for the time of harvesting the maize. Having fixed the positions exactly by these poles, they built columns of stone for perpetuity in their places, of the height of the poles and with holes in like places. All round it was ordered that the ground should be paved ; and on the stones certain lines were drawn, conforming to the movements of the sun entering through the holes in the columns. Thus the whole became an instrument serving for an annual time-piece, by which the times of sowing and harvesting were regulated. Persons were appointed to observe these watches, and to notify to the people the times they indicated[1].

Besides this, as he was curious about the things of antiquity, and wished to perpetuate his name, the Inca went personally to the hill of Tampu-tocco or Paccari-tampu, names for the same thing, and entered the cave whence it is held for certain that Manco Ccapac and his brethren came when they marched to Cuzco for the first time, as has already been narrated. After he had made

---

[1] The pillars at Cuzco to determine the time of the solstices were called *Sucanca*. The two pillars denoting the beginning of winter, whence the year was measured, were called *Pucuy Sucanca*. Those notifying the beginning of spring were *Chirao Sucanca*. *Suca* means a ridge or furrow and *sucani* to make ridges : hence *sucanca*, the alternate light and shadow, appearing like furrows. Acosta says there was a pillar for each month. Garcilasso de la Vega tells us that there were eight on the east, and eight on the west side of Cuzco (i. p. 177) in double rows, four and four, two small between two high ones, 20 feet apart. Cieza de Leon says that they were in the Carmenca suburb (i. p. 325).
To ascertain the time of the equinoxes there was a stone column in the open space before the temple of the Sun in the centre of a large circle. This was the *Inti-huatana*. A line was drawn across from east to west and they watched when the shadow of the pillar was on the line from sunrise to sunset and there was no shadow at noon. There is another *Inti-huatana* at Pisac, and another at Hatun-colla. *Inti*, the Sun God, *huatani*, to seize, to tie round, *Inti-huatana*, a sun circle.

a thorough inspection, he venerated the locality and showed his feeling by festivals and sacrifices. He placed doors of gold on the window Ccapac-tocco, and ordered that from that time forward the locality should be venerated by all, making it a prayer place and *huaca*, whither to go to pray for oracles and to sacrifice.

Having done this the Inca returned to Cuzco. He ordered the year to be divided into twelve months, almost like our year. I say almost, because there is some difference, though slight, as will be explained in its place.

He called a general assembly of the oldest and wisest men of Cuzco and other parts, who with much diligence scrutinized and examined the histories and antiquities of the land, principally of the Incas and their forefathers. He ordered the events to be painted and preserved in order, as I explained when I spoke of the method adopted in preparing this history.

XXXI.

PACHACUTI INCA YUPANQUI REBUILDS THE HOUSE OF THE SUN AND ESTABLISHES NEW IDOLS IN IT.

Having adorned the city of Cuzco with edifices, streets, and the other things that have been mentioned, Pachacuti Inca Yupanqui reflected that since the time of Manco Ccapac, none of his predecessors had done anything for the House of the Sun. He, therefore, resolved to enrich it with more oracles and edifices to appal ignorant people and produce astonishment, that they might help in the conquest of the whole land which he intended to subdue, and in fact he commenced and achieved the subjugation of a large portion of it. He disinterred the bodies of the seven deceased Incas, from Manco Ccapac to Yahuar-huaccac, which were all in the House of the Sun, enriching them with masks, head-dresses called *chuco*, medals, bracelets, sceptres called *yauri* or *champi*[1], and other ornaments of gold. He then placed them, in the order of their seniority, on a bench with a back, richly adorned with gold, and ordered great festivals to be celebrated with representations of the lives of each Inca. These festivals, which are called *purucaya*[2], were continued for more than four months. Great and sumptuous sacrifices were made to each Inca, at the conclusion of the representation of his acts and life. This gave them such authority that it made all strangers adore them, and worship them as gods. These strangers, when they beheld such majesty, humbled themselves, and put up their hands to worship or *mucha* as they say. The corpses were held in great respect and veneration until the Spaniards came to this land of Peru.

Besides these corpses, Pachacuti made two images of gold. He called one of them Viracocha Pachayachachi. It represented the creator, and was placed on the right of the image of the Sun. The other was called *Chuqui ylla*, representing lightning, placed on the left of the Sun. This image was most highly venerated by all. Inca Yupanqui adopted this idol for his *guauqui*[3], because he said that it had appeared and spoken in a desert place and had given him a serpent with two heads, to carry about with him always, saying that while he had it with him, nothing sinister could happen in his affairs. To these idols the Inca gave the use of lands, flocks, and servants, especially of certain women who lived in the same House of the Sun, in the manner of nuns. These all came as

---

[1] *Champi* means a one-handed battle axe (Garcilasso de la Vega, I. lib. ix. cap. 31). Novices received it at the festival of Huarachicu, with the word *Auccacunapac*, for traitors.

[2] According to Mossi *puruccayan* was the general mourning on the death of the Inca.

[3] *Huauqui*, brother.

virgins but few remained without having had connexion with the Inca. At least he was so vicious in this respect, that he had access to all whose looks gave him pleasure, and had many sons.

Besides this House, there were some *huacas* in the surrounding country. These were that of Huanacauri, and others called Anahuarqui, Yauira, Cinga, Picol, Pachatopan[1] [*to many they made the accursed sacrifices, which they called* Ccapac Cocha, *burying children, aged* 5 *or* 6, *alive as offerings to the devil, with many offerings of vases of gold and silver*].

The Inca, they relate, also caused to be made a great woollen chain of many colours, garnished with gold plates, and two red fringes at the end. It was 150 fathoms in length, more or less. This was used in their public festivals, of which there were four principal ones in the year. The first was called RAYMI or CCAPAC RAYMI, which was when they opened the ears of knights at a ceremony called *huarachico*. The second was called SITUA resembling our lights of St John[2]. They all ran

---

[1] Anahuarqui was the name of the wife of Tupac Inca Yupanqui. Yauira may be for Yauirca, a fabulous creature described by Yamqui Pachacuti. Cinga and Picol do not occur elsewhere. Pachatopan is no doubt *Pacha tupac*, beautiful land.

[2] The months and the festivals which took place in each month are given by several authorities. The most correct are those of Polo de Ondegardo and Calancha who agree throughout. Calancha gives the months as received by the first Council of Lima.

22 June—22 July.	INTIP RAYMI (*Sun Festival*).
22 July—22 Aug.	CHAHUAR HUARQUIZ—Ploughing month.
22 Aug.—22 Sept.	YAPAQUIZ (SITUA *or Moon Festival*)— Sowing month.
22 Sept.—22 Oct.	CCOYA RAYMI—Expiatory feast. Molina a month behind.
22 Oct.—22 Nov.	UMA RAYMI—Month of brewing chicha.
22 Nov.—22 Dec.	AYAMARCA—Commemoration of the dead.
22 Dec.—22 Jan.	CCAPAC RAYMI (HUARACHICU *festival*).
22 Jan.—22 Feb.	CAMAY—Month of exercises.
22 Feb.—22 March.	HATUN POCCOY (great ripening).
22 March—22 April.	PACHA POCCOY (MOSOC NINA *festival*).
22 April—22 May.	AYRIHUA (Harvest).
22 May—22 June.	AYMURAY (Harvest home).

at midnight with torches to bathe, saying that they were
thus left clean of all diseases. The third was called YNTI
RAYMI, being the feast of the Sun, known as *aymuray*.
In these feasts they took the chain out of the House of the
Sun and all the principal Indians, very richly dressed,
came with it, in order, singing, from the House of the
Sun to the Great Square which they encircled with the
chain. This was called *moroy urco*[1].

XXXII.

PACHACUTI INCA YUPANQUI DEPOPULATES TWO LEAGUES OF COUNTRY NEAR CUZCO.

After Pachacuti had done what has been described
in the city, he turned his attention to the people. Seeing
that there were not sufficient lands for sowing, so as to
sustain them, he went round the city at a distance of four
leagues from it, considering the valleys, situation, and
villages. He depopulated all that were within two leagues
of the city. The lands of depopulated villages were given
to the city and its inhabitants, and the deprived people
were settled in other parts. The citizens of Cuzco were
well satisfied with the arrangement, for they were given
what cost little, and thus he made friends by presents
taken from others, and took as his own the valley of
Tambo [*which was not his*].

The news of the enlargement of this city went far and
wide, and reached the ears of Viracocha Inca, retired in

---

[1] The great chain, used at festivals, is called by Sarmiento Muru-
urco. See also Molina. *Muru* means a coloured spot, or a thing
of variegated colours. Molina says that it was the house where the
chain was kept that was called Muru-urco, as well as the cable.
Huasca is another name for a cable (See G. de la Vega, ii. p. 422).

Caquia Xaquixahuana[1]. He was moved to go and see Cuzco. The Inca Yupanqui went for him, and brought him to Cuzco with much rejoicing. He went to the House of the Sun, worshipped at Huanacauri and saw all the improvements that had been made. Having seen everything he returned to his place at Caquia Xaquixahuana, where he resided until his death, never again visiting Cuzco, nor seeing his son Pachacuti Inca Yupanqui.

XXXIII.

PACHACUTI INCA YUPANQUI KILLS HIS ELDER BROTHER NAMED INCA URCO.

Pachacuti Inca Yupanqui found himself so powerful with the companies he had got together by liberal presents to all, that he proposed to subjugate by their means all the territories he could reach. For this he mustered all the troops that were in Cuzco, and provided them with arms, and all that was necessary for war. Affairs being in this state Pachacuti heard that his brother Urco was in a valley called Yucay, four leagues from Cuzco, and that he had assembled some people. Fearing that the movement was intended against him the Inca marched there with his army. His brother Inca Rocca went with him, who had the reputation of being a great necromancer. Arriving at a place called Paca in the said valley, the Inca went out against his brother Urco, and there was a battle between them. Inca Rocca hurled a stone which hit Urco on the throat. The blow was so

---

[1] This great plain to the north-west of Cuzco, called Xaquixahuana, and Sacsahuana, is now known as Surita. Most of the early writers call it Sacsahuana. Sarmiento always places the word Caquia before the name. *Capuchini* is to provide, *capuchic* a purveyor. Hence *Capuquey* means "my goods," abbreviated to *Caquey*, "my property." The meaning is "my estate of Xaquixahuana."

great that Urco fell into the river flowing down the ravine
where they were fighting. Urco exerted himself and fled,
swimming down the river, with his axe in his hand. In
this way he reached a rock called Chupellusca, a league
below Tampu, where his brothers overtook him and killed
him.

From thence the Inca Pachacuti Yupanqui, with his
brother Inca Rocca marched with their troops to Caquia
Xaquixahuana to see his father who refused ever to speak
with or see him, owing to the rage he felt at the death of
Inca Urco. But Inca Rocca went in, where Viracocha
was and said, "Father! it is not reasonable that you should
grieve so much at the death of Urco, for I killed him in
self defence, he having come to kill me. You are not to be
so heavy at the death of one, when you have so many sons.
Think no more of it, for my brother Pachacuti Yupanqui
is to be Inca, and I hold that you should favour him and
be as a father to him." Seeing the resolution of his son
Inca Rocca, Viracocha did not dare to reply or to con-
tradict him. He dismissed him by saying that that was
what he wished, and that he would be guided by him in
everything. With this the Inca Yupanqui and his brother
Inca Rocca returned to Cuzco, and entered the city
triumphing over the past victories and over this one.

The triumph was after this manner. The warriors
marched in order, in their companies, dressed in the best
manner possible, with songs and dances, and the captives,
their eyes on the ground, dressed in long robes with many
tassels. They entered by the streets of the city, which
were very well adorned to receive them. They went on,
enacting their battles and victories, on account of which
they triumphed. On reaching the House of the Sun, the
spoils and prisoners were thrown on the ground, and the
Inca walked over them, trampling on them and saying—
"I tread on my enemies." The prisoners were silent with-

out raising their eyes. This order was used in all their triumphs. At the end of a short time Inca Viracocha died of grief at the death of Inca Urco, deprived and despoiled of all honour and property. They buried his body in Caquia Xaquixahuana.

XXXIV.

THE NATIONS WHICH PACHACUTI INCA SUBJUGATED AND THE TOWNS HE TOOK: AND FIRST OF TOCAY CCAPAC, SINCHI OF THE AYAMARCAS, AND THE DESTRUCTION OF THE CUYOS.

Near Cuzco there is a nation of Indians called Ayamarcas who had a proud and wealthy Sinchi named Tocay Ccapac. Neither he nor his people wished to come and do reverence to the Inca. On the contrary, he mustered his forces to attack the Inca if his country was invaded. This being known to Inca Yupanqui, he assembled his *ayllus* and other troops. He formed them into two parties, afterwards called Hanan-cuzcos and Hurin-cuzcos, forming them into a corps, that united no one might be able to prevail against them. This done he consulted over what should be undertaken. It was resolved that all should unite for the conquest of all neighbouring nations. Those who would not submit were to be utterly destroyed; and first Tocay Ccapac, chief of the Ayamarcas, was to be dealt with, being powerful and not having come to do homage at Cuzco. Having united his forces, the Inca marched against the Ayamarcas and their Sinchi, and there was a battle at Huanancancha. Inca Yupanqui was victorious, assaulting the villages and killing nearly all the Ayamarcas. He took Tocay Ccapac as a prisoner to Cuzco, where he remained in prison until his death.

After this Inca Yupanqui took to wife a native of

Choco named Mama Añahuarqui. For greater pleasure and enjoyment, away from business, he went to the town of the Cuyos, chief place of the province of Cuyo-suyu. Being one day at a great entertainment, a potter, servant of the Sinchi, without apparent reason, threw a stone or, as some say, one of the jars which they call *ulti*, at the Inca's head and wounded him. The delinquent, who was a stranger to the district, was seized and tortured to confess who had ordered him to do it. He stated that all the Sinchis of Cuyo-suyu, who were Cuyo Ccapac, Ayan-quila-lama, and Apu Cunaraqui, had conspired to kill the Inca and rebel. This was false, for it had been extorted from fear of the torture or, as some say, he said it because he belonged to a hostile tribe and wished to do them harm. But the Inca, having heard what the potter said, ordered all the Sinchis to be killed with great cruelty. After their deaths he slaughtered the people, leaving none alive except some children and old women. Thus was that nation destroyed, and its towns are desolate to this day.

XXXV.

THE OTHER NATIONS CONQUERED BY INCA YU-PANQUI, EITHER IN PERSON OR THROUGH HIS BROTHER INCA ROCCA.

Inca Yupanqui and his brother Inca Rocca, who was very cruel, had determined to oppress and subdue all the nations who wished to be independent and would not submit to them. They knew that there were two Sinchis in a town called Ollantay-tampu, six leagues from Cuzco, the one named Paucar-Ancho and the other Tocori Tupac, who ruled over the Ollantay-tampus, but would not come to do homage, nor did their people wish to do so. The Inca marched against them with a large army and gave them battle. Inca Rocca was severely wounded, but at last the Ollantay-tampus were conquered. [*All were killed, the place was destroyed so that no memory was left of it*][1] and the Inca returned to Cuzco.

There was another Sinchi named Illacumpi, chief of two towns four leagues from Cuzco, called Cugma and Huata. Inca Yupanqui and Inca Rocca sent to him to do homage, but he replied that he was as good as they were and free, and that if they wanted anything, they must get it with their lances. For this answer the Inca made war upon the said Sinchi. He united his forces with those of two other Sinchis, his companions, named Paucar Tupac and Puma Lloqui, and went forth to fight the Inca. But they were defeated and killed, with nearly all their people. The Inca desolated that town with fire and sword, and with very great cruelty. He then returned to Cuzco and triumphed for that victory.

The Inca received information, after this, that there was a town called Huancara, 11 leagues from Cuzco, ruled by Sinchis named Ascascahuana and Urcu-cuna. So a message was sent to them, calling upon them to give reverence and obedience to the Inca and to pay tribute. They replied that they were not women to come and serve, that they were in their native place, and that if any one came to seek them they would defend themselves. Moved to anger by this reply, Inca Yupanqui and Inca Rocca made war, killed the Sinchis and most of their people and brought the rest prisoners to Cuzco, to force them into obedience.

Next they marched to another town called Toguaro, six leagues from Huancara, killing the Sinchi, named Alca-parihuana, and all the people, not sparing any but the children, that they might grow and repeople that land.

---

[1] This is untrue. The splendid ruins remain to this day. The place was long held against the Spaniards by Inca Manco.

With similar cruelties in all the towns, the Inca reduced
to pay tribute the Cotabambas, Cotaneras, Umasayus,
and Aymaraes, being the principal provinces of Cunti-
suyu.

The Inca then attacked the province of the Soras,
40 leagues from Cuzco. The natives came forth to resist,
asking why the invaders sought their lands, telling them to
depart or they would be driven out by force. Over this
question there was a battle, and two towns of the Soras
were subdued at that time, the one called Chalco, the other
Soras. The Sinchi of Chalco was named Chalco-pusaycu,
that of Soras Huacralla. They were taken prisoners to
Cuzco, and there was a triumph over them.

There was another place called Acos, 10 or 11 leagues
from Cuzco. The two Sinchis of it were named Ocacique
and Utu-huasi. These were strongly opposed to the
demands of the Inca and made a very strenuous resistance. The Inca marched against them with a great army.
But he met with serious difficulty in this conquest, for
the Acos defended themselves most bravely and wounded
Pachacuti on the head with a stone. He would not desist,
but it was not until after a long time that they were
conquered. He killed nearly all the natives of Acos, and
those who were pardoned and survived after that cruel
slaughter, were banished to the neighbourhood of Huamanca,
to a place now called Acos[1].

In all these campaigns which have been described, Inca
Rocca was the companion in arms, and participator in the
triumphs of Inca Yupanqui. It is to be noted that in all
the subdued provinces chiefs were placed, superseding or
killing the native Sinchis. Those who were appointed,
acted as guards or captains of the conquered places, holding office in the Inca's name and during his pleasure. In

---

[1] Acobamba, the present capital of the province of Angaraes.

this way the conquered provinces were oppressed and tyrannized over by the yoke of servitude. A superior was appointed over all the others who were nominated to each town, as general or governor. In their language this officer was called *Tucuyrico*[1], which means "he who knows and oversees all."

Thus in the first campaign undertaken by Pachacuti Inca Yupanqui, after the defeat of the Chancas, he subdued the country as far as the Soras, 40 leagues to the west of Cuzco. The other nations, and some in Cunti-suyu, from fear at seeing the cruelties committed on the conquered, came in to submit, to avoid destruction. [*But they ever submitted against their wills.*]

XXXVI.

PACHACUTI INCA YUPANQUI ENDOWS THE HOUSE OF THE SUN WITH GREAT WEALTH.

After Pachacuti Inca Yupanqui had conquered the lands and nations mentioned above, and had triumphed over them, he came to visit the House of the Sun and the Mama-cunas or nuns who were there. He assisted one day, to see how the Mama-cunas served the dinner of the Sun. This was to offer much richly cooked food to the image or idol of the Sun, and then to put it into a great fire on an altar. The same order was taken with the liquor. The chief of the Mama-cunas saluted the Sun with a small vase, and the rest was thrown on the fire. Besides this many jars full of that liquor were poured into a trough which had a drain, all being offerings to the Sun. This service was performed with vessels of clay. As

---

[1] *Tucuyricuc*, he who sees all. *Tucuy* means all. *Ricini* to see. Garcilasso de la Vega, I. lib. ii. cap. 14. Balboa, p. 115. Montesinos, p. 55. Santillana, p. 17.

Pachacuti considered that the material of the vases was too poor, he presented very complete sets of vases of gold and silver for all the service that was necessary. To adorn the house more richly he caused a plate of fine gold to be made, two *palmas* broad and the length of the court-yard. He ordered this to be nailed high up on the wall in the manner of a cornice, passing all round the court-yard. This border or cornice of gold remained there down to the time of the Spaniards.

XXXVII.

PACHACUTI INCA YUPANQUI CONQUERS THE PROVINCE OF COLLA-SUYU.

To the south of Cuzco there was a province called Colla-suyu or Collao, consisting of plain country, which was very populous. At the time that Pachacuti Inca Yupanqui was at Cuzco after having conquered the provinces already mentioned, the Sinchi of Collao was named Chuchi Ccapac or Colla Ccapac, which is all one. This Chuchi Ccapac increased so much in power and wealth among those nations of Colla-suyu, that he was respected by all the Collas, who called him Inca Ccapac.

Pachacuti Inca Yupanqui determined to conquer him from a motive of jealousy, together with all the provinces of the Collao. With this object he assembled his army and marched on the route to the Collao in order to attack Chuchi Ccapac who waited for him at Hatun-Colla, a town of the Collao where he resided, 40 leagues from Cuzco, without having taken further notice of the coming nor of the forces of Inca Yupanqui. When he came near to Hatun Colla, the Inca sent a message to Chuchi Colla, requesting him to serve and obey him or else to prepare for battle, when they would try their fortunes. This message caused much heaviness to Chuchi Colla, but he replied proudly that he waited for the Inca to come and do homage to him like the other nations that had been conquered by him, and that if the Inca did not choose to do so, he would prepare his head, with which he intended to drink in his triumph after the victory which he would win if they should come to a battle.

After this reply Inca Yupanqui ordered his army to approach that of Chuchi Ccapac the next day, which was drawn up ready to fight. Soon after they came in sight, the two forces attacked each other, and the battle continued for a long time without either side gaining any advantage. Inca Yupanqui, who was very dexterous in fighting, was assisting in every part, giving orders, combating, and animating his troops. Seeing that the Collas resisted so resolutely, and stood so firmly in the battle, he turned his face to his men saying in a loud voice: "O Incas of Cuzco! conquerors of all the land! Are you not ashamed that people so inferior to you, and unequal in weapons, should be equal to you and resist for so long a time?" With this he returned to the fight, and the troops, touched by this rebuke, pressed upon their enemies in such sort that they were broken and defeated. Inca Yupanqui, being an experienced warrior, knew that the completion of the victory consisted in the capture of Chuchi Ccapac. Although he was fighting, he looked out for his enemy in all directions and, seeing him in the midst of his people, the Inca attacked them at the head of his guards, took him prisoner, and delivered him to a soldier with orders to take him to the camp and keep him safe. The Inca and his army then completed the victory and engaged in the pursuit, until all the Sinchis and captains that could be found were captured. Pachacuti went to Hatun-colla, the residence and seat of government of Chuchi Ccapac, where he remained until all the provinces which obeyed Chuchi Ccapac, were reduced to obedience, and brought many rich presents of gold, silver, cloths, and other precious things.

Leaving a garrison and a governor in the Collao to rule in his name, the Inca returned to Cuzco, taking Chuchi Ccapac as a prisoner with the others. He entered Cuzco, where a solemn triumph was prepared. Chuchi Colla and the other Colla prisoners were placed before the Inca's litter dressed in long robes covered with tassels in derision and that they might be known. Having arrived at the House of the Sun, the captives and spoils were offered to the image of the Sun, and the Inca, or the priest for him, trod on all the spoils and captives that Pachacuti had taken in the Collao, which was great honour to the Inca. When the triumph was over, to give it a good finish, the Inca caused the head of Chuchi Ccapac to be cut off, and put in the house called *Llasa-huasi*[1], with those of the other Sinchis he had killed. He caused the other Sinchis and captains of Chuchi Ccapac to be given to the wild beasts, kept shut up for the purpose, in a house called *Samca-huasi*[2].

In these conquests Pachacuti was very cruel to the vanquished, and people were so terrified at the cruelties that they submitted and obeyed from fear of being made food for wild beasts, or burnt, or otherwise cruelly tormented rather than resist in arms. It was thus with the people of Cunti-suyu who, seeing the cruelty and power of Inca Yupanqui, humiliated themselves and promised obedience. It was for the cause and reason stated, and because they were threatened with destruction if they did not come to serve and obey.

---

[1] Llasa-huasi. *Llasa* means weight, from *llasani* to weigh. *Huasi* a house.

[2] Samgaguacy. This should be *Samca-huasi*, a prison for grave offences. Serpents and toads were put into the prison with the delinquents. Mossi, p. 233.

Chuchi Ccapac had subjugated a region more than 160 leagues from north to south, over which he was Sinchi or, as he called himself, Ccapac or Colla-Ccapac, from within 20 leagues of Cuzco as far as the Chichas, with all the bounds of Arequipa and the sea-coast to Atacama, and the forests of the Musus. For at this time, seeing the violence and power with which the Inca of Cuzco came down upon those who opposed him, without pardoning anyone, many Sinchis followed his example, and wanted to do the same in other parts, where each one lived, so that all was confusion and tyranny in this kingdom, no one being secure of his own property. We shall relate in their places, as the occasion offers, the stories of the Sinchis, tyrants, besides those of the Incas who, from the time of Inca Yupanqui, began to get provinces into their power, and tyrannize over the inhabitants.

Inca Yupanqui, as has already been narrated, had given the House of the Sun all things necessary for its services, besides which, after he came from Colla-suyu, he presented many things brought from there for the image of the Sun, and for the mummies of his ancestors which were kept in the House of the Sun. He also gave them servants and lands. He ordered that the *huacas* of Cuzco should be adopted and venerated in all the conquered provinces, ordaining new ceremonies for their worship and abolishing the ancient rites. He charged his eldest legitimate son, named Amaru Tupac Inca, with the duty of abolishing the *huacas* which were not held to be legitimate, and to see that the others were maintained and received the sacrifices ordered by the Inca. Huayna Yamqui Yupanqui, another son of Inca Yupanqui, was associated with the heir in this duty.

XXXVIII.

PACHACUTI INCA YUPANQUI SENDS AN ARMY TO CONQUER THE PROVINCE OF CHINCHAY-SUYU.

When Pachacuti Inca Yupanqui returned from the conquest of Colla-suyu and the neighbouring provinces, as has been narrated in the preceding chapter, he was well stricken in years, though not tired of wars, nor was his thirst for dominion satisfied. Owing to his age he chose to remain at Cuzco, as the seat of his government, to establish the lands he had subdued, in the way which he well knew how to establish. In order to lose no time in extending his conquests, he assembled his people, from among whom he chose 70,000 provided with arms and all things necessary for a military campaign. He nominated his brother, Ccapac Yupanqui, to be Captain-General, giving him for colleagues another of his brothers named Huayna Yupanqui, and one of his sons named Apu Yamqui Yupanqui. Among the other special captains in this army was one named Anco Ayllo of the Chanca nation, who had remained a prisoner in Cuzco from the time that the Inca conquered the Chancas at Cuzco and at Ichu-pampa. He had ever since been sad and brooding, thinking of a way of escape. But he dissimulated so well that the Inca treated him as a brother and trusted him. Hence the Inca nominated him as commander of all the Chancas in the army. For to each nation the Inca gave a captain from among their own people, because he would understand how to rule them and they would obey him better. This Anco Ayllo, seeing there was an opportunity for fulfilling his desire, showed satisfaction at receiving this commission from the Inca, and promised to do valuable service, as he knew those nations whose conquest was about to be undertaken. When the army was ready to march, the Inca gave the Captain-

General his own arms of gold, and to the other captains he gave arms with which to enter the battles. He made a speech to them, exhorting them to achieve success, showing them the honourable reward they would obtain, and the favours he, as a friend, would show them, if they served in that war. He gave special orders to Ccapac Yupanqui that he should advance with his conquering army as far as a province called Yana-mayu, the boundary of the nation of the Hatun-huayllas, and that there he should set up the Inca's boundary pillars, and he was on no account to advance further. He was to conquer up to that point and then return to Cuzco, leaving sufficient garrisons in the subjugated lands. He was also to establish posts at every half league, which they call *chasquis*, by means of which the Inca would be daily informed of what had happened and was being done[1].

Ccapac Yupanqui set out from Cuzco with these orders, and desolated all the provinces which did not submit. On arriving at a fortress called Urco-collac, near Parcos, in the country of Huamanca, he met with valorous resistance from the inhabitants. Finally he conquered them. In the battle the Chancas distinguished themselves so that they gained more honour than the Cuzcos *orejones* and the other nations.

This news came to the Inca, who was much annoyed that the Chancas should have distinguished themselves more, and had gained more honour than the Incas. He imagined that it would make them proud, so he proposed to have them killed. He sent a messenger ordering Ccapac Yupanqui to lay a plan for killing all the Chancas in the best way he could devise, and if he did not kill them, the Inca would kill him. The runner of the Inca reached

---

[1] For accounts of the *chasquis* or Inca couriers see Garcilasso de la Vega, ii. pp. 49, 60, 119, 120, 121. Balboa, p. 248. Polo de Ondegardo, p. 169.

Ccapac Yupanqui with this order, but it could not be kept a secret. It became known to a wife of Ccapac Yupanqui, who was a sister of Anco Ayllo, the captain of the Chancas. This woman told her brother, who always longed for his liberty, and now was urgently minded to save his life. He secretly addressed his Chanca soldiers, putting before them the cruel order of the Inca, and the acquisition of their liberty if they would follow him. They all agreed to his proposal. When they came to Huarac-tambo, in the neighbourhood of the city of Huanuco, all the Chancas fled with their captain Anco Ayllo, and besides the Chancas other tribes followed this chief. Passing by the province of Huayllas they pillaged it, and, continuing their route in flight from the Incas, they agreed to seek a rugged and mountainous land where the Incas, even if they sought them, would not be able to find them. So they entered the forests between Chachapoyas and Huanuco, and went on to the province of Ruparupa. These are the people who are settled on the river Pacay and, according to the received report, thence to the eastward by the river called Cocama which falls into the great river Marañon. They were met with by the captain Gomez d'Arias, who entered by Huanuco, in the time of the Marquis of Cañete, in the year 1556. Though Ccapac Yupanqui went in chase of the Chancas, they were so rapid in their flight that he was unable to overtake them[1].

In going after them Ccapac Yupanqui went as far as Caxamarca, beyond the line he was ordered not to pass by the Inca. Although he had the order in his mind, yet when he saw that province of Caxamarca, how populous it was and rich in gold and silver, by reason of the great Sinchi, named Gusmanco Ccapac, who ruled there and was

---

[1] Garcilasso de la Vega also gives an account of the flight of the Chancas under Anco-ayllu or Hanco-hualla, ii. pp. 82, 329.

a great tyrant, having robbed many provinces round
Caxamarca, Ccapac Yupanqui resolved to conquer it, although he had no commission from his brother for undertaking such an enterprise. On commencing to enter the
land of Caxamarca, it became known to Gusmanco Ccapac.
That chief summoned his people, and called upon another
Sinchi, his tributary, named Chimu Ccapac, chief of the
territory where now stands the city of Truxillo on the
coast of Peru. Their combined forces marched against
Ccapac Yupanqui, who by a certain ambush, and other
stratagems, defeated, routed and captured the two Sinchis
Gusmanco Ccapac and Chimu Ccapac, taking vast treasure
of gold, silver and other precious things, such as gems, and
coloured shells, which these natives value more than silver
or gold.

Ccapac Yupanqui collected all the treasure in the square
of Caxamarca, where he then was ; and when he saw such
immense wealth he became proud and vainglorious, saying
that he had gained and acquired more than his brother the
Inca. His arrogance and boasting came to the ears of his
sovereign, who, although he felt it deeply and desired
an opportunity to kill him, dissimulated for a time and
waited until the return to Cuzco. Inca Yupanqui feared
that his brother would rebel, and for this reason he
appeared to be pleased before the enyoys sent by Ccapac
Yupanqui. He sent them back with orders that Ccapac
Yupanqui should return to Cuzco with the treasure that
had been taken in the war, as well as the principal men of
the subdued provinces, and the sons of Gusmanco Ccapac
and Chimu Ccapac. The great chiefs themselves were to
remain in their territories with a sufficient garrison to keep
those lands obedient to the Inca. On receiving this order
Ccapac Yupanqui set out for Cuzco with all the treasure,
and marched to the capital full of pride and arrogance.
Inca Yupanqui, who himself subdued so many lands and

gained so much honour, became jealous, as some say afraid, and sought excuses for killing his brother. When he knew that Ccapac Yupanqui had reached Limatambo, eight leagues from Cuzco, he ordered his lieutenant-governor named Inca Capon, to go there and cut off the head of Ccapac Yupanqui. The reasons given were that he had allowed Anco Ayllo to escape, and had gone beyond the line prescribed. The governor went and, in obedience to his orders, he killed the Inca's two brothers Ccapac Yupanqui and Huayna Yupanqui. The Inca ordered the rest to enter Cuzco, triumphing over their victories. This was done, the Inca treading on the spoils, and granting rewards. They say that he regretted that his brother had gained so much honour, and that he wished that he had sent his son who was to be his successor, named Tupac Inca Yupanqui, that he might have enjoyed such honour, and that this jealousy led him to kill his brother.

XXXIX.

PACHACUTI INCA YUPANQUI PLANTS *MITIMAES* IN ALL THE LANDS HE HAD CONQUERED.

As all the conquests made by this Inca were attended with such violence and cruelties, with such spoliation and force, and the people who became his subjects by acquisition, or to speak more correctly by rapine, were numerous, they obeyed so long as they felt the force compelling them, and, as soon as they were a little free from that fear, they presently rebelled and resumed their liberty. Then the Inca was obliged to conquer them again. Turning many things in his mind, and seeking for remedies, how he could settle once for all the numerous provinces he had conquered, at last he hit upon a plan which, although adapted to the object he sought to attain, and coloured with some appearance of generosity, was really the worst tyranny he perpetrated. He ordered visitors to go through all the subdued provinces, with orders to measure and survey them, and to bring him models of the natural features in clay. This was done. The models and reports were brought before the Inca. He examined them and considered the mountainous fastnesses and the plains. He ordered the visitors to look well to what he would do. He then began to demolish the fastnesses and to have their inhabitants moved to plain country, and those of the plains were moved to mountainous regions, so far from each other, and each so far from their native country, that they could not return to it. Next the Inca ordered the visitors to go and do with the people what they had seen him do with the models. They went and did so.

He gave orders to others to go to the same districts, and, jointly with the *tucuricos*, to take some young men, with their wives, from each district. This was done and they were brought to Cuzco from all the provinces, from one 30, from another 100, more or less according to the population of each district. These selected people were presented before the Inca, who ordered that they should be taken to people various parts. Those of Chinchay-suyu were sent to Anti-suyu, those of Cunti-suyu to Colla-suyu, so far from their native country that they could not communicate with their relations or countrymen. He ordered that they should be settled in valleys similar to those in their native land, and that they should have seeds from those lands that they might be preserved and not perish, giving them land to sow without stint, and removing the natives.

The Incas called these colonists *mitimaes*[1], which

---

[1] The system of *mitimaes* was a very important part of the Inca polity. It is frequently referred to by Cieza de Leon, and described by Garcilasso de la Vega, ii. p. 215. See also Balboa, pp. 78, 114, 143, 249. Molina, pp. 4, 22, 23. Yamqui Pachacuti, pp. 95, 97. Polo de Ondegardo, p. 161.

means "transported" or "moved." He ordered them to
learn the language of the country to which they were
removed, but not to forget the general language, which
was the Quichua, and which he had ordered that all his
subjects in all the conquered provinces must learn and
know. With it conversation and business could be carried
on, for it was the clearest and richest of the dialects. The
Inca gave the colonists authority and power to enter the
houses of the natives at all hours, night or day, to see what
they said, did or arranged, with orders to report all to the
nearest governor, so that it might be known if anything was
plotted against the government of the Inca, who, knowing
the evil he had done, feared all in general, and knew that
no one served him voluntarily, but only by force. Besides
this the Inca put garrisons into all the fortresses of importance, composed of natives of Cuzco or the neighbourhood,
which garrisons were called *michecrima*[1].

XL.

THE COLLAS, SONS OF CHUCHI CCAPAC, REBEL AGAINST INCA YUPANQUI TO OBTAIN THEIR FREEDOM.

After Inca Yupanqui had celebrated the triumphs and
festivities consequent on the conquest of Chinchay-suyu,
and arranged the system of *mitimaes*, he dismissed the
troops. He himself went to Yucay, where he built the
edifices, the ruins of which may still be seen. These being
finished, he went down the valley of Yucay to a place
which is now called Tambo, eight leagues from Cuzco,
where he erected some magnificent buildings. The sons of
Chuchi Ccapac, the great Sinchi of the Collao, had to labour

---

[1] *Michec* a shepherd, hence a governor. *Rimay* to speak.

as captives at the masonry and other work. Their father, as has already been narrated, was conquered in the Collao and killed by the Inca. These sons of Chuchi Ccapac, feeling that they were being vilely treated, and remembering that they were the sons of so great a man as their father, also seeing that the Inca had disbanded his army, agreed to risk their lives in obtaining their freedom. One night they fled, with all the people who were there, and made such speed that, although the Inca sent after them, they could not be overtaken. Along the route they took, they kept raising the inhabitants against the Inca. Much persuasion was not needed, because, as they were obeying by force, they only sought the first opportunity to rise. On this favourable chance, many nations readily rebelled, even those who were very near Cuzco, but principally the Collao and all its provinces.

The Inca, seeing this, ordered a great army to be assembled, and sought the favour of auxiliaries from Gusmanco Ccapac and Chimu Ccapac. He collected a great number of men, made sacrifices *calpa*[1], and buried some children alive, which is called *capa cocha*, to induce their idols to favour them in that war. All being ready, the Inca nominated two of his sons as captains of the army, valorous men, named the one Tupac Ayar Manco, the other Apu Paucar Usnu. The Inca left Cuzco with more than 200,000 warriors, and marched against the sons of Chuchi Ccapac, who also had a great power of men and arms, and were anxious to meet the Incas and fight for their lives against the men of Cuzco.

As both were seeking each other, they soon met, and joined in a stubborn and bloody battle, in which there was great slaughter, because one side fought for life and liberty and the other for honour. As those of Cuzco were better

---

[1] *Calpa* means force, vigour ; also an army.

disciplined and drilled, and more numerous than their adversaries, they had the advantage. But the Collas preferred to die fighting rather than to become captives to one so cruel and inhuman as the Inca. So they opposed themselves to the arms of the *orejones*, who, with great cruelties, killed as many of the Collas as opposed their advance. The sons of the Inca did great things in the battle, with their own hands, on that day.

The Collas were defeated, most of them being killed or taken prisoners. Those who fled were followed to a place called Lampa. There the wounded were cared for, and the squadrons refreshed. The Inca ordered his two sons, Tupac Ayar Manco and Apu Paucar Usnu, to press onward, conquering the country as far as the Chichas, where they were to set up their cairns and return. The Inca then returned to Cuzco, for a triumph over the victory he had gained.

The Inca arrived at Cuzco, triumphed and celebrated the victory with festivities. And because he found that a son had been born to him, he raised him before the Sun, offered him, and gave him the name of Tupac Inca Yupanqui. In his name he offered treasures of gold and silver to the Sun, and to the other oracles and *huacas*, and also made the sacrifice of *capa cocha*. Besides this he made the most solemn and costly festivals that had ever been known, throughout the land. This was done because Inca Yupanqui wished that this Tupac Inca should succeed him, although he had other older and legitimate sons by his wife and sister Mama Anahuarqui. For, although the custom of these tyrants was that the eldest legitimate son should succeed, it was seldom observed, the Inca preferring the one he liked best, or whose mother he loved most, or he who was the ablest among the brothers.

XLI.

AMARU TUPAC INCA AND APU PAUCAR USNU CONTINUE THE CONQUEST OF THE COLLAO AND AGAIN SUBDUE THE COLLAS.

As soon as the Inca returned to Cuzco, leaving his two sons Tupac Amaru and Apu Paucar Usnu[1] in the Callao, those captains set out from Lampa, advancing to Hatun-Colla, where they knew that the Collas had rallied their troops to fight the Cuzcos once more, and that they had raised one of the sóns of Chuchi Ccapac to be Inca. The Incas came to the place where the Collas were awaiting them in arms. They met and fought valorously, many being killed on both sides. At the end of the battle the Collas were defeated and their new Inca was taken prisoner. Thus for a third time were the Collas conquered by the Cuzcos. By order of the Inca, his sons, generals of the war, left the new Inca of the Collas at Hatun-Colla, as a prisoner well guarded and re-captured. The other captains went on, continuing their conquests, as the Inca had ordered, to the confines of Charcas and the Chichas.

While his sons prosecuted the war, Pachacuti their father, finished the edifices at Tambo, and constructed the ponds and pleasure houses of Yucay. He erected, on a hill near Cuzco, called Patallata, some sumptuous houses, and many others in the neighbourhood of the capital. He also made many channels of water both for use and for pleasure ; and ordered all the governors of provinces who were under his sway, to build pleasure houses on the most convenient sites, ready for him when he should visit their commands.

---

[1] Tupac Amaru. *Tupac* means royal, and *amaru* a serpent. *Apu* a chief, *paucar* beautiful and *usnu* a judgment seat.

While Inca Yupanqui proceeded with these measures, his sons had completed the conquest of the Collao. When they arrived in the vicinity of Charcas, the natives of Paria, Tapacari, Cochabambas, Poconas and Charcas retreated to the country of the Chichas and Chuyes, in order to make a combined resistance to the Incas, who arrived where their adversaries were assembled, awaiting the attack. The Inca army was in three divisions. A squadron of 5000 men went by the mountains, another of 20,000 by the side of the sea, and the rest by the direct road. They arrived at the strong position held by the Charcas and their allies, and fought with them. The Incas were victorious, and took great spoils of silver extracted by those natives from the mines of Porco. It is to be noted that nothing was ever known of the 5000 *orejones* who entered by the mountains or what became of them. Leaving all these provinces conquered, and subdued, Amaru Tupac Inca and Apu Paucar Usnu returned to Cuzco where they triumphed over their victories, Pachacuti granting them many favours, and rejoicing with many festivals and sacrifices to idols.

XLII.

PACHACUTI INCA YUPANQUI NOMINATES HIS SON TUPAC INCA YUPANQUI AS HIS SUCCESSOR.

Pachacuti Inca Yupanqui was now very old ; and he determined to nominate a successor to take his place after his death. He called together the Incas his relations, of the *ayllus* of Hanan-cuzco and Hurin-cuzco and said, " My friends and relations ! I am now, as you see, very old, and I desire to leave you, when my days are over, one who will govern and defend you from your enemies. Some propose that I should name Amaru Tupac Inca, but it does not appear to me that he has the qualifications to govern so great a lordship as that which I have acquired. I, therefore, desire to nominate another with whom you will be more content." The relations, in their reply, gave thanks to the Inca, and declared that they would derive great benefit from his nomination. He then said that he named his son Tupac Inca, and ordered him to come forth from the house. He had been there for 15 or 16 years to be brought up, without any one seeing him except very rarely and as a great favour. He was now shown to the people, and the Inca presently ordered a fringe of gold to be placed in the hand of the image of the Sun, with the head-dress called *pillaca-llaytu*[1]. After Tupac Inca had made his obeisance to his father, the Inca and the rest rose and went before the image of the Sun where they made their sacrifices and offered *capa cocha* to that deity. Then they offered the new Inca Tupac Yupanqui, beseeching the Sun to protect and foster him, and to make him so that all should hold and judge him to be a child of the Sun and father of his people. This done the oldest and principal *orejones* took Tupac Inca to the Sun, and the priests took the fringe from the hands of the image, which they call *mascapaycha*, and placed it over the head of Tupac Inca Yupanqui until it rested on his forehead. He was declared Inca Ccapac and seated in front of the Sun on a seat of gold, called *duho*[2], garnished with emeralds and other precious stones. Seated there, they clothed him in the *ccapac hongo*[3], placed the *suntur paucar* in his hand, gave him the other insignia of Inca, and the priests raised him on their shoulders. When these ceremonies were completed, Pachacuti Inca Yupanqui ordered that his son Tupac Inca should remain shut up in the House of the Sun, performing the fasts which

---

[1] *Pillaca-llatu* is a cloth or cloak woven of two colours, black and brown.

[2] This word is corrupt. *Tiana* is the word for a seat.

[3] Ccapac uncu. The word *uncu* means a tunic.

it is the custom to go through before receiving the order of chivalry; which ceremony consisted in opening the ears. The Inca ordered that what had been done should not be made public until he gave the command to publish it.

XLIII.

HOW PACHACUTI ARMED HIS SON TUPAC INCA.

Pachacuti Inca Yupanqui found happiness in leaving memory of himself. With this object he did extraordinary things as compared with those of his ancestors, in building edifices, celebrating triumphs, not allowing himself to be seen except as a great favour shown to the people, for as such it was considered, on the day that he appeared. Then he ordered that no one should come to behold him without worshipping and bringing something in his hand to offer him. This custom was continued by all his descendants, and was observed inviolably. [*Thus, from the time of this Pachacuti began an unheard of and inhuman tyranny in addition to the tyrannies of his ancestors.*] As he was now old and desirous of perpetuating his name, it appeared to him that he would obtain his desire by giving authority to his son and successor named Tupac Inca. So the boy was brought up, confined in the House of the Sun for more than 16 years, seeing no one but his tutors and masters until he was brought and presented to the Sun, to be nominated as has already been explained. To invest him at the *huarachico*, the Inca ordered a new way of giving the order of chivalry. For this he built round the city four other houses for prayer to the Sun, with much apparatus of gold idols, *huacas* and service, for his son to perambulate these stations after he had been armed as a knight.

Affairs being in this state, there came to the Inca Pachacuti, his son Amaru Tupac Inca, who had been named by his father as his successor some years before, because he was the eldest legitimate son.   He said, "Father Inca! I understand that you have a son in the House of the Sun whom you have ordered to be your successor after your own days.   Order that he may be shown to me." The Inca, looking upon this as boldness on the part of Amaru Tupac, replied, "It is true, and I desire that you and your wife shall be his vassals, and that you shall serve and obey him as your Lord and Inca." Amaru replied that he wished to do so, and that, for this reason, he desired to see him and offer sacrifice to him, and that orders should be given to take him where his brother was.   The Inca gave permission for this, Amaru Tupac Inca taking what was necessary for the ceremony, and being brought to where Tupac Inca was fasting.   When Amaru saw him in such majesty of wealth and surroundings, he fell on his face to the earth, adoring, offering sacrifices and obedience. On learning that it was his brother, Tupac Inca raised him and saluted him in the face.

Presently Inca Yupanqui caused the necessary preparations to be made for investing his son with the order of chivalry.   When all was ready, the Inca, accompanied by all his principal relations and courtiers, went to the House of the Sun, where they brought out Tupac Inca with great solemnity and pomp.   For they carried with him all the idols of the Sun, Viracocha, the other *huacas*, the figures of the former Incas, and the great chain called *moro-urco*.   All being placed in order with such pomp as had never been seen before, they all went to the great square of the city, in the centre of which a bonfire was made.   All the relations and friends then killed many animals, offering them as sacrifices by throwing them into the flames.   They worshipped the heir, offering him rich gifts, the first that brought a gift being his father.   Following the example all the rest adored, seeing that his father had shown him reverence. Thus did the *orejones* Incas and all the rest who were present, seeing that for this they had been called and invited, to bring their gifts and offer them to their new Inca.

This being done, the festival called *Ccapac Raymi* was commenced, being the feast of kings, and consequently the most solemn festival kept by these people. When the ceremonies had been performed, they bored the ears of Tupac Inca Yupanqui, which is their mode of investiture into the order of chivalry and nobility. He was then taken to the stations of the Houses of the Sun, giving him the weapons and other insignia of war. This being finished his father the Inca Yupanqui gave him, for his wife, one of his sisters named Mama Ocllo, who was a very beautiful woman with much ability and wisdom.

XLIV.

PACHACUTI INCA YUPANQUI SENDS HIS SON TUPAC INCA YUPANQUI TO CONQUER CHINCHAY-SUYU.

The Inca Yupanqui desired that his son should be employed on some service that would bring him fame, as soon as he had been proclaimed his successor, and armed as a knight. He had information that Chinchay-suyu was a region where name and treasure might be acquired, especially from a Sinchi named Chuqui-Sota in Chachapoyas. He, therefore, ordered all preparations to be made for the conquest of Chinchay-suyu. He gave the prince for his tutors, captains, and captains-general of his army, two of his brothers, the one named Auqui Yupanqui and the other Tilca Yupanqui. The army being assembled and the preparations made, they set out from Cuzco.

Tupac went in such pomp and majesty that, where he passed, no one dared to look him in the face, in such veneration was he held. The people left the roads along which he had to pass and, ascending the hills on either side, worshipped and adored. They pulled out their eyebrows and eyelashes, and blowing on them, they made offering to the Inca. Others offered handfuls of a very precious herb called *coca*. When he arrived at the villages, he put on the dress and head-gear of that district, for all were different in their dress and head-gear as they are now. For Inca Yupanqui, so as to know each nation he had conquered, ordered that each one should have a special dress and head-gear, which they call *pillu*, *llaytu* and *chuco*, different one from the other, so as to be easily distinguished and recognized. Seating himself, Tupac Inca made a solemn sacrifice of animals and birds, burning them in a fire which was kindled in his presence ; and in this way they worshipped the sun, which they believed to be God.

In this manner Tupac Inca began to repeat the conquests and tyranny of all his ancestors and his father. For, although many nations were conquered by his father, almost all were again with arms in their hands to regain their liberty, and the rest to defend themselves. As Tupac Inca advanced with such power, force and pride, he not only claimed the subjection of the people, but also usurped the veneration they gave to their gods or devils, for truly he and his father made them worship all with more veneration than the Sun.

Tupac Inca finally marched out of Cuzco and began to proceed with measures for subduing the people in the near vicinity. In the province of the Quichuas[1] he conquered and occupied the fortresses of Tohara, Cayara, and Curamba, and in the province of Angaraes the fortresses

---

[1] The province of the Quichuas was in the valley of the Pachachaca, above Abancay.

of Urco-colla and Huaylla-pucara, taking its Sinchi named Chuquis Huaman prisoner. In the province of Xauxa he took Sisiquilla Pucara, and in the province of Huayllas the fortresses of Chuncu-marca and Pillahua-marca. In Chachapoyas the fortress of Piajajalca fell before him, and he took prisoner a very rich chief named Chuqui Sota. He conquered the province of the Paltas, and the valleys of Pacasmayu and Chimu, which is now Truxillo. He destroyed it as Chimu Ccapac had been subdued before. He also conquered the province of the Cañaris, and those who resisted were totally destroyed. The Cañaris submitted from fear, and he took their Sinchis, named Pisar Ccapac, Cañar Ccapac and Chica Ccapac, and built an impregnable fortress there called Quinchi-caxa.

Tupac Inca Yupanqui then returned to Cuzco with much treasure and many prisoners. He was well received by his father with a most sumptuous triumph, and with the applause of all the *orejones* of Cuzco. They had many feasts and sacrifices, and to please the people they celebrated the festival called Inti Raymi with feasts and dances, a time of great rejoicing. The Inca granted many favours for the sake of his son Tupac Inca, that he might have the support of his subjects, which was what he desired. For as he was very old and unable to move about, feeling the approach of death, his aim was to leave his son in the possession of the confidence of his army.

XLV.

HOW PACHACUTI INCA YUPANQUI VISITED THE PROVINCES CONQUERED FOR HIM BY HIS CAPTAINS.

It has been related how the Inca Yupanqui placed garrisons of Cuzco soldiers, and a governor called *tucuyrico* in all the provinces he conquered and oppressed. It must be known that owing to his absorbing occupations in conquering other provinces, training warriors, and placing his son in command for the conquest of Chinchay-suyu, he had not been able to put his final intentions and will into execution, which was to make those he oppressed submissive subjects and tributaries. Seeing that the people were in greater fear at beholding the valour of Tupac Inca, he determined to have a visitation of the land, and nominated 16 visitors, four for each of the four *suyus* or divisions of the empire, which are *Cunti-suyu* from Cuzco south and west as far as the South Sea, *Chinchay-suyu* from Cuzco to the north and west, *Anti-suyu* from Cuzco to the east, and *Colla-suyu* from Cuzco to the south, south-west, and south-east.

These visitors each went to the part to which he was appointed, and inspected, before all things, the work of the *tucuyricos* and the methods of their government. They caused irrigating channels to be constructed for the crops, broke up land where this had been neglected, built *andenes* or cultivated terraces, and took up pastures for the Sun, the Inca, and Cuzco. Above all they imposed very heavy tribute on all the produce, [*so that they all went about to rob and desolate property and persons*]. The visitations occupied two years. When they were completed the visitors returned to Cuzco, bringing with them certain cloths descriptive of the provinces they had visited. They reported fully to the Inca all that they had found and done.

Besides these, the Inca also despatched other *orejones* as overseers to make roads and hospices on the routes of the Inca, ready for the use of his soldiers. These overseers set out, and made roads, now called "of the Inca," over the mountains and along the sea coast. Those on the sea coast are all provided, at the sides, with high walls of *adobe*, wherever it was possible to build them, except in the deserts where there are no building materials.

These roads go from Quito to Chile, and into the forests of the Andes. Although the Inca did not complete all, suffice it that he made a great part of the roads, which were finished by his sons and grandsons.

XLVI.

TUPAC INCA YUPANQUI SETS OUT, A SECOND TIME, BY ORDER OF HIS FATHER, TO CONQUER WHAT REMAINED UNSUBDUED IN CHINCHAY-SUYU.

Pachacuti Inca Yupanqui knew from the report made by his son when he returned from the conquest of Chinchay-suyu, that there were other great and rich nations and provinces beyond the furthest point reached by Tupac Inca. That no place might be left to conquer, the Inca ordered his son to return with a view to the subjugation of the parts of Quito. He assembled the troops and gave his son the same two brothers as his colleagues, Tilca Yupanqui and Anqui Yupanqui, who had gone with him on the former expedition. [*Tupac inflicted unheard of cruelties and deaths on those who defended themselves and did not wish to give him obedience.*]

In this way he arrived at Tumipampa, within the territory of Quito, whose Sinchi, named Pisar Ccapac, was confederated with Pilla-huaso, Sinchi of the provinces and site of Quito. These two chiefs had a great army and were determined to fight Tupac Inca for their country and lives. Tupac sent messengers to them, demanding that they should lay down their arms and give him obedience. They replied that they were in their own native country, that they were free, and did not wish to serve any one nor be tributaries.

Tupac and his colleagues rejoiced at this answer, because their wish was to find a pretext to encounter

them with blows and to rob them, which was the principal
object of the war. They say that the Inca army numbered
more than 250,000 experienced soldiers. Tupac ordered
them to march against the men of Quito and the Cañaris.
They encountered each other, both sides fighting with
resolution and skill. The victory was for a long time
doubtful because the Quitos and Cañaris pressed stubbornly
against their enemies. When the Inca saw this he got out
of the litter in which he travelled, animated his people, and
made signs for the 50,000 men who were kept in reserve
for the last necessity. When these fresh troops appeared
the Quitos and Cañaris were defeated and fled, the pursuit
being continued with much bloodshed and cruelty, the
victors shouting, "Ccapac Inca Yupanqui! Cuzco! Cuzco!"
All the chiefs were killed. They captured Pilla-huaso in
the vanguard. No quarter was given, in order to strike
terror into those who heard of it.

Thence Inca Tupac marched to the place where now
stands the city of San Francisco de Quito, where they
halted to cure the wounded and give much needed rest
to the others. So this great province remained subject,
and Tupac sent a report of his proceedings to his father.
Pachacuti rejoiced at the success of his son, and celebrated
many festivals and sacrifices on receiving the tidings.

After Tupac Inca had rested at Cuzco, re-organized
his army, and cured the wounded he went to Tumipampa,
where his wife and sister bore him a son, to whom he gave
the name of Titu Cusi Hualpa, afterwards known as
Huayna Ccapac. After the Inca Tupac had rejoiced and
celebrated the birthday festivals, although the four years
were passed that his father had given him to complete the
conquests, he heard that there was a great nation towards
the South Sea, composed of Indians called Huancavelicas.
So he determined to go down to conquer. At the head
of the mountains above them he built the fortress of

Huachalla, and then went down against the Huancavelicas. Tupac divided his army into three parts, and took one by the most rugged mountains, making war on the Huancavelica mountaineers. He penetrated so far into the mountains that for a long time nothing was known of him, whether he was dead or alive. He conquered the Huancavelicas although they were very warlike, fighting on land and at sea in *balsas*, from Tumbez to Huañapi, Huamo, Manta, Turuca and Quisin.

Marching and conquering on the coast of Manta, and the island of Puna, and Tumbez, there arrived at Tumbez some merchants who had come by sea from the west, navigating in *balsas* with sails. They gave information of the land whence they came, which consisted of some islands called Avachumbi and Ninachumbi, where there were many people and much gold. Tupac Inca was a man of lofty and ambitious ideas, and was not satisfied with the regions he had already conquered. So he determined to challenge a happy fortune, and see if it would favour him by sea. Yet he did not lightly believe the navigating merchants, for such men, being great talkers, ought not to be credited too readily. In order to obtain fuller information, and as it was not a business of which news could easily be got, he called a man, who accompanied him in his conquests, named Antarqui who, they all declare, was a great necromancer and could even fly through the air. Tupac Inca asked him whether what the merchant mariners said was true. Antarqui answered, after having thought the matter well out, that what they said was true, and that he would go there first. They say that he accomplished this by his arts, traversed the route, saw the islands, their people and riches, and, returning, gave certain information of all to Tupac Inca.

The Inca, having this certainty, determined to go there. He caused an immense number of *balsas* to be constructed, in which he embarked more than 20,000 chosen men; taking with him as captains Huaman Achachi, Cunti Yupanqui, Quihual Tupac (all Hanan-cuzcos), Yancan Mayta, Quisu Mayta, Cachimapaca Macus Yupanqui, Llimpita Usca Mayta (Hurin-cuzcos); his brother Tilca Yupanqui being general of the whole fleet. Apu Yupanqui was left in command of the army which remained on land.

Tupac Inca navigated and sailed on until he discovered the islands of Avachumbi and Ninachumbi, and returned, bringing back with him black people, gold, a chair of brass, and a skin and jaw bone of a horse. These trophies were preserved in the fortress of Cuzco until the Spaniards came. An Inca now living had charge of this skin and jaw bone of a horse. He gave this account, and the rest who were present corroborated it. His name is Urco Huaranca. I am particular about this because to those who know anything of the Indies it will appear a strange thing and difficult to believe. The duration of this expedition undertaken by Tupac Inca was nine months, others say a year, and, as he was so long absent, every one believed he was dead. But to deceive them and make them think that news of Tupac Inca had come, Apu Yupanqui, his general of the land army, made rejoicings. This was afterwards commented upon to his disadvantage, and it was said that he rejoiced because he was pleased that Tupac Inca Yupanqui did not appear. It cost him his life.

These are the islands which I discovered in the South Sea on the 30th of November, 1567, 200 and more leagues to the westward, being the great discovery of which I gave notice to the Licentiate Governor Castro. But Alvaro de Mendaña, General of the Fleet, did not wish to occupy them[1].

---

[1] This story of the navigation of Tupac Inca to the islands of Ninachumpi and Avachumpi or Hahua chumpi is told by Balboa as well as by Sarmiento. They were no doubt two of the Galapagos Islands. *Nina chumpi* means fire island, and *Hahua chumpi*

After Tupac Inca disembarked from the discovery of the islands, he proceeded to Tumipampa, to visit his wife and son and to hurry preparations for the return to Cuzco to see his father, who was reported to be ill. On the way back he sent troops along the coast to Truxillo, then called Chimu, where they found immense wealth of gold and silver worked into wands, and into beams of the house of Chimu Ccapac, with all which they joined the main army at Caxamarca. Thence Tupac Inca took the route to Cuzco, where he arrived after an absence of six years since he set out on this campaign.

Tupac Inca Yupanqui entered Cuzco with the greatest, the richest, and the most solemn triumph with which any Inca had ever reached the House of the Sun, bringing with him people of many different races, strange animals, innumerable quantities of riches. But behold the evil condition of Pachacuti Inca Yupanqui and his avarice, for though Tupac Inca was his son whose promotion he had procured, he felt such jealousy that his son should have gained such honour and fame in those conquests, that he publicly showed annoyance that it was not himself who triumphed, and that all was not due to him. So he determined to kill his sons Tilca Yupanqui and Auqui Yupanqui who had gone with Tupac Inca, their crime being that they had disobeyed his orders by delaying longer than the time he had fixed, and that they had taken his son to such a distance that he thought he would never return to Cuzco. They say that he killed them, though some say that he only killed Tilca Yupanqui. At this Tupac Inca Yupanqui felt much aggrieved, that his father should have slain one who had worked so well for him. The death was concealed by many feasts in honour of the victories of Tupac Inca, which were continued for a year.

outer island.   See my introduction to the *Voyages of Sarmiento*, p. xiii; and *Las Islas de Galapagos* by Marco Jimenes de la Espada.

XLVII.

DEATH OF PACHACUTI INCA YUPANQUI.

Pachacuti Inca Yupanqui derived much comfort from his grandson, the son of Tupac Inca. He always had the child with him, and caused him to be brought up and cherished in his residence and dormitory. He would not let him out of his sight.

Being in the highest prosperity and sovereignty of his life, he fell ill of a grave infirmity, and, feeling that he was at the point of death, he sent for all his sons who were then in the city. In their presence he first divided all his jewels and contents of his wardrobe. Next he made them plough furrows in token that they were vassals of their brother, and that they had to eat by the sweat of their hands. He also gave them arms in token that they were to fight for their brother. He then dismissed them.

He next sent for the Incas *orejones* of Cuzco, his relations, and for Tupac Inca his son to whom he spoke, with a few words, in this manner:—"Son! you now see how many great nations I leave to you, and you know what labour they have cost me. Mind that you are the man to keep and augment them. No one must raise his two eyes against you and live, even if he be your own brother. I leave you these our relations that they may be your councillors. Care for them and they shall serve you. When I am dead, take care of my body, and put it in my houses at Patallacta. Have my golden image in the House of the Sun, and make my subjects, in all the provinces, offer up solemn sacrifice, after which keep the feast of *purucaya*, that I may go to rest with my father the Sun." Having finished his speech they say that he began to sing

in a low and sad voice with words of his own language.
They are in Castilian as follows :

> " I was born as a flower of the field,
> As a flower I was cherished in my youth,
> I came to my full age, I grew old,
> Now I am withered and die."

Having uttered these words, he laid his head upon a pillow
and expired, giving his soul to the devil, having lived 125
years. For he succeeded, or rather he took the Incaship
into his hands when he was 22, and he was sovereign
103 years.

He had four legitimate sons by his wife Mama Anahuarqui, and he had 100 sons and 50 daughters who
were bastards. Being numerous they were called *Hatun-
ayllu*, which means a "great lineage." By another name
this lineage is called *Inaca Panaca Ayllu*. Those who
sustain this lineage at the present time are Don Diego
Cayo, Don Felipa Inguil, Don Juan Quispi Cusi, Don
Francisco Chaco Rimachi, and Don Juan Illac. They live
in Cuzco and are Hanan-cuzcos.

Pachacuti was a man of good stature, robust, fierce,
haughty, insatiably bent on tyrannizing over all the world,
[*and cruel above measure. All the ordinances he made for
the people were directed to tyranny and his own interests*].
His conduct was infamous for he often took some widow as
a wife and if she had a daughter that he liked, he also took
the daughter for wife or concubine. If there was some
gallant and handsome youth in the town who was esteemed
for something, he presently made some of his servants
make friends with him, get him into the country, and kill
him the best way they could. He took all his sisters as
concubines, saying they could not have a better husband
than their brother.

This Inca died in the year 1191. He conquered more
than 300 leagues, 40 more or less in person accompanied by

his legitimate brothers, the captains Apu Mayta and Vicaquirao, the rest by Amaru Tupac Inca his eldest son, Ccapac Yupanqui his brother, and Tupac Inca his son and successor, with other captains, his brothers and sons.

This Inca arranged the parties and lineages of Cuzco in the order that they now are. The Licentiate Polo found the body of Pachacuti in Tococachi, where now is the parish of San Blas of the city of Cuzco, well preserved and guarded. He sent it to Lima by order of the Viceroy of this kingdom, the Marquis of Cañete. The *guauqui* or idol of this Inca was called *Inti Illapa*. It was of gold and very large, and was brought to Caxamarca in pieces. The Licentiate Polo found that this *guauqui* or idol had a house, estate, servants and women.

XLVIII.

THE LIFE OF TUPAC INCA YUPANQUI[1], THE TENTH INCA.

When Pachacuti Inca Yupanqui died, two *orejones* were deputed to watch the body, and to allow no one to enter or go out to spread the news of his death, until orders had been given. The other Incas and *orejones* went with Tupac Inca to the House of the Sun and then ordered the twelve captains of the *ayllus* of the Inca's guard to come. They came with 2200 men of the guard, under their command, fully armed, and surrounded the House of the Sun. The Incas again invested Tupac Inca

---

[1] All authorities agree that Tupac Inca Yupanqui was the successor of Pachacuti except Betanzos, Santillana and Garcilasso de la Vega. Betanzos has a Yamqui Yupanqui. Garcilasso gives the reign of another Inca named Inca Yupanqui between Pachacuti and Tupac Inca. He was ignorant of the fact that Pachacuti and Inca Yupanqui were the same person. Santillana follows Garcilasso but calls Pachacuti's other self Ccapac Yupanqui.

Yupanqui with the fringe, and gave him the other insignia of sovereignty, as he had now inherited and succeeded his father. Taking him in the midst of themselves, and of the guards, they escorted him to the great square, where he was seated, in majesty, on a superb throne. All the people of the city were then ordered to come and make obeisance to the Inca on pain of death.

Those who had come with the Inca, went to their houses to fetch presents to show reverence and do homage to the new Inca. He remained with his guards only, until they returned with presents, doing homage and adoring. The rest of the people did the same, and sacrifices were offered. [*It is to be noted that only those of Cuzco did this, and if any others were present who did so, they must have been forced or frightened by the armed men and the proclamation.*]

This having been done, they approached the Inca and said, " O Sovereign Inca! O Father! now take rest." At these words Tupac Inca showed much sadness and covered his head with his mantle, which they call *llacolla*, a square cloak. He next went, with all his company, to the place where the body of his father was laid, and there he put on mourning. All things were then arranged for the obsequies, and Tupac Inca Yupanqui did everything that his father had ordered at the point of death, touching the treatment of his body and other things.

XLIX.

TUPAC INCA YUPANQUI CONQUERS THE PROVINCE OF THE ANTIS.

Pachacuti Inca Yupanqui being dead, and Tupac Inca ruling alone, he caused all the Sinchis and principal men of the conquered provinces to be summoned. Those came who feared the fury of the Inca, and with them the Indians of the province of Anti-suyu, who are the dwellers in the forests to the eastward of Cuzco, who had been conquered in the time of Pachacuti his father.

Tupac Inca ordered them all to do homage, adore, and offer sacrifices. The Antis were ordered to bring from their country several loads of lances of palm wood for the service of the House of the Sun. The Antis, who did not serve voluntarily, looked upon this demand as a mark of servitude. They fled from Cuzco, returned to their country, and raised the land of the Antis in the name of freedom.

Tupac Inca was indignant, and raised a powerful army which he divided into three parts. He led the first in person, entering the Anti-suyu by Ahua-tona. The second was entrusted to a captain named Uturuncu Achachi, who entered Anti-suyu by a town they call Amaru. The third, under a captain named Chalco Yupanqui, advanced by way of Pilcopata. All these routes were near each other, and the three divisions formed a junction three leagues within the forest, at a place called Opatari, whence they commenced operations against the settlements of the Antis. The inhabitants of this region were Antis, called Opataris, and were the first to be conquered. Chalco Yupanqui carried an image of the Sun.

The forests were very dense and full of evil places; so that they could not force their way through, nor did they know what direction to take in order to reach the settlements of the natives, which were well concealed in the thick vegetation. To find them the explorers climbed up the highest trees, and pointed out the places where they could see smoke rising. So they worked away at road making through the undergrowth until they lost that sign of inhabitants and found another. In this way the Inca made a road where it seemed impossible to make one.

The Sinchi of the greater part of these provinces of the Antis was Condin Savana, of whom they say that he was a great wizard and enchanter, and they had the belief, and even now they affirm that he could turn himself into different shapes.

Tupac Inca and his captains penetrated into this region of the Antis, which consists of the most terrible and fearful forests, with many rivers, where they endured immense toil, and the people who came from Peru suffered from the change of climate, for Peru is cold and dry, while the forests of Anti-suyu are warm and humid. The soldiers of Tupac Inca became sick, and many died. Tupac Inca himself, with a third of his men who came with him to conquer, were lost in the forests, and wandered for a long time, without knowing whether to go in one direction or another until he fell in with Uturuncu Achachi who put him on the route.

On this occasion Tupac Inca and his captains conquered four great tribes. The first was that of the Indians called Opataris. The next was the Mano-suyu. The third tribe was called Mañaris or Yanasimis, which means those of the black mouth : and the province of Rio, and the province of the Chunchos. They went over much ground in descending the river Tono, and penetrated as far as the Chiponauas. The Inca sent another great captain, named Apu Ccurimachi, by the route which they now call of Camata. This route was in the direction of the rising of the sun, and he advanced until he came to the river of which reports have but now been received, called Paytiti, where he set up the frontier pillars of Inca Tupac. During the campaign against these nations, Tupac Inca took prisoners the following Sinchis : Vinchincayua, Cantahuancuru, Nutanhuari[1].

---

[1] This expedition of Tupac Inca Yupanqui into the montaña of Paucartambo, and down the River Tono is important. Garcilasso de la

During the campaign an Indian of the Collas, named Coaquiri, fled from his company, reached the Collao, and spread the report that Tupac Inca was dead. He said that there was no longer an Inca, that they should all rise and that he would be their leader. Presently he took the name of Pachacuti, the Collas rose, and chose him as their captain. This news reached Tupac Inca in Anti-suyu where he was in the career of conquest. He resolved to march against the Collas and punish them. He left the forests, leaving Uturuncu Achachi to complete the conquest, with orders to return into Peru when that service was completed, but not to enter Cuzco triumphing until the Inca should come.

L.

TUPAC INCA YUPANQUI GOES TO SUBDUE AND PACIFY THE COLLAS.

As the Collas were one of those nations which most desired their freedom, they entered upon attempts to obtain it whenever a chance offered, as has already been explained. Tupac Inca Yupanqui resolved to crush them once for all. Having returned from the Antis, he increased his army and nominated as captains Larico, the son of his cousin Ccapac Yupanqui, his brother Chachi, Cunti Yupanqui,

---

Vega describes it in chapters xiii., xiv., xv. and xvi. of Book vii. He says that five rivers unite to form the great Amaru-mayu or Serpent River, which he was inclined to think was a tributary of the Rio de la Plata. He describes fierce battles with the Chunchos, who were reduced to obedience. After descending the River Tono, Garcilasso says that the Incas eventually reached the country of the Musus (Moxos) and opened friendly relations with them. Many Incas settled in the country of the Musus. Garcilasso then gives some account of Spanish expeditions into the montaña, led by Diego Aleman, Gomez de Tordoya, and Juan Alvarez Maldonado.

The account in the text agrees, in the main, with that of Garcilasso de la Vega. Sarmiento gives the names of four Indian tribes who were encountered, besides the Chunchos.

and Quihual Tupac. With this army he advanced to the Collao. The Collas had constructed four strong places at Llallaua, Asillo, Arapa, and Pucara. The Inca captured the chiefs and the leader of all, who was Chuca-chucay Pachacuti Coaquiri, he who, as we have said, fled from Anti-suyu. Afterwards these were the drummers[1] of Inca Tupac. Finally, owing to the great diligence of Inca Tupac, although the war occupied some years, the Incas conquered and subdued all [*perpetrating great cruelties on them*].

Following up his victories, in pursuit of the vanquished, he got so far from Cuzco that he found himself in Charcas. So he determined to advance further, subduing every nation of which he received notice. He eventually prosecuted his conquests so far that he entered Chile, where he defeated the great Sinchi Michimalongo, and Tangalongo, Sinchi of the Chilians as far as the river Maule. He came to Coquimbo in Chile and to the banks of the Maule, where he set up his frontier columns, or as others say a wall, to show the end of his conquests. From this campaign he returned with great riches in gold, having discovered many mines of gold and silver. He then returned to Cuzco.

These spoils were joined with those of Uturuncu Achachi, who had returned from the forests of the Antis after a campaign of three years. He was at Paucar-tampu, awaiting the return of his brother, who entered Cuzco with a very great triumph. They made great feasts to commemorate the conquests, presenting gifts and granting many favours to the soldiers who had served with the Inca in these campaigns. As the provinces of the Chumpi-vilicas saw the power and greatness of Tupac Inca Yupanqui they came to submit with the rest of Cunti-suyu.

---

[1] *i.e.* their skins were made into drums.

Besides this the Inca went to Chachapoyas, and crushed those who had been suspected, visiting many provinces on the road.

On his return to Cuzco he made certain ordinances, as well for peace as for war time. He increased the *mitimaes* which his father had instituted, as has been explained in the account of his life, giving more privileges and liberty. Besides, he caused a general visitation to be made of all the land from Quito to Chile, registering the whole population for more than a thousand leagues; and imposed a tribute [*so heavy that no one could be owner of a* mazorca *of maize, which is their bread for food, nor of a pair of* usutas, *which are their shoes, nor marry, nor do a single thing without special licence from Tupac Inca. Such was the tyranny and oppression to which he subjected them*]. He placed over the *tucuricos* a class of officers called *Michu*[1] to collect the taxes and tributes.

Tupac Inca saw that in the districts and provinces the Sinchis claimed to inherit by descent. He resolved to abolish this rule, and to put them all under his feet, both great and small. He, therefore, deposed the existing Sinchis, and introduced a class of ruler at his own will, who were selected in the following way. He appointed a ruler who should have charge of 10,000 men, and called him *huanu*, which means that number. He appointed another ruler over 1000, and called him *huaranca*, which is 1000. The next had charge of 500, called *pichca-pachaca*, or 500. To another called *pachac* he gave charge of 100, and to another he gave charge of 10 men, called *chunca curaca*. All these had also the title of *Curaca*, which means "principal" or "superior," over the number of men of whom they had charge. These appoint-

---

[1] *Michu* should be *Michec* a shepherd, also a governor. *Michisca* the governed.

ments depended solely on the will of the Inca, who appointed and dismissed them as he pleased, without considering inheritance, or succession. From that time forward they were called *Curacas*, which is the proper name of the chiefs of this land, and not *Caciques*, which is the term used by the vulgar among the Spaniards. That name of *Cacique* belongs to the islands of Santo Domingo and Cuba. From this place we will drop the name of *Sinchi* and only use that of *Curaca*.

LI.

TUPAC INCA MAKES THE YANACONAS.

Among the brothers of the Inca there was one named Tupac Ccapac, a principal man, to whom Tupac Inca had given many servants to work on his farms, and serve on his estates. It is to be understood that Tupac Inca made his brother visitor-general of the whole empire that had been conquered up to that time. Tupac Ccapac, in making the visitation, came to the place where his brother had given him those servants. Under colour of this grant, he took those and also many more, saying that all were his *yana-cunas*[1], which is the name they give to their servants. He persuaded them to rebel against his brother, saying that if they would help him he would show them great favours. He then marched to Cuzco, very rich and powerful, where he gave indications of his intentions.

He intended his schemes to be kept secret, but Tupac

---

[1] Garcilasso de la Vega says that the meaning of *Yanacona* is "a man who is under the obligation to perform the duties of a servant." Balboa, p. 129, tells the same story of the origin of the *Yanaconas* as in the text. The amnesty was granted on the banks of the river Yana-yacu, and here they were called Yana-yacu-cuna, corrupted into Yana-cona. The Spaniards adopted the word for all Indians in domestic service, as distinguished from *mitayos* or forced labourers.

Inca was informed of them and came to Cuzco. He had
been away at the ceremony of arming one of his sons
named Ayar Manco. Having convinced himself that his
information was correct, he killed Tupac Ccapac with all
his councillors and supporters. Finding that many tribes
had been left out of the visitation by him, for this attempt,
Tupac Inca went in person from Cuzco, to investigate the
matter and finish the visitation.

While doing this the Inca came to a place called Yana-
yacu, which means "black water" because a stream of a
very dark colour flows down that valley, and for that
reason they call the river and valley Yana-yacu. Up to
this point he had been inflicting very cruel punishment
without pardoning any one who was found guilty either
in word or deed. In this valley of Yana-yacu his sister
and wife, Mama Ocllo, asked him not to continue such
cruelties, which were more butchery and inhumanity than
punishment, and not to kill any more but to pardon them,
asking for them as her servants. In consequence of this
intercession, the Inca ceased the slaughter, and said that
he would grant a general pardon. As the pardon was
proclaimed in Yana-yacu, he ordered that all the pardoned
should be called Yana-yacus. They were known as not
being allowed to enter in the number of servants of the
House of the Sun, nor those of the visitation. So they
remained under the Curacas. This affair being finished,
the visitation made by Tupac Ccapac was considered to
be of no effect. So the Inca returned to Cuzco with
the intention of ordering another visitation to be made
afresh.

LII.

TUPAC INCA YUPANQUI ORDERS A SECOND VISITA-TION OF THE LAND, AND DOES OTHER THINGS.

As the visitation entrusted to Tupac Ccapac was not to his liking, the Inca revoked it, and nominated another brother named Apu Achachi to be visitor-general. The Inca ordered him not to include the Yana-yacus in the visitation, because they were unworthy to enter into the number of the rest, owing to what they had done. Apu Achachi set out and made his general visitation, reducing many of the Indians to live in villages and houses who had previously lived in caves and hills and on the banks of rivers, each one by himself. He sent those in strong fastnesses into plains, that they might have no site for a fortress, on the strength of which they might rebel. He reduced them into provinces, giving them their Curacas in the order already described. He did not make the son of the deceased a Curaca, but the man who had most ability and aptitude for the service. If the appointment did not please the Inca he, without more ado, dismissed him and appointed another, so that no Curaca, high or low, felt secure in his appointment. To these Curacas were given servants, women and estates, submitting an account of them, for, though they were Curacas, they could not take a thing of their own authority, without express leave from the Inca.

In each province all those of the province made a great sowing of every kind of edible vegetable for the Inca, his overseers coming to the harvest. Above all there was a *Tucurico Apu*, who was the governor-lieutenant of the Inca in that province. It is true that the first Inca who obliged the Indians of this land to pay tribute of everything, and in quantity, was Inca Yupanqui. But Tupac Inca imposed rules and fixed the tribute they must pay, and divided it according to what each province was to contribute as well for the general tax as those for *Huacas*, and Houses of the Sun. [*In this way the people were so loaded with tributes and taxes, that they had to work perpetually night and day to pay them, and even then they could not comply, and had no time for sufficient labour to suffice for their own maintenance.*]

Tupac Inca divided the estates throughout the whole empire, according to the measure which they call *tupu*.

He divided the months of the year, with reference to labour in the fields, as follows. Three months in the year were allotted to the Indians for the work of their own fields, and the rest must be given up to the work of the Sun, of *huacas*, and of the Inca. In the three months that were given to themselves, one was for ploughing and sowing, one for reaping, and another in the summer for festivals, and for make and mend clothes days. The rest of their time was demanded for the service of the Sun and the Incas.

This Inca ordered that there should be merchants who might profit by their industry in this manner. When any merchant brought gold, silver, precious stones, or other valuable things for sale, they were to be asked where they got them, and in this way they gave information respecting the mines and places whence the valuables had been taken. Thus a very great many mines of gold and silver, and of very fine colours, were discovered.

This Inca had two Governors-General in the whole empire, called *Suyuyoc Apu*[1]; one resided at Xauxa and the other at Tiahuanacu in Colla-suyu.

---

[1] *Suyu* a great division of the empire, or a province. *Yoc* a terminal particle denoting possession or office.

Tupac Inca ordered the seclusion of certain women in the manner of our professed nuns, maidens of 12 years and upwards, who were called *acllas*[1]. From thence they were taken to be given in marriage to the *Tucurico Apu*, or by order of the Inca who, when any captain returned with victory, distributed the *acllas* to captains, soldiers and other servants who had pleased him, as gracious gifts which were highly valued. As they took out some, they were replaced by others, for there must always be the number first ordained by the Inca. If any man takes one out, or is caught inside with one they are both hanged, tied together.

This Inca made many ordinances, in his tyrannical mode of government, which will be given in a special volume.

LIII.

TUPAC INCA MAKES THE FORTRESS OF CUZCO.

After Tupac Inca Yupanqui had visited all the empire and had come to Cuzco where he was served and adored, being for the time idle, he remembered that his father Pachacuti had called the city of Cuzco the lion city. He said that the tail was where the two rivers unite which flow through it[2], that the body was the great square and the houses round it, and that the head was wanting. It would be for some son of his to put it on. The Inca discussed this question with the *orejones*, who said that the best head would be to make a fortress on a high plateau to the north of the city.

This being settled, the Inca sent to all the provinces,

---

[1] *Aclla* means chosen, selected.

[2] This district of Cuzco has always been called *Pumap chupan* or tail of the puma.

to order the *tucuricos* to supply a large number of people
for the work of the fortress. Having come, the workmen
were divided into parties, each one having its duties and
officers. Thus some brought stones, others worked them,
others placed them. The diligence was such that in a few
years, the great fortress of Cuzco was built, sumptuous,
exceedingly strong, of rough stone, a thing most admirable
to look upon. The buildings within it were of small worked
stone, so beautiful that, if it had not been seen, it would
not be believed how strong and beautiful it was. What
makes it still more worthy of admiration is that they did
not possess tools to work the stone, but could only work
with other stones. This fortress was intact until the
time of the differences between Pizarro and Almagro, after
which they began to dismantle it, to build with its stones
the houses of Spaniards in Cuzco, which are at the foot
of the fortress. Great regret is felt by those who see the
ruins. When it was finished, the Inca made many store
houses round Cuzco for provisions and clothing, against
times of necessity and of war; which was a measure of
great importance[1].

---

[1] This fortress of Cuzco, on the Sacsahuaman Hill, was well described by Cieza de Leon and in greater detail by Garcilasso de la
Vega, ii. pp. 305—318. Both ascribe it to Inca Yupanqui or his son
Tupac Inca, as does Sarmiento. The extensive edifices, built of
masonry of his period, were no doubt the work of Tupac Inca who
thus got credit for the whole. These later edifices were pulled down
by the Spaniards, for material for building their houses in the city.
But the wonderful cyclopean work that remains is certainly of much
more ancient date, and must be assigned, like Tiahuanacu, to the far
distant age of the monolithic empire.

LIV.

DEATH OF TUPAC INCA YUPANQUI.

Having visited and divided the lands, and built the fortress of Cuzco, besides edifices and houses without number, Tupac Inca Yupanqui went to Chinchero[1], a town near Cuzco, where he had very rich things for his recreation; and there he ordered extensive gardens to be constructed to supply his household. When the work was completed he fell ill of a grave infirmity, and did not wish to be visited by anyone. But as he became worse and felt the approach of death, he sent for the *orejones* of Cuzco, his relations, and when they had assembled in his presence he said: "My relations and friends! I would have you to know that the Sun my Father desires to take me to himself, and I wish to go and rest with him. I have called you to let you know who it is that I desire to succeed me as lord and sovereign, and who is to rule and govern you." They answered that they grieved much at his illness, that as the Sun his father had so willed it so must it be, that his will must be done, and they besought the Inca to nominate him who was to be sovereign in his place. Tupac Inca then replied: "I nominate for my successor my son Titu Cusi Hualpa, son of my sister and wife, Mama Ocllo." For this they offered many thanks, and afterwards the Inca sank down on his pillow and died, having lived 85 years.

Tupac Inca succeeded his father at the age of 18 years. He had two legitimate sons, 60 bastards, and 30 daughters.

---

[1] Chinchero is a village near Cuzco, on the heights overlooking the lovely valley of Yucay, with magnificent mountains in the background. The remains of the Inca palace are still standing, not unlike those on the Colcampata at Cuzco.

Some say that at the time of his death, or a short time before, he had nominated one of his illegitimate sons to succeed him named Ccapac Huari, son of a concubine whose name was Chuqui Ocllo.

He left a lineage or *ayllu* called *Ccapac Ayllu*, whose heads, who sustain it and are now living, are Don Andres Tupac Yupanqui, Don Cristobal Pisac Tupac, Don Garcia Vilcas, Don Felipe Tupac Yupanqui, Don Garcia Azache, and Don Garcia Pilco. They are Hanan-cuzcos.

The deceased Inca was frank, merciful in peace, cruel in war and punishments, a friend to the poor, a great man of indefatigable industry and a notable builder. [*He was the greatest tyrant of all the Incas.*] He died in the year 1258. Chalco Chima burnt his body in 1533, when he captured Huascar, as will be related in its place. The ashes, with his idol or *guauqui* called *Cusi-churi*, were found in Calispuquiu where the Indians had concealed it, and offered to it many sacrifices.

LV.

THE LIFE OF HUAYNA CCAPAC, ELEVENTH INCA[1].

As soon as Tupac Inca was dead, the *orejones*, who were with him at the time of his death, proceeded to Cuzco for the customary ceremonies. These were to raise the Inca his successor before the death of his father had become known to him, and to follow the same order as in the case of the death of Pachacuti Inca Yupanqui. As the wives and sons of Tupac Inca also went to Cuzco, the matter could not be kept secret. A woman who had been a concubine of the late Inca, named Ccuri Ocllo, a kins-

---

[1] All authorities agree that Huayna Ccapac was the son and successor of Tupac Inca.

woman of Ccapac Huari, as soon as she arrived at Cuzco, spoke to her relations and to Ccapac Huari in these words. "Sirs and relations! Know that Tupac Inca is dead and that, when in health, he had named Ccapac Huari for his successor, but at the end, being on the point of death, he said that Titu Cusi Hualpa, son of Mama Ocllo, should succeed him. You ought not to consent to this. Rather call together all your relations and friends, and raise Ccapac Huari, your elder brother, son of Chuqui Ocllo, to be Inca." This seemed well to all the relations of Ccapac Huari, and they sent to assemble all the other relations on his behalf.

While this was proceeding, the *orejones* of Cuzco, knowing nothing of it, were arranging how to give the fringe to Titu Cusi Hualpa. The plot of the party of Ccapac Huari became known to the late Inca's brother, Huaman Achachi. He assembled some friends, made them arm themselves, and they went to where Titu Cusi Hualpa was retired and concealed. They then proceeded to where the friends of Ccapac Huari had assembled, and killed many of them, including Ccapac Huari himself. Others say that they did not kill Ccapac Huari at that time, but only took him. His mother Chuqui Ocllo was taken and, being a rebel as well as a witch who had killed her lord Tupac Inca, she was put to death. Ccapac Huari was banished to Chinchero, where he was given a maintenance, but he was never allowed to enter Cuzco again until his death. They also killed the woman Ccuri Ocllo, who had advised the raising of Ccapac Huari to the Incaship.

LVI.

THEY GIVE THE FRINGE OF INCA TO HUAYNA CCAPAC, THE ELEVENTH INCA.

The city of Cuzco being pacified, Huaman Achachi went to Quispicancha, three leagues from Cuzco, where Titu Cusi Hualpa was concealed, and brought his nephew to Cuzco, to the House of the Sun. After the ˙sacrifices and accustomed ceremonies, the image of the Sun delivered the fringe to Titu Cusi Hualpa.

This being done, and the new Inca having been invested with all the insignia of Ccapac, and placed in a rich litter, they bore him to the *huaca* Huanacauri, where he offered a sacrifice. The *orejones* returned to Cuzco by the route taken by Manco Ccapac.

Arrived at the first square, called Rimac-pampa, the accession was announced to the people, and they were ordered to come and do homage to the new Inca. When they all assembled, and saw how young he was, never having seen him before, they all raised their voices and called him *Huayna Ccapac* which means "the boy chief" or "the boy sovereign." For this reason he was called Huayna Ccapac from that time, and the name Titu Cusi Hualpa was no longer used. They celebrated festivals, armed him as a knight, adored, and presented many gifts —as was customary.

LVII.

THE FIRST ACTS OF HUAYNA CCAPAC AFTER HE BECAME INCA.

As Huayna Ccapac was very young when he succeeded, they appointed a tutor and coadjutor for him named Hualpaya, a son of Ccapac Yupanqui, brother of Inca

Yupanqui. This prince made a plot to raise himself to the Incaship, but it became known to Huaman Achachi, then Governor of Chinchay-suyu. At the time he was in Cuzco, and he and his people killed Hualpaya and others who were culpable.

Huaman Achachi assumed the government, but always had as a councillor his own brother Auqui Tupac Inca. In course of time Huayna Ccapac went to the House of the Sun, held a visitation, took account of the officials, and provided what was necessary for the service, and for that of the *Mama-cunas*. He took the chief custodianship of the Sun from him who then held it, and assumed the office himself with the title of "Shepherd of the Sun." He next visited the other *huacas* and oracles, and their estates. He also inspected the buildings of the city of Cuzco and the houses of the *orejones*.

Huayna Ccapac ordered the body of his father Tupac Inca to be embalmed. After the sacrifices, the mourning, and other ceremonies, he placed the body in the late Inca's residence which was prepared for it, and gave his servants all that was necessary for their maintenance and services. The same Huayna Ccapac mourned for his father and for his mother who died nearly at the same time.

LVIII.

HUAYNA CCAPAC CONQUERS CHACHAPOYAS.

After Huayna Ccapac had given orders respecting the things mentioned in the last chapter, it was reported to him that there were certain tribes near the territory of the Chachapoyas which might be conquered, and that on the way he might subdue the Chachapoyas who had rebelled. He gave orders to his *orejones* and assembled a large army. He set out from Cuzco, having first offered sacrifices and observed the *calpa*[1]. On the route he took, he reformed many things. Arriving at the land of the Chachapoyas, they, with other neighbouring tribes, put themselves in a posture of defence. They were eventually vanquished and treated with great severity. The Inca then returned to Cuzco and triumphed at the victory gained over the Chachapoyas and other nations.

While he was absent on this campaign, he left as Governor of Cuzco one of his illegitimate brothers named Sinchi Rocca, an eminent architect. He built all the edifices at Yucay, and the houses of the Inca at Casana in the city of Cuzco. He afterwards built other edifices round Cuzco for Huayna Ccapac, on sites which appeared most convenient.

LIX.

HUAYNA CCAPAC MAKES A VISITATION OF THE WHOLE EMPIRE FROM QUITO TO CHILE.

Huayna Ccapac having rested in Cuzco for a long time and, wishing to undertake something, considered that it was a long time since he had visited the empire. He determined that there should be a visitation, and named his uncle Huaman Achachi to conduct it in Chinchay-suyu as far as Quito, he himself undertaking the region of Colla-suyu.

Each one set out, Huayna Ccapac, in person, taking the route to the Collao, where he examined into the government of his *tucuricos*, placing and dismissing governors and Curacas, opening lands and making bridges and irrigating channels. Constructing these works he

---

[1] *Calpa* means force, power. *Calpay* work. *Calparicu* " one who gives strength," used for a wizard. The Calpa was a ceremony connected with divination.

arrived at Charcas and went thence to Chile, which his father had conquered, where he dismissed the governor, and appointed two native Curacas named Michimalongo and Antalongo, who had been vanquished by his father. Having renewed the garrison, he came to Coquimbo and Copiapo, also visiting Atacama and Arequipa. He next went to Anti-suyu and Alayda, by way of Collao and Charcas. He entered the valley of Cochabamba, and there made provinces of *mitimaes* in all parts, because the natives were few, and there was space for all, the land being fertile. Thence he went to Pocona to give orders on that frontier against the Chirihuanas, and to repair a fortress which had been built by his father.

While engaged on these measures, he received news that the provinces of Quito, Cayambis, Carangues, Pastos, and Huancavilcas had rebelled. He, therefore, hurried his return and came to Tiahuanacu, where he prepared for war against the Quitos and Cayambis, and gave orders how the Urus[1] were to live, granting them localities in which each tribe of them was to fish in the lake. He visited the Temple of the Sun and the *huaca* of Ticci Viracocha on the island of Titicaca, and sent orders that all those provinces should send troops to go to that war which he had proclaimed.

LX.

HUAYNA CCAPAC MAKES WAR ON THE QUITOS, PASTOS, CARANGUES, CAYAMBIS, HUANCAVILCAS.

Knowing that the Pastos, Quitos, Carangues, Cayambis and Huancavilcas had rebelled, killed the *tucuricos*, and strengthened their positions with strong forces,

---

[1] The Urus are a tribe of fishermen, with a peculiar language, living among the reed beds in the S.W. part of Lake Titicaca.

Huayna Ccapac, with great rapidity, collected a great army from all the districts of the four *suyus*. He nominated Michi of the Hurin-cuzcos, and Auqui Tupac of the Hanan-cuzcos as captains, and left his uncle Huaman Achachi as governor of Cuzco. Others say that he left Apu Hilaquito and Auqui Tupac Inca in Cuzco, with his son who was to succeed named Tupac Cusi Hualpa Inti Illapa, and with him another of his sons named Titu Atanchi, who remained to perform the fasts before knighthood. It is to be noted that Huayna Ccapac was married, in conformity with custom and with the prescribed ceremonies to Cusi Rimay Coya, by whom he had no male child. He, therefore, took his sister Araua Ocllo to wife, by whom he had a son Tupac Cusi Hualpa, vulgarly called Huascar. Preparing for the campaign he ordered that Atahualpa and Ninan Cuyoche, his illegitimate sons, now grown men, should go with him. His other sons, also illegitimate, named Manco Inca and Paulu Tupac, were to remain with Huascar.

These arrangements having been made, the Inca set out for Quito. On the way he came to Tumipampa where he had himself been born. Here he erected great edifices where he placed, with great solemnity, the caul in which he was born. Marching onwards and reaching the boundary of the region where the Quitos were in arms, he marshalled his squadrons, and presently resolved to conquer the Pastos. For this service he selected two captains of the Collao, one named Mollo Cavana, the other Mollo Pucara, and two others of Cunti-suyu named Apu Cautar Canana and Cunti Mollo, under whose command he placed many men of their nations, and 2000 *orejones* as guards, under Auqui Tupac Inca, brother of Huayna Ccapac and Acollo Tupac of the lineage of Viracocha. They marched to the country of the Pastos who fell back on their chief place, leaving their old people, women and children, with a few men, that the enemy might think there was no one else. The Incas easily conquered these and, thinking that was all, they gave themselves up to idleness and pleasure. One night, when they were engaged in a great rejoicing, eating and drinking freely, without sentries, the Pastos attacked them, and there was a great slaughter, especially among the Collas. Those who escaped, fled until they came to the main army of the Incas which was following them. They say that Atahualpa and Ninan Cuyoche brought up assistance, and that, with the confidence thus gained, Huayna Ccapac ordered the war to be waged most cruelly. So they entered the country of the Pastos a second time, burning and destroying the inhabited places and killing all the people great and small, men and women, young and old. That province having been subdued, a governor was appointed to it.

Huayna Ccapac then returned to Tumipampa, where he rested some days, before moving his camp for the conquest of the Carangues, a very warlike nation. In this campaign he subdued the Macas to the confines of the Cañaris, those of Quisna, of Ancamarca, the province of Puruvay, the Indians of Nolitria, and other neighbouring nations.

Thence he went down to Tumbez, a seaport, and then came to the fortresses of Carangui and Cochisque. In commencing to subdue those of Cochisque he met with a stubborn resistance by valiant men, and many were killed on both sides. At length the place was taken, and the men who escaped were received in the fortress of Carangui. The Incas decided that the country surrounding this fortress should first be subdued. They desolated the country as far as Ancasmayu and Otabalo, those who escaped from the fury of the Incas taking refuge in the fortress. Huayna Ccapac attacked it with his whole force, but was repulsed by the garrison with much slaughter, and the *orejones* were forced to fly, defeated by the Cayambis, the Inca himself being thrown down. He would have been killed if a thousand of his guard had not come up with their captains Cusi Tupac Yupanqui and Huayna Achachi, to rescue and raise him. The sight of this animated the *orejones*. All turned to defend their Inca, and pressed on with such vigour that the Cayambis were driven back into their fortress. The Inca army, in one encounter and the other, suffered heavy loss.

Huayna Ccapac, on this account, returned to Tumipampa, where he recruited his army, preparing to resume the attack on the Cayambis. At this time some *orejones* deserted the Inca, leaving him to go back to Cuzco. Huayna Ccapac satisfied the rest by gifts of clothes, provisions, and other things, and he formed an efficient army.

It was reported that the Cayambis had sallied from their fortress and had defeated a detachment of the Inca army, killing many, and the rest escaping by flight. This caused great sorrow to the Inca, who sent his brother Auqui Toma, with an army composed of all nations, against the Cayambis of the fortress. Auqui Toma went, attacked the fortress, captured four lines of defence and the outer wall, which was composed of five. But at the entrance the Cayambis killed Auqui Toma, captain of the Cuzcos, who had fought most valorously. This attack and defence was so obstinate and long continued that an immense number of men fell, and the survivors had nowhere to fight except upon heaps of dead men. The desire of both sides to conquer or die was so strong that they gave up their lances and arrows and took to their fists. At last, when they saw that their captain was killed, the Incas began to retreat towards a river, into which they went without any care for saving their lives.

The river was in flood and a great number of men were drowned. This was a heavy loss for the cause of Huayna Ccapac. Those who escaped from drowning and from the hands of the enemy, sent the news to the Inca from the other side of the river. Huayna Ccapac received the news of this reverse with heavier grief than ever, for he dearly loved his brother Auqui Toma, who had been killed with so many men who were the pick of the army.

Huayna Ccapac was a brave man, and was not dismayed. On the contrary it raised his spirit and he resolved to be avenged. He again got ready his forces and marched in person against the fortress of the Cayambis. He formed the army in three divisions. He sent Michi with a third of the army to pass on one side of the fortress without being seen. This detachment consisted of Cuzco *orejones*, and men of Chinchay-suyu. They were to advance five marches beyond the fortress and, at a fixed time, return towards it, desolating and destroying. The Inca, with the rest of his army marched direct to the attack of the fortress, and began to fight with great fury. This continued some days, during which the Inca lost some men. While the battle was proceeding, Michi and those of Chinchay-suyu turned, desolating and destroying everything in the land of the Cayambis. They were so furious that they did not leave anything standing, making the very earth to tremble. When Huayna Ccapac knew that his detachment was near the fortress, he feigned a flight. The Cayambis, not aware of what was happening in their rear, came out of the fortress in pursuit of the Inca. When the Cayambis were at some distance from their stronghold, the Chinchay-suyus, commanded by Michi, came in sight. These met with no resistance in the fortress as the Cayambis were outside, following Huayna Ccapac. They easily entered it and set it on fire in several parts, killing or capturing all who were inside.

The Cayambis were, by this time, fighting with the army of Huayna Ccapac. When they saw their fortress on fire they lost hope and fled from the battle field towards a lake which was near, thinking that they could save themselves by hiding among the beds of reeds. But Huayna Ccapac followed them with great rapidity. In order that none might escape he gave instructions that the lake should be surrounded. In that lake, and the swamps on its borders, the troops of Huayna Ccapac, he fighting most furiously in person, made such havock and slaughter, that the lake was coloured with the blood of the dead Cayambis. From that time forward the lake has been called *Yahuar-cocha*, which means the "lake of blood," from the quantity that was there shed.

It is to be noted that in the middle of this lake there was an islet with two willow trees, up which some Cayambis climbed, and among them their two chiefs named Pinto and Canto, most valiant Indians. The troops of Huayna Ccapac pelted them with stones and captured Canto, but Pinto escaped with a thousand brave Cañaris.

The Cayambis being conquered, the Cuzcos began to select those who would look best in the triumphal entry into Cuzco. But they, thinking that they were being selected to be killed, preferred rather to die like men than to be tied up like women. So they turned and began to fight. Huayna Ccapac saw this and ordered them all to be killed.

The Inca placed a garrison in the fortress, and sent a captain with a detachment in pursuit of Pinto who, in his flight, was doing much mischief. They followed until Pinto went into forests, with other fugitives, escaping for a time. After Huayna Ccapac had rested for some days at Tumipampa, he got information where Pinto was in the forests, and surrounded them, closing up all entrances and exits. Hunger then obliged him, and those who were with him, to surrender. This Pinto was very brave and he had such hatred against Huayna Ccapac that even, after his capture, when the Inca had presented him with gifts and treated him kindly, he never could see his face. So he died out of his mind, and Huayna Ccapac ordered a drum to be made of his skin. The drum was sent to Cuzco, and so this war came to an end. It was at Cuzco in the *taqui* or dance in honour of the Sun.

LXI.

THE CHIRIHUANAS COME TO MAKE WAR IN PERU AGAINST THOSE CONQUERED BY THE INCAS.

While Huayna Ccapac was occupied with this war of the Cayambis, the Chirihuanas, who form a nation of the forests, naked and eaters of human flesh, for which they have a public slaughter house, uniting, and, coming forth from their dense forests, entered the territory of Charcas, which had been conquered by the Incas of Peru. They attacked the fortress of Cuzco-tuyo, where the Inca had a large frontier garrison to defend the country against them. Their assault being sudden they entered the fortress, massacred the garrison, and committed great havock, robberies and murders among the surrounding inhabitants.

The news reached Huayna Ccapac at Quito, and he received it with much heaviness. He sent a captain, named Yasca, to Cuzco to collect troops, and with them to march against the Chirihuanas. This captain set out for Cuzco, taking with him the *huaca* "Cataquilla[1]" of

---

[1] It was the policy of the Incas that the idols and *huacas* of conquered nations should be sent to Cuzco and deposited there. Catiquilla was an idol of the Caxamarca and Huamachuco people. Arriaga calls it Apu-cati-quilla. *Apu* the great or chief, *catic*

Caxamarca and Huamachuco, and "Curichaculla of the Chachapoyas; and the *huacas* "Tomayrica and Chinchay-cocha," with many people, the attendants of the *huacas*. He arrived at Cuzco where he was very well received by the Governors, Apu Hilaquito and Auqui Tupac Inca. Having collected his troops he left Cuzco for Charcas. On the road he enlisted many men of the Collao. With these he came up with the Chirihuanas and made cruel war upon them. He captured some to send to Huayna Ccapac at Quito, that the Inca might see what these strange men were like. The captain Yasca rebuilt the fortress and, placing in it the necessary garrison, he returned to Cuzco, dismissed his men, and each one returned to his own land.

LXII.

WHAT HUAYNA CCAPAC DID AFTER THE SAID WARS.

As soon as Huayna Ccapac had despatched the captain against the Chirihuanas, he set out from Tumipampa to organize the nations he had conquered, including Quito, Pasto, and Huancavilcas. He came to the river called Ancas-mayu, between Pasto and Quito, where he set up his boundary pillars at the limit of the country he had conquered. As a token of grandeur and as a memorial he placed certain golden staves in the pillars. He then followed the course of the river in search of the sea, seeking for people to conquer, for he had information that in that direction the country was well peopled.

---

follower, *quilla* the moon. Apu-cati-quilla appears to have been a moon god. The other *huacas* are local deities, all sent to Cuzco. Catiquilla had been kept as an oracle in the village of Tauca in Conchucos (Calancha, p. 471). *Cati-quilla* would mean "following moon." (See also *Extirpacion de la idolatria del Peru*, Joseph de Arriaga. Lima, 1627.)

On this road the army of the Inca was in great peril, suffering from scarcity of water, for the troops had to cross extensive tracts of sand. One day, at dawn, the Inca army found itself surrounded by an immense crowd of people, not knowing who they were. In fear of the unknown enemy, the troops began to retreat towards the Inca. Just as they were preparing for flight a boy came to Huayna Ccapac, and said: "My Lord! fear not, those are the people for whom we are in search. Let us attack them." This appeared to the Inca to be good advice and he ordered an impetuous attack to be made, promising that whatever any man took should be his. The *orejones* delivered such an assault on those who surrounded them that, in a short time, the circle was broken. The enemy was routed, and the fugitives made for their habitations, which were on the sea coast towards Coaques, where the Incas captured an immense quantity of rich spoils, emeralds, turquoises, and great store of very fine *mollo*, a substance formed in sea shells, more valued amongst them than gold or silver.

Here the Inca received a message from the Sinchi or Curaca of the island of Puna with a rich present, inviting him to come to his island to receive his service. Huayna Ccapac did so. Thence he went to Huancavilca, where he joined the reserves who had been left there. News came to him that a great pestilence was raging at Cuzco of which the governors Apu Hilaquito his uncle, and Auqui Tupac Inca his brother had died, also his sister Mama Cuca, and many other relations. To establish order among the conquered nations, the Inca went to Quito, intending to proceed from thence to Cuzco to rest.

On reaching Quito the Inca was taken ill with a fever, though others say it was small-pox or measles. He felt the disease to be mortal and sent for the *orejones* his relations, who asked him to name his successor. His reply was that his son Ninan Cuyoche was to succeed, if the augury of the *calpa* gave signs that such succession would be auspicious, if not his son Huascar was to succeed.

Orders were given to proceed with the ceremony of the *calpa*, and Cusi Tupac Yupanqui, named by the Inca to be chief steward of the Sun, came to perform it. By the first *calpa* it was found that the succession of Ninan Cuyoche would not be auspicious. Then they opened another lamb and took out the lungs, examining certain veins. The result was that the signs respecting Huascar were also inauspicious. Returning to the Inca, that he might name some one else, they found that he was dead. While the *orejones* stood in suspense about the succession, Cusi Tupac Yupanqui said: " Take care of the body, for I go to Tumipampa to give the fringe to Ninan Cuyoche." But when he arrived at Tumipampa he found that Ninan Cuyoche was also dead of the small-pox pestilence[1].

Seeing this Cusi Tupac Yupanqui said to Araua Ocllo— "Be not sad, O Coya! go quickly to Cuzco, and say to your son Huascar that his father named him to be Inca when his own days were over." He appointed two *orejones* to accompany her, with orders to say to the Incas of Cuzco that they were to give the fringe to Huascar. Cusi Tupac added that he would make necessary arrangements and would presently follow them with the body of Huayna Ccapac, to enter Cuzco with it in triumph, the order of which had been ordained by the Inca on the point of death, on a staff.

Huayna Ccapac died at Quito at the age of 80 years. He left more than 50 sons. He succeeded at the age

---

[1] Ninan Cuyoche is said by Cobos to have been legitimate, a son of the first wife Cusi Rimay Huaco, who is said by Sarmiento and others not to have borne a male heir.

of 20, and reigned 60 years. He was valiant though cruel.

He left a lineage or *ayllu* called *Tumipampa Ayllu*. At present the heads of it, now living, are Don Diego Viracocha Inca, Don Garcia Inguil Tupac, and Gonzalo Sayri. To this *ayllu* are joined the sons of Paulu Tupac, son of Huayna Ccapac. They are Hanancuzcos.

Huayna Ccapac died in the year 1524 of the nativity of our Lord Jesus Christ, the invincible Emperor Charles V of glorious memory being King of Spain, father of your Majesty, and the Pope was Paul III.

The body of Huayna Ccapac was found by the Licentiate Polo in a house where it was kept concealed, in the city of Cuzco. It was guarded by two of his servants named Hualpa Titu and Sumac Yupanqui. His idol or *guauqui* was called *Huaraqui Inca*. It was a great image of gold, which has not been found up to the present time.

LXIII.

THE LIFE OF HUASCAR, THE LAST INCA, AND OF ATAHUALPA.

Huayna Ccapac being dead, and the news having reached Cuzco, they raised Titu Cusi Hualpa Inti Illapa, called Huascar, to be Inca. He was called Huascar because he was born in a town called Huascar-quihuar, four and a half leagues from Cuzco. Those who remained at Tumipampa embalmed the body of Huayna Ccapac, and collected the spoils and captives taken in his wars, for a triumphal entry into the capital.

It is to be noted that Atahualpa, bastard son of Huayna Ccapac by Tocto Coca, his cousin, of the lineage of Inca Yupanqui, had been taken to that war by his father to prove him. He first went against the Pastos, and came back a fugitive, for which his father rated him severely. Owing to this Atahualpa did not appear among the troops, and he spoke to the Inca *orejones* of Cuzco in this manner. " My Lords ! you know that I am a son of Huayna Ccapac and that my father took me with him, to prove me in the war. Owing to the disaster with the Pastos, my father insulted me in such a way that I could not appear among the troops, still less at Cuzco among my relations who thought that my father would leave me well, but I am left poor and dishonoured. For this reason I have determined to remain here where my father died, and not to live among those who will be pleased to see me poor and out of favour. This being so you need not wait for me." He then embraced them all and took leave of them. They departed with tears and grief, leaving Atahualpa at Tumipampa[1].

The *orejones* brought the body of Huayna Ccapac to Cuzco, entering with great triumph, and his obsequies were performed like those of his ancestors. This being done, Huascar presented gold and other presents, as well as wives who had been kept closely confined in the house of the *acllas* during the time of his father. Huascar built edifices where he was born, and in Cuzco he erected the houses of Amaru-cancha, where is now the monastery of the "Name of Jesus," and others on the Colcampata, where Don Carlos lives, the son of Paulo.

After that he summoned Cusi Tupac Yupanqui, and the

---

[1] Atahualpa is said by Sarmiento and Yamqui Pachacuti to have been an illegitimate son of Huayna Ccapac by Tocto Coca his cousin, of the ayllu of Pachacuti. Cieza de Leon says that he was a son by a woman of Quilaco named Tupac Palla. Gomara, who is followed by Velasco, says that Atahualpa was the son of a princess of Quito. As Huayna Ccapac only set out for the Quito campaign twelve years before his death, and Atahualpa was then grown up, his mother cannot have been a woman of Quito. I, therefore, have no doubt that Sarmiento is right.

other principal *orejones* who had come with the body of his father, and who were of the lineage of Inca Yupanqui and therefore relations of the mother of Atahualpa. He asked them why they had not brought Atahualpa with them, saying that doubtless they had left him there, that he might rebel at Quito, and that when he did so, they would kill their Inca at Cuzco. The *orejones*, who had been warned of this suspicion, answered that they knew nothing except that Atahualpa remained at Quito, as he had stated publicly, that he might not be poor and despised among his relations in Cuzco. Huascar, not believing what they said, put them to the torture, but he extracted nothing further from them. Huascar considered the harm that these *orejones* had done, and that he never could be good friends with them or be able to trust them, so he caused them to be put to death. This gave rise to great lamentation in Cuzco and hatred of Huascar among the Hanan-cuzcos, to which party the deceased belonged. Seeing this Huascar publicly said that he divorced and separated himself from relationship with the lineages of the Hanan-cuzcos because they were for Atahualpa who was a traitor, not having come to Cuzco to do homage. Then he declared war with Atahualpa and assembled troops to send against him. Meanwhile Atahualpa sent his messengers to Huascar with presents, saying that he was his vassal, and as such he desired to know how he could serve the Inca. Huascar rejected the messages and presents of Atahualpa and they even say that he killed the messengers. Others say that he cut their noses and their clothing down to their waists, and sent them back insulted.

While this was taking place at Cuzco the Huanca-vilcas rebelled. Atahualpa assembled a great army, nominating as captains—Chalco Chima, Quiz-quiz, Incura Hualpa, Rumi-ñaui, Yupanqui, Urco-huaranca and Uña

Chullo. They marched against the Huancavilcas, conquered them, and inflicted severe punishment. Returning
to Quito, Atahualpa sent a report to Huascar of what had
taken place. At this time Atahualpa received news of
what Huascar had done to his messengers, and of the
death of the *orejones*; also that Huascar was preparing
to make war on him, that he had separated himself from
the Hanan-cuzcos, and that he had proclaimed him,
Atahualpa, a traitor, which they call *aucca*. Atahualpa,
seeing the evil designs entertained by his brother against
him, and that he must prepare to defend himself, took
counsel with his captains. They were of one accord that
he should not take the field until he had assembled
more men, and collected as large an army as possible,
because negotiations should be commenced when he was
ready for battle.

At this time an Orejon named Hancu and another
named Atoc came to Tumipampa to offer sacrifices before
the image of Huayna Ccapac, by order of Huascar. They
took the wives of Huayna Ccapac and the insignia of
Inca without communication with Atahualpa. For this
Atahualpa seized them and, being put to the torture, they
confessed what orders Huascar had given them, and that
an army was being sent against Atahualpa. They were
ordered to be killed, and drums to be made of their skins.
Then Atahualpa sent scouts along the road to Cuzco, to
see what forces were being sent against him by his brother.
The scouts came in sight of the army of Huascar and
brought back the news.

Atahualpa then marched out of Quito to meet his
enemies. The two armies encountered each other at
Riopampa where they fought a stubborn and bloody battle,
but Atahualpa was victorious. The dead were so numerous
that he ordered a heap to be made of their bones, as a
memorial. Even now, at this day, the plain may be seen,

covered with the bones of those who were slain in that battle.

At this time Huascar had sent troops to conquer the nations of Pumacocha, to the east of the Pacamoros, led by Tampu Usca Mayta and by Titu Atauchi, the brother of Huascar. When the news came of this defeat at Riopampa, Huascar got together another larger army, and named as captains Atoc, Huaychac, Hanco, and Huanca Auqui. This Huanca Auqui had been unfortunate and lost many men in his campaign with the Pacamoros. His brother, the Inca Huascar, to insult him, sent him gifts suited to a woman, ridiculing him. This made Huanca Auqui determine to do something worthy of a man. He marched to Tumipampa, where the army of Atahualpa was encamped to rest after the battle. Finding it without watchfulness, he attacked and surprised the enemy, committing much slaughter.

Atahualpa received the news at Quito, and was much grieved that his brother Huanca Auqui should have made this attack, for at other times when he could have hit him, he had let him go, because he was his brother. He now gave orders to Quiz-quiz and Chalco Chima to advance in pursuit of Huanca Auqui. They overtook him at Cusipampa, where they fought and Huanca Auqui was defeated, with great loss on both sides. Huanca Auqui fled, those of Atahualpa following in pursuit as far as Caxamarca, where Huanca Auqui met a large reinforcement sent by Huascar in support. Huanca Auqui ordered them to march against Chalco Chima and Quiz-quiz while he remained at Caxamarca. The troops sent by Huanca Auqui were Chachapoyas and many others, the whole numbering 10,000. They met the enemy and fought near Caxamarca. But the Chachapoyas were defeated and no more than 3000 escaped. Huanca Auqui then fled towards Cuzco, followed by the army of Atahualpa.

In the province of Bombon[1], Huanca Auqui found a
good army composed of all nations, which Huascar had
sent to await his enemies there, who were coming in
pursuit. Those of Atahualpa arrived and a battle was
fought for two days without either party gaining an
advantage. But on the third day Huanca Auqui was
vanquished by Quiz-quiz and Chalco Chima.

Huanca Auqui escaped from the rout and came to
Xauxa, where he found a further reinforcement of many
Indians, Soras, Chancas, Ayamarcas, and Yanyos, sent by
his brother. With these he left Xauxa and encountered
the pursuing enemy at a place called Yanamarca. Here a
battle was fought not less stubbornly than the former one.
Finally, as fortune was against Huanca Auqui, he was again
defeated by Chalco Chima, the adventurous captain of the
army of Atahualpa.

The greater part of the forces of Huanca Auqui was
killed. He himself fled, never stopping until he reached
Paucaray. Here he found a good company of *orejones*
of Cuzco, under a captain named Mayta Yupanqui who,
on the part of Huascar, rebuked Huanca Auqui, asking
how it was possible for him to have lost so many
battles and so many men, unless he was secretly
in concert with Chalco Chima. He answered that the
accusation was not true, that he could not have done more;
and he told Mayta Yupanqui to go against their enemy,
and see what power he brought. He said that Atahualpa
was determined to advance if they could not hinder his
captains. Then Mayta Yupanqui went on to encounter
Chalco Chima, and met him at the bridge of Anco-yacu
where there were many skirmishes, but finally the *orejones*
were defeated[2].

---

[1] Correctly Pumpu.

[2] This campaign is also fully described by Balboa, and in some
detail by Yamqui Pachacuti, pp. 113—116.

LXIV.

HUASCAR INCA MARCHES IN PERSON TO FIGHT CHALCO CHIMA AND QUIZ-QUIZ, THE CAPTAINS OF ATAHUALPA.

As the fortune of Huascar and his captains, especially of Huanca Auqui, was so inferior to that of Atahualpa and his adventurous and dexterous captains Chalco Chima and Quiz-quiz, one side meeting with nothing that did not favour them, the other side with nothing that was not against them, such terrible fear took possession of Huanca Auqui and the other Inca captains after the battle of Anco-yacu bridge, that they fled without stopping to Vilcas, 20 and more leagues from Anco-yacu, on the road to Cuzco.

Over the satisfaction that the captains of Atahualpa felt at the glory of so many victories that they had won, there came the news sent by Atahualpa that he had come in person to Caxamarca and Huamachuco, that he had been received as Inca by all the nations he had passed, and that he had assumed the fringe and the *Ccapac-uncu*. He was now called Inca of all the land, and it was declared that there was no other Inca but him. He ordered his captains to march onwards conquering, until they encountered Huascar. They were to give him battle, conquer him like the rest, and if possible take him prisoner. Atahualpa was so elated by his victories, and assumed such majesty, that he did not cease to talk of his successes, and no one dared to raise his eyes before him. For those who had business with him he appointed a lieutenant called " Inca Apu," which means " the Inca's lord," who was to take his place by the Inca when he was seated. Those who had business transacted it with him, entering with a load on their backs, and their eyes on the ground, and thus they spoke of their business with the *Apu*. He then reported to Atahualpa, who decided what was to be done. Atahualpa was very cruel, he killed right and left, destroyed, burnt, and desolated whatever opposed him. From Quito to Huamachuco he perpetrated the greatest cruelties, robberies, outrages, and tyrannies that had ever been done in that land.

When Atahualpa arrived at Huamachuco, two principal lords of his house came to offer sacrifice to the *huaca* of Huamachuco for the success that had attended their cause. These *orejones* went, made the sacrifice, and consulted the oracle. They received an answer that Atahualpa would have an unfortunate end, because he was such a cruel tyrant and shedder of so much human blood. They delivered this reply of the devil to Atahualpa. It enraged him against the oracle, so he called out his guards and went to where the *huaca* was kept. Having surrounded the place, he took a halberd of gold in his hand, and was accompanied by the two officers of his household who had made the sacrifice. When he came to where the idol was, an old man aged a hundred years came out, clothed in a dress reaching down to the ground, very woolly and covered with sea shells. He was the priest of the oracle who had made the reply. When Atahualpa knew who he was, he raised the halberd and gave him a blow which cut off his head. Atahualpa then entered the house of the idol, and cut off its head also with many blows, though it was made of stone. He then ordered the old man's body, the idol, and its house to be burnt, and the cinders to be scattered in the air. He then levelled the hill, though it was very large, where that oracle, idol or *huaca* of the devil stood.

All this being made known to Chalco Chima and Quiz-quiz, they celebrated festivals and rejoicings, and then resumed their march towards Cuzco. Huascar received reports of all that had happened, and mourned over the great number of men he had lost. He clearly saw that there only remained the remedy of going forth in person to try his fortune, which had hitherto been so adverse. In preparation he kept some fasts—for these gentiles also have a certain kind of fasting, made many sacrifices to the idols and oracles of Cuzco, and sought for replies. All answered that the event would be adverse to him. On hearing this he consulted his diviners and wizards, called by them *umu*, who, to please him, gave him hope of a fortunate ending. He got together a powerful army, and sent out scouts to discover the position of the enemy. The hostile army was reported to be at a place, 14 leagues from Cuzco, called Curahuasi[1]. They found there Chalco Chima and Quiz-quiz, and reported that they had left the main road to Cuzco, and had taken that of Cotabamba, which is on the right, coming from Caxamarca or Lima to Cuzco. This route was taken to avoid the bad road and dangerous pass by the Apurimac bridge.

Huascar divided his army into three divisions. One consisted of the men of Cunti-suyu, Charcas, Colla-suyu, Chuys, and Chile under the command of a captain named Arampa Yupanqui. His orders were to advance over Cotabamba towards another neighbouring province of the Omasayos, to harass the enemy on the side of the river of Cotabamba and the Apurimac bridge. The survivors of the former battles, under Huanca Auqui, Ahua Panti, and Pacta Mayta, were to attack the enemy on one flank, and to march into Cotabamba. Huascar in person commanded a third division. Thus all the forces of both Huascar and Atahualpa were in Cotabamba.

---

[1] Curahuasi is near the bridge over the Apurimac.

Arampa Yupanqui got news that the forces of Atahualpa were passing through a small valley or ravine which leads from Huanacu-pampa. He marched to oppose them, and fought with a strong squadron of the troops under Chalco Chima. He advanced resolutely to the encounter, and slew many of the enemy, including one of their captains named Tomay Rima. This gave Huascar great satisfaction and he said laughingly to the *orejones* — " The Collas have won this victory. Behold the obligation we have to imitate our ancestors." Presently the captains-general of his army, who were Titu Atauchi, Tupac Atao his brother, Nano, Urco Huaranca and others, marshalled the army to fight those of Atahualpa with their whole force. The armies confronted each other and attacked with skill and in good order.

The battle lasted from morning nearly until sunset, many being slain on both sides, though the troops of Huascar did not suffer so much as those of Chalco Chima and Quiz-quiz. The latter seeing their danger, many of them retreated to a large grassy plateau which was near, in Huanacu-pampa. Huascar, who saw this, set fire to the grass and burnt a great part of Atahualpa's forces.

Chalco Chima and Quiz-quiz then retreated to the other side of the river Cotabamba. Huascar, satisfied with what he had done, did not follow up his advantages, but enjoyed the victory which fortune had placed in his hands. For this he took a higher position. Chalco Chima and Quiz-quiz, who were experienced in such manœuvres, seeing that they were not followed, decided to rest their troops, and on another day to attack those who believed themselves to be conquerors. They sent spies to the camp of Huascar, and found from them that Huascar would send a certain division of his troops to take Atahualpa's captains without their being able to escape.

LXV.

THE BATTLE BETWEEN THE ARMIES OF HUASCAR AND ATAHUALPA. HUASCAR MADE PRISONER.

When the morning of the next day arrived Huascar determined to finish off the army of his brother at one blow. He ordered Tupac Atao to go down the ravine with a squadron, discover the position of the enemy, and report what he had seen. Tupac Atao received this order and entered the ravine in great silence, looking from side to side. But the spies of Chalco Chima saw everything without being seen themselves and gave notice to Chalco Chima and Quiz-quiz. Chalco Chima then divided his men into two parts and stationed them at the sides of the road where the *orejones* would pass. When Tupac Atao came onwards, they attacked him to such purpose that scarcely any one escaped. Tupac Atao himself was taken, badly wounded, by whom Chalco Chima was informed that Huascar would follow him with only a squadron of 5000 men, while the rest of his army remained in Huanacu-pampa.

Chalco Chima sent this information to Quiz-quiz, who was at a little distance, that they might unite forces. He told him that Tupac Atao was taken, that Huascar was expected with a small force, and that Quiz-quiz was wanted that both might take this enemy on the flanks. This was done. They divided their forces, placing them on both sides as in the attack on Tupac Atao. A short time after they entered the ravine, Huascar and his men came upon the dead bodies of the men of Tupac Atao who, being known to Huascar he wished to turn back, understanding that they were all dead and that there must have been some ambush. But it was too late, for he was surrounded by his enemies. Then he was attacked by the troops of Chalco Chima. When he tried to fly from those who fell upon his rear, he fell into the hands of Quiz-quiz who was waiting for him lower down. Those of Chalco Chima and those of Quiz-quiz fought with great ferocity, sparing none, and killing them all. Chalco Chima, searching for Huascar, saw him in his litter and seized him by the hands, and pulled him out of his litter. Thus was taken prisoner the unfortunate Huascar Inca, twelfth and last tyrant of the Inca Sovereigns of Peru, falling into the power of another greater and more cruel tyrant than himself, his people defeated, killed, and scattered.

Placing Huascar in safe durance with a sufficient guard, Chalco Chima went on in the Inca's litter and detached 5000 of his men to advance towards the other troops remaining on the plain of Huanacu-pampa. He ordered that all the rest should follow Quiz-quiz, and that when he let fall the screen, they should attack. He executed this stratagem because his enemies thought that he was Huascar returning victorious, so they waited. He advanced and arrived where the troops of Huascar were waiting for their lord, who, when they saw him, still thought that it was Huascar bringing his enemies as prisoners. When Chalco Chima was quite near, he let loose a prisoner who had been wounded, who went to the Inca troops. He told them what had happened, that it was Chalco Chima, and that he could kill them all by this stratagem. When this was known, and that Chalco Chima would presently order them to be attacked with his whole force, for he had let the screen fall, which was to be the sign, the Inca troops gave way and took to flight, which was what Chalco Chima intended. The troops of Atahualpa pursued, wounding and killing with excessive cruelty and ferocity, continuing the slaughter, with unheard of havock, as far as the bridge of Cotabamba. As the bridge was narrow and all could not cross it, many jumped into the water from fear of their ferocious pursuers, and were drowned. The troops of Atahualpa crossed the river, continuing the pursuit and rejoicing in their victory. During the pursuit they captured Titu Atauchi, the brother of Huascar. Chalco Chima and Quiz-quiz arrived at some houses called Quiuipay, about half a league from Cuzco, where they placed Huascar as a prisoner with a sufficient guard. Here they encamped and established their head-quarters.

The soldiers of Chalco Chima went to get a view of Cuzco from the hill of Yauina overlooking the city, where they heard the mourning and lamentation of the inhabitants, and returned to inform Chalco Chima and Quiz-quiz. Those captains sent a messenger to Cuzco to tell the inhabitants not to mourn, for that there was nothing to fear, it being well known that this was a war between two brothers for the gratification of their own passions. If any of them had helped Huascar they had not committed a crime, for they were bound to serve their Inca; and if there was any fault he would remit and pardon it, in the name of the great Lord Atahualpa. Presently he would order them all to come out and do reverence to the statue of Atahualpa, called *Ticci Ccapac* which means "Lord of the World."

The people of Cuzco consulted together, and resolved to come forth and obey the commands of Chalco Chima and Quiz-quiz. They came according to their *ayllus* and, on arriving at Quiuipay, they seated themselves in that order. Presently the troops of Atahualpa, fully armed, surrounded all those who had come from Cuzco. They took Huanca Auqui, Ahua Panti, and Paucar Usna, who had led the army against them in the battle at Tumipampa. Then they took Apu Chalco Yupanqui and Rupaca, Priests of the Sun, because these had given the fringe to Huascar. These being prisoners Quiz-quiz rose and said—" Now you know of the battles you have fought with me on the road, and the trouble you have caused me. You always raised Huascar to be Inca, who was not the heir. You treated evilly the Inca Atahualpa whom the Sun guards, and for these things you deserve death. But using you with humanity, I pardon you in the name of my Lord Atahualpa, whom may the Sun prosper."

But that they might not be without any punishment, he ordered them to be given some blows with a great stone on the shoulders, and he killed the most culpable. Then he ordered that all should be tied by the knees, with their faces towards Caxamarca or Huamachuco where Atahualpa was, and he made them pull out their eyelashes and eyebrows as an offering to the new Inca. All the *orejones*, inhabitants of Cuzco, did this from fear, saying in a loud voice, "Long live! Live for many years Atahualpa our Inca, may our father the Sun increase his life!"

Araua Ocllo, the mother of Huascar, and his wife Chucuy Huypa, were there, and were dishonoured and abused by Quiz-quiz. In a loud voice the mother of Huascar said to her son, who was a prisoner, "O unfortunate! thy cruelties and evil deeds have brought you to this state. Did I not tell you not to be so cruel, and not to kill nor ill-treat the messengers of your brother Atahualpa." Having said these words she came to him, and gave him a blow in the face.

Chalco Chima and Quiz-quiz then sent a messenger to Atahualpa, letting him know all that had happened, and that they had made prisoners of Huascar and many others, and asking for further orders.

LXVI.

WHAT CHALCO CHIMA AND QUIZ-QUIZ DID CON-CERNING HUASCAR AND THOSE OF HIS SIDE IN WORDS.

After Chalco Chima and Quiz-quiz had sent off the messengers to Atahualpa, they caused the prisoners to be brought before them, and in the presence of all, and of the mother and wife of Huascar, they declared, addressing themselves to the mother of Huascar, that she was the concubine and not the wife of Huayna Ccapac, and that, being his concubine, she had borne Huascar, also that she was a vile woman and not a Coya. The troops of Atahualpa raised a shout of derision, and some said to the *orejones*, pointing their fingers at Huascar—" Look there at your lord ! who said that in the battle he would turn fire and water against his enemies?" Huascar was then tied hand and foot on a bed of ropes of straws. The *orejones*, from shame, lowered their heads. Presently Quiz-quiz asked Huascar, " Who of these made you lord, there being others better and more valiant than you, who might have been chosen ? " Araua Ocllo, speaking to her son, said, " You deserve all this my son as I told you, and all comes from the cruelty with which you treated your own relations." Huascar replied, " Mother ! there is now no remedy, leave us," and he addressed himself to the priest Chalco Yupanqui, saying—" Speak and answer the question asked by Quiz-quiz." The priest said to Quiz-quiz, " I raised him to be lord and Inca by command of his father Huayna Ccapac, and because he was son of a Coya" (which is what we should call Infanta). Then Chalco Chima was indignant, and called the priest a deceiver and a liar. Huascar answered to Quiz-quiz, " Leave off these arguments. This is a question between me and my brother, and not between the parties of Hanan-cuzco and Hurin-cuzco. We will investigate it, and you have no business to meddle between us on this point."

Enraged at the answer Chalco Chima ordered Huascar to be taken back to prison, and said to the Incas, to re-assure them, that they could now go back to the city as they were pardoned. The *orejones* returned, invoking Viracocha in loud voices with these words—"O Creator! thou who givest life and favour to the Incas where art thou now? Why dost thou allow such persecution to come upon us? Wherefore didst thou exalt us, if we are to come to such an end?" Saying these words they beat their cloaks in token of the curse that had come upon them all.

LXVII.

THE CRUELTIES THAT ATAHUALPA ORDERED TO BE PERPETRATED ON THE PRISONERS AND CONQUERED OF HUASCAR'S PARTY.

When Atahualpa knew what had happened, from the messengers of Chalco Chima and Quiz-quiz, he ordered one of his relations named Cusi Yupanqui to go to Cuzco, and not to leave a relation or friend of Huascar alive. This Cusi Yupanqui arrived at Cuzco, and Chalco Chima and Quiz-quiz delivered the prisoners to him. He made inquiries touching all that Atahualpa had ordered. He then caused poles to be fixed on both sides of the road, extending not more than a quarter of a league along the way to Xaquixahuana. Next he brought out of the prison all the wives of Huascar, including those pregnant or lately delivered. He ordered them to be hung to these poles with their children, and he ordered the pregnant to be cut open, and the stillborn to be hung with them. Then he caused the sons of Huascar to be brought out and hung to the poles.

Among the sons of Huayna Ccapac who were prisoners there was one named Paullu Tupac. When they were going to kill him, he protested saying, it was unreasonable that he should be killed, because he had previously been imprisoned by Huascar; and on this ground he was released and escaped death. Yet the reason that he was imprisoned by Huascar was because he had been found with one of the Inca's wives. He was only given very little to eat, the intention being that he should die in prison. The woman with whom he was taken was buried alive. The wars coming on he escaped, and what has been related took place.

After this the lords and ladies of Cuzco who were found to have been friends of Huascar were seized and hanged on the poles. Then there was an examination of all the houses of deceased Incas, to see which had been on the side of Huascar, and against Atahualpa. They found that the house of Tupac Inca Yupanqui had sided with Huascar. Cusi Yupanqui committed the punishment of the house to Chalco Chima and Quiz-quiz. They seized the steward of the house, and the mummy of Tupac Inca, and those of his family and hung them all, and they burnt the body of Tupac Inca outside the town and reduced it to ashes. And to destroy the house completely, they killed many *mama cunas* and servants, so that none were left of that house except a few of no account. Besides this they ordered all the Chachapoyas and Cañaris to be killed, and their Curaca named Ulco Colla, who they said had rebelled against the two brothers.

All these murders and cruelties were perpetrated in the presence of Huascar to torment him. They murdered over 80 sons and daughters of Huascar, and what he felt most cruelly was the murder, before his eyes, of one of his sisters named Coya Miro, who had a son of Huascar in her arms, and another in her womb; and another very beautiful sister named Chimbo Cisa. Breaking his heart at the sight of such cruelty and grief which he was powerless to prevent, he cried, with a sigh, " Oh Pachayachachi Viracocha, thou who showed favour to me for so short a time, and honoured me and gave me life, dost thou see that I am treated in this way, and seest thou in thy presence what I, in mine, have seen and see."

Some of the concubines of Huascar escaped from this cruelty and calamity, because they had neither borne a child nor were pregnant, and because they were beautiful. They say that they were kept to be taken to Atahualpa. Among those who escaped were Doña Elvira Chonay, daughter of Cañar Ccapac, Doña Beatriz Carnamaruay, daughter of the Curaca of Chinchay-cocha, Doña Juana Tocto, Doña Catalina Usica, wife, that was, of Don Paullu Tupac, and mother of Don Carlos, who are living now. In this way the line and lineage of the unfortunate tyrant Huascar, the last of the Incas, was completely annihilated.

LXVIII.

NEWS OF THE SPANIARDS COMES TO ATAHUALPA.

Atahualpa was at Huamachuco celebrating great festivals for his victories, and he wished to proceed to Cuzco and assume the fringe in the House of the Sun, where all former Incas had received it. When he was about to set out there came to him two Tallanas Indians, sent by the Curacas of Payta and Tumbez, to report to him that there had arrived by sea, which they call *cocha*, a people with different clothing, and with beards, and that they brought animals like large sheep. The chief of them was believed to be Viracocha, which means the god of these people, and he brought with him many Viracochas, which is as much as to say "gods." They said this of the Governor Don Francisco Pizarro, who had arrived with 180 men and some horses which they called sheep. As the account in detail is left for the history of the Spaniards, which will form the Third Part to come after this, I will only here speak briefly of what passed between the Spaniards and Atahualpa.

When this became known to Atahualpa he rejoiced greatly, believing it to be the Viracocha coming, as he had promised when he departed, and as is recounted in the beginning of this history. Atahualpa gave thanks that he should have come in his time, and he sent back the messengers with thanks to the Curacas for sending the news, and ordering them to keep him informed of what might happen. He resolved not to go to Cuzco until he had seen what this arrival was, and what the Viracochas intended to do. He sent orders to Chalco Chima and Quiz-quiz to lose no time in bringing Huascar to Caxamarca, where he would go to await their arrival, for he had received news that certain Viracochas had arrived by sea, and he wished to be there to see what they were like.

As no further news came, because the Spaniards were forming a station at Tangarara, Atahualpa became careless and believed that they had gone. For, at another time, when he was marching with his father, in the wars of Quito, news came to Huayna Ccapac that the Viracocha had arrived on the coast near Tumbez, and then they had gone away. This was when Don Francisco Pizarro came on the first discovery, and returned to Spain for a concession, as will be explained in its place

LXIX.

THE SPANIARDS COME TO CAXAMARCA AND SEIZE ATAHUALPA, WHO ORDERS HUASCAR TO BE KILLED. ATAHUALPA ALSO DIES.

As the subject of which this chapter treats belongs to the Third Part (the history of the Spaniards), I shall here only give a summary of what happened to Atahualpa. Although Atahualpa was careless about the Spaniards they did not miss a point, and when they heard where Atahualpa was, they left Tangarara and arrived at Caxamarca. When Atahualpa knew that the Viracochas were near, he left Caxamarca and went to some baths at a distance of half a league that he might, from there, take the course which seemed best. As he found that they were not gods as he had been made to think at first, he prepared his warriors to resist the Spaniards. Finally he was taken prisoner by Don Francisco Pizarro, the Friar, Vicente Valverde, having first made a certain demand, in the square of Caxamarca.

Don Francisco Pizarro knew of the disputes there had been between Atahualpa and Huascar, and that Huascar was a prisoner in the hands of the captains of Atahualpa, and he urged Atahualpa to have his brother brought as quickly as possible. Huascar was being brought to Caxamarca by Atahualpa's order, as has already been said. Chalco Chima obeying this order, set out with Huascar and the captains and relations who had escaped the butchery of Cusi Yupanqui. Atahualpa asked Don Francisco Pizarro why he wanted to see his brother. Pizarro replied that he had been informed that Huascar was the elder and principal Lord of that land and for that reason he wished to see him, and he desired that he should come. Atahualpa feared that if Huascar came alive, the Governor Don Francisco Pizarro would be informed of what had taken place, that Huascar would be made Lord, and that he would lose his state. Being sagacious, he agreed to comply with Pizarro's demand, but sent off a messenger to the captain who was bringing Huascar, with an order to kill him and all the prisoners. The messenger started and found Huascar at Antamarca, near Yana-mayu. He gave his message to the captain of the guard who was bringing Huascar as a prisoner.

Directly the captain heard the order of Atahualpa he complied with it. He killed Huascar, cut the body up, and threw it into the river Yana-mayu. He also killed the rest of the brothers, relations, and captains who were with him as prisoners, in the year 1533. Huascar had lived 40 years. He succeeded his father at the age of 31 and reigned for 9 years. His wife was Chucuy Huypa by whom he had no male child. He left no lineage or *ayllu*, and of those who are now living, one only, named Don Alonso Titu Atauchi is a nephew of Huascar, son of Titu Atauchi who was murdered with Huascar. He alone sustains the name of the lineage of Huascar called the *Huascar Ayllu*. In this river of Yana-mayu Atahualpa had fixed his boundary pillars when he first rebelled, saying that from thence to Chile should be for his brother Huascar, and from the Yana-mayu onwards should be his. Thus with the death of Huascar there was an end to all the Incas of Peru and all their line and descent which they held to be legitimate, without leaving man or woman who could have a claim on this country, supposing them to have been natural and legitimate lords of it, in conformity with their own customs and tyrannical laws.

For this murder of Huascar, and for other good and sufficient causes, the Governor Don Francisco Pizarro afterwards put Atahualpa to death. He was a tyrant against the natives of this country and against his brother Huascar. He had lived 36 years. He was not Inca of Peru, but a tyrant. He was prudent, sagacious, and valiant, as I shall relate in the Third Part, being events which belong to the deeds of the Spaniards. It suffices to close this Second Part by completing the history of the deeds of the 12 Inca tyrants who reigned in this kingdom of Peru from Manco Ccapac the first to Huascar the twelfth and last tyrant.

LXX.

IT IS NOTEWORTHY HOW THESE INCAS WERE TYRANTS AGAINST THEMSELVES, BESIDES BEING SO AGAINST THE NATIVES OF THE LAND.

It is a thing worthy to be noted [*for the fact that besides being a thing certain and evident the general tyranny of these cruel and tyrannical Incas of Peru against the natives of the land, may be easily gathered from history*], and any one who reads and considers with attention the order and mode of their procedure will see, that their violent Incaship was established without the will and election of the natives who always rose with arms in their hands on each occasion that offered for rising against their Inca tyrants who oppressed them, to get back their liberty. Each one of the Incas not only followed the tyranny of his father, but also began afresh the same tyranny by force, with deaths, robberies and rapine. Hence none of them could pretend, in good faith, to give a beginning to time of prescription, nor did any of them hold in peaceful possession, there being always some one to dispute and take up arms against them and their tyranny. Moreover, and this is above all to be noted, to

CAPTURE OF ATAHUALPA, AND SIEGE OF CUZCO, ETC.

From the Rev. C. M. Cracherode's copy in the British Museum.

understand the worst aims of these tyrants and their horrid avarice and oppression, they were not satisfied with being evil tyrants to the natives, but also to their own proper sons, brothers and relations, in defiance of their own laws and statutes, they were the worst and most pertinacious tyrants with an unheard-of inhumanity. For it was enacted among themselves and by their customs and laws that the eldest legitimate son should succeed, yet almost always they broke the law, as appears by the Incas who are here referred to.

Before all things Manco Ccapac, the first tyrant, coming from Tampu-tocco, was inhuman in the case of his brother Ayar Cachi, sending him to Tampu-tocco cunningly with orders for Tampu-chacay to kill him out of envy, because he was the bravest, and might for that reason be the most esteemed. When he arrived at the valley of Cuzco he not only tyrannized over the natives, but also over Copali-mayta and Columchima who, though they had been received as natives of that valley were his relations, for they were *orejones*. Then Sinchi Rocca, the second Inca, having an older legitimate son named Manco Sapaca who, according to the law he and his father had made, was entitled to the succession, deprived him and nominated Lloqui Yupanqui the second son for his successor. Likewise Mayta Ccapac, the fourth Inca, named for his successor Ccapac Yupanqui, though he had an older legitimate son named Cunti Mayta, whom he disinherited. Viracocha, the eighth Inca, although he had an older legitimate son named Inca Rocca, did not name him as his successor, nor any of his legitimate sons, but a bastard named Inca Urco. This did not come about, Inca Urco did not enjoy the succession, nor did the eldest legitimate son, for there was a new tyranny. For Inca Yupanqui deprived both the one and the other, besides despoiling his father of his honours and estate. The same Inca Yupanqui, having an elder legitimate son named Amaru Tupac Inca, did not name him, but a young son, Tupac Inca Yupanqui. The same Tupac Inca, being of the same condition as his father, having Huayna Ccapac as the eldest legitimate son, named Ccapac Huari as his successor, although the relations of Huayna Ccapac would not allow it, and rose in his favour. If Ccapac Huari was legitimate, as his relations affirm, the evil deed must be fixed on Huayna Ccapac, who deprived his brother Ccapac Huari, and killed his mother and all his relations, making them infamous as traitors, that is supposing he was legitimate. Huayna Ccapac, though he named Ninan Cuyoche, he was not the eldest, and owing to this the succession remained unsettled, and caused the differences between Huascar and Atahualpa, whence proceeded the greatest and most unnatural tyrannies. Turning their arms against their own entrails, robbing, and with inhuman intestine wars they came to a final end. Thus as they commenced by their own authority, so they destroyed all by their own proper hands.

It may be that Almighty God permits that one shall be the executioner of the other for his evil deeds, that both may give place to his most holy gospel which, by the hands of the Spaniards, and by order of the most happy, catholic, and unconquered Emperor and King of Spain, Charles V of glorious memory, father of your Majesty, was sent to these blind and barbarous gentiles. Yet against the force and power of the Incas on foot and united, it appeared that it would be impossible for human force to do what a few Spaniards did, numbering only 180, who at first entered with the Governor Don Francisco Pizarro.

It is well established that it is a thing false and without reason, and which ought not to be said, that there is now, in these kingdoms, any person of the lineage of the Incas who can pretend to a right of succession to the Incaship of this kingdom of Peru, nor to be natural or legitimate lords. For no one is left who, in conformity with their laws, is able to say that he is the heir, in whole or in part of this land. Only two sons of Huayna Ccapac escaped the cruelty of Atahualpa. They were Paullu Tupac, afterwards called Don Cristóval Paullu, and Manco Inca. They were bastards, which is well known among them. And these, if any honour or estate had belonged to them or their children, your Majesty would have granted more than they had, their brothers retaining their estate and power. For they would merely have been their tributaries and servants. These were the lowest of all, for their lineage was on the side of their mothers which is what these people look at, in a question of birth[1].

And Manco Inca had been a traitor to your Majesty and was a fugitive in the Andes where he died or was killed. Your Majesty caused his son to be brought out, in peace, from those savage wilds. He was named Don Diego Sayri Tupac. He became a Christian, and provision was made for him, his sons and descendants. Sayri Tupac died as a Christian, and he who is now in the Andes in rebellion, named Titu Cusi Yupanqui, is not a legitimate son of Manco Inca, but a bastard and apostate. They hold that another son is legitimate who is with the same Titu, named Tupac Amaru, but he is incapable and the Indians called him *uti*. Neither one nor the other are heirs of the land, because their father was not legitimate.

Your Majesty honoured Don Cristóval Paullu with titles and granted him a good *repartimiento* of Indians, on which he principally lived. Now it is possessed by his son Don Carlos. Paullu left two legitimate sons who are now alive, named Don Carlos and Don Felipe. Besides these

---

[1] These statements about the illegitimacy of Manco and Paullu Inca are made to support the Viceroy's argument and have no foundation in fact. The two princes were legitimate ; their mother being a princess of the blood.

he left many illegitimate sons.   Thus the known grandsons
of Huayna Ccapac, who are now alive and admitted to be
so, are those above mentioned.   Besides these there are
Don Alonso Titu Atauchi, son of Titu Atauchi, and other
bastards, but neither one nor the other has any right to be
called a natural lord of the land.

For the above reasons it will be right to say to those
whose duty it may be to decide, that on such clear evidence is based the most just and legitimate title that your
Majesty and your successors have to these parts of the
Indies, proved by the actual facts that are here written, more
especially as regards these kingdoms of Peru without a
point to raise against the said titles by which the crown of
Spain holds them.   Respecting which your Viceroy of these
kingdoms, Don Francisco Toledo, has been a careful and
most curious enquirer, as zealous for the clearing of the
conscience of your Majesty, and for the salvation of your
soul, as he has shown and now shows himself in the general
visitation which he is making by order of your Majesty,
in his own person, not avoiding the very great labours and
dangers which he is suffering in these journeys, so long as
they result in so great a service to God and your Majesty.

LXXI.

SUMMARY COMPUTATION OF THE PERIOD THAT
THE INCAS OF PERU LASTED.

The terrible and inveterate tyranny of the Incas Ccapac
of Peru, which had its seat in the city of Cuzco, commenced
in the year 565 of our Christian redemption, Justin II
being Emperor, Loyva son of Athanagild the Goth being
King of Spain, and John III Supreme Pontiff.   It ended in
1533, Charles V being the most meritorious Emperor and
most Christian King of Spain and its dependencies, patron

of the church and right arm of Christendom, assuredly
worthy of such a son as your Majesty whom may God our
Lord take by the hand as is necessary for the Holy Christian
church. Paul III was then Pope. The whole period from
Manco Ccapac to the death of Huascar was 968 years.

It is not to be wondered at that these Incas lived for so
long a time, for in that age nature was stronger and more
robust than in these days. Besides men did not then
marry until they were past thirty. They thus reached such
an age with force and substance whole and undiminished.
For these reasons they lived much longer than is the case
now. Besides the country where they lived has a healthy
climate and uncorrupted air. The land is cleared, dry,
without lakes, morasses, or forests with dense vegetation.
These qualities all conduce to health, and therefore to the
long life of the inhabitants whom may God our Lord lead
into his holy faith, for the salvation of their souls. Amen[1].

> Maxima Tolleti Proregis gloria creuit
> Dum regni tenebras, lucida cura, fugat.
> Ite procul scioli, vobis non locus in istis!
> Rex Indos noster nam tenet innocue.

CERTIFICATE OF THE PROOFS AND VERIFICATION OF THIS HISTORY.

In the city of Cuzco, on the 29th day of February, 1572,
before the very excellent Lord Don Francisco de Toledo,
Mayordomo to His Majesty, and his Viceroy, Governor,
and Captain-General of these kingdoms and provinces of
Peru, President of the Royal Audience and Chancellory
that resides in the city of the Kings, and before me Alvaro

---

[1] Cieza de Leon and other authorities adopt a more moderate
chronology.

Ruiz de Navamuel his Secretary and of the Government and General Visitation of these kingdoms, the Captain Pedro Sarmiento de Gamboa presented a petition of the following tenor :

Most Excellent Lord,

I, the Captain Pedro Sarmiento, Cosmographer-General of these kingdoms of Peru, report that by order of your Excellency I have collected and reduced to a history the general chronicle of the origin and descent of the Incas, of the particular deeds which each one did in his time and in the part he ruled, how each one of them was obeyed, of the tyranny with which, from the time of Tupac Inca Yupanqui, the tenth Inca, they oppressed and subjugated these kingdoms of Peru until by order of the Emperor Charles V of glorious memory, Don Francisco Pizarro came to conquer them. I have drawn up this history from the information and investigations which, by order of your Excellency, were collected and made in the valley of Xauxa, in the city of Guamanga, and in other parts where your Excellency was conducting your visitation, but principally in this city of Cuzco where the Incas had their continual residence, where there is more evidence of their acts, where the *mitimaes* of all the provinces gathered together by order of the said Incas, and where there is true memory of their *ayllus*. In order that this history may have more authority, I pray that you will see, correct, and give it your authority, so that, wherever it may be seen, it may have entire faith and credit.

Pedro Sarmiento de Gamboa.

Having been seen by his Excellency he said that it may be known if the said history was in conformity with the information and evidence, which has been taken from the Indians and other persons of this city and in other parts, and he ordered that Doctor Loarte, Alcalde of the court of his Majesty should cause to appear before him the principal and most intelligent Indians of the twelve *ayllus* or lineages of the twelve Incas and other persons who may be summoned, and being assembled before me, the present Secretary, the said history shall be read and declared to them by an interpreter in the language of the said Indians, that each one may understand and discuss it among themselves, whether it is conformable to the truth as they know it. If there is anything to correct or amend, or which may appear to be contrary to what they know, it is to be corrected or amended. So I provide and sign

Don Francisco de Toledo

Before me Alvaro Ruiz de Navamuel.

Afterwards, on the abovesaid day, month, and year the illustrious Doctor Gabriel de Loarte, in compliance with the order of his Excellency and in presence of me the said Secretary, caused to appear before him the Indians of the names, ages and *ayllus* as follows:

Ayllu of Manco Ccapac.

	Aged
Sebastian Ylluc	30
Francisco Paucar Chima ...	30

Ayllu of Sinchi Rocca.

Diego Cayo Hualpa	70
Don Alonso Puzcon	40

Ayllu of Lloqui Yupanqui.

Hernando Hualpa	70
Don Garcia Ancuy	45
Miguel Rimachi Mayta	30

Ayllu of Mayta Ccapac.

Don Juan Tampu Usca Mayta	60
Don Felipe Usca Mayta ...	70
Francisco Usca Mayta ...	30

Ayllu of Ccapac Yupanqui.

	Aged
Don Francisco Copca Mayta ...	70
Don Juan Quispi Mayta ...	30
Don Juan Apu Mayta	30

Ayllu of Inca Rocca.

Don Pedro Hachacona	53
Don Diego Mayta	40

Ayllu of Yahuar-huaccac.

Juan Yupanqui	60
Martin Rimachi	26

Ayllu of Viracocha.

Don Francisco Anti-hualpa ...	89
Martin Quichua Sucsu ...	64
Don Francisco Chalco Yupanqui	45

Ayllu of Pachacuti.

Don Diego Cayo	68
Don Juan Hualpa Yupanqui ...	75
Don Domingo Pascac	90
Don Juan Quispi Cusi	45
Don Francisco Chanca Rimachi	40
Don Francisco Cota Yupanqui	40
Don Gonzalo Huacanhui ...	60
Don Francisco Quichua ...	68

Ayllu of Tupac Inca.

Don Cristoval Pisac Tupac ...	50
Don Andres Tupac Yupanqui	40
Don Garcia Pilco Tupac ..	40
Don Juan Cozco	40

Ayllu of Huayna Ccapac.

Don Francisco Sayri	28
Don Francisco Ninan Coro ...	24
Don Garcia Rimac Tupac ...	34

Ayllu of Huascar.

	Aged
Don Alonso Titu Atauchi ...	40

Besides these Ayllus.

Don Garcia Paucar Sucsu ...	34
Don Carlos Ayallilla	50
Don Juan Apanca	80
Don Garcia Apu Rinti... ...	70
Don Diego Viracocha Inca ...	34
Don Gonzalo Tupac	30

These being together in presence of his Excellency, the said Alcalde of the court, by the words of Gonzalo Gomez Ximenes, interpreter to his Excellency, in the general language of the Indians, said :—" His Excellency, desiring to verify and put in writing and to record the origin of the Incas, your ancestors, their descent and their deeds, what each one did in his time, and in what parts each one was obeyed, which of them was the first to go forth from Cuzco to subdue other lands, and how Tupac Inca Yupanqui and afterwards Huayna Ccapac and Huascar, his son and grandson became lords of all Peru by force of arms ; and to establish this with more authenticity, he has ordered that information and other proofs should be supplied in this city and other parts, and that the said information and proofs should be, by Captain Pedro Sarmiento to whom they were delivered, digested into a true history and chronicle. The said Pedro Sarmiento has now made it and presented it to his Excellency, to ascertain whether it is truthfully written in conformity with the sayings and declarations which were made by some Indians of the said *ayllus.* His Excellency is informed that the *ayllus* and descendants of the twelve Incas have preserved among themselves the memory of the deeds of their ancestors, and are those who best know whether the said chronicle is correct or defective, he has therefore caused you to assemble here, that it may be read in your presence and understood. You, among yourselves, will discuss what will be read and declared in the said language, and see if it agrees with the truth as you know it, and that you may feel a stronger obligation to say what you know, it is ordered that you take an oath."

The said Indians replied that they had understood why they had been sent for, and what it was that was required. They then swore, in the said language, by God our Lord, and by the sign of the cross, that they would tell the truth concerning what they knew of that history. The oaths being taken the reading was commenced in sum and substance. There was read on that and following days from their fable of the creation to the end of the history of the Incas. As it was read, so it was interpreted into their language, chapter by chapter. And over each chapter the Indians discussed and conferred among themselves in the said language. All were agreed in confirming and declaring through the interpreter, that the said history was good and true, and in agreement with what they knew and had heard their fathers and ancestors say, as it had been told to them. For, as they have no writing like the Spaniards, they conserve ancient traditions among themselves by passing them from tongue to tongue, and age to age. They heard their fathers and ancestors say that Pachacuti Inca Yupanqui, the ninth Inca, had verified the history of the former Incas who were before him, and painted their deeds on boards, whence also they had been able to learn the sayings of their fathers, and had passed them on to their children. They only amended some names of persons and places and made other slight corrections, which the said Alcalde ordered to be inserted as the Indians had spoken, and this was done. After the said corrections all the Indians, with one accord, said that the history was good and true, in conformity with what they knew and had heard from their ancestors, for they had conferred and discussed among themselves, verifying from beginning to end. They expressed their belief that no other history that might be written could be so authentic and true as this one, because none could have so diligent an examination, from those who are able to state the truth. The said Alcalde signed

The Doctor Loarte
Gonzalo Gomez Ximenes
Before me Alvaro Ruiz de Navamuel.

After the above, in the said city of Cuzco, on the 2nd of March of the same year, his Excellency having seen the declaration of the Indians and the affidavits that were made on them, said that he ordered and orders that, with the corrections the said Indians stated should be made, the history should be sent to his Majesty, signed and authenticated by me the said Secretary. It was approved and signed by the said Doctor Gabriel de Loarte who was present at the verification with the Indians, and then taken and signed

Don Francisco de Toledo
Before Alvaro Ruiz de Navamuel.

I the said Alvaro Ruiz de Navamuel, Secretary to his Excellency, of the Government, and to the general visitation of these kingdoms, notary to his Majesty, certify that the said testimony and verification was taken before me, and is taken from the original which remains in my possession, and that the said Alcalde, the Doctor Loarte, who signed, said that he placed and interposed upon it his authority and judicial decree, that it may be valued and accepted within his jurisdiction and beyond it. I here made my sign in testimony of the truth

Alvaro Ruiz de Navamuel.

Facsimile (reduced) of the
SIGNATURES OF THE ATTESTING WITNESSES TO THE SARMIENTO MS. 1572.
From the original, Göttingen University Library.

Reproduced and printed for the Hakluyt Society by Donald Macbeth.

ACCOUNT

OF THE

PROVINCE OF VILCAPAMPA

AND

A NARRATIVE OF THE EXECUTION

OF THE

INCA TUPAC AMARU

BY

CAPTAIN BALTASAR DE OCAMPO

(WRITTEN IN 1610)

Translated from a manuscript in the British Museum

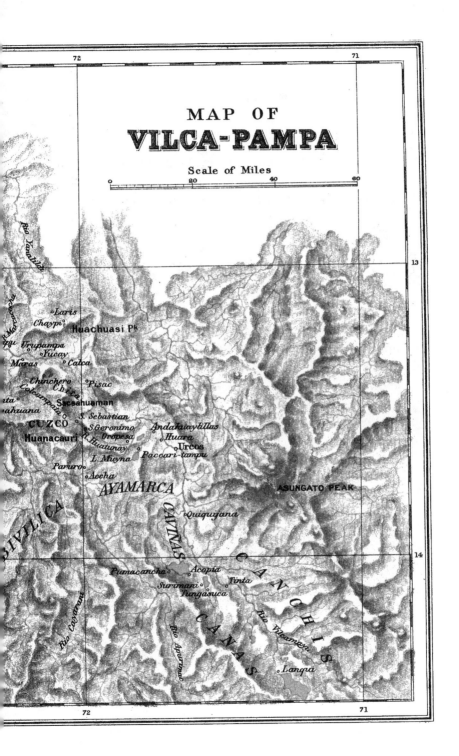

MAP OF
VILCA-PAMPA

Scale of Miles

0   20   40   60

72

71

13

R.Yanatili

R.Macao...

R....igu

Laris

Chaypi

Huachuasi Pk

Urupampa

Yucay

Maras

Calca

Chinchero

Chita

Cotampata

Pisac

ita

ahuana

Sacsahuaman

CUZCO

S.Sebastian

Huanacauri

S.Geronimo

Andahuaylillas

Oropesa

Huatunay

Jhuara

Urcos

L.Muyna

Paccari-tampu

Paruro

Aocha

AYAMARCA

ASUNGATO PEAK

CAYNAS

Quiquijana

SIVILICA

14

Pumacancha

Acopia

Surimani

Tinta

Tungasuca

Rio Cayarani

C A N G H I S

C A N A S

Rio Ayaurmac

Rio Vilcamayo

Langui

72

71

A DESCRIPTION OF THE PROVINCE

OF

ST FRANCIS OF VICTORY OF VILCAPAMPA

To the most excellent Lord Don Juan de Mendoza y Luna, Marquis of Montes Claros[1], lieutenant of the King our Lord, Viceroy, Governor, and Captain-General in these kingdoms and provinces of Peru and Chile, the Captain Baltasar de Ocampo, his servant, desires eternal felicity.

My age and white locks do not require that I should now treat of long past histories of bloodshed, but rather that I should seek for pleasant rest whereby I might finish my worn out life. In the service of the royal person of Philip II, our Lord and natural King, the true original transmitted to the third of that name, I have served in this country for more than 44 years, on all the occasions that the times and events have offered, seeking generally to be among the first to serve my King and Lord as a loyal vassal with my proper person, arms, horses and servants at my own cost, nor have I been rewarded or remunerated for such services. Although it is more than two years since I came to this coast to give an account to your Excellency of my condition and to make known my great necessities (owing to having disposed of my property by employing it in the way that I have said) I have before and do now present to your Excellency's person my memorials and proofs. Finding myself broken and altogether ruined, without any hope or remedy whatever, I ventured to kiss your Excellency's hand, and verbally to

---

[1] The third Marquis of Montes Claros was grandson of the first Marquis, who was a younger son of the third Duke of Infantado. He was Viceroy of Mexico from 1603 to 1607, and he came by sea from Acapulco to Callao to take up the appointment of Viceroy of Peru, owing to the death of the Count of Monterey, the former Viceroy. Solorzano praises him as a model of rectitude and prudence. In December, 1615, he gave up charge to the Prince of Esquilache and returned to Spain, where he received other high appointments.

give you an account of the city and province of San Francisco of the Victory of Vilcapampa, its origin and beginning, with information respecting it, as well as a rough estimate of the time occupied in its discovery. Your Excellency, having derived some pleasure from my narration, ordered me to put it in writing. Thinking that in doing so I should perform an agreeable service to your Excellency, I endeavoured that the memoir should consist of a narration of the memorable occurrences of those golden times, striving in all things to offer the truest history of the events that I am able to remember. For it is just that a Prince (such as your Excellency) should receive a frank account without any concealment whatever. May your Excellency receive it as a benign, amiable and most Christian Prince, from your servant who, in all things, desires to serve and please you. And I pray that your Excellency will not dwell upon the rustic style and language, but on the sincere, frank, and pure intention which animates me. So when I should suffer from hunger (more than I suffer at present) and, seeking help for God's sake, if I receive no other reward than kind words and acceptance, I shall remain well paid, and shall understand that I deserve nothing from God, from his Majesty, from his Excellency, nor from other men. This being granted, may your Excellency be served by passing your eyes over this writing and description of that land, that by chance it may have a pleasant sound in the ear of your Excellency whom may the Almighty Majesty of God preserve for many prosperous years, with the highest felicity of greater estates and lordships as your Excellency merits, and this your servant desires for you. Most excellent Lord

the servant of your Excellency

who kisses your feet and hands

Baltasar de Ocampo Conejeros.

DESCRIPTION

OF THE

PROVINCE OF SAN FRANCISCO OF THE VICTORY OF VILCAPAMPA.

HOW INTELLIGENCE WAS OBTAINED OF IT, OF ITS DISCOVERY, OF THE DEFEAT OF THE INCA TUPAC AMARU, OF HIS DEATH, AND OTHER MOURNFUL EVENTS.

May it please you, most excellent Prince, to give a favourable inclination, as of a pleasant taste on the palate, to my earnest desire to please you in relating this true history. If in anything I am faulty in what I say, it will not be from a want of desire to give complete satisfaction, but by reason of my limited understanding, being unable to reach a higher standard, as in my letter I have represented to your Excellency. And so I begin.

The Viceroy Don Francisco de Toledo being in the city of Cuzco, in the beginning of the year 1571, Don Carlos Inca, a resident in that city, legitimate son of Don Cristóval Paullu Cusi Tupac Inca and of Doña Catalina Usica Coya his wife, was leading a marital life, as he always did, with Doña Maria de Esquivel his legitimate wife, native of Truxillo of Estremadura, in the kingdom of Spain. She having conceived, and the time having been completed brought forth a son in the fortress of the city of Cuzco[1].

---

[1] That is, the palace of the Colcampata, at the foot of the fortress.

This caused great pleasure and rejoicing in the city, because Carlos Inca and his wife had been married for many years, and had never before had a child, the blessed fruit of their marriage. For the baptism of the infant its parents sought in the city for a godfather of sufficient rank, the Inca Don Carlos being grandson of Huayna Ccapac, the universal sovereign of these lands, in his time. They requested and besought the Lord Viceroy, Don Francisco de Toledo, that he would do them a signal favour by honouring them with his Excellency's presence and authority, in taking their son to the baptismal font, and being his godfather and their gossip[1]. They also requested that he would think it well that Doctor Friar Pedro Ordoñez y Flores, his chaplain and confessor of the order of Alcantara (brother of Don Pedro Ordoñez y Flores, formerly Apostolic Inquisitor of these kingdoms and now Archbishop of the new kingdom of Granada) should perform the baptismal service in the parish church of San Cristóval of the Colcampata, which is adjoining to the said fortress.

The said Lord Viceroy consented, with pleasure, to be godfather to the child, and gossip to its parents. On the day of the baptism, which was Epiphany Sunday, the 6th January of the said year 1571, when the child received the name of Melchior, there were festivals, rejoicings, fireworks, dances, and many newly invented and costly conceits, which they well knew how to get up very admirably at Cuzco in those days[2].

---

[1] Gossip from "God" and "sib," a relation through baptism. In Spanish the word used is *Compadre*, the relationship between the parents and the godparents, and of the godparents to each other.

[2] On an eminence called Carmenca, on the other side of the Huatanay stream to the fortress of Cuzco, there is a suburb with a small church dedicated to Santa Ana, possessing an altar of massive silver richly embossed. Most interesting paintings of the end of the 16th century line the walls, representing the procession of Corpus Christi in about the time of the Viceroy Toledo. The dresses give a

Invitations were sent out over all the land for more than forty leagues round Cuzco, and there assembled for the occasion all the Incas of the following parishes :

ACCHA (Paruro province)

ANTA (cap. Anta province)

ANTAHUAYLLAS (La Chica)

ARAYPALPA (Paruro province)

ATARAS

CHINCHERO (near Cuzco)

COLCHA (Paruro province)

CONCACALLA

CUCHARAYPAMPA

EQUEQUO

CUZCO

HUANUQUITI

HUAYHUACUNCA

MARCO

PACCARI-TAMPU (Quispicancha province)

PACOPATA

PALPA

PAMPACUCHU

PARCOS

PARURO (cap. Paruro province)

PILPINTO

PISAC (Calca province)

POCORAY

PUQUIURA

QUIQUISANA (Quispicancha province)

---

correct idea of the appearance of the assembly at the christening of Melchior Carlos Inca. First march the four religious orders' of Dominicans, Franciscans, Augustines, and Mercedarios, followed by the "Santissimo" under a canopy. Then an old cavalier in black with the insignia of the order of Alcantara, perhaps Toledo himself. Then follow people of each parish of Cuzco, drawing their patron saints in triumphal cars, and headed by principal Inca nobles in full ancient costume. On the head is the *chuccu* or head-dress with crimson fringe and plumes of feathers. Round the neck is a broad collar of several colours with a long yellow fringe. The tunic is of white cotton covered with ornaments, and confined round the waist by a very broad belt of richly worked cloth. On the breast there is a golden sun. Garters confine the pantaloons above the knee, which are of black cloth. The shoes are also of black cloth. Pumas' heads of gold, set with emeralds, on the shoulders, secure a long scarlet mantle with full white sleeves bordered with wide lace. There is a Ñusta or princess heading the procession of her parish, in one picture, with nearly the same dress but bare-headed, and a boy in front carrying her head-dress. The concluding picture represents the return of the "Santissimo" to the cathedral, with the whole Inca family looking on, magnificently dressed with huge plumes of egret's feathers on their heads. Heads and shoulders of the crowd are grouped along the lower parts of the pictures, Spaniards in black cloaks and broad *sombreros* mingling with Indian men and women in characteristic dresses.

RIMAC-TAMPU (Anta province)
SAN SALVADOR
SAN SEBASTIAN (Cuzco cercado)
SAN GERONIMO DE CORAMA
SURITE (Anta province)
URCOS (Quispicancha province)
URUPAMPA (cap. of Urubamba province)
XAQUIXAHUANA
YAURISCA (Paruro province)
YUCAY (Urubamba province).

All these are places where Incas reside. Canas, Canchis, and Collas were also invited, and men of all other nations that could be got together. Among the rest there came to the christening Titu Cusi Yupanqui Inca and his young brother Tupac Amaru Inca, who came from the province of Vilcapampa. They were infidel idolaters who worshipped the Sun, believing that he was the maker of all things, and they had an image of gold and a sanctuary. When these two last Incas saw the grandeur, majesty, and sumptuousness of the Christians, and that divine service was celebrated with such authority, and beheld the congregations of Christians assembled for public worship ; as men of good understanding they were deeply impressed, and easily deduced the sanctity and excellence of the Christian law.

Titu Cusi Yupanqui had the desire to enter the bosom of our holy mother church, and to be converted to our sacred catholic faith. The respect and reverence which the Lord Viceroy received from all his subjects appeared good to the Inca, who saw his person guarded by halberdiers. The Inca proposed in his heart to be a Christian, that he might realize his majesty and high rank, and feel that he was respected and esteemed in the land as its lord. As soon as the festivities, which lasted for many days in Cuzco, were concluded he retired to his native land of Vilcapampa with his brother Tupac Amaru Inca. Being a man full of ambition (a vice which is usually dominant in the characters of tyrants), he put his young brother into the House of the Sun with the chosen virgins and their matrons, a most ancient custom among all the rulers of these kingdoms before the arrival of the Spaniards. This younger brother was the natural and legitimate lord of these lands and grandson of Huayna Ccapac. But the elder brother, by his management and cunning, kept him secluded and imprisoned on the ground of his want of experience, usurping the government for himself. This Titu Cusi Yupanqui then sent ambassadors to the Lord Viceroy in the city of Cuzco, saying that he was very desirous of becoming a Christian, owing to having seen the grandeur and majesty displayed by the Christians in matters connected with divine worship.

As he was the Lord Inca of that land, he requested his Excellency to have the kindness to send him ministers who would instruct him respecting the holy catholic church ; as well as some persons who would teach and explain to him the rules of urbanity and courtesy that, after he had been instructed and trained, he might come to the city of Cuzco and offer obedience to his Majesty, and to his Excellency in his royal name.

Don Francisco de Toledo, full of joy and delight, called together the prelates of the monastic orders, with the members of the cathedral chapter and the magistracy of the city, and the words he spoke to them showed his pleasure. He gave them all to understand (like so prudent a Lord) the arrival of the new message which the Inca Titu Cusi Yupanqui had sent by his ambassadors, and that he would much like to send some religious priests to instruct the Inca, as well as some secular persons to accompany them, so that he might also be taught the customs of a court, and be trained in all things that were due to his position as the Inca. Each one of the prelates of the religious orders offered to appoint one or two monks from their convents.

Finally the persons chosen for this good work were the Father Friar Juano de Vivero[1], at that time Prior of the Convent of St Augustine, and Friar Diego Ortiz[2] (whom they afterwards martyred). The Lord Viceroy sent, as his Ambassadors, a citizen of Cuzco named Atilano de Añaya, a grave gentleman with an affable address and versed in the language of the Indians; Diego Rodriguez de Figueroa as Chief Magistrate, conferring upon him the privilege of bearing that staff of office during his life; and Francisco de las Veredas, public notary, a very courteous and discreet cavalier; that they might minister to the said Titu Cusi Yupanqui, and instruct him. As mayor-domo and master of the household a *mestizo* native of Cuzco, named Pedro Pando, was chosen, a great talker in their language. This was in the year 1571.

After the festivals on the occasion of the baptism of Don Melchior Carlos Inca, son of Don Carlos Inca and Doña Maria de Esquivel his wife (whom God pardon), to whom his Majesty the King our Lord has shown great favours, including the habit of Santiago and 10,000 ducats of rent in Spain, the embassy set out. Don Francisco de

---

[1] Juan de Vivero was a native of Valladolid, of an ancient Galician family, descended from Froila, King of Oviedo. He took the habit of St Augustine at Salamanca, and went out to Peru in 1557. He went to Cuzco and was the founder and first prelate of the Augustine monastery there, in 1559. The Marquis of Cañete committed to Vivero the duty of converting the Inca Sayri Tupac, and the baptism took place in 1558. Vivero accompanied the Viceroy Toledo in his visitations. His services were appreciated by Philip II who offered him a bishopric, which he declined. He returned to Spain and died at Toledo in 1577.

[2] Diego Ortiz was born near Seville, and came to Peru in 1560 as an Augustine friar. He was occupied for years in teaching and catechizing the Indians. When the Spaniards occupied Vilcapampa, the body of Ortiz was buried in the church they built, but in 1598 the Augustine friars removed it to Cuzco. Father Fulgencio Baldani wrote a life of Diego Ortiz in Italian.

Toledo sent with it many presents such as velvets, bro-
cades, and linen for the adornment of the Inca's person
and house ; as well as provision of wines, raisins, figs
and almonds, with other valuable things which were all
joyfully received by Titu Cusi Yupanqui. He showed
them to his principal courtiers as the gifts which the Lord
Viceroy had sent by his ambassadors. He ordered all his
vassals to show respect and hospitality to those who had
brought the presents, as persons coming from so great
a prince. The interpreter Pedro Pando explained to him
that they should treat the Priests with honour, respect and
veneration because they were ministers of another great
Prince who was the Lord of Heaven. On earth they were
Ministers of His Holiness the Roman Pontiff. He said
that they had come, at the will of the Viceroy and in the
service of God our Lord, to catechize, indoctrinate, baptize,
say mass, and publicly preach the evangelical law ; so as
to bring them to our holy catholic faith. For, he told
them, the Inca had hitherto been a slave of the devil,
worshipping the Sun which was one of God's creatures, not
a creator but created for the good of men. He gave them
to understand that their religion was idolatry. Such were
the hills, the *huacas*, and the *apachitas*[1], which are heaps of
stones made by the Indians on certain great cliffs and
rocks. They have a custom of throwing the *coca*, which
they hold in such estimation, on these heaps, carrying it in
their mouths solely with the object of offering it on the
said *apachitas*. They say that they leave there all the
fatigue of the road. Others leave their *usutos*, which in our
language means shoes. He went on to say that the said
Fathers, and the others who were in Christendom, were
respected, reverenced, and esteemed, and held in great
veneration by the Kings and great Lords, because they

---

[1] *Apacheta* or *pacheta* was a heap of stones at the summit of a pass.

were ministers of God, and did not occupy themselves in anything but the sacred work of the King of Heaven, that they were people who were held in such estimation by all the princes and powers of the earth, that they went down on their knees in their presence, and kissed their hands. He added that they had such influence with God that they received him in their hands from heaven, when they put him on the altar. They are consecrated with holy oil, and are permitted to treat familiarly with the Lord of heaven and earth, which the Emperor and all the other Monarchs in the world cannot do. They are blessed by all because they themselves bless the people and pardon by the authority of Almighty God, absolving and cleansing men from their sins and confessing them as the lieutenants of Jesus Christ, the Lord and Creator of all things in the universe.

As I have already said, this said province was discovered in the year 1571, through the same Titu Cusi Yupanqui having, God permitting, sent his ambassadors. He had seized and usurped the lordship of Tupac Amaru Inca, the natural and legitimate Lord of that land (he being a bastard) having no right. For the true Lord was the said Tupac Amaru Inca, his brother. Being a youth without experience his illegitimate brother oppressed him, and imprisoned him with the chosen virgins and their matrons in the House of the Sun, where he was when the Lord Viceroy Don Francisco de Toledo sent his embassy. The ambassadors persuaded Titu Cusi Yupanqui, with loving words and rich presents, to leave that province of Vilcapampa and come to the city of Cuzco to offer obedience to his Majesty, and to his Excellency in the royal name, as the said Inca had proposed to do through his envoys. He determined to comply but, owing to a fit of obstinacy, he delayed his departure for some time, putting it off from one day to another. The Father Friar

Juan de Vivero, seeing the perversity of the Inca, returned to Cuzco with Atilano de Añaya, Diego Rodriguez de Figueroa, Chief Magistrate, and Francisco de las Veredas. The Father Friar Diego Ortiz and Pedro Pando remained with the Inca.

The returning ambassadors reported what had taken place to his Excellency, who was piqued, as it appeared to him that the Inca was making fun of his person and authority. He ordered the Father Friar Juan de Vivero and Diego Rodriguez de Figueroa to go back with the wand of royal justice, that as chief magistrate he might overcome all difficulties, and bring the matter to a conclusion. He also sent Atilano de Añaya to administer the affairs connected with the Inca's property and person.

While these departures and returns were being arranged, Titu Cusi Yupanqui fell ill and was on the point of death. When the Indians saw his danger they said to the Father Friar Diego Ortiz that, as he was the Minister of God, he must ask Him to cure the said Inca of that infirmity. He replied that he would do so every day, and that if it was His pleasure God would restore him to health, and if not all would be in conformity with His will. For His Majesty knew what was best for the salvation of souls. For the Inca, at his own request, had been baptized by the Father Friar Juan de Vivero in the said province of Vilcapampa, receiving the name of Don Felipe Titu Cusi Yupanqui. As a baptized Christian the Fathers said a mass every day. The chapel in which they performed these services was near my house and on my own land in the place called Puquiura, near the metal works of Don Cristóval de Albornoz, formerly Precentor of the cathedral of Cuzco.

Affairs being in this state, the Inca died. When his chief people and captains saw that the Inca Don Felipe Titu Cusi Yupanqui was dead, and that the prayers and sacrifices of the said Father Friar Diego Ortiz were of no

avail, an Indian named Quispi, who is still living, came to
the said Friar, and asked him why his God had not cured
the Inca if he was so powerful? and, without giving the
Father time to answer, the Indian struck him. Our Lord
permitted that his hand and his arm up to the shoulder
should wither. It is dried up to this day, and the Indian
knew his sin. The Friar went down on his knees, and
turned the other cheek to the smiter. He received another
blow and they tied his hands behind his back and dragged
him along. They opened a place under the beard with
a kind of knife which they call *tumi*, and fastened a rope
in his mouth by which they dragged him, making him
suffer an unheard of martyrdom. The blessed Father took
it smiling, with his eyes raised to heaven. His age was 33,
a man of holy life and fame, for he had performed many
and great miracles in that province, as well on women
as on children and other persons. His body remained
fragrant, being placed in a box of cedar, lined with crimson
satin, in the tabernacle of the convent of St Augustine, in
the city of Cuzco, on the gospel side of the principal
chapel of the transept. On the same day they killed the
interpreter Pedro Pando with unheard of cruelties, like
barbarous people without laws or beliefs.

After they had performed certain ceremonies which the
Incas had established on the occasions of the interment of
the Lords of that land, which they called *Purucaya*[1] in
their language, meaning the honours only shown to the
Incas, they brought out the insignia of their Sovereigns.
These were:

TUMI—The battle axe	YACOLLA—Robe
CHUQUI—The lance	ACHIHUA—The parasol of
CHIPANA—Bracelet	various colours wonder-
LLAUTU—The fringe	fully worked

---

[1] General mournings on the death of an Inca.

HUALLCANCA—The shield   MASCAPAYCHU—The crown
USUTA—The shoes   HUANTUY—The litter.
DUHO[1]—The throne

Carrying each of the insignia in the hands of the
greatest lords in deep mourning, with muffled drums, and
sounds of grief, they proceeded to the House of the Sun,
where was the Inca Tupac Amaru, the true and legitimate
Lord, brother of the now deceased Titu Cusi Yupanqui.
Tupac Amaru was with the *Acllus* or selected women.
These *Acllus* were women chosen for the service of the
Sun, under the *Mama-cunas*, who were matrons to keep
guard over them, for they were very beautiful.

The said Inca Tupac Amaru was there in the fortress
of Pitcos, which is on a very high mountain whence the view
commanded a great part of the province of Vilcapampa.
Here there was an extensive level space, with very sumptuous and majestic buildings, erected with great skill and
art, all the lintels of the doors, as well the principal as
the ordinary ones, being of marble, elaborately carved.

They took the Inca Tupac Amaru out of this place, and
did him homage as their natural Lord, telling what had
happened with respect to the Father Friar Diego Ortiz
and Pedro Pando. I am unable to tell your Excellency
what then happened. When tidings came that people
were coming from Cuzco to act as spies[2], seven captains
went out along the road to that city. One was named
Puri Paucar. With him there was a native of the valley
of Xauxa, a Huanca Indian of a very warlike tribe. I do
not remember the names of the other five captains. They
guarded the bridge of Chuqui-chaca, over the Vilcamayu
river, which is the key to the province of Vilcapampa.

---

[1] This form of the word is corrupt. It should be TIANA.
[2] *Chapas* or *caunihuas*. *Chapa* or *Chapatiyoc* is a sentry. The
word is also used for a spy. *Caunihua* is not in Holguin or Mossi.

The Ambassador Atilano de Añaya, with the Friar Juan de Vivero and Diego Rodriguez de Figueroa, was coming a second time to the province of Vilcapampa, with an embassy to Titu Cusi Yupanqui, who was dead. Friar Juan de Vivero and Diego Rodriguez de Figueroa, being in the town of Ollantay-tampu, which is on the road to the bridge, received certain tidings of what had happened there, which caused them not to wish to enter with the Ambassador, and they required further news before they went on. But Atilano de Añaya, being a sober-minded man, affable in his intercourse with the Indians, did not desist from continuing the prosecution of the duty assigned to him by the Viceroy. He proceeded to the bridge of Chuqui-chaca: he intended to pass the night there, as there was a house for him to lodge in, and pasture for his horses. After he had put in order all that he brought as presents and provisions for the Inca, he saw the Peruvian captains approaching with hostile determination and ready for war. Before they could arrive an Indian came apparently to warn him of what had happened. Not trusting them, he ordered a negro servant to saddle a good mule, gave him a token of gold, with orders to return quickly to the city of Cuzco and deliver it to Doña Juana Machuca, his wife, as a sign that she would never see him again, because this was the warning he had from the Indian who had disappeared, by which he knew that it was an angel sent from heaven. The negro went.

The captains came to where the Ambassador was, who gave them to eat and drink, receiving them with much kindness, and giving them presents. After they had received this hospitality they killed him as a return for it. He thought it better to suffer death than to fail in the execution of the orders he had received from his prince. For he could have escaped with his negro, but he did not do so.

Three days afterwards the negro arrived with the sad news of the death of the Ambassador, and of what had happened to the blessed martyr Diego Ortiz and to Pedro Pando. When the Viceroy was informed, he called together the magistracy and municipality of the city of Cuzco, to assemble in the palace where he lodged. He announced the sad news that had arrived of the death of the priest and the others, declaring that he would despatch a warlike force to punish those who had taken part in the events described in my narrative.

After the consultation with the said officials he adopted the resolution to prepare an armed force with captains and officers. He nominated Martin Hurtado de Arbieto[1] as general, a citizen and magistrate of the city, a leading knight and one of the conquerors. The Camp Master was Juan Alvarez Maldonado[2], also a citizen of Cuzco and governor of the province of the Chunchos. As Coadjutor of the council of war he named his nephew, Don Geronimo de Figueroa. The captains were Martin Garcia Oñez de Loyola[3], captain of the Viceroy's guard, and knight of the

---

[1] Martin Hurtado de Arbieto was a Biscayan. He served under Centeno against Gonzalo Pizarro and was wounded and taken prisoner at the battle of Huarina. He escaped and was with Gasca at the rout of Sucsahuana. He also served against Giron. He founded a new city in Vilcapampa. He was a magistrate of Cuzco.

[2] Juan Alvarez Maldonado was a citizen of Cuzco. He led an expedition into the montaña of Paucartampu ; and was followed by Gomez de Tordoya. A dispute arose between the two expeditions and they fought a desperate battle. The wild Chunchos fell upon the survivors and killed Tordoya. Maldonado escaped by way of Caravaya, and returned to Cuzco. Leon Pinelo is said, by Antonio, to have written a *Relacion de la jornada de Alvarez Maldonado*, 1617.

[3] Don Martin Garcia Oñez de Loyola was a native of Guipuzcoa, of the same family as Ignatius. He had seen some service in Europe, and went out to Peru with the Viceroy Toledo, as the captain of his guard. After the Vilcapampa campaign he married the Inca Princess Beatriz Clara Coya, niece of Tupac Amaru, her dowry being an estate in the valley of Yucay. In 1579 Loyola was Governor of Potosi, and acquired great wealth. He raised 200 men and went with them to Chile ; where he was appointed Captain-General, in 1592. He was killed by the Araucanian Indians who surprised his camp in 1598. By the Inca Princess he had an only daughter, Ana Maria Coya de

order of Calatrava; Captain Ordoño Ordoñez of Valencia, a citizen of Lima, who went as captain of artillery; the Captain Juan Ponce de Leon, a citizen of Huamanca and brother-in-law of the general, who was Provost Marshal; Captain Don Juan Palomino[1]; Captain Don Gomez de Tordoya[2]; Captain Don Antonio Pereyra; Captain Mancio Sierra de Leguisano[3]; Captain Don Alonso de Mesa[4], Lord of the town of Piedra-buena; Captain Martin Dolmas, a Knight of Santiago; Captain Martin de Meneses, and Captain Julian de Umuran. The general and his captains, with their camp in order, marched from

---

Loyola, who was born at Cuzco. She went to Spain in 1622 and was created by Philip III Marchioness of Oropesa and Yucay, with remainder, in default of children, to the heirs general of her uncle Tupac Amaru. She married Don Juan Henriquez de Borja, son of the Marquis of Alcanizes and of a daughter of Don Francisco de Borja, Duke of Gandia. Ana had three children, Juan Marquis of Alcanizes and Oropesa and descendant of the Incas, Alvaro, and Francisca married to the Marquis of Peña Alba. In the church of Copacabana at Lima there is a picture of the marriage of Loyola with the Inca princess.

[1] If this is the same Juan de Palomino whose name often occurs in the civil wars of the conquerors, he must have been well advanced in years.

[2] Gomez de Tordoya is the same cavalier who was at the battle of Chupas, and made the disastrous entry into the forests of the Chunchos.

[3] Mancio Sierra de Leguisano was one of the first conquerors and a first settler at Cuzco in 1534. He received a golden sun as his share of the spoils, which he gambled away in one night. When he was elected a Magistrate he left off gambling, and never touched a card again. He served in the defence of Cuzco. He married an Inca Princess, Doña Beatriz Coya, and had a son Juan. But his memory is chiefly worthy of praise because, in his will, he recognized the virtues of the Indians and denounced the cruelties of his own country-men. His son was a schoolfellow of the Inca Garcilasso de la Vega.

[4] This must have been the son of Alonso de Mesa, the conqueror who came to Caxamarca with Pizarro. The father was a native of the Canary Islands. He received 135 marcs of silver and 3350 *pesos* of gold out of Atahualpa's ransom. He became a citizen and had a house in Cuzco. He behaved with great gallantry during the siege, and at the battles of Salinas and Chupas. He did good service in the campaign against Gonzalo Pizarro and also opposed Giron. The son Alonso went to Spain, and co-operated with the Incas Garcilasso de la Vega and Melchior Carlos in an effort to obtain concessions for the Inca family.

Cuzco down the valley by Yucay and Ollantay-tampu to
the bridge of Chuqui-chaca and province of Vilcapampa.
The Captain Gaspar de Sotelo, uncle of the President of
Charcas Don Diego de Portugal, a very leading knight and
native of Zamora, with Captain Nuño de Mendoza, a
citizen of Cuzco, entered by way of Curahuasi and
Huamancay[1], to stop the way if by chance the Inca should
wish to fly by it to the province of Antahuaylla, where he
might take shelter. Thence he might take refuge in the
valley of Maya-marca, very near the province of the
Pilcones[2], very warlike Indians inhabiting an extensive
tract of country, which I shall mention presently.

The force which marched from Cuzco by way of the
valley of Yucay, reached the Chuqui-chaca bridge. Here
they found Tupac Amaru Inca prepared, having been taken
out of the House of the Sun, with his camp formed.
Our troops had an encounter with his people, though the
river was between them. For with four shots from our
small field guns, and the arquebuses of the soldiers, the
Peruvians were routed, and were obliged to retreat to their
camp. Our men then occupied the bridge, which was a
measure of no small importance for the royal force. For
the enemy did not remember to burn and destroy the said
bridge. God permitted this, because of the great trouble
the Spaniards would have had in making one over the
very full river. Leaving some of our men to guard it, and
to forward supplies to the front, the rest of the force continued the pursuit, the Inca and his people being routed
and in flight. The road was narrow in the ascent, with
forest on the right, and on the left a ravine of great depth.
Our troops could not advance in formation of squadrons,
but only two and two.

The Captain Martin Garcia Oñez de Loyola, who was

---

[1] Abancay?   [2] Further on he has Pilcosones.

in the vanguard, was advancing alone like a good and well-armed captain, when an Inca captain, named Hualpa, came out of the forest without being seen by anyone, and tackled our captain with such an embrace that he could not get at his arms, the object being to hurl him down the ravine. He would have been dashed to pieces and hurled into the river, but an Indian servant of the captain, named Corillo, who is still alive, with property in the valley of Yucay, and who was then with him, drew Loyola's sword from the scabbard and, with much dexterity and animation, killed the Indian Hualpa, who was thus vanquished and failed in his evil intent. To this day the place where this happened is called "the leap of Loyola."

Continuing the pursuit the troops arrived at a place called Onccoy, where there are some wide and fertile open spaces. Here there were herds of cattle, and llamas with their lambs ; at which the captains and soldiers were contented and delighted on finding supplies of meat for the camp. Continuing in pursuit of the enemy, many prisoners, both captains and common people, were taken. Being pressed to say what road the Inca had taken, they replied that he had gone inland towards the valley of Simaponte ; and that he was flying to the country of the Mañaries Indians, a warlike tribe and his friends, where balsas and canoes were posted to save him and enable him to escape.

Having received this information, the Spaniards held a council of war, at which Captain Martin Garcia Oñez de Loyola was appointed to continue the pursuit. He accepted and went on with 50 soldiers. Loyola overtook the fugitives, capturing the Inca and many other prisoners. None escaped, because detachments were stationed all round. Only two Spaniards were killed. One was called Ribadeneira, but there is no memory of the name of the other.

The Inca and the other Indians were collected and

brought back to the valley of Hoyara. Here the Indians were settled in a large village, and a city of Spaniards was founded. It was called San Francisco of the Victory of Vilcapampa for two sacred and honest reasons. The first was because the victory was on the 4th of October, 1571, the day of San Francisco, the second being the name of the Viceroy to whom the victory was due. Great festivities were held in the city of Cuzco when the news of the victory arrived.

This city was founded on an extensive plain near a river, with an admirable climate. From the river channels of water were taken for the service of the city, the water being very good. Owing to the discovery of important silver mines in the hills of Huamani and Huamanape, the site of the city was moved nearer to the mines, to the Villa-rica de Argeta, which was founded by order of Don Garcia Hurtado de Mendoza, Marquis of Cañete, and Viceroy of these kingdoms. By assent of the municipality formed in the said city of San Francisco of the Victory, four priests became members of it. One was Don Cristóval de Albornoz, Precentor of the cathedral of Cuzco. It was decided by the governor that the site of the said city should be moved to that of Villa-rica de Argeta, which was at the place called Onccoy, where the Spaniards who first discovered this land found the flocks and herds. In this municipality it was resolved to send a procurator-general to obtain permission and the good will of Don Luis de Velasco[1], who was at that time Viceroy. For the negotiation there was sent as Procurator myself, Baltasar de Ocampo, and I came to the city and treated with the said Viceroy. The change of site appeared convenient for

---

[1] Don Luis de Velasco, afterwards Marquis of Salinas, was Viceroy of Mexico, whence he was transferred to Peru in 1595, relieving the Marquis of Cañete. He was Viceroy of Peru from 1595 to 1604, when he was relieved by the Count of Monterey. In 1609 he was created Marquis of Salinas by Philip III.

the service of God our Lord and of his Majesty, and for the increase of his royal fifths, as well as beneficial to the inhabitants of the said city. Having examined the capitulations and reasons, the said Don Luis de Velasco granted the licence to move the city to where it is now founded, ordering that it should have the title and name of the city of San Francisco of the Victory of Vilcapampa, which was its first name. By this change of site I, the said Baltasar de Ocampo, performed a great service to God our Lord and his Majesty. Through my care, industry and solicitude a very good church was built, with its principal chapel and great doors. For previously there was only a small chapel in the city, with barely room for the citizens and miners, while the Indian *mitayos* were exposed to sun or rain. The sacrament is now placed on the high altar, and on the occasion of this divine worship our Lord was served by ordaining that affairs should be in much prosperity for the common good, and that there should be a large increase of the royal fifths, as will presently be mentioned. For until our conquest all was idolatry and worship of the devil, at which the majesty of God was greatly offended. The martyr, Father Friar Diego Ortiz, had destroyed many sanctuaries from which devils were seen to come out, unable to resist the prayers, exhortations and exorcisms offered up by the said Father, and the fumigations with which he tormented and afflicted them.

After the General Martin Hurtado de Arbieto left off using cords, he began the foundation of the city and named citizens to receive *encomiendas*, among whom he divided more than 1500 Indians for personal service. Until he should make his report to Don Francisco de Toledo he placed things in martial order, leaving a garrison of more than 50 soldiers in that city. He then marched to Cuzco with the Inca Tupac Amaru and his captains, who were prisoners. On reaching the archway of Carmenca, which is the entrance to the city of Cuzco, he marshalled all his troops. The said governor Juan Alvarez Maldonado, as Master of the Camp, chained Tupac Inca Amaru and his captains together. The Inca was dressed in a mantle and doublet of crimson velvet. His shoes were made of wool of the country, of several colours. The crown or head-dress, called *mascapaychu*, was on his head, with fringe over his forehead, this being the royal insignia of the Inca, in the same way as a crown is used by kings. So they proceeded in triumph over their victory straight to the palace where the Viceroy Don Francisco de Toledo then lived. It formed the houses of Don Tristan de Silva y Guzman and Juan de Pancorvo Celiorigo, citizens of the city of Cuzco. They are the principal and best houses in the city, as Doctor Alonso Perez Marchan, President of Guadalaxara, can inform your Excellency, for he lived in one of them.

In form of an ordered force, the General and his captains marched there in triumph, and presented their prisoners to the Viceroy. After his Excellency had felt the pleasure of conquest, he ordered that the Inca and his captains should be taken to the fortress which is in the parish of San Cristóval of the Colcampata, where the Viceroy's uncle, Don Luis de Toledo, was castellan. This fortress consisted of grand and majestic houses belonging to Don Cristóval Paullu Inca, citizen of Cuzco, father of Don Carlos Inca, and grandfather of Don Melchior Carlos Inca, who was born there. Don Carlos Inca was despoiled of them in order that they might be converted into a royal fortress and barrack for the city guard. The pretext was that he had Titu Cusi Yupanqui and Tupac Amaru Inca, his first cousins, concealed in his house without reporting their presence, at the time of the baptism. These houses commanded a view of the whole city of Cuzco and its parishes, and of more than four leagues of the valley beyond, as far as the *tampu* of Quispicancha, on the road to Potosi.

This fortress was owned by his Majesty for many years, but after a lawsuit respecting the houses, brought by Don Melchior Carlos Inca against the crown, it was decreed that they should be restored to the said Don Melchior Carlos Inca[1], and they were restored.

To return to our history : at the end of some days after the triumph, having considered the evidence respecting the deaths of the Father Friar Diego Ortiz, of Pedro Pando, and of the ambassador Atilano de Añaya, the Doctor Gabriel de Loarte[2], Magistrate of this court, who was then Governor of the city of Cuzco, sentenced the homicidal captains to be hanged, and Tupac Amaru Inca to be beheaded.

The sentences were executed. The captains were led through the streets to the place of execution, while the town crier proclaimed their offences. Three died in the public streets, and two at the foot of the gallows, because they had been tortured in prison until they were dying. Notwithstanding their condition their bodies were taken to comply with the law, while two, namely Ccuri Paucar and the Huanca Indian were hanged when still alive.

At the end of two or three days, after being taught and catechized, Tupac Amaru was baptized. This was done by

---

[1] Melchior Carlos Inca went to Spain to seek justice for himself and his family from the King. The Inca Garcilasso de la Vega, the historian, and Alonso de Mesa the younger, co-operated with him. He came with a complete pedigree of the Incas in 1603. He died, without obtaining any of his requests, at Alcala de Henares, leaving a son who died young.

[2] Gabriel de Loarte had been a judge at Panama and Quito, and was one of the four first criminal judges in the Audience of Lima, in 1570. He came with the Viceroy Toledo to Cuzco. He acted as the Viceroy's accomplice in preparing false charges against Tupac Amaru. Having perpetrated this crime he was sent to Huancavelica to seize the quicksilver mine for the government, the owner being robbed, and appealing to the Council of the Indies.

two monks of our Lady of Mercy. One was the first Creole who was born after the seige of Cuzco, named Friar Gabriel Alvarez de la Carrera, son of a soldier of the first conquest, and the other Friar Melchior Fernandez. They spoke the language so well that they excelled the Incas themselves, especially Friar Gabriel Alvarez de la Carrera. To this day no other has been found who could speak with such grace and eloquence. In short the Inca was converted, for the two religious were such great adepts in their office, that they fed the Inca, as it were, with a spoon.

The Inca was taken from the fortress, through the public streets of the city, with a guard of 400 Cañari Indians, having their lances in their hands. The Cañaris were great enemies of the Incas. He was accompanied by the two monks, one on either side, by Father Alonso de Barzana, of the Company of Jesus, and by Father Molina, preacher to the Indies and priest of the hospital of our Lady of the remedies. They went along teaching and saying things of much consolation to the soul, until they reached the scaffold, which was reared on high in the centre of the great square, fronting the cathedral. Here they got down, and the fathers remained with the Inca, comforting his soul with holy preparation.

The open spaces, roofs, and windows in the parishes of Carmenca and San Cristóval were so crowded with spectators that if an orange had been thrown down it could not have reached the ground anywhere, so closely were the people packed. The executioner, who was a Cañari Indian, having brought out the knife with which he was to behead Tupac Amaru, a marvellous thing happened. The whole crowd of natives raised such a cry of grief that it seemed as if the day of judgment had come, and all those of Spanish race did not fail to show their feelings by shedding tears of grief and pain.

When the Inca beheld the scene, he only raised his

right hand on high and let it fall. With a lordly mind he alone remained calm, and all the noise was followed by a silence so profound that no living soul moved, either among those who were in the square or among those at a distance. The Inca then spoke with a self-possession unlike one about to die. He said that now his course was run, and that he merited that death. He besought and charged all present who had children, on no account to curse them for any bad conduct, but only to chastise them. For when he was a child, having angered his mother, she had put a malediction on him by saying that he would end by being put to death and would not die a natural death; and it had come true. The Fathers Carrera and Fernandez rebuked him, saying that his fate was the will of God and was not due to the curse of his mother. As these Fathers were, like St Paul, so eloquent in their preaching, they easily convinced him, and he repented of what he had said. He asked them all to forgive him, and that they would tell the Viceroy and the Magistrate that he would pray to God for them.

Things being in this state along the principal streets, the most reverend Friar Don Agustin de la Coruña[1], Bishop of Popayan, who was one of the famous twelve Augustine Friars who were the first to enter Mexico preaching the gospel; Father Friar Gonzalo de Mendoza, Provincial of the order of our Lady of Mercy; Father Friar Francisco

---

[1] Friar Agustin de la Coruña y Gormaz was a native of Coruña, son of Hernando de Gormaz and Catalina de Velasco. He took the Augustine habit at Salamanca in 1524, and went to Mexico with other friars in 1533, where he was Prior of several convents and Provincial in 1560. He returned to Spain to urge the better treatment of the Indians, and was consecrated Bishop of Popayan where he went to reside. But in 1567 he had to go to Lima to be present at the second Council, and he afterwards assisted the Viceroy Toledo in his visitation, and the preparation of his "Ordinances." He did all in his power to prevent the murder of Tupac Amaru, and returned to his diocese declining to be longer associated with Toledo. He died at Timana in 1590.

Corrol, Prior of St Augustin in this city; Father Friar Gabriel de Oviedo, Prior of San Domingo; Father Friar Francisco Velez, Guardian of San Francisco; Father Friar Geronimo de Villa Carrillo, Provincial of San Francisco; Father Friar Gonzalo Ballastero, Vicar Provincial of the Order of Mercy; and Father Luis Lopez, Rector of the Company of Jesus, all went to the Viceroy. They went down on their knees and besought him to show mercy and spare the life of the Inca. They urged that he should be sent to Spain to be judged by the King in person. But no prayers could prevail with the Viceroy.

Juan de Soto, chief officer of the court and a servant of his Excellency, was sent on horseback with a pole to clear the way, galloping furiously and riding down all kinds of people. He ordered the Inca's head to be cut off at once, in the name of the Viceroy. The Inca then received consolation from the Fathers who were at his side and, taking leave of all, he put his head on the block, like a lamb. The executioner then came forward and, taking the hair in his left hand, he severed the head with a knife at one blow, and held it on high for all to see. As the head was severed the bells of the cathedral began to ring, and were followed by those of all the monasteries and parish churches in the city. The execution caused the greatest sorrow and brought tears to all eyes.

They carried the body of Tupac Amaru to the house of Doña Maria Cusi Huarcay, the Inca's mother and aunt, for brother was married to sister in heathen times. Afterwards, by a bull of Pope Paul III, the marriage was ratified by Friar Geronimo de Loaysa, first Archbishop of Lima, being then Viceroy Don Andres Hurtado de Mendoza, Marquis of Cañete and Chief Guard of Cuenca. On the next day, after mass, the body of the Inca was interred in the high chapel of the cathedral, the services being performed by the chapter. Pontifical mass was said by the Bishop Agustin de la Coruña. The epistle was read by the Canon Juan de Vera, the gospel by the Canon Estevan de Villalom. All the religious of the city attended the funeral, and each one said his vigils and joined in the singing at the mass, in presence of the corpse. There had been a great council before he was baptized, when on the point of being taken out to be beheaded. Now there was a universal feeling of sorrow; and the masses were sung, with the organ, as for a Lord and Inca.

On the 9th day all the funeral honours were repeated, the religious coming to join in the vigils and masses of their own accord; from which it may be inferred that the Inca is with God our Lord.

When the head was cut off, it was put on a spike, and set up on the same scaffold in the great square, where the execution had taken place. There it became each day more beautiful, the Inca having had a plain face in life. The Indians came by night to worship the head of their Inca. At last, one night, towards the dawn, Juan Sierra[1] came to his window and saw the idolatries practised by the people. He reported it to Don Francisco de Toledo, who then ordered the head to be taken down and buried with the body. This was done with no less solemnity than on the occasion of the interment of the body. Thus the inconvenience of the Inca's head being worshipped by the people was avoided. In this city there is a monk of our Lady of Mercy, named Father Nicolas de los dichos, who witnessed all I have here related, touched it with his hands, trod there with his feet, and heard everything. Your Excellency can well inform yourself from him, as he possesses a very good memory, and is an excellent authority on all these events, being an eye-witness of good repute[2].

---

[1] Juan Sierra de Leguizamo. See p. 219 and footnote.

[2] The judicial murder of the Inca Tupac Amaru was a blunder as well as a crime. King Philip II seems to have heard of it in-

Returning to our subject, which is to give an account to
your Excellency of the disposition of the land and the
government of the province of Vilcapampa, I have to
inform your Excellency that this land covers more than
300 leagues, with much fertile and fairly level spaces. The
discovered and conquered part is suited for the cultivation
of sugar cane in the valleys, with an annual rent making a
large sum of money. For one inhabitant alone, named
Toribio de Bustamante, has an annual rent, free of all
demands, of $10,000. He is a man who has built two
houses in Cuzco for God and his servants, a grand thing,
much to be admired. One is a monastery for bare foot
Franciscans, all complete with ornaments necessary for the
performance of divine service. The best part of his labours
is for the adornment of the church; for all wood work for
the doors, windows and chapels is of very fine cedar from
the province of Vilcapampa. At present he is building a
convent for Dominican nuns of our Lady of the remedies
which, when finished, will not be less curious and perfect
than the monastery for the bare foot Franciscans. These
are heroic works, worthy of praise throughout the world,

---

directly, most probably through the ecclesiastical dignitaries who
protested against it. Judging from the narrative of Sarmiento the
Viceroy kept silence. Philip resented the action of Toledo, who was
disgraced on his return.

Tupac Amaru was the legitimate son of Inca Manco, grandson of
Huayna Ccapac, and the rightful Sovereign of Peru.

Dr Justiniani, the descendant of this Inca's sister, had a portrait of
Tupac Amaru in 1853 with these words under it—*Ccollanap Pachacamac ricuay auccacunac yahuarniy hichascancuta* (Creator of the
world behold how my enemies spill my blood).

The youthful Inca had two little daughters, Juana and Magdalena,
who found a refuge with Dr Loaysa, the Archbishop of Lima. Juana
married the Curaca of Surimani named Condorcanqui. Their
descendant Josè Gabriel Condorcanqui, Cacique or Curaca of
Surimani and Tungasuca, was born in 1742. He established his
claim to the Marquisate of Oropesa, before the Royal Audience of
Lima in 1770. Taking the name of Tupac Amaru he led the Indian
revolt in 1780, and suffered death by torture in the great square
of Cuzco on May 18th, 1781. Two of his sons were put to death with
him, and the youngest was sent to Spain and died in prison.

he having been a soldier who arrived very poor. Yet he has done such good work that many nobles and grandees of Spain could not have shown more generosity than this soldier. He had been kept a prisoner for more than two years by the savages on the island of Dominica, and was many times in danger of his life, especially when his captors had their drinking bouts. But it pleased God that a fleet of Castille should come to the island, and boats came on shore for water. He ran shouting to the Spaniards, with nothing on but plantain leaves, and thus he escaped to perform works so lofty and worthy that they deserve eternal memory. All this has happened from his being a citizen of San Francisco of the Victory of Vilcapampa.

Besides this soldier there are others who have factories of much grandeur and richness. The province is important both for its size and fertility. For this reason it may be understood why this land was chosen by the Incas, it being the richest and most opulent in all Peru.

This province has farms for coca, lands for wheat, barley, potatoes, *yucas* and all kinds of vegetables, and many hills containing rich lodes of silver, besides the mines on the hill of Huamani and Huamanape. A very great quantity of silver was taken out of these mines in the time of the Marquis Don Garcia Hurtado de Mendoza[1], and of Don Luis de Velasco[2], which largely increased the royal fifths of his Majesty. There have been years when they have yielded to the royal treasury over $30,000, with only 300 Indians subjected to forced labour; this being the total amount of labour for the mines, factories, and to cut wood and make charcoal. The 200 from the province of Andahuaylas the great[3], of the royal crown, and the 100 of the

---

[1] Viceroy from 1590 to 1596.

[2] Viceroy from 1596 to 1604.

[3] Andahuaylas is an extensive and fertile valley on the road from

province of Chumpivilcas from the *encomienda* of Don
Diego de Vargas de Carbazal were taken away as your
Excellency well knows. The 200 of Andahuaylas were
transferred to the quicksilver mines of Huancavelica by
order of the Count of Monterey[1], who was not informed of
the great injury this would cause to the royal fifths, and to
the settlers and owners of mines in this province. The
information should have come from the Governor and the
royal officers of Cuzco, where the fifths were calculated by
provision of the Viceroys, that they might have an annual
account of the fifths. Serious losses have been the result,
of which your Excellency may satisfy yourself by calling
for a return from the royal official judges of Cuzco, of the
fifths for each year. The truth will then be known.

There is in this province, most excellent Lord, a report
concerning great treasure in a *huaca* of the Incas of which
there are expectations that it will be discovered, our Lord
being served, together with a ravine yielding gold, called the
ravine of Purumata. From this place the Spaniards have
already taken a great quantity of very fine gold. Four
years ago a nugget was found the size of a hen's egg.
When the Camp Master Diego Garcia de Paredes was
Governor he took to Spain a purse full of bits of gold,
including the one just mentioned, that the King might see
them. These riches are not found owing to the want of
Indians; and it is desired beyond measure that, in the
time of your Excellency, favoured by the help of your
Excellency in granting some Indians for the province,
great riches may be found. It will be the most important
thing that has happened in this kingdom, for by it all these

Ayacucho to Cuzco. Ocampo calls it "the great" to distinguish
it from Andahuaylas "the little," a village south of Cuzco, now called
Andahuaylillas.

[1] Viceroy from 1604 to 1607, and predecessor of the Marquis of
Montes Claros to whom Ocampo addresses his narrative.

Indies and our Spain may return to that opulence and grandeur they enjoyed at the beginning, when these provinces of Peru were first discovered. There then went to Spain very powerful men by reason of their estates and possessions. When necessitous knights came to them to ask for charity, they gave it with minds greater than those of most men, not considering whether they or their children would be losers ; and they gave $3000 or $4000 to the necessitous, thinking nothing of it.

In these days a man's wealth is well placed, when he is not considered poor, and performs deeds worthy of praise. There was a knight, a citizen of Cuzco named Don Luis Palomino, who, having given a soldier as a present (Doña Mayor Palomino his sister being a maiden) a very handsome harpsichord, this cavalier gave in return 2000 *cestos* of coca placed in Potosi, at a time when coca was worth $12 to $14 the *cesto*. For this soldier rose from great poverty, but went back to Castille very rich and influential.

The same knight performed another piece of magnificence, publicly in the great square, being then an ordinary magistrate of the city of Cuzco. Being on horseback a soldier came to him and besought him to order an official to return his sword which he had taken from him on the previous night, and offered to let him have it back for a mark, which he did not care to pay. The good knight told him that such things were perquisites of the officials, and he took his own sword with a belt embroidered in gold and pearls, and all the fittings of silver gilt, and gave it to the soldier that the official might not lose his perquisite on the other sword, though this one was worth an ingot of silver. When the minister of justice saw the magistrate's very munificent act, he returned the soldier's sword without demanding any fee, and the soldier restored the rich sword to its master. These things deserve to be recorded in history and kept in eternal memory, for there is nothing

that shines so brightly as a generous mind doing a good
work.   As the theologians say, a good work has four
effects on him who performs it.   The first is to make him
good as the act he has performed is good.   The second is
to cure the vices which would lead him to act in a contrary
way.   The third and greater effect is to make him deserve
grace and glory.   The fourth is to give satisfaction for the
pain he may have to suffer in this world or in purgatory.
I could tell your Excellency many other things about the
prodigality of citizens in this kingdom, but I leave them in
order to avoid prolixity.

The province of Mañaries, most excellent prince, is one
of Indians friendly to our Spanish nation.   The people are
fair and well disposed, amatory both men and women, the
latter being very beautiful.   All are well and honestly
dressed.   Their country is very pleasant and fertile, with
extensive grounds, suited for growing all kinds of fruits,
and corn, excellent for sugar cane, with delightful rivers of
sweet water, abundant pastures for flocks and herds, and of
great extent.   The soldiers who enter it will do so without
shedding blood, skirmishes and encounters being un-
necessary, for they will be received with affability, love,
and charity.   Though they will have their arms, death,
cruelties and atrocities should not occur as in former times,
for they will be given what they want without resistance.
The occupation of this province would cause a large extension of the royal patrimony and sovereignty.

The reason that I am moved to say this is that I was
an eye-witness.   After the pacification of the province of
Vilcapampa and the foundation of the city, when all the
Indian population had become peaceful and quiet, two
captains with only two soldiers, named Captain Anton de
Alvarez and Captain Alonso Suarez, with Pedro Gudiño,
a Portuguese, and another soldier whose name I do not
remember, penetrated into the country of the Mañaries.

The people received them with much willingness and love, giving them plenty of food, *vacas de anta* (tapirs), peccaries, which have their navels on their backs, turkeys, ducks and other game, fish in great quantity. They were also regaled with yuca, mani, maize toasted and boiled, many delicious fruits of that land, especially from trees planted by the Indians yielding *paltas, guayavas, paccays,* quantities of almonds much larger and better than those of Castille, and trees of *cacao.*

The Indians showed themselves to be so affable and friendly that the four Spaniards brought an image of our Lady on canvas and, to commend them to God, they ordered the Indians to construct a small chapel. They did this, placed the picture in the chapel, and set up a great cross outside, on a heap of stones, and other smaller crosses inside. Here they prayed and commended themselves to God every morning and also in the afternoons. Seeing this devotion the Indians came to the chapel to perform acts of prayer, raising their hands to heaven and striking their breasts. The Spaniards rejoiced to see them so friendly and so desirous to become Christians. When these four soldiers went back to the province of Vilca-pampa, the principal chief, called *Apu,* which means lord or governor, prayed that they would receive them as their vassals ; and if they wanted to enter the province of Pilco-sones with arms, they could easily do so, as it was near. The chief gave his word that he would assist them in an enterprise against these warlike Indians. There were two reasons for this invasion. One was to make them Christians that they might know the word of God ; and the other was to stop the injuries done by the Pilcosones to the Mañaries.

After more than eight years the governor, owing to this report, wrote to Don Martin Henriquez, Viceroy of these kingdoms[1], asking for permission to go in person

---

[1] Viceroy from 1581 to 1583, the successor of Toledo.

to discover these provinces of the Pilcosones and Yscay-
singas, concerning which the Mañaries gave information to
the said captains Anton de Alvarez and Alonso Saurez.
He reported that he could raise a force, and he recapitu-
lated certain reasons for the enterprise being of service to
his Majesty.

About a hundred soldiers were raised in the city of
Cuzco and neighbouring valleys, besides mestizos, mulattos,
and free negroes. With these an entry might be made, for
the Spaniards are very good soldiers. Starting on our
enterprise from the valley of Quillapampa, we descended
the river in balsas and canoes made with great trouble and
cost, which appeared like an armed fleet. After having
navigated for four or five days, we lost them at some rapids
formed in the turns which the river makes, on rocks and
shoals, the Captain Anduaca, and several Spaniards, Indians,
and mulattos being drowned. There were lost also the
cash belonging to the Governor, the ornaments of the
Father Pedro de Cartagena of the Company of Jesus,
brother of Don Fernando de Cartagena, a citizen of Cuzco ;
and of Dr Montoya Romano, of the said Company. The
soldiers also lost much property. We landed on a beach
and held a council of war.

It was agreed that we should make a road through the
forest with wood knives and axes. We suffered from
hunger, exposure and cold, our clothes being torn to pieces
by thorns on the trees, and we were left without any covering or food. For it is a wild country without road. If
a hundred friendly Mañaries, who had been apprised by
the Governor that he was coming to conquer the Pilcosones,
had not come to our rescue we should all have perished.

Coming in search of us with two of their chiefs, they
brought us succour, and put us on the Inca road to the land
of the Pilcosones, with supplies.

If your Excellency would be served that in this time of

your government all that land should be conquered with little cost to his Majesty, you might nominate a General, Camp Master, and Officers. With all my grey hairs and advanced age I would take order to join the expedition. The roads in the jurisdiction of the city of Huamanca being open, the conquest would be easy, and the virile energy which God has given me, combined with industry and the experience I possess, would ensure the enterprise having a better result than before.

Treating of the Pilcosones I say, most excellent Lord, that we received information from a Pilcosone Indian, named Oparo, that we had arrived near their settlements. But he was treacherous, deserting us in the night. We were in a convenient place where we made a good fort, with trenches, bastions at the angles, and loopholes in all parts whence to discharge the arquebuses. The Pilcosone came with great demonstrations of peace, simulating profound humility, and bringing provisions for the camp. He promised the Governor obedience, and embraced him with smiles and professions of content. He also embraced me as Camp Master. In this kingdom it is the custom to give this title to principal and meritorious soldiers, there not being over many such in the militia. When we least expected it, one day at two in the afternoon, they gave us a volley of arrows and darts. They hit the Governor badly, and other soldiers, who went to guard the door of the fort, where he had stationed himself as a spirited and valiant knight.

The Governor was made into a San Sebastian with arrows that stuck in his *escaupil*. This is harness made of cotton cloth well stuffed with wool until it resists as well as steel. With a partisan in his hand (being a large man) he did more even than Mucius Scævola, wounding and killing with great valour and elevation of his knightly spirit ; showing him to be Hurtado and Mendoza by the heroic deeds which are worthy of eternal memory.

We were warned by the Mañaries of the great risk we ran from being so reduced in numbers and without resources. The shipwreck we suffered in the river caused the loss of property and supplies, and the death of soldiers We were torn by the forest, in want of food and the means of nourishing our bodies. The enemy was numerous. In the village called Hatun Pilcosone alone they were in overpowering force. For great and small had taken up arms, sending notice throughout the province, and they were a very warlike people.

It was, therefore, resolved to raise the camp, and retreat in all haste by the Inca road which the Mañaries had shown us. Leaving their province on one side, we entered our own, more that the Fathers of the Company might be placed in safety than from fear of our own lives. If we had not suffered such great losses of powder, shields, and muskets, we did not doubt that we should have conquered those people, even if they had been much more warlike than they were. According to the information we collected, and from a sight of their farms and cultivation, and of the many flocks, and the lay of the land, it appeared to us that they were a hill people, in a country of very great mineral wealth, and that there were also people of the valleys where there was a marvellous climate for the cultivation of grains and sugar cane. It is land with abundant streams of water, and a great river having quantities of fish.

Returning to our campaign, most excellent Lord, if we had not been rescued and guided by those friends, not a single one of us would have come out alive, owing to the overpowering numbers of our enemies, who would have inflicted cruel deaths upon us without sparing one. God our Lord delivered us from that danger[1].

---

[1] The Mañaries and Pilcosones were two forest tribes near the skirts of the mountains, between the rivers Vilcamayu and Apurimac in their lower courses. The Mañaries are mentioned by Sarmiento as

It is eight years, most excellent Lord, since we were
visited by the worst calamity it was possible for us to suffer,
over and above the misfortunes and labours this city has
had to endure, caused by the necessity for changing the
site which has already been mentioned. In this province
there are many factories all peopled by African slaves,
whose disposition is soul-less, without God or conscience.
We saw six Spaniards and one priest (nephew of the precentor Don Cristóval de Albornoz), engaged in a great
conflict, the commencement of a general rising of negroes
of all the factories in the valleys of Quillapampa, Hondará,
Amaypampa and Huayupampa[1]. They were working in
concert with the negroes of Cuzco, Arequipa, and Huamanca, that they might enter into that land and convert it
into another Vallano, of which your Excellency will have
had notice. I received warnings as Magistrate of the Holy
Brotherhood, a post I then held, and had done for 14 years
with orders from the Viceroy, Marquis of Cañete and Don
Luis de Velasco, which I now submit. I had ordered the
imprisonment of a woman, wife of a negro highwayman,
and of another Indian woman who was apprehended in
a sugar cane farm, by my order, because they had murdered
their two Indian husbands and a free mulatto, robbing them
of their clothes and their provisions in the farms where
they were killed. The actual murderers were an Indian
Pilcosone named Francisco Chichima, and a negro slave of
the widow of Melchior del Pero, who had a factory there.

I had them in irons, and threatened that next day they
would be quartered unless they told me where were their
husbands. The negress, fearing death, and having seen
justice executed on the others that same night, the captain
Nicolas de Ormachea being with me, a person who possessed

occupying country near the banks of the Tono. I have not met with
the name of Pilcosones in any other writer.

[1] Huayupata?

a large estate, she called to him, and begged him to ask me not to quarter her if she told a truth which involved the lives of all the owners of factories and mayor-domos, besides many others. I went to where the prisoners were secured, and asked the said captain Ormachea what the negress had told him, although I had heard everything. He answered that she was a drunken lying creature who did not know what she was saying. In order to find out the truth I used flattering words, telling her that if she would speak the truth I would not only release her, but also give her liberty in the name of his Majesty. She then told me that, in the middle of that night, all the negroes of Ormachea and of Toribio de Bustamente, and those of the widow of Melchior del Pero and of all the other factories in the valleys of Hondará, Amaypampa, and Huayupampa, had conspired among themselves, and, with the negroes of the cities of Cuzco, Arequipa, and Huamanca, to rise that night.

This they actually did, burning the houses and factory of Toribio de Bustamente, whom they intended to have killed. That night they killed 24 Indians and a chief who came to put out the fire. Then they intended to kill Toribio de Bustamente, and four Spaniards and a priest who were with him. Next, at midnight, they would attack Captain Ormachea and all that were with him.

Asking her how she knew this, she declared on oath that on Sundays and festivals when the negroes assembled for drinking bouts, they talked in their mother tongue, and went about to collect arms and stores of maize, *mani*, and *oca* which they had in granaries in the forests.

Using good diligence I sent the tidings to the Governor Diego de Aquilar y de Cordova at Vilcapampa by two Indians who were very well paid, and two negroes born in the house. The latter never appeared again, for they were killed and thrown into the river. But the Indians, knowing the country, reached Vilcapampa and gave the message.

As soon as succour arrived we made a wooden fort, in which we assembled a number of Indian natives, posting sentries that we might not be taken by surprise. Here we were besieged for 30 days, defending ourselves with muskets and other arms. The Indians pointed out to us the direction from the top of the fort, without showing their faces. The Governor Don Diego de Aquilar y Cordova sent 50 well armed soldiers with their muskets, ammunition, and a good supply of cheese, biscuit, dried mutton, maize, and other things; also a number of friendly Indians with bows and arrows. With this we were able to raise the seige and put down the mutiny. For certain reasons given by Toribio de Bustamente, who was then building the bare foot monastery at Cuzco, the negroes cutting cedars and other trees for the work, justice was only executed on eight or ten of the ringleaders, and on the Pilcosone Indian, Francisco Chichima, who was one of the murderers, and the most bellicose Indian we ever had to do with in our time. His valour was such that the negroes themselves chose him as their captain, and obeyed his orders, though generally Indians were down-trodden by the negroes, with ill-treatment both of word and deed. So that the Indians called the negroes their lords, and the negroes called the Indians dogs. Such was the bravery of this Francisco Chichima that, being alone, and the negroes so many, he was their captain and chief, and they obeyed him in all things, and feared him like death.

To this city of Vilcapampa, when it was first peopled, there came the monks of our Lady of Mercy and founded a convent. They were given land for building and for sowing. They built a living house and a church where they said mass. They were more than 15 years established there, being the Fathers Friars Juan de Rivas, Francisco Guerrero, Nicolas Gomez, and Gonzalo de Toro Cavallero. As they had no servants, nor labourers to cultivate the land, nor even one to bring them a jar of water, they agreed in council to abandon that place, leaving the ornaments, chalices, bells, and images in charge of a secular priest. They went from that province to Cuzco, and to this day the church is there. Though they have tried to return four or five times, for great devotion is felt for these fathers, being the first monks, servants of our Lady, who planted the faith in these kingdoms of Peru, Chili, Tucuman, Paraguay, and Santa Cruz de la Sierra, but as they had no servants, they did not come back for fear they should die of hunger. The other religious communities saw that the fathers of our Lady of Mercy had given up the place, and no others have come lest they should be in the same straits as the said fathers. Hence this city remains with only a parish church. The inhabitants cannot hear mass early as they would wish, but only when it is said in the parish church. This is an intolerable grievance which ought to be remedied. The monastery of our Lady of Mercy should be re-established, for it would be a great boon to the citizens. If your Excellency would order some servants and labourers to be granted, the desired result could be secured.

All that I have written until now, most excellent Prince, is what I have been well able to recollect respecting things far back but within my weak memory. I understand that I have related the events nearly as they happened, but describing only the soul of those things which are most pleasant to hear about. I am well able to describe the parades, reviews, and other imitations of war which took place in the city of Cuzco previous to the despatch of that expedition, and to depict to your Excellency the great and celebrated festivals which took place, including bull fights, tournaments, and other displays[1]. There were imitations

---

[1] These festivities are in the wrong place. They were celebrated before the Viceroy Toledo became "an execrable regicide" as the Inca pedigrees call him.

of Moorish castles, forests of very lofty trees that seemed to reach the sky, set up in the great square of Cuzco. Among the trees were fastened tigers, lions, bears, peacocks, tapirs, large and small monkeys, armadillos, ferrets, ducks of varied plumage, macaws and parrots green, red, blue, brown and yellow, talking parrots of different kinds, small paroquets, and other birds of many colours, large and small. They were subtly fastened in the trees, and all made such resounding music as enchanted every one. There was a fountain from which mountain girls and others drew their jars of water. Then the Moors issued from their castle and captured the girls. Then, after the tournaments, all the knights made skirmishes against the Moors, taking them prisoners and releasing the Christian captives. The show was very pleasant and delightful for those who witnessed it from the windows and balconies, as well as for those who saw it standing in the square. Don Francisco de Toledo jousted with canes on that day, which added much to the pleasure and enjoyment of the people. It was the day of St John the Baptist. The costumes and liveries were very costly, adorned with gold and silver, very rich harness inlaid with pearls and precious stones. The bars within which the knights made mimic war were adorned with silver. There came forth 48 knights from among the most distinguished in the kingdom. The Lord Viceroy was on the most beautiful horse for prancing and speed, yet the safest, gentlest, and most loyal that was ever born of a mare. They called it the hobby of the silver feet, for it had white marks from below the knees, and one on the forehead, which added to its beauty, all the rest of the body being dark chestnut, with the finest tail that ever was seen in a horse. As the Viceroy's companions there came the following knights :

Ayala, Gonzalo Mexia de, second son of the Count of La Gomera (the elder),

Barrasa, Francisco de, the Viceroy's Chamberlain,

Berrio, Juan de,

Berrio, Miguel de,

Carbajal, Pablo de,

Carrasco, Pablo Alonso, now of the order of Santiago,

Castilla[1], General Geronimo, of the order of Santiago,

Davila, the Governor Melchior Vasquez,

Dolmos, Captain Martin, of the order of Santiago,

Esquivel, Captain Rodrigo de,

Figueroa, Don Geronimo, the Viceroy's nephew,

Frias, General Geronimo de,

Grado, Captain Francisco de,

Loaysa[2], Captain Alonso, cousin of the Archbishop of Lima,

Loaysa, Don Geronimo,

Maldonado, the Governor Juan Alvarez,

Manuel, Pedro Nuñez,

Marañon, Don Geronimo, a much esteemed knight,

Mendoza, Captain Nuño de,

Meneses, Captain Martin de,

Nocedo, Pedro Castilla de,

Orozco, Sancho de, brother of the Loaysas,

Pacheco, Captain Geronimo,

Palomino, Don Luis,

Pancorvo, Juan de, citizen of Cuzco,

Pereyran, Captain Don Antonio de,

Quinos, Captain Juan de,

---

[1] Geronimo Castilla was a native of Zamora. He was a magistrate of Cuzco and owned the estate of Asillo in the Collao. His name occurs frequently in the civil wars. His descendant was created Marquis of San Juan de Buena Vista.

[2] Alonso de Loaysa, nephew of the first Archbishop of Lima, was concerned in the civil wars, and went through strange adventures, especially on his wedding day at Cuzco, when the house was attacked by the rebels under Giron. His uncle the Archbishop was a native of Talavera of good family. Another uncle was Archbishop of Seville, and another confessor to Charles V.

Salas de Valdas, the Factor Juan de, brother of Cardinal
  Don Fernando de Valdas, Archbishop of Seville,
Sanchez, Miguel, the Treasurer,
Silva, Don Juan de, of the order of Santiago,
Sotomayor, Juan de, of the order of Santiago,
Suaso, Lope de,
Tordoya, Don Gomez de,
Umaran, Captain Julian de,
Valençuela, Gonzalo Hernandez de, son of Miguel
  Sanchez,
Valveorde, Francisco de, of the order of Santiago,

and other very distinguished knights whose names I cannot
remember, all the rest being citizens of Cuzco. There were
also others of the household of the Viceroy, and representatives of other cities, people of condition.

There came out, at the turn into the square, six cava-
liers attired as very ferocious demons, and behind their
horses there were other demons made of paste, seated in
their saddles with very short stirrups, looking as if they
had been born on horseback, going shoulder to shoulder.
These also tilted with the cane lance. Next came a boy
aged twelve years, dressed in the finest brocade, with the
mitre of a bishop made of cloth of silver, with gloves made
in the city, and many rings of emeralds set in gold, on his
fingers. He went along, on a mule, giving benedictions,
with his face behind and his back in front. Further back
there came six sheep in the dress of choristers, mounted on
horseback, with singing books in their hands. They were
made to give out groans by means of cords, raising and
lowering the song according to the ideas of those who had
charge of the affair. Next came I know not how many
satyrs very well attired, and last came a *Hirco* dressed
all in crimson, with his shirt and cloak of a black colour,
bordered with velvet, and a cap of the same. He had

a crown of gilt paste, and a gilt sword. Many servants
followed.

After having paraded round the square, they took up
their positions in order for entering the lists. The game
then commenced, the Viceroy coming first, who only ran
three courses. He then dismounted and went up to the
corredor of Diego de los Rios, a citizen and principal
cavalier. From thence his Excellency witnessed the tilting.
Afterwards they let out a most ferocious bull, one of the
bravest I ever saw, which took charge for a long time. At
last it went in among the trees where it saw the wild
beasts. It attacked the tiger with great impetus and fury.
As the beast was tied up very short it could not well use
its claws, nor take advantage of its superior quickness ; but
it defended itself, also taking the offensive, until the bull
was so tired and baffled that it gave up the encounter and
came out again into the square, where it was irritated by
the bull baiters until darkness put an end to the amuse-
ments and rejoicings. For a long time people talked of
nothing else.

One would wish, most excellent Lord, to have the
eloquence of that great orator Cicero, and the wisdom of
Solomon, so as to be able to shape this history into a neat
and pleasant style, and in language so that all the world
would be pleased with it. I must be satisfied if your
Excellency will receive it with your benign consideration,
and excuse the faults which I have made, numerous as
they must be. I supplicate that it may be thus received.
If I have been prolix in my narration, I submit that I may
be pardoned because in a history of the events which have
occurred in this kingdom I could do no less ; this requiring
the cream of the truth. There is, in this city, an old monk
of the order of Mercy, as I have said before, who was an
eye-witness of all these things, and heard them with his
ears, and touched them with his hands. I have made bold

to mention him, because your Excellency could get from him some more particulars, as he is younger than I am, and would remember things that I have forgotten. I have done my duty without stating anything that is unauthentic, or that may be wide of the truth. I have eschewed fabulous things for fear of losing the esteem of sensible men, for this course is advantageous, though the vulgar may not think so. For my straightforward procedure I await your Excellency's full approval, and hope for it. For besides having served their Majesties the Kings our Lords, your Excellency will have performed one of the most meritorious acts of mercy that can be done in this life, by recognizing my loyal service, in having given the flower of my youth to my Kings and Lords, until these last years which find me in poverty and old age. For this approval may our Lord grant to your Excellency the greatest felicity in this life, and in the life to come may you find eternal rest for ages and ages.

Amen.

PLACE NAMES.

Abancay, capital of the province. Nearly the same latitude as Cuzco. Height about 8,300 ft. There was a battle here between Orgoñez and Alvarado, 13 July, 1537, 220

Accha, in the province of Paruro (dept. of Cuzco) near the right bank of the Apurimac. Molina spells it Aycha (174, 176), 208

Acos, 10 to 11 leagues from Cuzco according to Sarmiento. Acomayu is now a province. Most of the people were moved by the Inca to Acobamba, 109

Acobamba, now the capital of the province of Angaraes (dept. Huancavelica), 109

Ahua-chumbi. *See* Avachumpi.

Ahuatuna (Aguatona), on one of the roads to the forests of Anti-suyu, 142

Ahuayro-cancha, a town of the Ayamarcas near Cuzco, to which the Inca's kidnapped son was taken, 75

Alayde, Huayna Ccapac at, 159

Alcabisas, one of the original tribes settled in the valley of Cuzco. The Incas had some trouble with them, 59, 60; crushed by Manco Ccapac 62; and finally subdued by Mayta Ccapac. *See* Cieza de Leon, ii. 105, 106, Balboa, 25, 26. Balboa has Allcay-villcas, 40, 58, 66, 67

Amaru, on one of the roads to the forests of Anti-suyu, 75, 142

Amaru-cancha, in Cuzco. Palace built by Huascar. *Amaru* a serpent, *cancha* a place, 170

Amaru-mayu, river, 144

Amaybamba, valley of, 239

Ancamarca, subdued by Huayna Ccapac, 161

Ancasmarca, 4 leagues from Cuzco, subdued by Ccapac Yupanqui, 69

Anco-mayu, country as far as, desolated by the Incas. Northern limit of the empire, 31, 161, 166

Anco-yacu, bridge over the river between Huanta and Acobamba. Defeat of the army of Huascar at, 174, 175

Andahuaylas, capital of the modern department of Apurimac. There are three villages in the beautiful and fertile valley, Andahuaylas, Talavera, and San Geronima. The river flows north to the Pampas. This valley was the original home of the powerful tribe of Chancas. It is on the road from Ayacucho to Cuzco, between the Pampas and Pachachaca river, xviii, 86, 87, 231, 232

Andahuaylas el chico, now called Andahuaylillas, owing to Chancas from Andahuaylas having been settled there, 22 miles S.S.W. of Cuzco, in the province of Quispicanchi. It is in an oval valley, nearly level, 18 miles long by 3 to 6 wide watered by rills from the surrounding mountains, which collect in a single stream and reach the Vilcamayu—the valley was once, no doubt, a lake, 232

Andes, the chains of mountains or *cordilleras* in Peru ; so called from the *anduaria* or terraced cultivation, 8, 34, 133, 193

Anta, capital of a province, about 7 miles N.W. of Cuzco. The little town is on the side of a hill facing north, overlooking the great swampy plain of Sasahuana. A daughter of the Sinchi of Anta contrived the rescue of the Inca's little son Yahuar-huaccac, from the Ayamarcas. Antas to be called relations of the Incas. Viracocha Inca married a native of, 77, 81, 208

Antahuaylas. *See* Andahuaylas.
Antamarca, murder of Inca Huascar at, 189
Antasay, a tribe settled on the site of Cuzco, 40
Anti-suyu, the eastern division of the empire, V.L.B., 132, 159
Apurimac, the great river drains the coast *cordillera* from Canas to Lucanas receiving large tributaries from the south and east, Cayaruni, Catabamba, Huayllati, Pachachaca, Abancay, and Pampas. It finally unites with the Vilcamayu, forming the Ucayali. Flowing through a profound gorge it divides the country, and there is a famous cable bridge on the road from Cuzco westward, xxi, 70, 177, 238
Arapa, in the Collao, on the lake of Arapa ; in the modern province of Azangaro. O.B., 145
Araypalpa, province of Paruro, 208
Arequipa, 16° 24' S., 7,266 ft. above the sea. Founded 1534. Subjugated by the Collas. Visited by Huayna Ccapac. V.L.B., 66, 114, 159, 239
Asillo, in the Colla, province of Azangaro. V.L.B., 145, 244
Atacama, the coast desert between Peru and Chile, c.v. Under the dominion of the Collas. Huayna Ccapac in, 114, 159
Atañaris, Indians
Ataras, 208
Avachumpi Island, News of Tupac Inca's voyage to, 135, 136
Ayamarcas, a powerful tribe, 3 leagues S.S.W. of Cuzco, 64. V.L.M.P. Wife of Ccapac Yupanqui from, 69. War with the Huayllacans, 73. Kidnapping of the Inca's son; 74. His rescue, 77. Final subjugation by Pachacuti, 106, etc.
Ayavilla, in the valley of Cuzco, 83
Aymara, a tribe in the upper basin of the river Pachachaca, tributary of the Apurimac. Some Aymaras were taken as colonists (*mitimaes*) to the Collao, their children adopted the Colla dialect, and, through a blunder, the Jesuits at Juli gave the name to the Colla dialect, and later to the Collas themselves. None of the older writers give the name of Aymara to the Collas. Tributary to Pachacuti, 109

Bimbilla, a village where the mummies of Manco Ccapac and Sinchi Rocca were found, near Cuzco, 61, 63
Bombon, correctly Pumpu. Height on the right bank of the river Pampas, 174

Cabiñas. *See* Caviñas
Cacha, ruins of a remarkable temple in the basin of the upper Vilcamayu. Province of Canchis, below Sicuani. Viracocha's miracle at, 35. The temple is fully described by Squier (pp. 408 to 414)
Calca, capital of a province, in the valley of Vilcamayu. It includes the districts of Calca, Pisac, and Laris. Conquered by Viracocha, 85, 208. V.M.
Calis puquio, the ashes of Tupac Inca were found there, 154
Camal, conquered by Viracocha Inca, 85
Camata, on one of the routes into Anti-suyu, 143
Cañaris, a turbulent tribe near Tumipampa. Conquered by Tupac Inca, 131. Fight with the Cayambi chief, 164. At Cuzco in Spanish times, because they hated the Incas, 226. Executioner of Tupac Amaru, 226. V.L.B. Fable of their origin, 30.
Caquia Xaquixahuana. *See* Sacsahuana
Caranques, a warlike Quito tribe, in rebellion, 159
Carmenca, suburb of Cuzco, 82, 99, 207, 223, 226
Casacancha, conquered by Viracocha, 84
Casana, in Cuzco. Edifices built by Sinchi Rocca, 158
Caviñas, a tribe in the Vilcamayu valley, south of Urcos. Made tributary to Yahuar-huaccac, 81
Caxamarca, a province in Chinchaysuyu, 140, 165, 166, 173, 188, 219. Conquered by the Incas, 117, 118. Atahualpa at, 175
Cayambis, a warlike Quito tribe, in rebellion, 62, 159. Defeat the Inca, 162, 163. Siege, 163. Final rout, 164
Cayancachi, suburb of Cuzco, 40, 59, 60, 82
Cayara, a fortress in the Quichua province. Taken by Tupac Inca, 130

quest, 135. In rebellion, 159.
March of Huayna Ccapac to, 160,
Organized, 166. Huayna Ccapac
at, 165. Death at, 168. Atahualpa
at, 176
Quiuipay, headquarters of Atahualpa's generals near Cuzco, 181

Rarapa, body of Inca Rocca found
at, 72
Rimac-pampa, Huayna Ccapac at,
156. The most S. square in Cuzco
Rimac-tampu, 119, 209. *See also*
Limatambo
Rio, province in Anti-suyu, 143
Riobamba, army of Huascar defeated
by Atahualpa at, 172, 173
Rondo-cancha. *See* Runta-cancha
Runta-cancha, conquered for Vira-
cocha, 84. Five leagues from
Cuzco
Ruparupa, B. Flight of the Chancas
to, 117

Sacsahuana (Surita, Caquia Xaqui-
xahuana), 85, 86, 91, 95, 104, 184,
209. Battle of, 218
Sanaseras, first settlers in the valley
of Cuzco, 40, 57, 62.
Sanca-huasi, wild beasts kept in,
113
San Geronimo de Carama, 209
Saño, B., wife of Sinchi Rocca a
native of, 63
San Salvador, Peru, 209
San Sebastian, Cuzco cercado, 209
Sauseray, 40, 57, 62
Sayri-cancha, B. Division of land
at Cuzco between the rivers, 58
Sisiquilla–pucara, B. In Xauxa,
taken by Tupac Inca, 131
Simaponte, 221
Socma, subdued by Viracocha Inca,
85
Soras, L.B. Province of, attacked by
Pachacuti, 109, 174. In the
province of Lucanas, dept. Aya-
cucho
Surita (Sacsahuana), 104, 218
Susur-puquio, M. Pachacuti sees a
vision there, 90
Sutic-tocco, the side window at
Tambo-tocco, out of which came
the *ayllu* of that name, and also
the Tambos, 44, 45, 46

Tacucaray, native place of the wife
of Mayta Ccapac, 68
Tallanas, Indians brought news of
the Spaniards to Atahualpa, 186

Tambo, valley of, 103. *See* Ollantay-
tambo
Tambo-quiro, L. Second stage of
the march of Manco Ccapac to
Cuzco. Sinchi Rocca born there,
48
Tampucuncas, 64
Tampu-tocco, B., at Paccari-tambo.
A hill. Not, as Sarmiento says,
"the house of windows," but
"the window tavern." The
three windows out of which issued
Manco Ccapac, his brethren and
followers. A legend, 49, 50.
Visited by Pachacuti, 99. *See
also* Paccari-tampu
Tangarara, Spaniards at, 187. Name
disappeared. Same as Puira?
Taocamarca, conquered by Yahuar-
huaccac, 81
Tiahuanacu, V.L.B., 34, 37. Viceroy
resided at, 150. Huayna Ccapac
at, 159
Titicaca, island, V.L.B.M. "Rock of
lead." Viracocha created sun and
moon, 32, 159. Huayna Ccapac
at, 159
Tococachi, V. Body of Pachacuti
found in, 140
Toguaro, six leagues from Huancara.
Subdued by Pachacuti, 108
Tohara, B., fortress occupied by
Tupac Inca, 130
Tono, V., river in Anti-suyu, 143,
239
Truxillo, on the site of Chimu, 118,
131, 137, 206. Capital of dept.
Libertad, six provinces, Huama-
chuco, Otus-co, Pacasmayo, Patas,
Santiago de Chuco, Truxillo
Tumbez, V.L.B. Tupac Inca at, 135.
Huayna Ccapac at, 161. Spaniards
reported at, 186. "A Littoral
Province."
Tumipampa, V.L.S., 30. Arrival
of Tupac Inca at, 154. Huayna
Ccapac born at, 134, 158. Huayna
Ccapac's buildings at, 160. Death
of Ninan Cuyoche at, 168. Atahu-
alpa remained at, 172. Surprise
attack, 173, 181
Turuca, Tupac Inca at, 135

Umasayus, become tributary to
Pachacuti, 109, 177
Urco-colla, B., near Parcos, in the
Guamanga country. Inca army
valorously resisted at, 116. Con-
quered by Tupac Inca, 131
Urcos, V.L.M.O. Viracocha at, 36.

QUICHUA WORDS IN SARMIENTO.

	Incas	Coyas (Queens)	Ayllus (Lineages)	Huauqui (or familiar spirit)
1	Manco Ccapac, A.D. 565—665	Mama Ocllo, sister	Chima Panaca Ayllu	Indi (*bird*)
2	Sinchi Rocca, 665—684	Mama Cuca, of Saño	Raura Panaca	Huanachiri Amaru (*fish*)
3	Lloqui Yupanqui, 684—795	Mama Cava, of Uma	Avayni Panaca	Apu Mayta
4	Mayta Ccapac, 795—905	Mama Tacucaray, of Tacucaray	Usca Mayta Panaca	
5	Ccapac Yupanqui, 905—994	Ccuri-hilpay, of Ayamarca	Apu Mayta Panaca	
6	Inca Rocca, 994—1097	Mama Micay, of Huayllacan	Vicaquirau Panaca	
7	Titu Cusi Hualpa (Yahuar-huaccac), 1097—1193	Mama Chicya, of Ayamarca	Aucaylli Panaca	
8	Viracocha Inca, 1193—1294	Mama Runtucaya, sister	Socso Panaca	Inca Amaru
9	Inca Yupanqui Pachacuti, 1294—1397	Mama Anahuarqui, of Choco, sister	Inaca Panaca	Chuqui Ylla
10	Tupac Inca Yupanqui, 1397—1464	Mama Chimpa Ocllo, sister	Ccapac	Cusi Churi
11	Huayna Ccapac, 1464—1524	Cusi Rimay Coya s. p. Araua Ocllo	Tumipampa Panaca	Huaraqui Inca
12	Huascar Inca, 1524—1533	Chucuy Huypa	Huascar Panaca	
13	Manco Inca, crowned by Pizarro 24 March 1534, *ob.* 1544	Ataria Cusi Huarcay, niece		
14	Sayri Tupac, *ob.* 1560	Cusi Huacutay		
15	Tupac Amaru, *ob.* Dec. 1571			

The chronology for Nos. 1—11 is according to Sarmiento.

INCAS LIVING IN 1572.

Ayllu or Gens:

The 10 Companies which came from Paccari-tampu with Manco Ccapac,
46, 47

  1. *Chauin Cuzco.* From Ayar Cachi   ⎫ Brothers of
  2. *Arayraca Cuzco-Callan.* From Ayar Uchu ⎭ Manco Ccapac.
  3. *Tarpuntay.*
  4. *Huacaytaqui.*
  5. *Sañoc.*
  6. *Sutic-tocco.*
  7. *Maras.*
  8. *Cuycusa.*
  9. *Masca.*
 10. *Oro.*

The 12 *Ayllus* or Lineages from the 12 Incas

  1. *Chima Panaca*   from *Manco Ccapac,* 62.
  2. *Raura Panaca*   ,,   *Sinchi Rocca,* 63.
  3. *Avayni Panaca*   ,,   *Lloqui Yupanqui,* 65.
  4. *Usca Mayta Panaca* ,,   *Mayta Ccapac,* 68.
  5. *Apu Mayta Panaca*   ,,   *Ccapac Yupanqui,* 70.
  6. *Vicaquirau Panaca*   ,,   *Inca Rocca,* 72.
  7. *Aucaylli Panaca*   ,,   *Yahuar-huaccac,* 81.
  8. *Socso Panaca*   ,,   *Viracocha,* 86.
  9. *Inaca Panaca*   ,,   *Pachacuti,* 139.
 10. *Ccapac Ayllu Panaca* ,,   *Tupac Yupanqui,* 154.
 11. *Tumipampa Panaca* ,,   *Huayna Ccapac,* 169.
 12. *Huascar Panaca*   ,,   *Huascar,* 189.

83 INCAS LIVING IN 1572.

(NAMES GIVEN BY SARMIENTO.)

† Witnesses to the History, 39.
‡ Witnesses also in the lists under each Inca, 12.

Aclari, Cristóval (Cuycusa Ayllu), 46
Amaru Titu (Socso Panaca), 86
Ampura Llama Oca, Don Gonzalo (Maras Ayllu), 46
†Ancay, Don Garcia (Avayni Panaca), 197
‡†Anti Hualpa Don Francisco (Socso Panaca), 198
†Apu Mayta, Don Juan (Apu Mayta Panaca), 198
†Apu Riuti, Don Garcia, 199
Avca Michu Avra Sutic, Don Francisco (Sutic-tocco Ayllu), 46
Avcaylli Titu Putisuc (Avayni Panaca) 65
Ayachi, Don García (Ccapac Ayllu), 154
†Ayallilla, Don Carlos, 199

‡†Cayo, Don Diego (Inaca Panaca), 198
Cayo Hualpa, Don Diego (Raura Panaca), 197
‡†Chalco Yupanqui, Don Francisco (Socso Panaca), 86, 198
Checo, Don Diego (Chima Panaca), 62
Chima Huarhua, Don Juan (Chima Panaca), 62
Chucumbi, Martin (Chima Cuzco Ayllu), 46
Cocasaca, Don Francisco (Apu Mayta Panaca), 70
Concha Yupanqui, Don Juan (Aucaylli Panaca), 81
Conde Mayta, Don Agustin (Avayni Panaca), 65
†Copca Mayta, Don Francisco (Apu Mayta Panaca), 198
†Cota Yupanqui, Don Francisco (Inaca Panaca), 198

†Cozco, Don Juan (Ccapac Ayllu Panaca), 198
Cusi Hualpa, Don Cristóval (Apu Mayta Panaca), 70

†Hachacoma, Don Pedro (Vicaquirau Panaca), 198
†Huacanqui, Don Gonzalo (Inaca Panaca), 198
Hualpa, Don Alonso (Sutic-tocco Ayllu), 46
†Hualpa, Hernando (Avayni Panaca), 197
†Hualpa Yupanqui, Don Juan (Inaca Panaca), 198
Huaman Mayta, Don Antonio (Vicaquirau Panaca), 72
Huaman Paucar, Don Diego (Chauin Cuzco Ayllu), 46
Huaman Rimachi Hachicona, Don Francisco (Vicaquirau Panaca), 72

Illac, Don Juan (Inaca Panaca), 139
Inguil, Don Felipe (Inaca Panaca), 139
Inguil Tupac, Don García (Tumipampa Panaca), 169

Llama Oca, Don Alonso (Maras Ayllu), 46

†Mayta, Don Diego (Vicaquirau Panaca), 198

†Ninan Coro, Don Francisco (Tumipampa Panaca), 198

†Pascac, Don Domingo (Inaca Panaca), 198
Paucar Aucaylli, Don Gonzalo (Aucaylli Ayllu), 81

NAMES OF INDIANS IN SARMIENTO.

GODS—HUACAS—IDOLS OF INCAS.

BIBLIOGRAPHY OF PERU.

A.D. 1526—1907.

PART I.

CHRONOLOGICALLY ARRANGED.

1907.

BIBLIOGRAPHY.

NOTE. The following Bibliography is not exhaustive, but is intended to elucidate references in this volume.

1526.

1. **Fernández de Oviedo y Valdés,** Gonzalo.—Oviedo de la natural hystoria de las Indias. ff. 52.
   Por industria de maestre Remõ de Petras: en la cibdad de Toledo, MDXXVI. fol.
   [G. 6268.—With a large plate of the arms of Charles V on the title-page.]

1527.

2. **Valera,** Diego de.—La cronica de España abreviada por mandado dla catholica & muy poderosa Señora doña Isabel Reyna de Castilla &cetera. Por mossen Diego de Valera. ff. 100. [With the coat of arms of Charles V on the title.] MS. NOTES.
   Fue impressa...en Sevilla en casa de Juan varela de Salamanca, 1527. fol.
   [C. 62. f. 3.—With the coat of arms in gold, on the covers, and with the book-plate, of Joachim Gomez de la Cortina, Marqués de Morante.—1542. K. 179. f. 16.—1562. 9180. h. 7.]

1533.

3. **Pizarro,** Hernando.—Carta de Hernando Pizarro a los magníficos señores, los señores oidores de la audiencia real de S. M., que reside en la ciudad de Santo Domingo. ([Nov. 1533.] Sacada de Oviedo, que la inserta en el cap. 15 de su parte tercera, ó lib. 43 de su *Historia General* [which exists only in manuscript].)
   See 1535, No. 11; 1547, No. 21; 1830, No. 158.

4. **Sancho,** Pedro.—Testimonio de la Acta de reparticion del rescate de Atahualpa, otorgado por el escribano Pedro Sancho. 1533.
   See 1830, No. 159.

1534.

5. **Peru.**—Copia delle Lettere del Prefetto della India la nova Spagna detta, alla Cesarea Maesta rescritte. Alla Sereniss. & Catho. Maestra Cesarea. E arrivata una nave, &c. (fol. 73 & 74 of "Isolario di Benedetto Bordone." ff. 74). [With the news of the Conquest of Peru by Francisco Pizarro.]
   Impresse in Vinegia per Nicolo d' Aristotile, detto Zoppino, nel mese di Giugno, del MDXXXIIII. fol.
   [571. i. 23.]

6. **Peru.**—Nouvelles certaines des Isles du Péru. [An account of the Conquest of Peru by Francisco Pizarro.] 8 leaves. **𝕮.𝕷.**
   On les vend à Lyon ches Fräcoys Juste devāt Nostre dame de Confort, 1534· 12°.
   [G. 6492. (1).]

7. **Spain.**—Newe Zeytung aus Hispanien und Italien. 4 leaves. **𝕭.𝕷.**
   [With the news of the Conquest of Peru by Francisco Pizarro.]
   [*Nürnberg,*] *Mense Februario,* 1534· 4°.
   [C. 32. d. 4.—Purchased July 1, 1853.]

8. **West Indies.**—Libro Ultimo del Summario delle Indie Occidentali.
   (Libro Ultimo del Summario de le cose de le Indie occidentali, dove si narra di tutto quello ch' è stato fatto nel Arovar la provincia de Peru, over del Cusco, chiamata hoggi nuova Castiglia, dalli capitani del Imperatore.) 15 leaves.
   In Vinegia, Del mese d' Ottobre, MDXXXIIII. 4°.
   [G. 6907.—9771. bb. 10. From the Library of Henry Stevens, of Vermont, F.S.A., with his book-plate, 1882, and with a facsimile by J. Harris of the rare map, "La carta universale della terra ferma & Isole delle Indie occidětali...cavata da due carte da navicare fatte in Sibilia da li piloti della Majesta Cesarea. Del mese di Dicembre MDXXXIIII." 17¼ × 21½ inches.—The Libro Ultimo forms Book III of a Summary of Pietro Martire d' Anghiera, Gonzalo Fernandez de Oviedo y Valdés, & other writers.]

9. **Xéres,** Francisco de.—[Verdadera Relacion de la Conquista del Peru, y Provincia del Cuzco, llamada la nueva Castilla...Embiada a su majestad por Francisco de Xerez, natural...de Sevilla, secretario del sobre dicho señor (Francisco piçarro), &c.—La relaciõ del viage que hizo el señor capitan Hernādo piçarro por mādado del señor governador su hermano desde el pueblo de Caxamalca a Parcama y de alli a Xauxa. (Por Miguel de estete.)] With 42 five-line stanzas relating to the author, at the end, by Gonzalo Fernández de Oviedo y Valdés. 19 unnumbered leaves.
   Impressa en casa de Bartholome perez en el mes de Julio: Sevilla, 1534· fol.
   [C. 33. m. 4.—Wanting the title-page, which has been supplied in facsimile by John Harris.]

10. **Zhaval.**—LETERA DE La nobil cipta : novamente ritrovata alle Indie con li costumi & modi del suo Re & soi populi : Li modi del suo adorare con la bella usanza de le donne loro : & de la dua ꝑ sone ermafrodite donate da quel Re al Capitano de larmata. El V. S. V. Al suo D. L. S. Data in Peru adi. XXV. de Novembre. Del. MDXXXIIII. [4 leaves. Without the woodcut of the 1535 edition.] 1534· 4°.
    [G. 7173.—There is a copy in the John Carter Brown Library, Providence, Rhode Island.] *See* 1535, No. 14; 1700, No. 119; 1850, No. 172.

1535.

11. **Fernández de Oviedo y Valdés,** Gonzalo.—La historia general de las Indias. (Escripta por el capitan gonçalo hernandez de Oviedo y Valdes.) ff. 193.
    En la emprēta de Juan Cromberger: Sevilla, 1535. fol.
    [C. 20. d. 4.—From the Library of Sir Joseph Banks. With a fine engraved title-page, with the arms of Charles V, and the Pillars

of Hercules, surrounded by an ornamental border. On fol. cxciii
is the autograph signature of the author, and on the *verso* is a large
plate of the author's coat of arms.]

12. **Xéres**, Francisco de.—Libro Primo de la Conquista del Peru & provincia del Cuzco de le Indie occidentali (per Francesco de Xerez...
Tradotta novaměte in lingua Italiana per Dominico de Gaztelu gentilhomo Spagnolo de la citta de Tudela del reame de Navarra secretario
del illustrissimo signor don Lope de Soria cŏsigliero & imbasciadore
della prefata Cesarea Majesta.—La Relatione del Viaggio che fece il
Signore capitano Ferdinando Picciarro per comandamento del signor
Governatore suo fratello de la terra de Caxamalca fina a Parcama & de
li a Xauxa. (Per Michael de Stette.) Con gratia & privilegio per
anni X. 62 unnumbered leaves.

Stampato in Vinegia per Maestro Stephano da Sabio del MDXXXV.
Nel mese di Marzo.

[G. 6338.—K. 145. a. 11.—On the title are the arms of Charles V,
with the Pillars of Hercules, and on the *verso* of fol. 2 are the arms
of Domenico de Gaztelu.]

13. **Xéres**, Francisco de.—Libro Primo de la Conquista del Peru & Provincia
del Cuzco de le Indie occidentali. (Traducta novamente in lingua
Italiana per Dominico de Gaztelu, gentilhomo Spagnolo, de la citta
de Tudela, del reame de Navara, secretario de...don Lope de Soria,
cŏsiglierio & imbasciadore de la p̄fata Cesarea Majesta...Allo illustrissimo & Serenissimo Principe messer Andrea Gritti Dominico de
Gaztelu salute & felicita perpetua.)—La relatione del viaggio che fece
il Signore Capitano Ferdinando Piciarro per comădaměto del signor
Governatore suo fratello de la terra de Caxamalca fin a Parcama & de
li a Xauxa. (Per Michael de Stette.) 40 unnumbered leaves.

*Impresso in Milano per Domino Gotardo da Ponte a compagnia de
Domino Io. Ambrosio da Borsano nel Anno del Mille cinquecento
e trentacinque.* [1535.] 4°.

[9781. b. 22.—With the arms of Charles V, and the Pillars of
Hercules, on the title, and the arms of Dominico de Gaztelu on
the *verso* of fol. 2.—Purchased June 10, 1857.]

14. **Zhaval.**—Lettera de La nobil Citta nuovamente ritrovata alle Indie con
li suoi costumi & modi del suo Re & soi popoli : Li modi del suo
adorare con la bella usanza delle donne loro. Et de le dua persone
ermafrodite donate da quel Re al Capitano della Armata. Il V. S. V.
Al suo D. L. S. Data in Zhaval. Adi XXV. di Settembre, MDXXXV.
[4 leaves. With a woodcut on the title-page.] 1535. 4°.

[G. 7174.—C. 32. h. 4. This copy is slightly cropped.—There is a
copy in the John Carter Brown Library, Providence, Rhode Island.]

See 1534, No. 10 ; 1700, No. 119 ; 1850, No. 172.

1538.

15. **Beuter**, Pedro Antonio.—Primera Part d'la historia de Valěcia q̃ tracta
de les Antiquitats de Spanya, y fundacio de Valěcia, ab tot lo discurs,
fins al těps q̃ lo inclit rey dŏ Jaume primer la cŏquista. Cŏpilada p̃ lo
reverět maestre, Pere Antoni Beuter, maestre en sacra theologia. ff. 70.
MS. NOTES.

Estampat en Valencia, Anno MDXXXVIII. fol.

[593. g. 18.]

16. **Mercadillo**, Alonso.—La Jornada del Capitán Alonso Mercadillo á los
Indios Chupachos é Iscaicingas. 1538.

See 1897, No. 272.

17. **Ravenna, Th.**—Mali Galeci sanandi, vini ligni, et aquae: unctionis, ceroti, suffumigii, praecipitati, ac reliquorum modi omnes. [With an account of Peru.] 33 leaves.

Per Nicolinis de Sabio: Venetis, 1538. 4º.

[Not in the British Museum.—Karl W. Hiersemann, *Katalog* 336. No. 1865. 1907.—Not in Brunet, Graesse, Harrisse or Lowndes.]

1539.

18. **Marineo, Lucio,** *Siculo.*—Obra Compuesta por Lucio Marineo Siculo Coronista ő sus Majestades de las cosas memorables de España. ff. 192.

En casa de Juan de Brocar: en la noble Villa de Alcala de Henares, Año de MDXXXIX. fol.

[K. 179. f. 20.—On the title-page are the arms of Charles V, with the Pillars of Hercules.]

1540.

19. **Andagoya, Pascual de.**—Relacion de los sucesos de Pedrarias Dávila en las provincias de Tierra firme ó Castilla del oro, y de lo ocurrido en el descubrimiento de la mar del Sur y costas del Perú y Nicaragua, escrita por el Adelantado Pascual de Andagoya.

See 1829, No. 154; 1865, No. 201.

1546.

20. **Beuter, Pedro Antonio.**—Primera Parte de la Coronica general de toda España, y especialmente del reyno de Valencia...Compuesta por el Dotor Pero Anton Beuter, Maestro en sacra Theologia. ff. 118.

Impresso en la muy noble ciudad de Valencia, en casa de Joan Mey Flandro, Año del Nascimiento de nuestro señor Jesu Christo, MDXLVI. fol.

[593. g. 1. (1).—From the Library of King Edward VI.]

1547.

21. **Fernández de Oviedo y Valdés, Gonzalo.**—Coronica de las Indias. La hystoria general de las Indias agora nuevamente impresa corregida y emendada. (Libros de los infortunios y naufragios de casos acaecidos en las mares de las Indias, yslas y tierra firme del mar oceano, con el qual se da fin a la primera parte de la general & natural hystoria de las Indias.—Libro XX. De la segunda parte de la general historia de las Indias...que trata del estrecho de Magallans.) Y con la conquista del Peru [por Francisco de Xéres]. 𝔊.𝔏. Pts. 1, 2.

Juan de Junta: Salamanca, 1547; *Francisco Fernandez de Córdova: Valladolid,* 1557. fol.

[C. 33. m. 3. (1).—This work was arranged for publication in three parts, forming together 50 "Libros," numbered consecutively. The "Libro de los infortunios y naufragios," of which chapters I.—XI. only are here printed with Part 1, was to form Libro L. No more was published after Book 1 of Part 2, which forms "Libro XX." of the entire work. The "Conquista del Peru" was bound up with this edition.—K. 146. e. 10. Another copy of Part 1.—G. 6269. Another copy of Part 2.—On the title-page of Part 1 is a large plate of the arms of Charles V, with the Pillars of Hercules.]

22. **Xéres, Francisco de.**—Conquista del Peru. Verdadera relacion de la conquista del Peru & Provincia del Cuzco llamada la nueva Castilla conquistada por Francisco piçarro: capitan de la S. E. C. M. del Emperador nuestro señor. Embiada a su magestad por Francisco de

Xerez, natural de la muy noble y leal ciudad de Sevilla: secretario del sobre dicho capitan en todas las provincias y conquista de la nueva Castilla: y uno de los primeros conquistadores della. **G. L. ff. 22.**

Fue Impreso en Salamanca por Juan de Junta, 1547. fol.

[C. 33. m. 3. (2).—After folio 22 is a leaf, containing stanzas addressed by the author to the Emperor Charles V.]

1548.

23. **Medina, Pedro de.**—Libro de grandezas y cosas memorables de España. Agora de nuevo fecho y copilado per el Maestro Pedro de Medina, vezino de Sevilla. Dirigido al Serenissimo y muy esclarecido Señor, Don Filipe, Principe de España, &c. Nuestro señor. [With woodcuts.]

Impresso en casa de Dominico ỏ Robertis: Sevilla, Año del Virgineo parto, MDXLVIII. fol.

[573. l. 1.—With a second title-page, containing a coloured woodcut map of Spain. On the first title-page is a large plate of the arms of Charles V.]

1549.

24. **Tiraquellus, Andreas.**—Andreæ Tiraquelli Regii in Curia Parisiensi Senatoris Commentarii. De Nobilitate, et jure Primigeniorum. pp. 690.

Apud Jacobum Keruer: Parisiis, 1549. fol.

[Not in the British Museum.—In King George the Third's Library there is a copy of the 1573 edition, *Apud Guliel. Rovillium: Lugduni.*—K. 17. d. 4.]

1552.

25. **Casas, Bartolomé de las,** *Bishop of Chiapa.*—Aqui se contiene una disputa o controversia: entre el Obispo dõ fray Bartholome de las Casas o Casaus obispo q̃ fue dela ciudad Real de Chiapa que es en las Indias parte de la nueva España; y el doctor Gines de Sepulveda Coronista del Emperador nuestro señor: sobre q̃ el doctor contendia: q̃ las conquistas de las Indias contra los Indios eran licitas: y el obispo por el cõtrario dfendío y affirmo aver sido y ser ipossible no serlo: Airanicas injustas & iniquis. La qual questiõ se vẽtilo & disputo en presencia d muchos letrados theologos & juristas en una cõgregacion q̃ mando su magestad juntar el año de mil & quiẽtos y cincuẽta en la villa de Valladolid. Año 1552. **G. L. 61 leaves.**

En casa de Sebastian Trugillo: Sevilla, 1552. 4°.

[G. 6342. (3).—K. 279. h. 27. (2).—672. d. 14. (2).—493. g. 13. (5).] This is no. 3 of the 9 Tracts by Las Casas, and Mr Thomas Grenville only knew of one other copy with the 9 tracts, the Duke of Grafton's, afterwards in Mr Richard Heber's Library.]

26. **López de Gómara, Francisco.**—La istoria de las Indias y conquista de México. [Por Francisco López de Gómara.] ff. 139.

Fue impressa en casa de Agustin Millan: Çaragoça, 1552. fol.

[983. g. 17.—On the title-page is a large woodcut of the arms of Charles V, with the Pillars of Hercules, 7 × 9¼ inches.]

1553.

27. **Cieza de Leon, Pedro de.**—Parte Primera de la chronica del Peru. Que tracta la demarcacion de sus provincias: la descripcion dellas. Las fundaciones de las nuevas ciudades. Los ritos y costumbres de los

indios. Y otras cosas estrañas dignas de ser sabidas. Fecha por Pedro d̄ Cieça de Leon, vezino de Sevilla. ff. 134.

Impressa en Sevilla en casa de Martin de montesdoca, 1553. fol.

[G. 6416.—983. g. 18.—From the Library of Sir Joseph Banks. With a large plate of the arms of Charles V on the title-page.]

28. **Ocampo, Florian de.**—Los Cinco Libros primeros de la Cronica general de España, que recopila el maëstro Florian do Campo, Cronista del Rey nuestro señor, por mandado de su Magestad, en Camora.(que continuaua Ambrosio de Morales, natural de Cordova). 4 tom.

Impresso en Medina del Campo por Guillermo de Millis; Ano 1553; *en casa de Juan Iñiquez de Lequerica: en Alcala de Henares, en Setiembre, del año* MDLXXIII; *en Abril, del año* MDLXXVII; *impresso en Cordoua por Gabriel Ramos Bejarano, impressor de libro, á costa de Francisco Roberte, mercader de libros, Año* 1586. 1553–86. fol.

[686. h. 17–20.—Tom. 1 has on the title a large plate, coloured, of the coat of arms of Charles V, with the Pillars of Hercules.]

1554.

29. **Alcocer, Pedro de.**—Hystoria o Descripcion del Imperial cibdad de Toledo, &c. [Por Pedro de Alcocer.] ff. 124.

Por Juan Ferrer: en Toledo, 1554. fol.

[10161. f. 9.—10161. g. 3.—573. l. 12.—With a large plate of the arms of Charles V on the title-page.]

30. **Cieza de Leon, Pedro de.**—Parte Primera de la Chronica del Peru... Hecha por Pedro de Cieça de Leon, vezino de Sevilla. Añadiose de nuevo la descripcion y traça de todas las Indias, con una Tabla alphabetica, &c. ff. 285.

En casa de Juan Steelsio; [impresso por Juan Lacio]; en Anvers, MDLIIII. 12°.

[G. 6310.—K. 279. a. 31.—1061. b. 20.—1196. b. 23.—1061. b. 19.]

1555.

31. **Zarate, Augustin de.**—Historia del Descubrimiento y Conquista del Peru, con las cosas naturales que señaladamente alli se hallan, y los sucessos que ha avido. La qual escrivia Augustin de Çarate, exerciendo el cargo de Contador general de cuentas por su Magestad en aquella provincia, y en la de Tierra firme. ff. 273.

En casa de Martin Nucio, a las dos Cigueñas: en Anvers, Año M.D.LV. 12°.

[G. 6311.—1061. b. 22.]

1557.

32. **Franciscus, à Victoria.**—Relectiones Theologicae tredecim partibus per varias sectiones in duos libros divisæ. Authore R. P. F. Francisco a Victoria ordinis Prædicatorum, &c. (Relectio v. De Indis.) pp. 521.

Jac. Boyer: Lyon, 1557. 8°.

[Not in the British Museum.—1587. *Expensis Petri Landry: Lugduni,* 4374. aaa. 18.]

1560.

33. **Domingo,** *de Santo Tomas.*—Grammatica o Arte de la lengua general de los Indios de los Reynos del Peru. Nuevamente compuesta por el Maestro fray Domingo de S. Thomas, De la orden de S. Domingo, Morador en los dichos Reynos. ff. 96.

Impresso en Valladolid, por Francisco Fernandez de Cordova, Impressor de la M. R., 1560. 12°.

[C. 33. c. 39.]

34. **Domingo,** *de Santo Tomas.*—Lexicon o Vocabulario de la lengua general del Peru. Cõpuesto por el Maestro F. Domingo de S. Thomas de la orden de S. Domingo. ff. 179.

Impresso en Valladolid, por Francisco Fernandez de Cordova, Impressor de la M. R., 1560. 12°.

[C. 33. c. 39.]

35. **Ondegardo,** Polo de.—Report by Polo de Ondegardo on the lineage, conquests, edifices, fortresses, &c., of the Yncas. From the MS. in the Biblioteca Nacional, Madrid. B. 135. 1560.

See 1873, No. 220.

1563.

36. **Beuter,** Pedro Antonio.—Primera Parte de la Coronica general de todo España, y especialmente del reyno de Valencia...Compuesta por el Doctor Pero Anton Beuther, maestro en sacra Theologia. (Segunda Parte, 1551.) 2 pts. [With woodcuts.]

Impresso en la muy noble ciudad de Valencia, en casa de Joan Mey Flandro, Año del Nascimiento de nuestro señor Jesu Christo, 1563, 1551. fol.

[593. g. 2.]

1565.

37. **Benzoni,** Girolamo.—La Historia del Mondo Nuovo, di M. Girolamo Benzoni, Milanese. La qual tratta dell' Isole, & Mari nuovamente ritrovati, et delle nuove Città da lui proprio vedute, per acqua & per terra in quatordeci anni. [With woodcuts, among others "Come gl' Indiani del Peru adorano il Sole, & lo tengono per il suo principal Iddio" (f. 166); & "Il modo che tengono gli orefici nel lavorare, & fondere l' oro, & l' argento." (ff. 169). ff. 175.

Appresso (Fr. Rampazetto, ad instantia di) Gabriel Benzoni: in Venetia, MDLXV. 8°.

[K. 278. a. 39.—Another edition.—1061. a. 7.]

1569.

38. **Toledo,** Francisco de, *Viceroy of Peru.*—[Documents relating to the appointment and administration of Francisco de Toledo, Viceroy of Peru, 1569–1581.—Biblioteca Nacional, Madrid. MS. J. 113.]

See 1867, No. 207.

1570.

39. **Molina,** Christoval de.—An Account of the Fables and Rites of the Yncas. By Christoval de Molina. 1570–1584.

See 1873, No. 220.

1571.

40. **Fernández,** Diego, *de Palencia.*—Primera y Segunda Parte de la Historia del Peru, que se mando escrevir à Diego Fernandez, vezino de

la ciudad de Palencia. Côtiene la primera, lo succedido en la Nueva
España y en el Perù, sobre la execucion de las nuevas leyes : y el
allanamiento, y castigo, que hizo el Presidente Gasca de Gonçalo
Piçarro y sus sequaces. La Segunda, contiene la Tyrannia y Alça-
miento de los Contreras, y don Sebastiã de Castilla, y de Francisco
Hernãdez Giron: con otros muchos acaescimientos y successos. Dirigido
à la C. R. M. del Rey Don Philippe nuestro Señor. 2 parts.

*Fue impresso en Sevilla en casa de Hernando diaz en la calle de la
Sierpe, Año de* 1571. fol.

[G. 6392.—K. 147. d. 8.—601. l. 6.—This book was prohibited by
the Council of the Indies, and never reprinted, and is now very
rare. The author served in Peru against Pizarro. There is a
copy in the John Carter Brown Library, Providence, Rhode
Island. On the title-page of each part is a large plate of the arms
of Philip II, and at the end of Part 2 is the author's autograph
signature.]

41. **Incas.**—Informacion de las Idolatrias de los Incas e Indios y de como se
enterraban, *etc.* Año de 1571.

See 1874, No. 222.

42. **Ondegardo, Polo de.**—Relacion de los Fundamentos acerca del notable
Daño que resulta de no guardar á los Indios sus fueros. Junio 26
de 1571.

[Por Polo de Ondegardo.—Biblioteca Nacional, Madrid. Manuscritos
de Indias, T. 9.]

See 1872, No. 218.

43. **Toledo, Francisco de,** *Viceroy of Peru.*—Memorial que D. Francisco de
Toledo dió al Rey nuestro Señor del estado en que dejó las cosas
del Pirú despues de haber sido en él virey y capitan general trece años,
que comenzaron el de 1569.

See 1855, No. 180.

1572.

44. **Benzoni, Girolamo.**—La Historia del Mondo Nuovo, di M. Girolamo
Benzoni, Milanese...Nuovamente ristampata, et illustrata con la giunta
d' alcune cose notabile dell' Isole di Canaria. [Dedicated to Scipio
Simoneta, Senator.] ff. 179. MS. Notes.

*Appresso gli Heredi di Giovan Maria Bonelli, ad instantia di Pietro
& Francesco Tini, fratelli: in Venetia,* MDLXII. 8°.

[G. 6902.—978. a. 22. From the Library of Sir Joseph Banks.]

45. **Sarmiento de Gamboa, Pedro.**—Segunda parte de la Historia general
llamada Índica, la cual por mandado del excelentísimo señor Don
Francisco de Toledo, virrey, gobernador y capitán general de los reinos
del Pirú y mayordomo de la casa real de Castilla, compuso el capitán
Pedro Sarmiento de Gamboa. MS. 1572.

See 1906, No. 289 ; 1907, No. 290.

1577.

46. **Zarate, Augustin de.**—Historia del Descubrimiento y Conquista de las
Provincias del Peru, y de los successos que enella ha avido, desde que se
conquistò, hasta que el Licenciado de la Gasca Obispo de Siguença
bolvio a estos reynos : y de las cosas naturales que en la dicha provincia
se hallan dignas de memoria. La qual escrevia Augustin de Çarate,

Contador de mercedes de su Magestad, siendo Contador general de cuentas en aquella provincia, y en la de Tierrafirme. Imprimiose el año de cincuenta y cinco en la villa de Anvers, &c. (Tabla.) ff. 117. *En casa de Alonso Escrivano: en Sevilla, Año de* M.D.LXXVII. fol. [601. k. 19.]

1581.

47. **Zarate**, Augustin de.—The strange and delectable History of the discoverie and Conquest of the Provinces of Peru, in the South Sea. And of the notable things which there are found : and also of the bloudie civill warres which there happened for government. Written in foure bookes, by Augustine Sarate, Auditor for the Emperour his Maiestie in the same provinces and firme land. And also of the ritche Mines of Potosi. Translated out of the Spanish tongue, by T. Nicholas. [Dedicated to Thomas Wilson, D.C.L., one of the principal Secretaries to Queen Elizabeth.] ff. 92. [With woodcuts.]

Imprinted at London by Richard Jhones, dwelling over against the Fawlcon, by Holburne bridge, 1581. 4°.

[G. 6337.—1061. b. 23.—With a second title, and woodcut of "The Riche Mines of Potossi." The second copy is cropped, and is imperfect, wanting ff. 17-20, sig. F.]

1584.

48. **Catecisma.**—[Catecismo y Doctrina Cristiana en los Idiomas Castellano, y Qquechua, y Aymara. Ordenado por autoridad del Concilio Provincial de Lima del año de 1583.] ff. 84.

Impresso en la Ciudad de los Reyes, por Antonio Ricardo, primero Impressor en estos Reynos del Piru. Año de MDLXXXIIII. 4°.

[C. 53. c. 26. (1).—The first book printed in Peru, according to the British Museum Catalogue. But *see* 1604, No. 67; and 1829, No. 155. This copy wants the title-page. At the back of the colophon is a plate with the arms of Philip II, and the Pillars of Hercules. Purchased October 13, 1891.]

1585.

49. **Indios.**—Confessionario para los Curas de Indios. Con la instrucion contra sus Ritos : y Exhortacion para ayudar a bien morir : y summa de sus Privilegios : y forma de Impedimentos del Matrimonio. Compuesto y traduzido en las Lenguas Quichua, y Aymara. Por autoridad del Concilio Provincial de Lima, del año de 1583. ff. 65.

Impresso con Licencia de la Real Audiencia, en la Ciudad de los Reyes, por Antonio Ricardo, primero Impressor en estos Reynos del Piru, Año de MDLXXXV. 4°.

[C. 53. c. 59.—C. 53. c. 26 (2).—In this work is contained : " Instrucion contra las Ceremonias y Ritos que usan los Indios conforme al tiempo de su infidelidad."]

50. **Catecismo.**—Tercero Cathecismo y Exposicion de la Doctrina Christiana, por Sermones. Para que los Curas y otros ministros prediquen y enseñen a los Yndios y a las demas personas. Conforme a lo que en el Sancto Concilio Provincial de Lima se proveyo. ff. 1-207.

Impresso con licencia de la Real Audiencia, en la Ciudad de los Reyes, por Antonio Ricardo, primero Impressor en estos Reynos del Piru, Año de MDLXXXV. 4°.

[C. 53. c. 26 (3).—At the bottom right-hand corner of the title-page is written : *Joseph de Acosta*, which may be the autograph of the famous historian of the Indies. This copy wants all after fol. 207.— C. 53. d. 8.—This is a perfect copy, with 213 folios.]

See 1774, No. 139.

278 BIBLIOGRAPHY

1586.

51. **Cavello Balboa,** Miguel.—Miscellanea austral. [Part III. Historia del Perú.] MS. 1586.
    See 1840, No. 162.

52. **Quichua.**—Arte y Vocabulario en la lengua general del Peru llamada Quichua, y en la lengua española. El mas copioso y elegante que hasta agora se ha impreso. pp. 223.
    Por Antonio Ricardo: en Los Reyes, Año de MDLXXXVI. 8°.
    [Not in the British Museum.—There is a copy in the Biblioteca Nacional, and the Biblioteca del Museo de Ultramar, Madrid.]
    See 1614, No. 85.

53. **Sarmiento de Gamboa,** Pedro.—Copy of a Letter translated from the English, written in London, 10th November 1586, taken by Pedro Sarmiento de Gamboa, and with a note of his visit to Queen Elizabeth at Windsor Castle.
    See 1896, No. 271.

1590.

54. **Acosta,** Joseph de, *S.J.*—Historia natural y moral de las Indias, en que se tratan las cosas notables del cielo, y elementos, metales, plantas, y animales dellas : y los ritos, y ceremonias leyes, y govierno, y guerras de los Indios. Compuesta por el Padre Joseph de Acostà, Religioso de la Compañia de Jesus. Dirigida a la Serenissima Infanta Doña Isabella Clara Eugenia dè Austria. pp. 535.
    Impresso en Sevilla en casa de Juan de Leon, Año de 1590. 4°.
    [G. 6341.—K. 146. a. 3.]

55. **Valera,** Blas, *S.J.*—Historia imperii Peruani. MS. c. 1590.
    [The author went to Spain, to superintend the printing of this work, but the greater part of the MS. was lost in the siege of Cadiz by the English in 1596. Father Pedro Maldonado de Saavedra, Professor of Theology at Cordova, in 1600, gave some leaves of the MS. to Garcilasso de la Vega.]

1591.

56. **Acosta,** Joseph de, *S.J.*—Historia Natural y Moral de las Indias... Compuesta por el Padre Joseph de Acosta, Religioso de la Compañia de Jesus. Dirigida al Illustrissimo Señor Don Enrique de Cardona, Governador por su Magestad en el Principado de Cathaluña. pp. 345.
    Acosta de Lelio marini, Veneciano, al Carrer de la Boqueria: en Barcelona, 1591. 12°.
    [978. a. 13.—Two pages of the Introduction are supplied in MS.—From the Library of Sir Joseph Banks.]

1593.

57. **Jesuits.**—Lettres du Japon, et de la Chine, des années 1589 & 1590. Et certains advis du Péru, des années 1588 & 1589. Envoyez au Reverend Père Général de la Compagnie de Jésus. pp. 310.
    Par Jean Pillehotte, à l'enseigne du nom de Jésus: à Lyon, M.D.XCIII. 8°.
    [G. 6685. (1).—Formerly in the Library of Richard Heber.—On the covers are the Crown and Cipher of Louis XIII, King of France, and his wife, Anne of Austria, with the later addition of the arms of Paulin Prondre de Guermante.]

1594.

58. **Jesuits.**—Recueil de Quelques Missions des Indes Orientales, & Occidentales : extraict d'aucuns Avertissemens escrits és années 1590 & 1591, par les Pères Pierre Martinez, Provincial de l'Inde Orientale, Jean d'Atienza, Provincial du Péru, & Pierre Diaz, Provincial du Messic. Au Révérend Père Claude Aquaviva, Général de la Compagnie de Jésus. Traduict maintenant d'Italien en François. (Table.) pp. 172.
   Par Jean Pillehotte : à Lyon, M.D.XCIIII. 8°.
   [G. 6685. (2).—Bound up with 1593, No. 57.]

1598.

59. **Oré,** Luis Gerónimo de.—Symbolo Catholico Indiano, en el qual se declaran los mysterios de la Fé contenidos en los tres Symbolos Catholicos, Apostolico, Niceno, y de S. Athanasio. Contiene assi mesmo una descripcion del nuevo orbe, y de los naturales del. Y un orden de enseñarles la doctrina Christiana en las dos lenguas Generales, Quichua y Aymara, con un Confessionario breve y Catechismo de la Communion. Todo lo qual esta approbado por los Reverendissimos señores Arçobispo de los Reyes, y Obispos del Cuzco, y de Tucuman. Compuesto por el Padre Fray Luis Hieronymo de Oré, predicador de la orden de sant Francisco, de la provincia de los doze Apostoles del Piru. [On the *verso* of the title is : Por el Señor don Luys de Velasco Vissorrey del Piru esta tassado a real el pliego.] ff. 193.
   Impresso en Lima por Antonio Ricardo; a costa de Pedro Fernandez de Valençuela, Año 1598. 4°.
   [C. 58. e. 9.—The Permission to print from the Viceroy, the Marquis de Cañete, is signed by Alvaro Ruyz de Navamuel.]

1599.

60. **Vargas Machuca,** Bernardo de.—Milicia y Descripcion de las Indias. Por el Capitan don Bernardo de Vargas Machuca, Cavallero Castellano, natural de la villa de Simancas. Dirigido al Licenciado Paulo de Laguna, Presidente del Consejo Real de las Indias. (Compendio de la Sphera.) ff. 186.
   En casa de Pedro Madrigal : en Madrid, Año MDXCIX.
   [G. 7159.—K. 278. f. 23.—1046. c. 1. (2).]

1601.

61. **Herrera Tordesillas,** Antonio de.—Historia General de los Hechos de los Castellanos en las Islas i Tierra Firme del Mar Oceano. Escrita por Antonio de Herrera, Coronista Mayor de su M^d : de las Indias y su Coronista de Castilla. En quatro [or rather, nine] Decadas desde el Ano de 1492 hasta el de 1531. Al Rey Nu^ro. Señor.
   En Ma^d: en la Emplenta Rea[l] ; por Juan de la Cuesta; 1601, 1615, 1601. fol.
   [G. 7206-8.—601. k. 12-15.—601. k. 8-11.—The Decades have finely engraved title-pages, with medallion portraits, and battle-scenes, &c.—Decade 5 has 13 medallion portraits of the Incas of Peru, which Dr Richard Pietschmann thinks may have been copied from the three cloths sent by Sarmiento to Philip II, as on p. ix of the Introduction to the present volume, where there is a reproduction of the Herrera title-page.
   See 1859, No. 188; 1906, No. 289 ; 1907, No. 290.

1602.

62. **Avalos y Figueroa**, Diego d'.—Primera Parte de la Miscelanea Austral de Don Diego d' Avalos y Figueroa, en varios Coloquios, Interlocutores, Delio, y Cilena. Con la Defensa de Damas, Dirigida a l' excellentissimo señor Don Luys de Velasco, Cavallero de la Orden de Santiago, Visorey, y Capitan general de los Reynos del Piru, Chile, y Tierra firme. 2 vols. *Con Licencia de su Excelencia: Impresso en Lima por Antonio Ricardo, Año* M.DC.II., M.DCIII. 4°.

 [C. 58. e. 15.]

1603.

63. **Bertonio**, Ludovico.—Arte Breve de la Lengua Aymara. Para introduction del Arte Grande de la misma Lengua. Compuesta por el P. Ludovico Bertonio, Romano de la compañia de Jesus en la Provincia del Piru, de la India Occidental. pp. 30. *En Roma por Luis Zannetti, Año de* 1603. 8°.

 [C. 33. d. 19.]

64. **Bertonio**, Ludovico.—Arte y Grammatica muy copiosa de la Lengua Aymara. Con muchos, y varios modos de hablar para su mayor declaracion, con la tabla de los capitulos, y cosas que en ella se contienen, &c. Compuesta por el P. Ludovico Bertonio, Romano de la compañia de Jesus en la Provincia del Piru, de la India Occidental. (Registro.) pp. 348. *En Roma por Luis Zannetti, Año de* 1603. 8°.

 [C. 33. d. 19.] *See* 1879, No. 231.

65. **Torres Rubio**, Diego de, *S.J.*—Grammatica y Vocabulario en la Lengua general del Peru, llamada Quichua y en la Lengua Española, el mas copioso y elegante que hasta agora se ha impresso. [Por Diego de Torres Rubio.] *Clemente Hidalgo: Sevilla,* 1603. 12°.

 [Not in the British Museum.—*See* Aug. & Al. de Backer. *Bibl. Comp. de Jésus.* tom. 8. 1898. col. 135.—*See* also Bernard Quaritch, *Catalogue No.* 112, May 1891, No. 1633.]

1604.

66. **Acosta**, Joseph de.—The Naturall and Morall Historie of the East and West Indies. Intreating of the remarkeable things of Heaven, of the Elements, Mettalls, Plants and Beasts which are proper to that Country : Together with the Manners, Ceremonies, Lawes, Governements, and Warres of the Indians. Written in Spanish by Joseph Acosta, and translated into English by E. G[rimston]. pp. 590. *Printed by Val: Sims for Edward Blount and William Aspley: London,* 1604. 4°.

 [G. 15020.—K. 279. h. 35.—978. f. 9. From the Library of Sir Joseph Banks.]

67. **Catecismo**.—Catecismo en la Lengua Española, y Aymara del Piru. Ordenado por autoridad del Concilio Provincial de Lima, y impresso en la dicha ciudad el año de 1583. ff. 49. *En Sevilla, por Bartolome Gomez, Año de* 1604. 12°.

 [C. 58. a. 14. (2).—With the crest and initials of Henri Ternaux-Compans on the covers.]

68. **Quichua.**—Vocabulario en la Lengua General del Peru, llamada Quichua, y en la lengua Española. Nuevamente emendado y añadido de algunas cosas que faltavan por el Padre Maestro Fray Juan Martinez, Cathedratico de la Lengua, de la orden del señor Saint Augustin. (Arte de la Lengua General del Peru, &c.) 3 pts.

Por Antonio Ricardo : en los Reyes, Año de MDCIIII. 8°.

[C. 63. a. 13.]

1607.

69. **García, Gregorio.**—Origen de los Indios de el Nuevo Mundo, e Indias Occidentales. Averiguado con discurso de opiniones por el Padre Presentado Fray Gregorio Garcia, de la orden de Predicadores... Dirigido al Angelico Dotor Santo Thomas de Aquino. pp. 535.

En casa de Pedro Patricio Mey, junto a San Martin : en Valencia, MDCVII. 12°.

[1061. b. 11.] *See* 1729, No. 125.

70. **Gonzaléz Holguin, Diego,** *S.J.*—Gramatica y Arte Nueva de la Lengua General de todo el Peru, llamada lengua Qquichua, o lengua del Inca. Añadida y cumplida (Dedicada al Doctor Hernando Arias de Ugarte)...Compuesta por el Padre Diego Gonçalez Holguin, de la Compañia de Jesus, natural de Caçeres. ff. 144.

Impressa en la Ciudad de los Reyes del Peru por Francisco del Canto impressor, Año MDCVII. 4°.

[C. 58. e. 14.] *See* 1842, No. 165.

71. **Peruvian Ritual.**—Rituale, seu Manuale Peruanum, et Forma Brevis Administrandi apud Indos sacrosancta Baptismi, Pœnitentiæ, Eucharistiæ, Matrimonii, & Extremæ unctionis Sacramenta. Juxta ordinem Sanctæ Romanæ Ecclesiæ. Per R. P. F. Ludovicum Hieronymum Orerium, Ordinis Minorum Concionatorem, & Sacræ Theologiæ Lectorem accuratum : et quæ indigent versione, vulgaribus Idiomatibus Indicis, secundum diversos situs omnium Provinciarum novi orbis Perù, aut per ipsum translata, aut ejus industria elaborata. pp. 418.

Apud Jo. Jacobum Carlinum, & Constantinum Vitalem : Neapoli, 1607. 4°.

[C. 52. c. 13.—3365. g. 3. This copy is printed on thin paper, and has been cropped in binding.] *See* 1894, No. 265.

1608.

72. **Acosta, Joseph de,** *S.J.* Historia Natural y Moral de las Indias... Compuesta por el Padre Joseph de Acosta, Religioso de la Compañia de Jesus, Dirigida a la Serenissima Infanta Doña Isabela Clara Eugenia de Austria. (Tabla de las Cosas.) pp. 535.

Impresso en Madrid en casa de Alonso Martin ; a costa de Juan Berrillo, mercader de libros, Año 1608. 4°.

[978. k. 6.]

73. **Avila, Francisco de.**—A Narrative of the errors, false gods, and other superstitions and diabolical rites, in which the Indians of the province of Huarochiri lived in ancient times. By Dr Francisco de Avila. 1608.

See 1873, No. 220.

74. **Gonzalez Holguin, Diego,** *S.J.*—Vocabulario de la Lengua General de todo el Peru llamada lengua Qquichua, o del Inca. Corregido y renovado conforme a la propriedad cortesana del Cuzco. Dividido en dos libros...Van añadidos al fin los privilegios concedidos a los Indios. Compuesto por el Padre Diego Gonçalez Holguin, de la Compañia de

Jesus, natural de Caçeres. Dedicado al Doctor Hernando Arias de Vgarte, &c. (Summario de los Privilegios y Facultades concedidas para los indios.) 2 pts. *Impresso en la Ciudad de los Reyes. Por Francisco del Canto, Año* MDCVIII. 4°. [C. 58. e. 5.—With the crest and initials of Henri Ternaux-Compans on the covers.]

1609.

75. **Garcilasso de la Vega,** *el Inca.*—Primera Parte de los Commentarios Reales, que tratan del Origen de los Yncas, Reyes que fueron del Peru, de su Idolatria, Leyes, y govierno en paz y en guerra : de sus vidas y conquistas, y de todo lo que fue aquel Imperio y su Republica, antes que los Españoles passaran a el. Escritos por el Ynca Garcilasso de la Vega, natural del Cozco, y Capitan de su Magestad. Dirigidos a la Serenissima Princesa Doña Catalina de Portugal, Duqueza de Bargança, &c. ff. 264. [The colophon is dated : MDCVIII.]

Con licencia de la Sancta Inquisicion, Ordinario, y Paço : en la officina de Pedro Crasbeeck : en Lisboa, Año de MDCIX. 4°.

—Segunda Parte de los Comentarios Reales que tratan del Origen de los Incas, Reyes que fueron del Peru, de su Idolatria, Leyes, y Govierno en paz, y en guerra ; de sus Vidas, y Conquistas, su Descubrimiento, y como lo ganaron los Españoles ; las Guerras Civiles que huvo entre Pizarros, y Almagros, sobre la partiga de la Tierra ; Castigo, y Levantamiento de Tyranos, y de todo lo que fue aquel Imperio, y Republica, antes que los Españoles passaran à èl. Escritos por el Inca Garcilasso de la Vega, Natural del Cozco, y Capitan de su Magestad. Dirigida a la Limpissima Virgen Maria Madre de Dios, y Señora Nuestra. ff. 300.

En la Oficina de Pedro Crasbeeck : en Lisboa, Año MDCIX. 4°.

[601. i. 15, 16.] *See* 1723, No. 124 ; 1829, No. 156.

76.—[Another copy of Primera Parte.—With a large plate, 6¾ × 9¼ inches, of the arms of Garcilasso de la Vega, as on his memorial chapel at Cordova, showing the coats of the families of Vargas, Figueroa, Counts of Feria, Saavedra, Counts of Castellar, Mendoza, Counts of Tendilla, and the coat of the Incas, granted by the Emperor Charles V.—This plate has been reproduced in facsimile by Mr Donald Macbeth for the Hon. Secretary of the Hakluyt Society, from whom copies can be obtained at 1*s.* each.

[601. i. 17.]

77.—[Another edition of Segunda Parte : entitled :] Historia General del Peru. Trata el Descubrimiento del ; y como lo ganaron los Españoles. Las Guerras civiles que huvo entre Piçarros, y Almagros, sobre la partija de la tierra. Castigo y levantamiẽto de tiranos : y otros sucessos particulares que en la Historia se contienen. Escrita por el Ynca Garcilasso de la Vega, Capitan de su magestad, *etc.* Dirigida à la Limpissima Virgen Maria, Madre de Dios, y Señora nuestra. ff. 300.

Por la Viuda de Andres Barrera, y a su costa, en Cordova, Año MDCXVII. fol.

[601. l. 7.—From the Library of King James I.]

1610.

78. **Lopez de Caravantes,** Francisco.—Noticia General del Perú, Tierra firme y Chile. Por Francisco Lopez de Caravantes, Contador de Cuentas en el Tribunal de la Contaduría mayor de las mismas provincias. MS. c. 1610.

["Esta obra estuvo antes en la librería del colegio mayor de Cuenca de Salamanca, y ahora existe en la particular de S. M."] *See* 1830, No. 159.

79. **Muñiz, Pedro.**—Discurso del Dr Muñiz, decan de Lima, sobre el servicio de los indios en el beneficio de obrajes, trapiches, viñas, sementeras, guarda de ganados, beneficio de las minas de Azogue en Guancabelica de la Plata en Potosí. [Holograph MS. with the signature of the author.] c. 1610.

    [B.M. Sloane MSS. 3055, fol. 20. *See* Gayangos, P. de, *Catalogue*, vol. 2, p. 477. 1877.]

80. **Ocampo, Baltasar de.**—Descripcion de la provincia de Sant Francisco de la Vitoria de Villcapampa (Vilcabamba), por el capitan Baltasar de Ocampo, dirigida al Marques de Montesclaros [Don Juan de Mendoza y Luna], virrey, gobernador y capitan general de los Reynos del Perú y Chile. ff. 36. MS. c. 1610.

    [Add. MSS. 17,585. Tract 1 in a volume : PERU : Tratados Varios. 1557–1610. From the Bauzá Collection. This MS., of which an English translation now first appears, gives an account by an eyewitness of the execution of the Inca Tupac Amaru, 1571. This volume belonged originally to Don Juan Bautista Muñoz, the historian of Spanish America (1745–1799). The MS. in question appears to be a copy made at the end of the 18th century. *See* Gayángos, Pascual de, *Catalogue*, vol. 11 p. 461. 1877. 8°. There are many other MSS. on Peru in the same catalogue, which are at present lost in the absence of a complete general index of authors, titles, and subjects, as is also the case with the MS. maps of Peru and South America, in the British Museum. The printed Catalogue (1844–1861) ends at vol. 3, 1861, and is not yet complete, and even for these three volumes there is no Index.]

81. **Suarez de Salazar, Juan Bautista.**—Grandezas y Antiguedades de la Isla y Ciudad de Cadiz...Por Joan Baptista Suarez de Salazar, Racionero en la santa Iglesia de Cadiz. Dirigido al illustrissimo Cardenal don Antonio Çapata. pp. 317.

    Impresso por Clemente Hidalgo: en Cadiz, Año 1610. 4°.

    [K. 281. g. 26.—574. f. 20.]

1612.

82. **Bertonio, Ludovico.**—Arte de la Lengua Aymara. Con una silva de Phrases de la misma lengua, y su declaracion en Romance. Por el Padre Ludovico Bertonio, Italiano de la Compañia de Jesus en la Provincia del Peru natural de Rocca contrada de la Marca de Ancona. Dedicado al Illustrissimo y Reverendissimo señor don Hernando de Mendoça Obispo del Cuzco de la mesma Compañia. pp. 263.

    Impresso en la casa de la Côpañia de Jesus de Juli en la Provincia de Chucuyto. Por Francisco del Canto, 1612. 8°.

    [C. 33. a. 51.—With the book-plate of Sir Woodbine Parish, F.R.S.]

83. **Bertonio, Ludovico.**—Vocabulario de la Lengua Aymara. Primera parte, donde por Abecedario se ponen en primer lugar los Vocablos de la lengua Española para buscar los que les corresponden en la lengua Aymara. Compuesto por el P. Ludovico Bertonio, Italiano, de la Compañia de Jesus, en la Provincia del Piru, de las Indias Occidentales, Natural de la Roca contrada de la Marca de Ancona. Dedicado al Illustrissimo y Ræverendissimo Señor Don Fray Domingo Valderrama Centeno Maestro en sancta Theologia, Arçobispo, y primer obispo de la Paz, del Consejo de su Magestad. 2 pts.

    Impresso en la casa de la Compañia de Jesus de Juli Pueblo en la Provincia de Chucuito. Por Francisco del Canto, 1612. 4°.

    [C. 58. e. 6.—With the crest and initials of Henri Ternaux-Compans on the covers.] *See* 1879, No. 232.

84. **Villegas**, Alonso de.—Libro de la Vida y Milagros de Nuestro Señor
Jesu Christo en dos Lenguas, Aymara, y Romance, traducido de el que
recopilo el Licenciado Alonso de Villegas, quitadas, y añadidas algunas
cosas, y acomodado a la capacidad de los Indios. Por el Padre
Ludovico Bertonio, Italiano de la Compañia de Jesus en la Provincia de
el Piru, natural de Rocca Contrada de la Marca de Ancona. Dedicado
al Illustrissimo y Reverendissimo Señor don Alonso de Peralta primer
Arçobispo de los Charcas. (Tabla.) pp. 659.

*Impresso en la Casa de la Compañia de Jesus de Juli Pueblo en
la Provincia de Chucuyto por Francisco del Canto, 1612.* 4°.

[C. 58. d. 23.—Purchased August 3, 1893.]

1614.

85. **Quichua.**—Arte, y Vocabulario en la Lengua General del Peru, llamada
Quichua, y en la lengua Española. El mas copioso y elegante, que
hasta agora se ha impresso. 3 pts.

*En los Reyes, Con Licencia del Excellentissimo Señor Marques de
Montes Claros, Virrey del Peru, por Francisco del Canto, Ano
de* MDCXIIII. 12°.

[C. 58. b. 3. (1).] *See* 1586, No. 52.

1616.

86. **Huerta**, Alonzo de.—Arte de la Lengua Quechua General de los Yndios
de este Reyno del Piru. Dirigido al Illustrissimo Señor Don Bartholome
Lobo Guerrero, Arçobispo Tercero del. Compuesto por el Doctor Alonso
de Huerta Clerigo Presbytero Predicador de la dicha Lengua en esta
Sancta Yglesia Cathedral,...natural de la muy noble y muy leal Ciudad
de Leõ de Huanuco. ff. 35.

Impresso por Francisco del Canto : en los Reyes, Año MDCXVI. 4°.

[C. 58. e. 4.—The last leaf has a large Printer's Device, with the
Cross, three nails, and a skull at the base.—The crest and initials of
Henri Ternaux-Compans are on the covers.]

87. **Torres Rubio**, Diego de, *S.J.*—Arte de la Lengua Aymara. Compuesto
por el Padre Diego de Torres Rubio, de la Compañia de Jesus. Con
Licencia del Señor Principe de Esquilcahe Virrey destos Reynos. ff. 98.

En Lima, por Francisco del Canto, Año de 1616. 12°.

[C. 58. a. 14. (1).—With the crest and initials of Henri Ternaux-
Compans on the covers.]

1619.

88. **Torres Rubio**, Diego de, *S.J.*—Arte de la Lengua Quichua. Compuesto
por el Padre Diego de Torres Rubio, de la Compañia de Jesus. Con
Licencia del Senor Principe de Esquilache Virrey destos Reynos. 3 pts.

Por Francisco Lasso : en Lima, Año de 1619. 16°.

[C. 33. a. 50.—*See* 1700, No. 118 ; 1754, No. 134.

1620.

89. **Santa Cruz Pachacuti Yamqui**, Juan de.—-Relacion de Antigüedades
deste Reyno del Pirú. Por Don Juan de Santacruz Pachacuti Yamqui.
1620.

See 1873, No. 220 ; 1879, No. 235 ; 1892, No. 259.

1621.

90. **Arriaga**, Pablo Joseph de, *S.J.*—Extirpacion de la Idolatria del Piru. Dirigido al Rey N.S. en su Real Conseio de Indias. Por el Padre Pablo Joseph de Arriaga, de la Compañia de Jesus. pp. 147.

Por Ceronymo de Contreras, Impressor de Libros: en Lima, Año 1621. 8°.

[C. 25. e. 5.—The MS. was in the Library of Ephraim George Squier in 1876. (No. 723, Catalogue of the Library of E. G. Squier. Edited by Joseph Sabin. Bangs, Merwin & Co.: New York, 1876. 8°.—011899. k. 25.)]

91. **Ramos Gavilan**, Alonso.—Historia del Celebre Santuario de Nuestra Señora de Copacabana, y sus Milagros, è Invencion de la Cruz de Carabuco. A Don Alonso Bravo de Sarabia y Sotomayor, del Abito de Santiago, del Consejo de su Magestad, Consultor del Santo Oficio, y Oydor de Mexico. Por el P. F. Alonso Ramos Gavilan, Predicador, del Orden de N. P. S. Agustin. (Tabla. Soneto.) pp. 432.

Por Geronymo de Contreras: en Lima, Año 1621. 4°.

[4744. dd. 10.]

1622.

92. **Lopez de Haro**, Alonso.—Nobiliario Genealogico de los Reyes y Titulos de España. Dirigido a la Magestad del Rey Don Felipe Quarto nuestro señor. Compuesto por Alonso Lopez de Haro, Criado de su Magestad, y Ministro en su Real Consejo de las Ordenes. 2 tom.

Por Luis Sanchez, Impressor Real: en Madrid, Año MDCXXII. fol.

[K. 136. c. 12, 13.—607. k. 17, 18.—2119. f.—Tom. ii, pp. 40–44. Coat of arms and pedigree of Don Francisco de Toledo, Viceroy of Peru, 1569–1581.

1625.

93. **Leon Pinelo**, Antonio de.—Libros Reales de Govierno y Gracia de la Secretaria del Perù, que por mandado del Real Consejo de las Indias, y orden del señor Licenciado don Rodrigo de Aguiar y Acuña, a cuyo cargo està la Recopilaciõ de leyes dellas, ha leydo y passado el Licenciado Antonio de Leon. ff. 11.

[*Madrid*, 1625.] fol.

[1324. i. 13. (2).]

94. **Matienzo de Peralta**, Juan.—Relacion del libro intitulado Govierno de el Perú, que hizo el Lic^do. Matienço, oydor de la audiencia de la ciudad de la Plata. 2 pts. ff. 137.

[Pt. 1, in 52 chapters, treats of the history of Peru before the Spanish Conquest. Pt. 2 has 32 chapters.] MS. c. 1625.

[B.M. Add. MSS. 5469. *See* Gayangos, P. de, *Catalogue*, vol. 2, p. 470. 1877.]

1627.

95. **Simon**, Pedro.—Primera Parte de las Noticias historiales de las Conquistas de tierra firme en las Indias Occidentales. Compuesto por el Padre Fray Pedro Simon, Provincial de la Serafico Orden de San Francisco, del Nuevo Reyno de Granada en las Indias...Natural de la Parrilla Obispado de Cuenca. Dirigido a nuestro invictissimo y major Monarca del Antiguo y nuebo Mundo, Philippo quarto en su Real y supremo Consejo de las Indias. pp. 671.

En Cuenca por Domingo de la Iglesia, Año de 1627. fol.

[G. 6418.—601. l. 20.—With a fine engraved title, representing the King of Spain holding the crown of the Indies on his knees before the Pope.—K. 147. d. 12. This copy wants the original title. In place of this, has been substituted a theological engraved title by Marcus de Orozco, 1660, representing Veritas, Sol Justitiæ, Aurora Consurgens, &c. The last fly-leaf has the tax stamp of Philip V, with the Spanish arms.] See 1861, No. 194.

1630.

96. **Salinas y Cordova**, Buenaventura de.—Memorial des las Historias del Nuevo Mundo: Piru. Meritos, y Excelencias de la Ciudad de Lima, cabeça de sus ricos, y estendidos Reynos, y el estado presente en que se hallan. Para inclinar a la Magestad de su Catolico Monarca Don Felipe IV. Rey poderoso de España, y de las Indias, a que pida a su Santidad la Canonizacion de su Patron Solano. Por el Padre F. Buenaventura de Salinas, de la Orden de nuestro Serafico Padre san Francisco, Letor de Teologia, en el Convento de Jesus de Lima, y Calificador del Santo Oficio. pp. 308.

Impresso en Lima, Por Geronymo de Contreras: Año de 1630. 4°.
[1061. g. 46.]

1631.

97. **Oliva**, Anello, *S. J.*—Vidas de varones ilustres de la Compañia de Jesus de la Provincia del Peru. Repartidas en cuatro libros: En el primero se trata del Reyno y Provincias del Peru, de sus Incas, Reyes, descubrimiento y conquista por les Españoles de la corona de Castilla con otras singularidades concernientes à la historia, y en los otros tres las vidas de los dichos Padres. Por le R. P. Anello Oliva, de la Compañia de Jesus. 2 tom.

MS. *Lima*, 1631. fol.
[B. M. Add. MSS. 25327. *Lima*, Feb. 25, 1631. Part 1 only.]
See 1857, No. 184.

1633.

98. **Garcilasso de la Vega**, *el Inca.*—Le Commentaire Royal on L'Histoire des Yncas, Roys du Peru; contenant leur origine, depuis le premier Ynca Manco Capac, leur Establissement, leur Idolatrie, leurs Sacrifices, leurs Vies, leurs Loix, leur Gouvernement en Paix & en Guerre, leurs Conquestes; les merveilles du Temple du Soleil; ses incroyables richesses & tout l'Estat de ce grand Empire avant que les Espagnols s'en fissent maistres, au temps de Huascar, & d'Atahuallpa. Ensemble une description particuliere des Animaux, des Fruicts, des Mineraux, des Plantes, & des singularitez du Païs. Oeuvre curieuse & tout à faict necessaire à l'intelligence de l'Histoire des Indes. Escritte en langue Peruvienne, par l'Ynca Garcillasso de la Vega, natif de Cozco; & fidellement traduitte sur la version Espagnolle [1609], par J. Baudouin. Avec deux Tables, fort amples, l'une des Chapitres, & l'autre des principales Matières. 2 tom.

A Paris, chez Augustin Courbé, Libraire & Imprimeur de Monseigneur Frère du Roy, au Palais, dans la petite Salle, à la Palme. MDCXXXIII. 4°.

[There is a copy in the John Carter Brown Library, Providence, Rhode Island; and two copies in the Bibliothèque Nationale, Paris: Ol. 774. & P. Angrand 354.—Mr Henry N. Stevens, F.R.G.S., had a fine copy, with the arms of the Duke of Sutherland stamped on the covers.—There is a second engraved title, with a view of the Temple of the Sun, and portraits of the Inca Manco Capac, & Coya Mama Oclho.—This copy has been acquired by the British Museum, July 9, 1907.—*See* Karl W. Hiersemann, *Katalog* 336, No. 1802, 1907.]

99. **Olmos**, Diego de.—Gramatica de la Lengua General. Por Fr. Diego de Olmos, Franciscano, Natural del Cuzco.
En Lima, 1633. 4°.
[Not in the British Museum.—Ant. de Leon Pinelo, *Epitome*, col. 727. 1737.]

1634.

100. **Cardenas**, Bernardino de, *Bishop of Paraguay*.—Memorial y Relacion verdadera para el Rei N.S. y su Real Consejo de las Indias, de cosas del Reino del Perù, mui importantes à su Real servicio, y conciencia. Por el P. F. Bernardino de Cardenas, Predicador general de la Orden de S. Francisco, y Legado del Santo Concilio Provincial Argentino. ff. 64.
Por Francisco Martinez: en Madrid, Año M.DC.XXXIV. 4°.
[8180. e. 14.]

1638.

101. **Calancha**, Antonio de la.—Coronica Moralizada del Orden de San Augustin en el Peru, con Sucesos egenplares en esta Monarquia. Dedicada a Nuestra Señora de Gracia, singular Patrona i Abogada de la dicha Orden. Compuesta por el muy Reverendo Padre Maestro Fray Antonio de la Calancha, de la misma Orden, i Difinidor actual. Primer tomo.
Por Pedro Lacavalleria, en la calle de la Libreria: en Barcelona, 1638. fol.
[K. 203. f. 6.—With a second engraved title-page, larger than the book, with many illustrations.]

1639.

102. **Calancha**, Antonio de la.—Chronica Moralizada den Orden de S. Augustin en el Peru, con sucesos exemplares vistos en esta Monarchia...Por el Pe Mo F. Antonio de la Calancha...Dedicada a Nřa Sa de Gratia Virgen Maria, Madre de Dios, Patrona de la Religion de Nro. Pe S. Augustin. (Tomo Segundo. [Edited by Bernardo de Torres.])
Por Pedro Lacavalleria, en la Calle de la Libreria: en Barcelona, 1639, 1653. fol.
[493. k. 11.—Tom. 1 has a second engraved title-page, larger than the book, with many illustrations.]

1641.

103. **Acuña**, Cristoval de.—Nuevo Descubrimiento del Gran Rio de las Amazonas. Por el Padre Chrstoval [sic] de Acuña, Religioso de la Compañia de Jesus, y Calificador de la Suprema General Inquisicion, al qual fue y se hizo por orden de su Magestad, el año de 1639, por la Provincia de Quito en los Reynos del Perù. Al Excelentissimo Señor Conde Duque de Olivares. ff. 46.
En Madrid, en la Imprenta del Reyno, Año de 1641. 4°.
[G. 6936.—C. 7. a. 19. On the covers of this copy are two Austrian coats of arms, the one with the Bohemian crown, the double-headed eagle, and the arms of Austria and Ragusa ; the other, an Archducal crown, and the arms of the Archduchy of Unter der Ens, and of Austria.]—10480. b. 19. (1). This copy was purchased February 5, 1849.]
See 1859, No. 188.

1644.

104. **Carrera,** Fernando de la.—Arte de la Lengua Yunga de los Valles del Obispado de Truxillo del Peru, con un Confessonario, y todas las Oraciones Christianas, traducidas en la lengua, y otras cosas. Autor el Beneficiado Don Fernando de la Carrera, natural de la dicha ciudad de Truxillo, &c....Dirigido al Rey N. Señor en su Real Consejo de las Indias. pp. 265.

Impresso en Lima, por Joseph de Contreras, Año de 1644. 16°. [C. 58. b. 4.]

1647.

105. **Escalona Aguero,** Gaspar de.—Gazophilatium Regium Perubicum. I. Administrandum. II. Calculandum. III. Conservandum. (Gazofilacio Regio Perubico, en Latin, y Ramance.)...Edytum a Gaspare d' Escalona Aguero...nunc Senatore Chilensi. 3 parts.

[*Matriti,* 1647.] fol.

[501. g. 8.—With a fine engraved title-page, with a border of 22 types of Indians, engraved by Juan de Noort. This copy wants pp. 1—10, and the title and prefatory leaves are mutilated.]

1648.

106. **Avendaño,** Fernando de.—Sermones de los Ministerios de Nuestra Santa Fe Catolica, en lengua Castellana y la General del Inca. Impugnanse los errores particulares que los Indios han tenido. Parte Primera. Por el Doctor Don Fernando de Avendaño, Arcediano de la Santa Iglesia Metropolitana de Lima, Calificador del Santo Oficio, Catedratico de Prima de Teologia, y Examinador Sinodal. Dedicase al Illustrissimo Señor Doctor Don Pedro de Villagomez, Arcobispo de Lima, del Consejo del Rey N. S. Part I, 129 leaves. Part II, 94 leaves.

Impresso en Lima, por Jorge Lopez de Herrera, Impressor de Libros, en la Calle de la Carcel de Corte, 1648. fol.

[Not in the British Museum.—A copy in the John Carter Brown Library, Providence, Rhode Island.]

107. **Solorzano Pereyra,** Juan de.—Politica Indiana. Sacada en lengua Castellana de los dos tomos del Derecho, i Govierno Municipal de las Indias Occidentales que mas copiosamente escribio en la Latina el Dotor Don Juan de Solorzano Pereira, Caballero del Orden de Santiago, del Consejo del Rey Nuestro Señor en los Supremos de Castilla, i de las Indias. Por el mesmo Autor. Dividida en seis Libros. [With a second fine engraved title-page dated 1647.] (Indice.) pp. 1040.

Por Diego Diaz de la Carrera: en Madrid, Año MDCXLVIII. fol.

[K. 23. b. 16.—521. l. 11.—1703. 521. m. 10.—1776. 2 tom. 711. h. 16, 17.]

1650.

108. **Soleto Pernia,** Alonso.—Alonso Soleto Pernia. Memoria de lo que han hecho mis padres y yo en busca del Dorado, que ansi se llama esta conquista, y dicen que es el Paytiti. MS. *Archivo de Indias.* c. 1650.

See 1905, No. 286.

1653.

109. **Cobo,** Bernabé.—Historia del Nuevo Mundo. Por el P. Bernabé Cobo, de la Compañía de Jesús. 1653.

See 1890, No. 254.

1658.

110. **Leon Pinelo**, Antonio de.—Politica de las Grandezas y Govierno del Supremo y Real Consejo de las Indias. Dirigida al Rey Nuestro Señor en el mismo Real Consejo, &c. Por el Licenciado Antonio de Leon. ff. 20.

[Madrid, 1658.] 4°.

[8155. c. 45.]

1661.

111. **Padilla**, Juan de, *Alcalde.*—Carta, que tiene por titulo, Trabajos, agravios, e injusticias, que padecen los Indios del Peru, en lo espiritual, y temporal. [Por Juan de Padilla.—Ordered to be printed by Don Luis Enriquez de Guzman, Conde de Alva, Virrey destos Reynos del Peru, September 21, 1660.] ff. 70.

[Lima, 1661.] fol.

[600. l. 14.—With the book-plate of the Duke of Sussex.]

1668.

112. **Avendaño**, Diego de.—R. P. Didaci de Avendaño Societatis Jesu, Segoviensis, in Peruvio jam pridem publici & primarij S. Theologiæ Professoris, & in Sacro Inquisitionis Sanctæ Tribunali adlecti Censoris, Thesaurus Indicus, seu Generalis Instructor pro regimine conscientiæ, in iis quæ ad Indias spectant. Tom. 1, 2.

Apud Jacobum Meursium: Antverpiæ, Anno MDCLXVIII. fol.

[K. 14. c. 6.—Tom. 3–6, 1675, are mentioned by Antonio de Leon Pinelo, *Epitome*, col. 675, 1737.]

1677.

113. **Courtot**, François.—La Vie du bien-heureux père Francisco Solano, religieux de l' ordre de Saint François, Patron du Pérou, composée sur les mémoires présentées au Saint Siège pour sa béatification, et le récit du Martyre d'onze Religieux du mesme Ordre...l'an 1572. pp. xvi. 157.

Paris, 1677. 12°.

[Not in the British Museum.—Karl W. Hiersemann, Leipzig, *Katalog* 336, No. 1792. 1907.]

114. **Kellen**, Ludovicus.—Erzehlung des Lebens, Tugenden, und Wunderwercken des Apostels von Peru, des S. Vatters Francisci Solani, S. Francisci Ordens, erwehlten Patrons der Haupt- u. Königlichen Stadt Limae in Peru. 14 plates. pp. 378.

Maeyntz, 1677. fol.

[Not in the British Museum.—Karl W. Hiersemann, Leipzig. *Katalog* 336, No. 1810. 1907.]

1688.

115. **Fernandez de Piedrahita**, Lucas, successively *Bishop of Santa Marta and of Panama.*—Historia general de las Conquistas del Nuevo Reyno de Granada. A la S. C. R. M. de D. Carlos Segundo, Rey de las Españas, y de las Indias. Por el Doctor D. Lucas Fernandez Piedrahita. Primera Parte. pp. 599.

Por Juan Baptista Verdussen: Amberes, [1688]. fol.

[9781. f. 29.—601. l. 14.—Two engraved title-pages, with medallion portraits of Chiefs of Bogota. These are apparently only copies of the portraits of the Incas, in " Historia general de los Hechos

de los Castellanos en las Islas y Tierra Firme del Mar Oceano,"
by Antonio de Herrera Tordesillas, *Madrid*, 1615. Lucas
Fernandez de Piedrahita's great-grandmother, Francisca Nusta,
was a niece of the Inca Huayna Ccapac.]
See 1601, No. 61 ; 1906, No. 289; 1907, No. 290.

116. **Garcilasso de la Vega**, *El Inca.*—The Royal Commentaries of
Peru. In two Parts. The First Part treating of the Original of their
Incas or Kings : of their Idolatry : of their Laws and Government both
in Peace and War : of the Reigns and Conquests of the Incas : with
many other Particulars relating to their Empire and Policies before
such time as the Spaniards invaded their Countries. The Second Part
describing the manner by which that New World was conquered by
the Spaniards. Also the Civil Wars between the Piçarrists and the
Almagrians, occasioned by Quarrels arising about the Division of that
Land. Of the Rise and Fall of Rebels ; and other Particulars contained in that History. Illustrated with Sculptures. Written originally
in Spanish, by the Inca Garcilasso de la Vega, and rendred into
English, by Sir Paul Ricaut, Kt. pp. 1019.

*Printed by Miles Flesher, for Jacob Tonson at the Judge's-Head in
Chancery-Lane near Fleetstreet: London,* MDCLXXXVIII. fol.

[K. 146. g. 8.—King George the Third's copy, with a second title-
page : *Printed by Miles Flesher, for Christopher Wilkinson at the
Black Boy against St. Dunstan's Church in Fleetstreet: London,*
1688.—G. 2875. With the autograph and book-plate of George
Grenville.—Without the Jacob Tonson title-page.]

1691.

117. **Melgar**, Estevan Sancho de.—Arte de la Lengua General del Ynga,
llamada Qquechhua. Compuesto por el Bac. D. Estevan Sancho de
Melgar, natural de esta Ciudad de los Reyes...Consagrale a Don
Francisco de Oyague, Cavallero del Orden de Santiago, &c. ff. 55.

*Impresso de Lima, en la Calle de las Mantas, por Diego de Lyra, Año
de* 1691. 12°.

[12943. aa. 12.—12907. a. 43. This copy wants fol. 1, 2 of the
Dedication.]

1700.

118. **Torres Rubio**, Diego de, *S.J.*—Arte de la Lengua Quichua. Por
el P. Diego de Torres Rubio, de la Compañia de Jesus. Y nuevamente van añadidos los Romances, el Cathecismo pequeño, todas las
Oraciones, los dias da fiesta, y ayunos de los Indios, el Vocabulario
añadido, y otto Vocabulario de la lengua Chinchaisuyo. Por el M. P.
Juan de Figueredo Professo de la misma Compañia...Consagrale al
Senor D. D. Miguel Nuñez de Sanabria...A Costa de Francisco Farfan
de los Godos, Mercader de Libros, &c. ff. 114.

*En Lima por Joseph de Contreras y Alvarado, Impressor Real, de el
S. Oncio, de la Santa Cruzada,* [1700]. 12°.

[C. 33. a. 49.] *See* 1619, No. 88 ; 1754, No. 134.

119. **Zhaval.** LETERA DE LA nobil cipta : novamente ritrovata alle Indie
con li costumi & modi del suo Re & soi populi : Li modi del suo
adorare con la bella usanza de le donne loro : & de le dua persone
ermafrodite donate da quel Re al Capitano de larmata. El V. S. V.
Al Suo. D. L. S. Data in Peru adi. xxv. de Novembre. Del.
MDXXXIIII. 4 leaves.

[*Florence,* 1700.] 4°.

[697. g. 34. (6).—Purchased Nov. 6, 1841.] *See* 1534, No. 10.
1850, No. 172 ; 1535, No. 14.

1706.

120. **Garcilasso de la Vega,** *el Inca.*—Histoire des Guerres Civiles des Espagnols dans les Indes, entre les Piçarres & les Almagres, qui les avoient conquises. Traduite de l'Espagnol de l'Ynca Garcillasso de la Vega [*Comentarios Reales*, Pt. 2], par J. Baudouin. [With two maps of North and South America.] 2 vols.

Chez Gerard Kuyper, Marchand Libraire à côté de la Maison de Ville: à Amsterdam, MDCCVI. 8º.

[K. 278. a. 27, 28.—With a second engraved title.] *See* 1633, No. 98; 1715, No. 122; 1737, No. 127; 1830, No. 157.

1709.

121. **Cieza de Leon,** Pedro de.—The Seventeen Years Travels of Peter de Cieza, through the mighty Kingdom of Peru, and the large Provinces of Cartagena and Popayan in South America, from the city of Panama, on the Isthmus, to the Frontiers of Chile. Now first translated from the Spanish [by John Stevens], and illustrated with a Map, and several Cuts. [Dedicated to the Honourable Edmund Poley, of Badley, Suffolk.] pp. 244.

London: Printed in the Year MDCCIX. 4º.

[981. c. 18.—From the Library of Sir Joseph Banks.] *See* 1553, No. 27.

1715.

122. **Garcilasso de la Vega,** *el Inca.*—Histoire des Yncas, Rois du Pérou, contenant leur origine, depuis le premier Ynca Manco Capac, leur Etablissement, leur Idolâtrie, leurs Sacrifices, leurs Loix, leurs Conquêtes; les merveilles du Temple du Soleil; & tout l'Etat de ce grand Empire, avant que les Espagnols s'en rendissent Maîtres. Avec une Description des Animaux, des Fruits, des Minéraux, des Plantes, &c. Traduite de l'Espagnol de l'Ynca Garcillasso de la Vega [*Comentarios Reales*, Pt. 1], par Jean Baudouin. [With a map of Peru, and three plates.] 2 tom.

Chez Jaques Desbordes, sur le Pont de la Bourse: à Amsterdam, MDCCXV. 8º.

1196. b. 24, 25.—With a second engraved title.]

1716.

123. **Zarate,** Augustin de.—Histoire de la Découverte et de la Conquête du Pérou. Traduite de l'Espagnol d'Augustin de Zarate, par. S. D. C. [Samuel de Broé, Seigneur de Citry & de La Guette]. 2 tom.

Par la Compagnie des Libraires: à Paris, MDCCXVI. 8º.

K. 278. a. 11, 12.—The names of 10 booksellers, of the Compagnie des Libraires, occur on the *verso* of the title-page.—Tom. 1 has one map and eight plates.] *See* 1555, No. 31.

1723.

124. **Garcilasso de la Vega,** *El Inca.*—Primera Parte de los Commentarios Reales que tratan de el Origen de los Incas, Reies, que fueron del Perù, de su Idolatria, Leies y Govierno en Paz y en Guerra, de sus Vidas, y Conquistas y de todo lo que fue aquel Imperio y su Republica, antes que los Españoles pasaran, à èl. Escritos por el Inca Garcilaso de la Vega, Natural del Cozco, y Capitan de su Magestad. Dirigidos a el Rei Nuestro Señor. Segunda Impresion, enmendada, y añadida la Vida de Inti Cusi Titu Iupanqui, Penultimo Inca. Con dos Tablas; una, de los Capitulos, y otra, de las Cosas Notables. ([Segunda Parte:] Historia General del Perù, trata, el Descubrimiento de el, y como lo ganaron los

Españoles: las Guerras Civiles, que huvo entre Pizarros y Almagros sobre la Partija de la Tierra. Castico, y Levantamiento de Tyranos, y otros sucesos particulares, que en la Historia se contienen...Dirigida a la Limpisima Virgen Maria, Madre de Dios, y Señora Nuestra. Segunda Impresion, &c. 1722.) [Edited by Gabriel de Cardenas, pseud., i.e. Andrès Gonzalez de Barcia Carballido y Zuñiga.] *En la Oficina Real, y à Costa de Nicolas Rodriguez Franco, Impresor de Libros: en Madrid,* CIƆIƆCCXXIII, 1722. fol.

[K. 145. f. 13.—688. h. 7, 8. From the Library of the Rev. Clayton Mordaunt Cracherode.] *See* 1609, No. 75; 1829, No. 156.

1729.

125. **García, Gregorio.**—Origen de los Indios de el Nuevo Mundo, e Indias Occidentales. Averiguado con discurso de opiniones por el Padre Presentado Fr. Gregorio Garcia, de la Orden de Predicadores... Segunda Impresion. Enmendada, y añadida de algunas opiniones ò cosas notables, en major prueba de lo que contiene...Dirigido al Angelico Doct. Sto Tomas de Aquino. pp. 336.

En la Imprenta de Francisco Martinez Abad: en Madrid, Año de 1729. fol.

[G. 7225.—K. 146. e. 4.] *See* 1607, No. 69.

1732.

126. **Peralta Barnuevo Rocha y Benavides,** Pedro José de.—Lima Fundada, o Conquista del Perú. Poema Heroico. En que se decanta toda la Historia del Descubrimiento, y sugecion de sus Provincias por Don Francisco Pizarro, Marques de los Atabillos Inclyto y Primer Governador de este vasto Imperio. Y se contine la serie de los Reyes, la historia de los Virreyes y Arzobispos, que ha tenido; y la memoria de los Santos, y Varones ilustres, que la Ciudad y Reyno han producido. La qual ofrece, dedica, y consagra al Excelentissimo Señor Don Joseph de Armendariz, Marquès de Castelfuerte, Commendador de Chiclana y Montizon en el Orden de Santiago, Capitan General de los Reales Exercitos de S. Magestad, y Virrey de estos Reynos del Perù, Tierra firme, y Chile. El Doctor D. Pedro de Peralta Barnuevo Rocha y Benavides, &c. 2 pts.

En la Imprenta de Francisco Sobrino y Bados: en Lima, 1732. 4º.

[G. 11, 318.—K. 87. b. 11, 12.] *See* 1863, No. 196.

1737.

127. **Garcilasso de la Vega,** *el Inca.*—Histoire des Yncas, Rois du Pérou, depuis le premier Ynca Manco Capac, Fils du Soleil, jusqu'à Atahualpa, dernier Ynca: où l'on voit leur Etablissement, leur Religion, leurs Loix, leurs Conquêtes; les merveilles du Temple du Soleil; & tout l'Etat de ce grand Empire, avant que les Espagnols s'en rendissent maîtres. Traduite de l'Espagnol [*Comentarios Reales,* Pt. 1] de l'Ynca Garcillasso de la Vega. [Par Jean Baudoin.] On a joint à cette Edition l'Histoire de la Conquête de la Floride. Par le même Auteur, &c. [1605.—Translated by Pierre Richelet.] Avec des Figures dessinées par feu B. Picart, le Romain. [Three maps, and fourteen plates.]—(Nouvelle Découverte d'un Pays plus grand que l'Europe, situé dans l'Amérique. [By Louis Hennepin.]) 2 tom.

Chez Jean Frederic Bernard: à Amsterdam, MDCCXXXVII. 4º.

K. 145. b. 3, 4.—The date on the imprint of tom. 2 is misprinted: MDCCXXVII.] *See* 1609, No. 75.

128. **Leon Pinelo**, Antonio de.—Epitome de la Bibliotheca oriental y occidental, nautica y geografica de Don Antonio de Leon Pinelo, del Consejo de su Mag. en la Casa de la Contratacion de Sevilla, y Coronista Major de las Indias. Añadido, y enmendado nuevamente, en que se contienen los Escritores de las Indias Orientales y Occidentales y Reinos convecinos...Al Rey Nuestro Señor. Por Mano del Marques de Torre-Nueva, su Secretario del Despacho Universal de Hacienda, Indias y Marina. [Edited by Andrès Gonzalez de Barcia Carballido y Zuñiga.]
En la Oficina de Francisco Martinez Abad: en Madrid, Año de MDCCXXXVII.–VIII. fol.
[G. 489.—K. 125. g. 14.—620. i. 5.]

1741.

129. **Alcedo y Herrera**, Dionysio de.—Aviso Historico, Politico, Geographico, con las Noticias mas particulares del Peru, Tierra-Firme, Chile, y Nuevo Reyno de Granada, en la Relacion de los Sucessos de 205 años, por la Chronologia de los Adelantados, Presidentes, Governadores y Virreyes de aquel Reyno Meridional desde el año de 1535 hasta el de 1740, &c. Dedicado al Rey Nuestro Señor...y escrito en virtud de Real Orden de S. M. por Don Dionysio de Alcedo y Herrera. pp. 382.
En la Oficina de Diego Miguel de Peralta: Madrid, [1741]. 4°.
[9772. bbb. 3.]

1744.

130. **Garcilasso de la Vega**, *el Inca.*—Histoire des Incas, Rois du Pérou. Nouvellement traduite de l'Espagnol de Garcillasso de la Vega. Et mise dans un meilleur ordre; avec des Notes & des Additions sur l'Histoire Naturelle de ce Pays. [Translated by Thomas François Dalibard. With two maps, by Philippe Buache.] 2 tom.
Chez Prault fils, Quai de Conti, vis-à-vis la descente du Pont-Neuf, à la Charité: à Paris, MDCCXLIV. 8°.
[9772. de. 1.]

1747.

131. **Campbell**, John, *LL.D.*— The Spanish Empire in America; containing a succinct relation of the discovery and settlement of its several colonies; a view of their respective situations, extent, commodities, trade, *etc.*, and a full and clear account of the commerce with Old Spain by the Galleons, Flota, *etc.*; as also of the contraband trade with the English, Dutch, French, Danes and Portuguese. With an exact description of Paraguay. By an English Merchant. [John Campbell, LL.D.]
John Stagg and Daniel Browne: London, 1747. 8°.
[Not in the British Museum.—This is another edition of Dr John Campbell's "A Concise History of the Spanish America," pp. viii. 330. *John Stagg and Daniel Browne: London,* 1741. 8°.—1061. c. 18.]

1748.

132. **Ulloa**, Antonio de, *Admiral.*—Relacion Historica [by Antonio de Ulloa] del Viage á la América Meridional, hecho [1735–1746] de orden de S. Mag. para medir algunos grados de Meridiano Terrestre, y venir por ellos en conocimiento de la verdedera Figura, y Magnitud de la Tierra, con otras varias Observaciones Astronomicas, y Phisicas. Por Don Jorge Juan, Comendador de Aliaga, en el Orden de San Juan...y Don Antonio de Ulloa, de la Real Sociedad de Londres, ambos

Capitanes de Fragata de la Real Armada. (Resumen Historico del Origen, y Succession de los Incas, y demas Soberanos del Perú, con Noticias de los Sucessos mas notables en el Reynado de Cada Uno. pp. cxcv. With an engraved plate, 24 × 17¾ inches, of the 14 Incas, and 8 Kings of Spain, from Charles V to Ferdinand VI, in 22 numbered medallions. "Didacus Villanova invenit et delineavit. I^s. Palom^o. sculp^r. Regius inv^t. excudit, et Iconibus incidit. Mat^{ti}. Anno MDCCXLVIII.") 5 tom. [With maps, charts, and plans.]

Impressa de Orden del Rey Nuestro Señor en Madrid por Antonio Marin, Año de M.DCC.XLVIII. fol.

[983. g. 19, 20.—From the Library of Sir Joseph Banks. This copy has inserted, in Vol. I, an engraved plate, 8¾ × 13¼ inches, " Dame Créole du Pérou vétue selon l'usage de Lima. S$^{ra.}$ Criolla de Lima. Dedicado al S$^{or.}$ D$^{n.}$ Joseph Perfecto de Salas...por...Pedro M***. Julian Davila Lim. Pinx. Ingouf Junior Parisinus sculpsit anno 1774."—K. 215. a. 6–9. King George the Third's copy wants Vol. 5, 1748.—K. 144. e. 14 is the 1773 folio edition of Vol. 5.—687 k. 10–14. From the Library of the Rev. Clayton Mordaunt Cracherode.—568. g. 1–4, wanting Vol. 5.]

1752.

133. **Ulloa,** Antonio de, *Admiral.*—Voyage Historique de l'Amérique Meridionale fait par ordre du Roi d'Espagne, par Don George Juan... et par Don Antoine de Ulloa...Ouvrage orné des figures, plans et cartes nécessaires, et qui contient une Histoire des Yncas du Pérou, et les Observations Astronomiques & Physiques, faites pour déterminer la Figure & la Grandeur de la Terre. [Dedicated to "Son Altesse Royale Monseigneur le Prince Royale de Pologne [Friedrich Christian, Elector of Saxony.]" Translated by Eléazar de Mauvillon.] 2 tom.

Chez Arkstée and Merkus: à Amsterdam et à Leipzig, MDCCLII.   4°.

[K. 211. c. 7, 8.]

1754.

134. **Torres Rubio,** Diego de, *S.J.*—Arte y Vocabulario de la Lengua Quichua General de los Indios de el Perú. Que compuso el Padre Diego de Torres Rubio, de la Compañia de Jesus. Y añadio el P. Juan de Figueredo, de la misma Compañia. Ahora nuevamente Corregido, y Aumentado...Por un Religioso de la misma Compañia. Dedicado al Doct. D. Bernardo de Zubieta y Roxas, &c. ff. 254.

Reimpresso en Lima, en la Imprenta de la Plazuela de San Christoval, Año de 1754.   12°.

[G. 7452.—826. a. 13.] *See* 1700, No. 118.

1762.

135. **American Gazetteer.**—The American Gazetteer. Containing a distinct Account of all the parts of the New World: their Situation, Climate, Soil, Produce, Former and present Condition; Commodities, Manufactures, and Commerce. Together with an accurate Account of the Cities, Towns, Ports, Bays, Rivers, Lakes, Mountains, Passes, and Fortifications. The whole intended to exhibit the Present State of Things in that Part of the Globe, and the Views and Interests of the several Powers who have Possessions in America. Illustrated with proper Maps. 3 vols.

Printed for A. Millar, and J. & R. Tonson, in the Strand: London, 1762.   12°.

[798. d. 2–4.]

1763.

136. **American Gazetteer.**—Il Gazzettiere Americano. Contenente un distinto ragguaglio di tutte le parti del Nuovo Mondo della loro Situazione, Clima, Terreno, Prodotti, Stato antico e moderno, Merci, Manifatture, e Commercio. Con una esatta descrizione delle Città, Piazze, Porti, Baje, Fiumi, Laghi, Montagne, Passi, e Fortificazione. Il tutto destinato ad esporre lo stato presente delle cose in quella parte di Globo, e le mire, e interessi delle diverse Potenze, che hanno degli stabilimenti in America. Tradotto dall' Inglese [1762] e arricchito di Aggiunte, Note, Carte e Rami. 3 tom. 78 maps. 𝕃.𝕡.

Per Marco Coltellini, all' Insegna della Verità: in Livorno MDCCLXIII. 4°.

[K. 145. f. 2–4.—Tom. 1 has an engraved frontispiece, by Carlo Coltellini & F. Gregorii, of four Indians offering homage to Pizarro.]

137. **El Conocimiento de los Tiempos.**—[Descripcion del Reyno del Perù, y de el de Chile por Obispados y provincias, y en igual conformidad de las del Rio de la Plata, y sus respectivas Dependencias, que en los 15 años contados de 1763 à 1772, y de 1774 à 1778. Diò à luz en la Ciudad de los Reyes, Capital del Virreynato, el Doctor Don Cosme Bueno, Catedratico de Prima de Matematicas, Cosmografo mayor de dicho Reyno, y socio de la Real Academia Medica Matritense. 1763 año primero comprehensibo del Catalogo de los Ex^mos. S^res. Virreyes del Perù.]

["*El Conocimiento de los Tiempos*": Lima, 1763–78.] 12°.

[C. 28. a. 17.—Bound in red silk, ribbed, with two metal clasps.— Purchased February 5, 1849.] *See* 1863, No. 196.

138.—[Another copy, with the addition of "Dissertacion Physico experimental sobre la Naturaleza del Agua, y sus propriades"; "Continuacion de la Disertacion del Agua"; and "Dissertacion sobre los Antojos de las Mugeres Preñades." With a manuscript note by Robert Southey: "This book, of which perhaps a duplicate is nowhere to be found, was given me by Mr Murray. It contains the fullest account which has yet been published of the old Viceroyalty of Peru, Province by Province. The information was obtained from the respective Corregidores, and printed for many successive years in the Lima Almanack [*El Conocimiento de los Tiempos*], from whence some Curioso cut out the whole collection, and formed them into this most valuable little volume. Even the Catalogue of Viceroys contains some facts which I have not seen elsewhere.

"There are a few physical essays at the end, printed in the same almanack. Some curious notices are to be found in them.

"R. SOUTHEY.

"I have frequently been beholden to this book, in writing the History of Brazil."]

[C. 28. a. 2.—Purchased July 27, 1844.]

1774.

139. **Catecismo.**—Tercero Catecismo y Exposicion de la Doctrina Christiana por Sermones. Paraque los Curas, y otros Ministros prediquen, y enseñen à los Indios, y à las demàs Personas: Conforme a lo que se proveyo en el Santo Concilio Provincial de Lima el año pasado de 1583. Mandado reimprimir por el Concilio Provincial del año de 1773. pp. 515.

En la Oficina de la Calle de San Jacinto: [Lima, 1774]. 4°.

[4425. aa. 14.] *See* 1585, No. 50.

1777.

140. **Marmontel, Jean François.**—Les Incas, ou La Destruction de l'Empire du Pérou. Par M. Marmontel, Historiographe de France, l'un des Quarante de l'Académie Françoise. [Dedicated to Gustavus III, King of Sweden.] 2 tom.

Chez Lacombe, Libraire, rue de Tournon, près le Luxembourg: à Paris, M.DCC.LXXVII. 12°.

[12512. aaa. 9.]

1783.

141. **Antonio, Nicholas.**—Bibliotheca Hispana Nova...1500 ad 1684. [Edited by T. A. Sanchez, J. A. Pellicer, and R. Casalbonus.] 2 tom.

Apud Joachimum de Ibarra: Matriti, 1783-88. 4°.

[G. 53.—K. 128. h. 4, 5.—K. 126. h. 5, 6.—2049. e.]

1785.

142. **Gronovius, Abrahamus.**—Bibliothecæ Gronovianæ pars reliqua et præstantissima...quorum publice fiet auctio...Die 30 Majii et seqq. 1785.

Haak and Co.: Lugduni Bat., 1785. 8°.

[Not in the British Museum.—There is a copy in the Göttingen University Library. The Sarmiento MS., 1572, is No. 60 on p. 7 of the MSS.]

1789.

143. **Velasco, Juan de.**—Historia del Reino de Quito. 1789.

See 1840, No. 164.

1791.

144. **Eder, Franciscus Xavier,** *S.J.*—Descriptio Provinciæ Moxitarum in Regno Peruano, quam e scriptis posthumis Franc. Xav. Eder e Soc. Jesu annis XV. sacri apud eosdem Curionis digessit, expolivit, & adnotatiunculis illustravit Abb. & Consil. Reg. Mako. [With 9 plates & 1 map.] pp. xviii. 383.

Typis Universitatis: Budæ, 1791. 8°.

[10480. e. 5.]

145. *Mercurio Peruano.*—Mercurio Peruano de Historia, Literatura, y Noticias Públicas que da á luz la Sociedad Academica de Amantes de Lima, y en su nombre D. Jacinto Calero y Moreira. 12 tom.

En la Imprenta Real de los Niños Huérfanos: Lima, 1791-95. 4°.

[P. P. 4095.—This publication was suppressed by the Spanish Government.] *See* 1861, No. 193.

1792.

146. **Acosta, Joseph de.**—Historia Natural y Moral de las Indias...Por el Padre Joseph de Acosta, de la extinguida Compañía de Jesus. Dala a luz en esta sexta edicion. D. A. V. C. 2 tom.

Por Pantaleon Aznar: Madrid, Año de MDCCXCII. 8°.

[9551 f. 3.]

1793.

147. **Bombelli, Pietro.**—Breve ed esatta notizia della miracolosa immagine di Maria Santissima di Copacavana nel Perú, cavata dalla raccolta delle immagini della Bma Vergine. pp. 12.

Roma, 1793. 12°.

[Not in the British Museum.—Karl W. Hiersemann, Leipzig, *Katalog* 336, No. 1781. a. 1907.]

1800.

148. **Hervás y Panduro, Lorenzo.**—Catálogo de las Lenguas de las Naciones Conocidas, y numeracion, division, y clases de estas segun la diversidad de sus idiomas y dialectos. Su Autor el Abate Don Lorenzo Hervás, Teólogo del Eminentísimo Señor Cardenal Juan Francisco Albani, Decano del Sagrado Colegio Apostólico, y Canonista del Eminentísimo Señor Cardenal Aurelio Roverella, Pro-datario del Santo Padre. 6 vols.

En la Imprenta de la Administracion del Real Arbitrio de Beneficencia: Madrid, Año 1800–1805. 4°.

[623. h. 6-8.]

1807.

149. **Humboldt, Friedrich Heinrich Alexander von, Baron.**—Voyage de Humboldt et [Aimé] Bonpland. [Aux Régions Équinoxiales du Nouveau Continent, fait en 1799–1804.] 6 pts. in 24 vols.

Chez Fr. Schoell: Paris; et chez J. G. Cotta: Tübingue, 1814, 1807–1833. 4° and fol.

[K. 149. h. 1-10 ; i. 1, 2 ; and K. 148. i. 1-12.]

1808.

150. **Beauchamp, Alphonse de.**—Histoire de la Conquête et des Révolutions du Pérou. Par Alphonse de Beauchamp, avec Portraits. [Dedicated to Madame Louise de Salaberry, au Château de Meslay, près Vendôme.] 2 tom.

Chez Lenormant, Imprimeur-Libraire, rue des Prêtres Saint-Germain-l'Auxerrois, No. 17 ; Lerouge, Libraire, Cour du Commerce: à Paris, M.DCCC.VIII. 8°.

[1061. c. 24, 25.]

1821.

151. **Tupac-Amaru, Juan.**—Ventajas de la Constitucion Española. En la Tertulia patriótica de la Isle de Leon se inserta una noticia muy interesante sobre la suerte de D. Juan Tupac-Amaro, descendiente de los antiguos Incas del Perú, que encerrado durante 35 años en el presidio de Ceuta, acaba de ser restituido á la libertad por los ciudadanos de buenos principios que hay en aquella plaza. (Miscelanea, numeros 333 y 334.) pp. 8.

Imprenta de I. Sancha: Madrid; Reimpresa en la Imprenta Imperial: México, 1821. 4°.

[9180. dd. 3. (10).—Tract 10 in a volume, lettered : Papeles Varios. 11.—Historia de España, 11.]

1826.

152. **Juan y Santacilla, Jorge.**—Noticias Secretas de America, sobre el estado naval, militar, y politico de los Reynos del Perú y Provincias de Quito, Costas de Nueva Granada y Chile : Gobierno y Regimen particular de los Pueblos de Indios : Cruel Opresion y Extorsiones de sus Corregidores y Curas : Abusos escandalosos introducidos entre estos habitantes por los misioneros : Causas de su origen y motivos de su continuacion por el espacio de tres siglos. Escritas fielmente segun las instrucciones del Excelentisimo Señor Marques de la Ensenada, Primer Secretario de Estado, y presentadas en informe secreto á S. M. C. el Señor Don Fernando VI por Don Jorge Juan, y Don Antonio de Ulloa, Tenientes Generales de la Real Armada, Miembros de la Real Sociedad de Londres, &c. Sacadas a luz para el verdadero conocimiento del Gobierno de los Españoles en la America Meridional.

Por Don David Barry. [With portraits of D. Jorge Juan, and D. Antonio de Ulloa, engraved by Edwd. Scriven, after J. Maea.] 2 pts. ꝯ.ꝓ.
En la Imprenta de R. Taylor: Londres, 1826. fol.
[G. 6270.—795. m. 5. This copy has on the title-page the imprint of *John Murray, Albemarle Street: London.*]

1827.

153. **Ranking,** John.—Historical Researches on 'the Conquest of Peru, Mexico, Bogota, Natchez, and Talomeco, in the Thirteenth Century, by the Mongols, accompanied with Elephants...containing...History of Peru and Mexico, to the Conquest by Spain.—Grandeur of the Incas, and of Montezuma...With two Maps, and Portraits of all the Incas, and Montezuma. By John Ranking. (Bibliography.—Supplement.) pp. 479. 51.
Longman, Rees, Orme and Co.: London, 1827–34. 8°.
[1061. i. 31.—1061. i. 32.]

1829.

154. **Andagoya,** Pascul de.—Relacion de los sucesos de Pedrarias Dávila en las provincias de Tierra firme ó Castilla del oro, y de lo ocurrido en el descubrimiento de la mar del Sur y costas del Perú y Nicaragua, escrita por el Adelantado Pascual de Andagoya. [1540.] (Orig. en el Arch. de Ind. en Sevilla, Relac. y Descripc., leg. 11.—In Tom. III, Núm. VII, pp. 393–459, " Coleccion de los Viages y Descubrimientos, que hicieron por Mar los Españoles desde fines del siglo XV...Coordinada é ilustrada por Don Martin Fernandez de Navarrete.")
En la Imprenta Real: Madrid, Año 1829. fol.
[G. 6826.—790. g. 3.]

155. **Catecismo.**—Catecismo y Doctrina Cristiano en los Idiomas Castellano, y Qquechua. Ordenado por autoridad del Concilio Provincial de Lima, e impreso en dicha ciudad el año de 1583. Le da nuevamente a luz (habiendole ajustado con el mayor cuidado a su orijinal) el D. D. Carlos Gallegos, &c. pp. 34.
Imprenta del Gobierno: Cuzco, 1829. 4°.
[3506. c. 31.]

156. **Garcilasso de la Vega,** *el Inca.*—Primera (Segunda) Parte de los Comentarios Reales, que tratan del origen de los Incas, reyes que fueron del Perú, de su idolatría, leyes y gobierno, en paz y en guerra, de sus vidas y conquistas, y de todo lo que fue aquel imperio y su republica antes que los españoles pasáran á él. Escritos por el Inca Garcilaso de la Vega, natural del Cozco, y capitan de S. M. Nueva edicion. 4 tom. (Tom. 2–5, " Historia de la Conquista del Nuevo Mundo.")
Imprenta de los Hijos de Doña Catalina Piñuela: Madrid, 1829. 8°.
[1196. b. 10, 11.] *See* 1609, No. 75; 1723, No. 124.

1830.

157. **Garcilasso de la Vega,** *el Inca.*—Histoire des Incas, Rois du Pérou. (Histoire des Guerres Civiles des Espagnols dans les Indes.) Par Garcillasso de la Vega. [Translated from the *Comentarios Reales* by Jean Baudoin.] 7 tom.
Imprimé aux frais du Gouvernement pour procurer du travail aux Ouvriers Typographes: Paris, Aout 1830. 8°.
[790. e. 17–19.—The Printed Catalogue of the Bibliothèque Nationale ascribes this translation to Jean Baudoin.] *See* 1633, No. 98; 1706, No. 120; 1715, No. 122; 1737, No. 127.

158. **Pizarro**, Hernando.—Carta de Hernando Pizarro a los magníficos
señores, los señores oidores de la audiencia real de S. M. que reside en
la ciudad de Santo Domingo. [Nov. 1533.] (Sacada de Oviedo, que
la inserta en el cap. 15. de su parte tercera, ó lib. 43 de su Historia
General [which exists only in manuscript].) [Apendice v. pp. 392–406.
Tom. II, "Vidas de Españoles Célebres. (Francisco Pizarro.) Por
Don Manuel Josef Quintana." 3 tom. 1807–1833.]
   Imprenta de Don Miguel de Burgos : Madrid, 30 julio 1830. 8°.
   [614. b. 29, 30.—Another edition : "Coleccion de los Mejores
   Autores Españoles." Tom. XXXIV. *Baudry : Paris, 1845.* 8°.
   12220. i.]

159. **Sancho**, Pedro.—Testimonio de la Acta de reparticion del rescate
de Atahualpa, otorgado, por el escribano Pedro Sancho. [1533.]
(Extractado de la obra inédita, *Noticia general del Perú, Tierre firme y
Chile*, por Francisco Lopez de Caravantes, Contador de Cuentas en el
tribunal de la contaduría mayor de las mismas provincias. Esta obra
estuvo antes en la librería del colegio mayor de Cuenca de Salamanca,
y ahora existe en la particular de S. M.) [Apendice VI, pp. 407–415.
Tom. II, "Vidas de Españoles Célebres. (Francisco Pizarro.) Por
Don Manuel Josef Quintana." 3 tom. 1807–1833.]
   Imprenta de Don Miguel de Burgos : Madrid, 30 julio 1830. 8°.
   [614. b. 29, 30.—Another edition : "Coleccion de los Mejores
   Autores Españoles." Tom. XXXIV. *Baudry : Paris, 1845.* 8°.—
   12230. i.]

1836.

160. **Tupac Amaru**, José Gabriel.—Relacion Historica de los Sucesos de la
Rebellion de José Gabriel Tupac-Amaru en las Provincias del Perú, el
Año de 1780. Primera Edicion. pp. viii. 113.—Documentos para la
Historia de la Sublevacion de José Gabriel Tupac-Amaru, Cacique de
la Provincia de Tinta, en el Peru. Primera Edicion. pp. 286, v.
(Tom. v, Coleccion de Obras y Documentos relativos á la Historia
Antigua y Moderna de las Provincias del Rio de La Plata, ilustrados
con notas y disertaciones por Pedro de Angelis.)
   Imprenta del Estado : Buenos-Aires, 1836. fol.
   [600. m. 12. (3, 4).]—*See* 1863, No. 197.

1837.

161. **Xeres**, Francisco de.—Relation Véridique de la Conquête du Pérou et de
la Province du Cuzco, nommée Nouvelle-Castille. Par François Xérès.
Salamanque. 1547. pp. viii. 198. (Tom. IV, "Voyages, Relations et
Mémoires Originaux pour servir à l'histoire de la découverte de
l'Amérique, publiés pour la première fois en français par H. Ternaux-
Compans.")
   Arthus Bertrand : Paris, M.DCCC.XXXVII. 8°.
   [G. 15806.—1196. i. 4.]

1840.

162. **Cavello Balboa**, Miguel.—Histoire du Pérou. Par Miguel Cavello
Balboa. Inédite. (Part III of *Miscellanée Australe [Miscellanea
austral].* 1586.) pp. viii. 331. (In "Voyages, Relations et Mémoires
Originaux, pour servir à l'histoire de la découverte de l'Amérique,
publiés pour la première fois en Français par H. Ternaux-Compans."
Tom. 15.)
   Arthus Bertrand : Paris, 1840. 8°.
   [G. 15817.—1196. i. 8.] *See* 1586, No. 51.

163. **Montesinos**, Fernando de.—Mémoires Historiques sur l'ancien Pérou. [Memorias antiguas historiales y políticas del Perú.] Par le Licencié Fernando Montesinos. Inédits. pp. xv. 235. (In "Voyages, Relations et Mémoires Originaux, pour servir à l'histoire de la découverte de l'Amérique, publiés pour la première fois en Français par H. Ternaux-Compans." Tom. 17.)
    Arthus Bertrand: Paris, 1840. 8°.
    [G. 15819.—1196. i. 9.] *See* 1882, No. 244.

164. **Velasco**, Juan de.—Histoire du Royaume de Quito. [Historia del Reino de Quito.] Par Don Juan de Velasco, Natif de ce royaume... Inédite. (1789.) 2 tom. (In "Voyages, Relations et Mémoires Originaux, pour servir à l'histoire de la découverte de l'Amérique, publiés pour la première fois en Français par H. Ternaux-Compans." Tom. 18, 19.)
    Arthus Bertrand: Paris, MDCCCXL. 8°.
    [G. 15821–2.—1196. i. 9, 10.]

1842.

165. **Gonzalez Holguin**, Diego, *S.J.*—Gramática y Arte Nueva de la Lengua General de todo el Peru, llamada Lengua Qquichua o Lengua del Inca...Compuesta por el Padre Diego Gonzales Holguin, de la Compañia de Jesus, natural de Caceres. Nueva edicion revista y corregida. (Dedicada al Doctor Hernando Arias de Ugarte, &c.) pp. 288.
    [*Lima*,] MDCCCXLII. 8°.
    [12910. cc. 5.] *See* 1607, No. 70.

1843.

166. **Xéres**, Francisco de.—Geschichte der Entdeckung und Eroberung Peru's. Von Francisco de Xerez, Pizarro's Geheimschreiber. Aus dem Spanischen von Dr Ph. H. Külb. Nebst Ergänzung aus Augustins de Zarate und Garcilasso's de la Vega Berichten. pp. viii. 252. (Lieferung 27. Reisen und Länderbeschreibungen der älteren und neuesten Zeit...Herausgegeben von Dr Eduard Widenmann...und Dr Hermann Hauff.)
    Druck und Verlag der J. G. Cotta'schen Buchhandlung: Stuttgart und Tübingen, 1843. 8°.
    [1294. c. 6.]

1846.

167. **Tschudi**, Johann Jakob von.—Peru. Reiseskizzen aus den Jahren 1838–1842. Von J. J. von Tschudi. 2 Bde.
    Scheitlin und Zollikofer: St Gallen, 1846. 8°.
    [1430. i. 17.]

1847.

168. **Prescott**, William Hickling.—History of the Conquest of Peru. With a preliminary view of the Civilization of the Incas. By William H. Prescott. 2 vols.
    Richard Bentley: London, 1847. 8°.
    [9771. eee. 7.—The original American edition does not appear to be in the British Museum. There is a copy in the Boston Public Library, Massachusetts.]

169. **Tschudi, Johann Jakob von.**—Travels in Peru, during the years 1838–1842, on the Coast, in the Sierra, across the Cordilleras and the Andes, into the Primeval Forests. By Dr J. J. von Tschudi. Translated from the German by Thomasina Ross. pp. xii. 506.
　　David Bogue: London, MDCCCXLVII. 8°.
　　[1430. i. 11.]

170. **Vater, Johann Severin.**—Litteratur der Grammatiken, Lexica und Wörtersammlungen aller Sprachen der Erde. Von Johann Severin Vater. [1815.] Zweite, völlig umgearbeitete Ausgabe von B. Jülg. (Verbesserungen.) pp. xii. 592.
　　In der Nicolaischen Buchhandlung: Berlin, 1847. 8°.
　　[BB. T. d. 10.—825. g. 12.]

1850.

171. **Castelnau, François de,** *Comte.*—Expédition dans les Parties Centrales de l'Amérique du Sud, de Rio de Janeiro à Lima, et de Lima au Para. Exécutée par ordre du Gouvernement Français pendant les années 1843 à 1847. Sous la direction de Francis de Castelnau. Histoire du Voyage. 6 tom.
　　P. Bertrand: Paris, 1850–51. 8°.
　　[1295. d. 3–5.]

—Deuxième Partie. Vues et Scènes. Les planches lithographiées par Champin. 60 plates. Troisième Partie. Antiquités des Incas et autres peuples anciens. Les planches lithographiées par Champin. 62 plates.
　　P. Bertrand: Paris, 1852. 4°.
　　[1295. h. 11, 12.—Plate 57. Prince Incas, en costume national, d'après un tableau conservé à Cuzco.—Plates, 58, 60. Princesse Incas, en costume national, d'après un tableau conservé à Cuzco.—Plate 59. Prince Incas, en costume espagnol du temps de la conquête, d'après un tableau conservé à Cuzco.]

—Quatrième Partie. Itinéraires et Coupe Géologique. 76 plates. Cinquième Partie. Géographie. Les cartes gravées par Bouffard. 30 maps.
　　P. Bertrand: Paris, 1852–53. fol.
　　[1295. i. 1, 2.]

—Sixième Partie. Botanique. pp. 231. 90 plates.

—Septième Partie. Zoologie. 3 tom.
　　P. Bertrand: Paris, 1855–59. 4°.
　　[1295. h. 13–16.]

172. **Zhaval.**—LETERA DE LA nobil cipta : novamente ritrovata alle Indie con li costumi & modi del suo Re & soi populi : Li modi del suo adorare con la bella usanza de le donne loro : & de le dua persone ermafrodite donata da quel Re al Capitano de larmata. [Signed:] El. V. S. V. Al Suo. D. L. S. Data in Peru adi. xxv de Novembre. Del. MDXXXIIII. [A Reprint of the 1700 edition.] 4 leaves.
　　[*Milano,* 1850.] 4°.
　　[10055. b. 10.—One of 25 copies. Purchased July 18, 1863.] *See* 1534, No. 7; 1700, No. 119; 1535, No. 14.

1851.

173. **Rivero y Ustariz**, Mariano Eduardo de. Antigüedades Peruanas. Por Mariano Eduardo de Rivero...y Juan Diego de Tschudi. pp. xiv. 328.
Imprenta Imperial de la Corte y del Estado: Viena, 1851. 4°.
[579. i. 27.]

—Atlas. 58 coloured plates. *Viena*, 1851. *obl.* fol.
[569. i. 24.] *See* 1853, No. 175.

174. **Sarmiento de Gamboa**, Pedro.—[Bibliography in:] Biblioteca Marítima Española. Obra póstuma del Excmo. Señor Don Martin Fernandez de Navarrete...Impresa de Real Orden. Tom. II. pp. 616–625.
Imprenta de la Viuda de Calero: Madrid, 1851. 8°.
[8806. f. 24.]

1853.

175. **Rivero y Ustariz**, Mariano Eduardo de. Peruvian Antiquities. By Mariano Edward Rivero...and John James von Tschudi...Translated into English from the original Spanish [1851] by Francis L. Hawks, D.D., LL.D. Illustrated. pp. xxii. 306.
George P. Putnam and Co.: New York, 1853. 8°.
[9772. d. 7.] *See* 1851, No. 173.

176. **Squier**, Ephraim George.—Ancient Peru. Its People and its Monuments. [With 29 illustrations, of the Temple of the Sun, Cuzco, Ruins of Pachacamac, Ruins in Titicaca Island, &c. By E. G. Squier.] (In *Harper's New Monthly Magazine*, Vol. VII. June 1853. pp. 7–38.)
Harper and Brothers: New York, 1853. 8°.
[P. P. 6383.]

177. **Tschudi**, Johann Jakob von.—Die Kechua-Sprache. Von J. J. von Tschudi. (Sprachlehre.—Sprachproben.—Wörterbuch.) 3 Abth.
Aus der Kaiserlich-Königlichen Hof- und Staatsdruckerei: Wien, 1853. 8°.
[12907. bbb. 37.]

1854.

178. **Bollaert**, William, *F.R.G.S.*—Observations on the History of the Incas of Peru, on the Indians of South Peru, and on some Indian Remains in the Province of Tarapaca. By W. Bollaert, F.R.G.S. Read 12th May 1852. (*Journal of the Ethnological Society of London*, Vol. III. 1854. pp. 132–164.)
W. Watts, Printer: London, 1854. 8°.
[Ac. 6234/2.]

1855.

179. **Helps**, *Sir* Arthur, *K.C.B.*—The Spanish Conquest in America, and its relation to the history of Slavery, and to the government of Colonies. By Arthur Helps. 4 vols.
John W. Parker and Son: London, 1855–61. 8°.
[09555. cc. 7.] *See* 1900, No. 275.

180. Toledo, Francisco de, *Viceroy of Peru.*—Memorial que D. Francisco de Toledo dió al Rey nuestro Señor del estado en que dejó las cosas del Pirú despues de haber sido en él virey y capitan general trece años, que comenzaron el de 1569. (Sacado de una copia de letra coetánea de un tomo fol. pergamino, señalado N. 2, de la Biblioteca de D. Luis de Salazar.) [1571.] (In "Coleccion de Documentos Inéditos para la Historia de España. Por Los Sres. Marqués de Pidal y D. Miguel Salvá." Tom. XXVI. pp. 122–161.)

Imprenta de la Viuda de Calero: Madrid, 1855. 8°.

[9197 f.]

1856.

181. Markham, Sir Clements Robert, *K.C.B., F.R.S.*—Cuzco. A Journey to the ancient Capital of Peru. With an account of the history, language, literature, and antiquities of the Incas. And Lima. A visit to the Capital and Provinces of Modern Peru. With a sketch of the Viceregal Government, History of the Republic, and a review of the literature and society of Peru. With illustrations and a map. By Clements R. Markham, F.R.G.S., author of "Franklin's Footsteps," pp. iv, 419.

Chapman and Hall: London, 1856. 8°.

[2374. a. 6.]

1857.

182. Benzoni, Girolamo.—History of the New World. By Girolamo Benzoni, of Milan. Shewing his travels in America, from A.D. 1541 to 1566 : with some particulars of the Island of Canary. [Dedicated to the Senator, Scipio Simoneta, 1572.] Now first translated, and edited by Rear-Admiral W. H. Smyth, K.S.F., D.C. L., *etc., etc., etc.* [With woodcuts.] pp. iv. 280. (Hakluyt Society Publications. First Series. Vol. 21.)

Hakluyt Society: London, 1857. 8°.

[Ac. 6172/19.] *See* 1572, No. 44.

183. Mossi de Cambiano, Honorio.—Ensayo sobre las escelencias y perfeccion del Idioma llamado comunmente Quichua. Por el R. P. F. Honorio Mossi, Misionero Apostolico del Colejio de Propaganda Fide, de la esclarecida y opulenta ciudad de Potosí. pp. 54.

Imprenta de Lopez: Sucre, 1857. fol.

[12901. k. 28. (2).]

184. Oliva, Anello, *S.J.*—Histoire du Pérou. Par le P. Anello Oliva. [1631.] Traduite de l'espagnol sur le manuscrit inédit par M. H. Ternaux-Compans. pp. 128. (Bibliothèque Elzevirienne.)

P. Jannet: Paris, MDCCCLVII. 12°.

[12234. b. 7.] *See* 1631, No. 97.

1858.

185. Castro y Rossi, Adolfo de.—Historia de Cádiz y su Provincia desde los remotos tiempos hasta 1814. Escrita por Don Adolfo de Castro. [With a plan of Cadiz, 1609, and 6 plates.] pp. xvi. 826.

Imprenta de la Revista Médica: Cádiz, 1858. 8°.

[10161. e. 22.—The cover is dated : 1859.]

304   BIBLIOGRAPHY

186. **Desjardins**, Antonie Émile Ernest.—Le Pérou avant la conquête espagnole, d'après les principaux historiens originaux, et quelques documents inédits sur les antiquités de ce pays.
Arthus Bertrand: Paris, 1858. 8°.
[Not in the British Museum.]

187. **Ludewig**, Hermann Eduard.—The Literature of American Aboriginal Languages. By Hermann E. Ludewig. With additions and corrections by Professor Wm. W. Turner. Edited by Nicolas Trübner. (Trübner's Bibliotheca Glottica, I.) pp. xxiv. 258.
Trübner and Co.: London, MDCCCLVIII. 8°.
[BB. T. c. 10.]

1859.

188. **Markham**, *Sir* Clements Robert, *K.C.B.*, *F.R.S.*—Expeditions into the Valley of the Amazons, 1539, 1540, 1639. [Expedition of Gonzalo Pizarro to the land of Cinnamon, A.D. 1539–42, translated from the second part of Garcilasso Inca de la Vega's *Royal Commentaries of Peru* [1609]. The Voyage of Francisco de Orellana down the river of the Amazons, A.D. 1540–1, translated from the Sixth Decade of Antonio de Herrera's *General History of the Western Indies* [1615.]—New Discovery of the Great River of the Amazons, by Father Cristoval de Acuña, A.D. 1639, translated from the Spanish edition of 1641.] Translated and edited, with notes, by Clements R. Markham, F.R.G.S., author of "Cuzco and Lima." pp. lxiv. 190. (Hakluyt Society Publications. Series 1, Vol. 24.)
Printed for the Hakluyt Society: London, 1859. 8°.
[Ac. 6172/22.] *See* 1609, No. 75; 1641, No. 103.

1860.

189. **Auteo**, Bartolomé.—Arte de Lingua Quiche, ó Utlatica. Compuesto por U. M. R. P. Fray Bartolomé Auteo Religioso Minor de N. S. Pe San Francisco. With an Essay on the Quichís by Ephraim George Squier, in MS.
1860. 8°.

190. **Bollaert**, William, *F.R.G.S.*—Antiquarian, Ethnological and other Researches in New Granada, Equador, Peru, and Chile. With observations on the Pre-Incarial, Incarial, and other Monuments of Peruvian Nations. By William Bollaert, F.R.G.S....With plates. pp. 279.
Trübner and Co.: London, 1860. 8°.
[10481. d. 22.]

191. **Mossi de Cambiano**, Honorio.—(Diccionario Quichua-Castellano. (Castellano-Quichua.) Por el R. P. Fr. Honorio Mossi, Misionero Apostólico del Colejio de Propaganda Fide de la ilustre y Heróica Ciudad de Sucre. 2 pts.
Imprenta Boliviana: Sucre, Abril 28 de 1860. fol.
[12901. k. 28. (3).]

192. **Mossi de Cambiano**, Honorio.—Gramática de la Lengua General del Perú, llamada comunmente Quichua. Por el R. P. Fr. Honorio Mossi, Misionero Apostólico del Colejio de Propaganda Fide de la esclarecida y opulenta ciudad de Potosi. pp. 72.
Imprenta de Lopez: Sucrr [Sucre, 1860]. fol.
[12901. k. 28. (1).]

1861.

193. *Mercurio Peruano.*—Biblioteca Peruana de Historia, Ciencias y Literatura. Coleccion de Escritos del Anterior y Presente Siglo de los mas acreditados Autores Peruanos. Por Manuel A. Fuentes...Antiguo *Mercurio Peruano.* 9 tom.

Felipe Bailly: Lima, 1861–64. 8°.

[P. P. 4095. b.] *See* 1791, No. 145.

194. **Simon,** Pedro.—The Expedition of Pedro de Ursua & Lope de Aguirre in search of El Dorado and Omagua in 1560–1. Translated from Fray Pedro Simon's "Sixth Historical Notice of the Conquest of Tierra Firme." [1627.] By William Bollaert, Esq., F.R.G.S....With an Introduction by Clements R. Markham, Esq. [With a map showing the Track of the Expedition.] pp. liii. 237. (Hakluyt Society Publications. Series I. Vol. 28.)

Printed for the Hakluyt Society: London, 1861. 8°.

[Ac. 6172/26.] *See* 1627, No. 95.

1862.

195. **Markham,** *Sir* Clements Robert, *K.C.B., F.R.S.*—Travels in Peru and India, while superintending the collection of Chincona plants and seeds in South America, and their introduction into India. By Clements R. Markham, F.S.A., F.R.G.S., Corr. Mem. of the University of Chile; author of "Cuzco and Lima." With maps and illustrations. pp. xviii. 572.

John Murray: London, 1862. 8°.

[2356. e. 13.]

1863.

196. **Odriozola,** Manuel de.—Coleccion de Documentos Literarios del Peru. Colectados y arreglados por el Coronel de Caballeria de Ejercito, Fundador de la Independencia, Manuel de Odriozola. 8 tom.

Establecimiento de tipografía y encuadernacion de Aurelio Alfaro: Lima, 1863–76. 8°.

[12231. ddd. 3.—Tom. 1, 1863, contains a reprint of *Lima Fundada,* by Pedro José de Peralta Barnuevo Rocha y Benavides, 1732. *See* 1732, No. 126.—Tom. 3, 1872, contains *Descripcion de las provincias pertenecientes al Arzobispado de Lima,* por el Doctor don Cosme Bueno, 1763–78. *See* 1763, Nos. 137, 138.—Tom. 7. 1875, contains *Las Tres Epocas del Peru ó Compendio de su Historia,* por José María Córdova y Urrutia, Contador de segunda clase del Tribunal Mayor de Cuentas del Peru, 1844. The chronology of the Incas, and of the Viceroys of Peru is given.—Tom. 8, 1876, contains a reprint of *Primera y Segunda Parte de la Historia del Peru,* por Diego Fernández, de Palencia, 1571. *See* 1571, No. 40.—Karl W. Hiersemann, Leipzig, *Katalog* 336, No. 1786 (1907), quotes this Coleccion, with 11 volumes, 1863–78.]

197. **Odriozola,** Manuel de.—Documentos Historicos del Peru en las Epocas del Coloniaje despues de la Conquista y de la Independencia hasta la presente. Colectados y arreglados por el Coronel de Caballería de Ejército Fundador de la Independencia Manuel de Odriozola. Tom. 1. Tom. 2. Entr. 1–7.

Tipografia de Aurelio Alfaro: Lima, 1863–64. 8° and 4°.

[9772. f. 25.—Tom. 1 contains: "Relacion Historica de los Sucesos de la Rebelion de José Gabriel Tupac-Amaru contra las Provincias del Peru en 1780."—"Documentos para la Historia de la Sublevacion de José Gabriel de Tupac-Amaru, Cacique de la Provincia de Tinta en el Peru," &c.] *See* 1836, No. 160.

1864.

198. **Cieza de Leon,** Pedro de.—The Travels of Pedro de Cieza de Leon, A.D. 1532–50, contained in the First Part of his Chronicle of Peru. (The Second Part of the Chronicle of Peru.) Translated and edited, with notes and an introduction, by Clements R. Markham, F.S.A., F.R.G.S., author of "Cuzco and Lima," "Travels in Peru and India," and a "Quichua Grammar and Dictionary." [With a map of Peru, Quito, and New Granada, to illustrate the travels of Pedro de Cieza de Leon, A.D. 1532–50.] 2 vols. (Hakluyt Society Publications. Series I. Vols. 33, 68.)

Printed for the Hakluyt Society: London, 1864, 1883. 8°.

[Ac. 6172/31.] *See* 1553, No. 27; 1880, No. 239.

199. **Markham,** *Sir* Clements Robert, *K.C.B., F.R.S.*—Contributions towards a Grammar and Dictionary of Quichua, the language of the Yncas of Peru. Collected by Clements R. Markham, F.S.A., F.R.G.S., Secretary to the Royal Geographical Society; Honorary Secretary to the Hakluyt Society; Foreign Member of the Geographical Society of Berlin; Corresponding Member of the University of Chile; author of "Cuzco and Lima," and "Travels in Peru and India." pp. 223.

Trübner and Co.: London, 1864. 8°.

[12907. b. 33.]

1865.

200. **Agustinos.**—Relacion de la Religion y Ritos del Peru, hecha por los primeros Religiosos Agustinos que alli pasaron para la conversion de los Naturales. [Tom. 87. *Coleccion* de D. Juan Bautista Muñoz.] (In "Coleccion de Documentos Inéditos relativos al descubrimiento conquista y colonizacion de las posesiones Españolas en América y Oceanía, sacados, en su mayor parte, del Real Archivo de Indias, bajo la direccion de los Sres. D. Joaquin F. Pacheco y D. Francisco de Cárdenas, &c." Tom. III. pp. 5–58.)

Imprenta de Manuel B. de Quirós: Madrid, 1865. 8°.

[9551. g.]

201. **Andagoya,** Pascual de.—Narrative of the Proceedings of Pedrarias Davila in the provinces of Tierra Firme or Castilla del Oro, and of the Discovery of the South Sea and the Coasts of Peru and Nicaragua. Written by the Adelantado Pascual de Andogaya. [1540.] Translated and edited, with notes and an introduction, by Clements R. Markham. pp. xxix. 88. (Hakluyt Society Publications. Series I. Vol. 34.)

Printed for the Hakluyt Society: London, 1865. 8°.

[Ac. 6172/32.] *See* 1540, No. 19.

202. **Bollaert,** William, *F.R.G.S.*—Introduction to the Palæography of America: or, Observations on Ancient Picture and Figurative Writing in the New World; on the Fictitious Writing in North America; on the Quipu of the Peruvians, and Examination of Spurious Quipus. By William Bollaert, F.A.S.L., &c. (*Memoirs read before the Anthropological Society of London.* 1863–64. Vol. I. pp. 169–194.)

Trübner and Co.: London, 1865. 8°.

[Ac. 6235/3.]

203. **John Carter Brown Library,** Providence, Rhode Island.—Bibliotheca Americana. A Catalogue of Books relating to North and South America, in the Library of the late John Carter Brown, of Providence,

R. I. With notes by John Russell Bartlett. Part I, 1493 to 1600.
Part II, 1601 to 1700. 2 vols.

Providence [Rhode Island], 1865, 1866. 8°.

[11901. d. 10.—Second edition. 1482 to 1800. 3 pts. in 4 vols.
1875, 1882, 1870–71. 8°. 11901 d. 11.—The transcriptions of
the titles are not always accurate.]

204. **Martin de Moussy,** V.—Coup d'œil sur l'Histoire du Bassin de La
Plata avant la découverte. Par le Dr Martin de Moussy. (*Annuaire
du Comité d'Archéologie Américaine.* 1863–65. pp. 65–82.)

Au Bureau du Comité ; Maisonneuve et Cie: Paris [1865]. 8°.

[Ac. 5351.—The British Museum set of this *Annuaire* is sadly
defective.]

205. **Paz Soldan,** Mariano Felipe.—Atlas Geográfico del Perú. Por
Mariano Felipe Paz Soldan, Director General de Obras Publicas, &c.
pp. 81. 68 plates. [With a Bibliography of Peru.]

Fermin Didot Hermanos, Hijos y Ca.: Paris, 1865. fol.

[Maps 2. d. 17.—With the autograph of the author.] *See* 1865,
No. 206 ; 1869, No. 210.

206. **Paz Soldan,** Mariano Felipe.—Atlas Géographique de la République
du Pérou. Par Mariano Felipe Paz Soldan...Publié aux frais du
Gouvernement Péruvien sous la Présidence du Libérateur le Grand
Maréchal Ramon Castilla. Edition française par P. Arsène Mouqueron
...avec la collaboration de Manuel Rouaud y Paz Soldan, neveu de
l'auteur. pp. 82. 68 plates.

Auguste Durand: Paris, 1865. fol.

[Maps 30. e. 25.] *See* 1865, No. 205 ; 1869, No. 210.

1867.

207. **Toledo,** Francisco de, *Viceroy of Peru.*—[Documents relating to the
appointment and administration of Francisco de Toledo, Viceroy of
Peru, 1569–81.—Biblioteca Nacional, Madrid. MS. J. 113.] (In
Tom. VIII, pp. 212–293. "Coleccion de Documentos Ineditos,
relativos al descubrimiento, conquista y organizacion de las antiguas
posesiones Españolas de América y Oceanía, sacados de los Archivos
del Reino, y muy especialmente del de Indias. Por D. Luis Torres de
Mendoza.")

Imprenta de Frias y compañia: Madrid, 1867. 8°.

[9551. g.]

1868.

208. **Squier,** Ephraim George.—Quelques Remarques sur la Géographie et
les Monuments du Pérou. Par E. G. Squier, Ancien commissaire des
États-Unis au Pérou. Extrait du Bulletin de la Société de Géographie.
Janvier 1868. pp. 28. [With the autograph of the author.]

Imprimerie de E. Martinet: Paris, 1868. 8°.

[7704. i. 6. (9).] *See* 1870, No. 213.

1869.

209. **Garcilasso de la Vega,** *el Inca.*—First Part of the Royal Commentaries of the Yncas. By the Ynca Garcilasso de la Vega. Translated and edited, with notes and an introduction, by Clements R.
Markham, Vol. I containing Books I, II, III, and IV, Vol. II
containing Books V, VI, VII, VIII, and IX. [With a plan of Cuzco,

ancient and modern, with references to the Houses of Spanish Conquerors, A.D. 1555.] 2 vols. (Hakluyt Society Publications. Series I. Vols. 41, 45.)

Printed for the Hakluyt Society : London, 1869, 1871. 8°.

[Ac. 6172/36.] *See* 1609, No. 75.

210. **Paz Soldan,** Mariano Felipe.—Atlas Géográphico de la República del Perú. Por Mariano Felipe Paz Soldan, Director General de Obras Publicas...Nueva Edicion. pp. 81. 68 plates.

F. Brachet : Paris, 1869. fol.

·[Maps 109. d. 14.] *See* 1865, Nos. 205, 206.

1870.

211. **Forbes,** David, *F.R.S.*—On the Aymara Indians of Bolivia and Peru. By David Forbes, Esq., F.R.S., F.G.S., *etc.* Read June 21st, 1870. (*Journal of the Ethnological Society of London.* New Series. Vol. II. Session 1869–70. pp. 193–305. With 7 plates.)

Trübner and Co.: London, 1870. 8°.

[Ac. 6234.]

212. **Peru.**—Relacion de todo lo sucedido en la Provincia del Piru desde que Blasco Nuñez Vela fue enviado por S. M. a ser Visorey della, que se embarco a primero de Noviembre del año de M.D.X.L.III.

Imprenta del Estado : Lima, 1870.

[9781. f. 11.]

213. **Squier,** Ephraim George.—Observations on the Geography and Archæology of Peru. By E. G. Squier, M.A., F.S.A., late Commissioner of the United States in Peru. A paper read before the American Geographical Society, February 1870. pp. 27.

Trübner and Co.: London, 1870. 8°.

[10480. c. 7.]—*See* 1868, No. 208.

214. **Squier,** Ephraim George.—The Primeval Monuments of Peru, Compared with those in other parts of the world. By E. G. Squier, M.A. From the *American Naturalist.* Vol. IV. 1870. pp. 19. [With illustrations, and the autograph of the author.]

Essex Institute Press : [Salem, Mass., 1870]. 8°.

[7704. f. 41. (9).]

1871.

215. **Markham,** *Sir* Clements Robert, *K.C.B., F.R.S.*—On the Geographical Positions of the Tribes which formed the Empire of the Yncas. With an Appendix on the name : Aymara. By Clements R. Markham, C.B., Secretary R.G.S. Read 10th July, 1871. (In *The Journal of the Royal Geographical Society.* Vol. 41. pp. 281–338.)

John Murray : London, 1871. 8°.

[Ac. 6170.]

216. **Ollanta.**—Ollanta. An ancient Ynca Drama. Translated from the original Quichua. By Clements R. Markham, C.B., Corresponding Member of the University of Chile. pp. 128.

Trübner and Co.: London, 1871. 8°.

[11791. c. 42.]

1872.

217. **Markham,** *Sir* Clements Robert, *K.C.B., F.R.S.*—Reports on the Discovery of Peru. I. Report of Francisco de Xeres, Secretary to Francisco Pizarro. [1534.] II. Report of Miguel de Astete on the Expedition to Pachacamac. [1534.] III. Letter of Hernando Pizarro to the Royal Audience of Santo Domingo. [Nov. 1533.] IV. Report of Pedro Sancho on the partition of the Ransom of Atahualpa. [1533.] Translated and edited, with notes and an introduction, by Clements R. Markham, C.B. [With a map of a part of Peru, showing the Marches of Francisco and Hernando Pizarro, May 1532 to May 1533.] pp. xxii. 143. (Hakluyt Society Publications. Series I. Vol. 47.)
Printed for the Hakluyt Society: London, 1872. 8°.
[Ac. 6172/41.] *See* 1534, No. 9; 1535, No. 11; 1547, No. 21.

218. **Ondegardo,** Polo de.—Relacion de los Fundamentos acerca del notable Daño que resulta de no guardar á los Indios sus fueros. Junio 26 de 1571. [By Polo de Ondegardo.]—Biblioteca Nacional, Madrid. Manuscritos de Indias. T. 9. (In "Coleccion de Documentos Inéditos relativos al descubrimiento conquista, y organizacion de las antiguas posesiones Españolas de América y Oceania, sacados de los Archivos del Reino y muy especialmente del de Indias. Competentemente autorizada.") Tom. XVII. pp. 5–177.
Imprenta del Hospicio: Madrid, 1872. 8°.
[9551. g.]

1873.

219. **Hutchinson,** Thomas Joseph.—Two years in Peru. With exploration of its antiquities. By Thomas J. Hutchinson, F.R.G.S....With Map by Daniel Barrera, and numerous illustrations. 2 vols.
Sampson Low, Marston and Co.: London, 1873. 8°.
[2374. e. 9.]

220. **Markham,** *Sir* Clements Robert, *K.C.B., F.R.S.*—Narratives of the Rites and Laws of the Yncas. (I. An Account of the Fables and Rites of the Yncas. By Christoval de Molina. [1570–84.] II. An Account of the Antiquities of Peru. By Juan de Santa Cruz Pachacutiyamqui Salcamayhua. [1620.] III. A Narrative of the errors, false gods, and other superstitions and diabolical rites in which the Indians of the province of Huarochiri lived in ancient times. By Dr Francisco de Avila. [1608.] IV. Report by Polo de Ondegardo, on the lineage, conquests, edifices, fortresses, &c. of the Yncas. From the MS. in the Madrid Biblioteca Nacional. B. 135. [1560.]) Translated from the original Spanish Manuscripts, and edited, with notes and an introduction, by Clements R. Markham, C.B., F.R.S. pp. xx. 220. (Hakluyt Society Publications. Series I. Vol. 48.)
Printed for the Hakluyt Society: London, 1873. 8°.
[Ac. 6172/43.] *See* 1879, No. 235.

1874.

221. **Anchorena,** José Dionisio.—Grámatica Quechua ó del Idioma del Imperio de los Incas. Compuesta por el Dr José Dionisio Anchorena, Abogado de los Tribunales de Justicia de la Republica. pp. viii. 187.
Imprenta del Estado: Lima, 1874. 8°.
[12910. cc. 2.]

310 BIBLIOGRAPHY

222. **Incas.**—Informacion de las Idolatrias de los Incas e Indios y de como se enterraban, *etc.* Año de 1571. (In "Coleccion de Documentos Inéditos relativos al Descubrimiento, Conquista y Organizacion de las antiguas posesiones Españolas de América y Oceanía, sacados de los Archivos del Reino, y muy especialmente del de Indias. Competentemente autorizada." [Edited by Joaquin Francisco Pacheco.]) Tom. XXI. pp. 131–220.

Imprenta de Manuel G. Hernandez: Madrid, 1874. 8°.

[9551. g.]

223. **Markham**, *Sir* Clements Robert, *K.C.B.*, *F.R.S.*—A memoir of the Lady Ana de Osorio, Countess of Chinchon, and Vice-Queen of Peru (A.D. 1629–39). With a plea for the Correct Spelling of the Chinchona Genus. By Clements R. Markham, C.B., F.R.S., Commendador da Real Ordem de Christo ; Socius Academiæ Cæsareæ Naturæ Curiosorum, Cognomen *Chinchon*. [With 10 illustrations and 1 map.] pp. xi. 99.

Trübner and Co.: London, 1874. 4°.

[10632. eee. 3.]

224. **Mendiburu**, Manuel de.—Diccionario Historico-Biografico del Peru. Formado y redactado por Manuel de Mendiburu. Parte Primera, que corresponde a la epoca de la Dominacion Española. 8 tom.

Imprenta de J. Francisco Solis; Imp. de Torres Aguirre: Lima 1874–90. 8°.

[9771. de. 3.]

225. **Wiener**, Charles.—Essai sur les Institutions Politiques, Religieuses, Économiques et Sociales de l'Empire des Incas. Par Charles Wiener. pp. 104. 5 plates.

Maisonneuve et Cie: Paris, 1874. 4°.

[9772. f. 1.]

1875.

226. **British Museum.**—Catalogue of the Manuscripts in the Spanish Language in the British Museum. By Don Pascual de Gayángos. Vols. 1–4.

Printed by order of the Trustees: London, 1875–93. 8°.

[Cat. Desk A.—11908. s. 6.—This valuable work still lacks "the copious Index," promised by Sir Edward A. Bond in August 1875, as well as a supplementary volume for the additions from 1875 to 1907.]

1877.

227. **Cieza de Leon**, Pedro de.—Guerras Civiles del Perú por Pedro de Cieza de Leon, natural de Llerena. I. Guerra de las Salinas. Publicada por vez primera conforme al MS. coetáneo propiedad de los señores Marqués de la Fuensanta del Valle y D. José Sancho Rayon. pp. vi. 534. (Tom. 68. Coleccion de Documentos Inéditos para la Historia de España. Por el Marqués de la Fuensanta del Valle, D. José Sancho Rayon y D. Francisco de Zabalburu.)

Imprenta de Miguel Ginesta: Madrid, 1877. 8°.

[9197. g.]

228. **Cieza de Leon, Pedro de.**—Tercero Libro de las Guerras civiles del Perú, el cual se llama la Guerra de Quito, hecho por Pedro de Cieza de Leon, Coronista, de las cosas de las Indias, y publicado por Márcos Jiménez de la Espada. Tomo I. (Apéndices.) pp. cxix. 176. 120. (*Biblioteca Hispano-Ultramarina.*)

   Imprenta de M. G. Hernandez: Madrid, 1877. 8°.

   [9771. ee. 16.]

229. **Paz Soldan, Mariano Felipe.**—Diccionario Geográfico Estadístico del Perú. Contiene ademas la Etimologia Aymara y Quechua de las principales Poblaciones, Lagos, Rios, Ceros, *etc.*, *etc.* Por Mariano Felipe Paz Soldan. (Apéndices.—I. De la declinacion y conjugacion en las lenguas Aymará y Quechua.—II. Diccionarios orográfico é hidrográfico.—III. Biblioteca Geográfica del Perú.) pp. xxix. 1077.

   Imprenta del Estado: Lima, 1877. 4°.

   [Maps 1. c. 44.—10480. g. 2.—With the autograph of the author.]

230. **Squier, Ephraim George.**—Peru. Incidents of Travel and Exploration in the Land of the Incas. By E. George Squier, M.A., F.S.A....With illustrations. pp. xx. 599.

   Macmillan and Co.: London, 1877. 8°.

   [2374. e. 14.]

1879.

231. **Bertonio, Ludovico.**—Arte de la Lengua Aymara. Compuesta por el P. Ludovico Bertonio. [1603.] Publicada de nuevo por Julio Platzmann. Edicion facsimilaria. (Registro.) pp. 348.

   B. G. Teubner: Leipzig, 1879. 8°.

   [12907. eee. 19.] *See* 1603, No. 64.

232. **Bertonio, Ludovico.**—Vocabulario de la Lengua Aymara. Compuesto por el P. Ludovico Bertonio. [1612.] Publicado de nuevo por Julio Platzmann...Edicion facsimilaria. [Dedicated to Leopold II, King of the Belgians.] 2 pts.

   B. G. Teubner: Leipzig, 1879. 8°.

   [12910. d. 55.] *See* 1612, No. 83.

233. **Cuzco.**—Relacion del Sitio del Cuzco, y principio de las Guerras Civiles del Perú hasta la muerte de Diego de Almagro, 1535 á 1539.— Biblioteca Nacional, sala de MS., J. 130. (pp. 1–195. "Varias Relaciones del Perú y Chile y Conquista de la Isla de Santa Catalina, 1535 á 1658." Edited by Feliciano Ramirez de Arellano, Marqués de Fuensanta del Valle, & José Sancho Rayon.—*Coleccion de Libros Españoles Raros ó Curiosos.* Tom. 13.)

   Imprenta de Miguel Ginesta: Madrid, 1879. 8°.

   [12230. aa.]

234. **Hernandez Giron, Francisco.**—Rebelion de Francisco Hernandez Giron en el Perú en 1553. (Relacion de lo Acaecido en Perú desde que Francisco Hernandez Giron se alzó hasta el dia que murió.) (pp. 197– 235. "Varias Relaciones del Perú y Chile y Conquista de la Isla de Santa Catalina, 1535 á 1658." Edited by Feliciano Ramirez de Arellano, Marqués de Fuensanta del Valle, & José Sancho Rayon.— *Coleccion de Libros Españoles Raros ó Curiosos.* Tom. 13.)

   Imprenta de Miguel Ginesta: Madrid, 1879. 8°.

   [12230. aa.]

235.   **Jiménez de la Espada**, Márcos.—Tres Relaciones de Antigüedades Peruanas. Publícalas el Ministerio de Fomento. Con motivo del Congreso Internacional de Americanistas que ha de celebrarse en Bruselas el presente año. Al Excmo. Señor Don Francisco de Borja Queipo de Llano, Conde de Toreno, Ministro de Fomento. (I. Relacion del Órigen, Descendencia, Política y Gobierno de los Incas. Por el Licenciado Fernando de Santillan.—[From the MS. in the Biblioteca del Escorial, L. j. 5, fol. 301.] II. Relacion de las Costumbres Antiguas de los Naturales del Pirú. Anónima. [By the Anonymous Jesuit.] III. Relacion de Antigüedades deste Reyno del Pirú. Por Don Juan de Santacruz Pachacuti Yamqui. [1620.]) [Edited by Márcos Jiménez de la Espada.] pp. xliv, 328.

Imprenta y Fundicion de M. Tello: Madrid, 1879.   8°.

[7706. de. 24.]

1880.

236.   **Acosta**, Joseph de.—The Natural and Moral History of the Indies. By Father Joseph de Acosta. Reprinted from the English translated edition of Edward Grimston, 1604, and edited, with notes and an introduction, by Clements R. Markham, C.B., F.R.S. Vol. I. The Natural History (Books I–IV). pp. xlv. 295. Vol. II. The Moral History (Books V–VII). pp. xii. 295–551. Map of Peru. (Hakluyt Society Publications. Series I. Vols. 60, 61.)

Printed for the Hakluyt Society: London, 1880.   8°.

[Ac. 6172/54.]   *See* 1604, No. 66.

237.   **Betánzos**, Juan de.—Suma y Narracion de los Incas, que los Indios llamaron Capaccuna, que fueron Señores de la Ciudad del Cuzco y de todo lo á ella subjeto. Escrita por Juan de Betánzos. Publícala Márcos Jiménez de la Espada. pp. 140. (*Biblioteca Hispano-Ultra-marina*. Tom. 5.)

Imprenta de Manuel G. Hernandez: Madrid, 1880.   8°.

[9771. ee. 11.]

238.   **Chile.**—*Oficina Hidrográfica*. Noticias sobre las Provincias Litorales correspondientes a los Departamentos de Arequipa, Ica, Huancavelica i Lima. Por la Oficina Hidrográfica. [Edited by Francisco Vidal Gormáz. With a map.] pp. 40.

Imprenta Nacional: Santiago, 1880.   8°.

[10481. ff. 16. (5).]

239.   **Cieza de Leon**, Pedro de.—Segunda Parte de la Crónica del Perú, que trata del Señorío de los Incas Yupanquis y de sus grandes hechos y gobernacion. Escrita por Pedro de Cieza de Leon. La publica. Márcos Jiménez de la Espada. pp. 279. (*Biblioteca Hispano-Ultramarina.* Tom. 5.)

Imprenta de Manuel Gines Hernandez: Madrid, 1880.   8°.

[9771. ee. 11.]

240.   **Markham**, *Sir* Clements Robert, *K.C.B.*, *F.R.S.*—Peru. By Clements R. Markham, C.B. With illustrations. (*Foreign Countries and British Colonies.*) pp. viii. 192.

Sampson Low and Co.: London. 1880.   8°.

[2370. a. 16.]

241. **Reiss, Wilhelm.**—The Necropolis of Ancon in Peru. A contribution to our knowledge of the culture and industries of the Empire of the Incas. Being the results of excavations made on the spot by W. Reiss and A. Stübel. Translated by Professor A. H. Keane, B.A., F.R.G.S., Vice-President of the Anthropological Institute, with the aid of the General Administration of the Royal Museums of Berlin. 3 vols. [Coloured plates of mummies, garments & textiles, head-dress, toys, pottery, &c.]

   A. Asher and Co.: Berlin, 1880–87. fol.

   [1704. c. 15.]

242. **Wiener, Charles.**—Pérou et Bolivie. Récit de Voyage, suivi d'études archéologiques et ethnographiques et de notes sur l'écriture et les langues des populations indiennes. Par Charles Wiener. Ouvrage contenant plus de 1100 gravures, 27 cartes et 18 plans. pp. xi. 796.

   Hachette et Cie: Paris, 1880. fol.

   [2374. h. 4.]

1881.

243. **Spain.**—*Ministerio de Fomento.*—Relaciones Geográficas de Indias. Publícalas el Ministerio de Fomento. Perú. Tomo I–IV.

   Tipografía de Manuel G. Hernandez: Madrid, 1881–97. fol.

   [10480. 5. 1.]

1882.

244. **Montesinos, Fernando de.**—Memorias antiguas historiales y políticas del Perú. Por el Licenciado D. Fernando Montesinos. Seguidas de las Informaciones acerca del Señorío de los Incas, hechas por mandado de D. Francisco de Toledo, Virey del Perú. (Informaciones acerca del Señorío y Gobierno de los Ingas, hechas, por mandado de Don Francisco de Toledo, Virey del Perú. 1570–72.) [Edited by Márcos Jiménez de la Espada.] pp. xxxii. 259. (Tom. XVI. *Coleccion de Libros Españoles Raros ó Curiosos.* Edited by Feliciano Ramirez de Orellana, Marqués de Fuensanta del Valle, and José Sancho Rayon.)

   Imprenta de Miguel Ginesta: Madrid, 1882. 8°.

   [12230. aa.] *See* 1840, No. 163.

1883.

245. **Falb, Rudolf.**—Das Land der Inca in seiner Bedeutung für die Urgeschichte der Sprache und Schrift. Von Rudolf Falb. pp. xxxvi. 455.

   J. J. Weber: Leipzig, 1883. 8°.

   [7706. ee. 9.]

1884.

246. **Inwards, Richard.**—The Temple of the Andes. [Tiahuanaco.] pp. 32. 19 plates.

   Printed for the Author by Vincent Brooks, Day and Son: London, 1884. 4°.

   [7708. de. 27.]

247. **Tschudi, Johann Jakob von.**—Organismus der Khetšua-Sprache. Von J. J. von Tschudi. pp. xvi, 534.

   F. A. Brockhaus: Leipzig, 1884. 8°.

   [12907. cc. 20.]

1885.

248. **Adams**, William Henry Davenport.—The Land of the Incas and the City of the Sun, or, The Story of Francisco Pizarro and the Conquest of Peru. By W. H. Davenport Adams. [Illustrated.] pp. 256.
The Book Society: London, 1885. 8°.
[9771. bb. 9.]

249. **Brehm**, Reinhold Bernhard.—Das Inka-Reich. Beiträge zur Staats- und Sittengeschichte des Kaiserthums Tahuantinsuyu. Nach den ältesten spanischen Quellen bearbeitet von Dr med. Reinhold Bernhard Brehm...Mit einer Karte in Chromodruck und Holzschnitten. pp. xxxi. 842.
Fr. Mauke's Verlag (A. Schenk): Jena, 1885. 8°.
[9772. b. 4.]

1887.

250. **Encyclopedias.**—Diccionario Enciclopedico Hispano-Americano de Literatura, Ciencias y Artes. Edicion profusamente ilustrada. 25 tom.
Montaner y Simón: Barcelona, 1887–99. 4°.
[1878. c.]

251. **Villar**, Leonardo, *del Cuzco.*—Lexicologia Keshua, Uirakocha. (A la Sociedad de Arqueología y Lingüística Cuzqueña.) pp. 16.
Imprenta del "Comercio": Lima, 1887. 8°.
[12902. h. 27. (1).]

1889.

252. **Mossi.** Miguel Angel.—Manuel del Idioma General del Perú. Gramática razonada de la Lengua Qíchua, comparada con las lenguas del antiguo continente; con notas especiales sobre la que se habla en Santiago del Estero y Catamarca. Por el Presbítero Don Miguel Angel Mossi, Cura y Vicario interino de Atamizki en la Provincia de Santiago del Estero (República Argentina), Autor de varias otras obras. Mandada imprimir para enviar á la Exposicion Universal de Paris por el Exmo. Gobierno de la Provincia de Santiago del Estero. pp. 219.
Imprenta "La Minerva" de A. Villafañe: Córdoba, 1889. 8°.
[12910. v. 12.]

253. **Toledo**, Francisco de, *Viceroy of Peru.*—[Despatches concerning Peru from Francisco de Toledo, Viceroy, to Philip II of Spain, 1569–81.] (In "Coleccion de Documentos Inéditos para la Historia de España. Por el Marqués de la Fuensanta del Valle, D. José Sancho Rayon y D. Francisco de Zabálburu." Tom. 94. pp. 225–532.)
M. Ginesta Hermanos: Madrid, 1889. 8°.
[9197. h.]

1890.

254. **Cobo**, Bernabé.—Historia del Nuevo Mundo. Por el P. Bernabé Cobo, de la Compañía de Jesús. [1653.] Publicada por primera vez con notas y otras ilustraciones de D. Marcos Jiménez de la Espada. 4 tom. (Sociedad de Bibliófilos Andaluces. Primera Serie. Tom. 19–22.)
Imp. de E. Rasco: Sevilla, 1890–95. 8°.
[9770. cc.] *See* 1653, No. 109.

255. **Vivien de Saint Martin, Louis.**—Nouveau Dictionnaire de Géographie Universelle...Ouvrage commencé par M. Vivien de Saint Martin...et continué par Louis Rousselet. (Tom. 4. Pérou. pp. 713–731. With a valuable bibliography of books and of maps.)
Hachette et Cie: Paris, 1890. 4°.
[2056. g.]

1891.

256. **Domingo, de Santo Tomas.**—Arte de la Lengua Quichua. Compuesta por Domingo, de Sancto Thomas. [1560.] Publicada de nuevo por Julio Platzmann. Edicion facsimilar. ff. 96.
B. G. Teubner: Leipzig, 1891. 8°.
[12910. aa. 38.] *See* 1560, No. 33.

257. **Jiménez de la Espada, Márcos.**—Las Islas de los Galápagos y otras más á poniente. [Por] Márcos Jiménez de la Espada. (In *Boletín de la Sociedad Geográfica de Madrid.* Tom. XXXI. pp. 351–402.)
Fortanet: Madrid, 1891. 8°.
[Ac. 6018.]

1892.

258. **Casas, Bartolomé de las,** *Bishop of Chiapa.*—De las antiguas gentes del Perú [extracted from the *Apologética Historia Sumaria*]. Por el Padre Fray Bartolomé de las Casas. [Edited by Márcos Jiménez de la Espada.] pp. lix. 290. (Tom. 21. *Coleccion de Libros Españoles Raros ó Curiosos.* Edited by Feliciano Ramirez de Orellana, Marqués de Fuensanta del Valle & José Sancho Rayon.)
Tipografía de Manuel G. Hernández: Madrid, 1892. 8°.
[12230. aa.]

259. **Lafone y Quevedo, Samuel Alexander.**—Ensayo Mitológico. El Culto de Tonapa. Los Himnos sagrados de los Reyes del Cuzco según el Yamqui-Pachacuti. Por Samuel A. Lafone Quevedo. (*Revista del Museo de La Plata.* Del Tomo III. Página 320 y siguientes.) pp. 59.
Talleres del Museo de La Plata, 1892. 8°.
[Ac. 3091.]

260. **Markham,** *Sir* Clements Robert, *K.C.B., F.R.S.*—A History of Peru. (*Latin-American Republics.*) Illustrations and maps. pp. xvi. 566.
C. H. Sergel and Co.: Chicago, 1892. 8°.
[2398. d. 11.]

261. **Muñoz Manzano, Cipriano,** *Conde de la Viñaza.*—Bibliografía Española de Lenguas Indígenas de América. Por el Conde de la Viñaza. Obra premiada por la Biblioteca Nacional en el Concurso Público de 1891 é impresa á expensas del Estado. pp. xxv. 427.
Sucesores de Rivadeneyra: Madrid, 1892. 8°.
[11900. i. 38.]

262. **Stübel, Alphons.**—Die Ruinenstaette von Tiahuanaco, im Hochlande des alten Perú. Eine kulturgeschichtliche Studie auf Grund selbstaendiger Aufnahmen von A. Stübel und M. Uhle. Mit einer Karte und 42 Tafeln in Lichtdruck. 2 Thle.
C. T. Wiskott: Breslau, 1892. fol.
[1706. c. 15.]

1893.

263. **Meyer**, Wilhelm, *Professor in Göttingen.*—Die in der Goettinger
Bibliothek erhaltene Geschichte des Inkareiches von Pedro Sarmiento
de Gamboa. [1572.] Von Wilhelm Meyer, aus Speyer. (In *Nach-
richten von der Königlichen Gesellschaft der Wissenschaften und der
Georg-Augusts-Universität zu Göttingen.* No. 1. 18 Januar 1893.
pp. 1-18.)
        Dieterichsche Verlags-Buchhandlung: Göttingen, 1893. 8º.

  [P. P. 4672.—The MS. was sent to Philip II in 1572, was purchased
  by Göttingen University in 1785, remained unnoticed for 108 years,
  was edited with German notes, but without a translation, in
  August 1906, and was translated into English in September 1906.]

264. **Prussia.**—Verzeichniss der Handschriften im Preussischen Staate. I.
Hannover. 2. Göttingen. 2. (Hannover. Die Handschriften in
Göttingen. 2. Universitäts-Bibliothek.)
        A. Bath: Berlin, 1893. 8º.

  [011910. g.—pp. 268-9. *Histor.* 809 gives the first notice in print
  since 1785 of the MS. of the *Indica*, by Pedro Sarmiento de Gamboa,
  1572, with a collation.]

1894.

265. **Peruvian Ritual.**—Langues Américaines. Langue Puquina. Textes
Paquina, contenus dans le Rituale seu Manuale Peruanum de Geronimo
de Ore, publié à Naples en 1607, d'après un exemplaire trouvé à la
Bibliothèque Nationale de Paris. Avec texte espagnol en regard,
traduction analytique interlinéaire, vocabulaire et essai de grammaire.
Par Raoul de la Grasserie. pp. 67.
        K. F. Koehler: Leipzig [*Vannes* printed], 1894. 8º.
  [12910. dd. 35.] *See* 1607, No. 71.

266. **Prussia.**—Verzeichniss der Handschriften im Preussischen Staate. I.
Hannover. 3. Göttingen. 3. (Hannover. Die Handschriften in
Göttingen. 3. Universitäts-Bibliothek, &c.)
        A. Bath: Berlin, 1894. 8º.

  [011901. g.—pp. 540-1. *Jurid.* 160 b. Spanish MS. 14-15 cent., and
  leaves relating to the Decretum Gratiani, found in the binding of the
  Sarmiento 1572 MS. (*Histor.* 809.)]

1895.

267. **Martens**, Oscar.—Ein sozialistischer Grossstaat vor 400 Jahren. Die
geschichtliche, soziale und politische Grundlage des Inkareiches
Tahuantinsuŷu, das Staatswesen der Incas auf dem südamerikanischen
Hochlande. 2 Auflage. pp. 84.
        E. Streisand: Berlin, 1895. 8º.
  [Not in the British Museum.]

268. **Philippi**, Rudolph Amandus.—Descripcion de los Ídolos Peruanos de
Greda Cocida. Por el Dr R. A. Philippi. Con 7 Láminas [coloured].
(*Anales del Museo Nacional de Chile.* Publicados por Orden del
Gobierno de Chile. Entr. 11.) pp. 22.
        Imprenta de F. A. Brockhaus: Leipzig; Santiago de Chile,
        1895. 4º.
  [Ac. 3092. b.]

269. **Sarmiento de Gambóa**, Pedro.—Narratives of the Voyages of Pedro Sarmiento de Gambóa to the Straits of Magellan. Translated and edited, with notes and an introduction, by Clements R. Markham, C.B., F.R.S. With a map. pp. xxx. 401. (Hakluyt Society Publications. Series I. Vol. 91.)

Printed for the Hakluyt Society: London, 1895. 8°.

[Ac. 6172/72.—Page xxi notes the re-discovery of the *Indica* MS. of 1572.]

1896.

270. **René-Moreno**, Gabriel.—Biblioteca Peruana. Apuntes para un Catálogo de Impresos. I. Libros y Folletos Peruanos de la Biblioteca del Instituto Nacional. [Por Don Gabriel René-Moreno.] pp. viii. 558.

En la Biblioteca del Instituto Nacional: Santiago de Chile, 1896. 8°.

[11899. dd.]

271. **Sarmiento de Gamboa**, Pedro.—Copy of a Letter translated from the English, written in London, 10th November 1586, taken by Pedro Sarmiento de Gamboa, and with a note of his visit to Queen Elizabeth at Windsor Castle. (In "Calendar of Letters and State Papers relating to English Affairs, preserved principally in the Archives of Simancas. Vol. III. Elizabeth. 1580–1586. Edited by Martin A. S. Hume." No. 505. pp. 651–6.)

H.M. Stationery Office: London, 1896. 8°.

[2076. f.—9507. a. 13.] *See* 1586, No. 53.

1897.

272. **Jiménez de la Espada**, Márcos.—La Jornada del Capitán Alonso Mercadillo á los Indios Chupachos é Iscaicingas [1538]. Al Excmo. Sr. D. Eugenio Larrabure y Unánue. [Por] M. Jiménez de la Espada. pp. 40.

Imprenta de Fortanet: Madrid [1897]. 8°.

[10412. gg. 22. (6).]

273. **Meyer**, Wilhelm, *Professor in Göttingen.*—Die Buchstaben-Verbindungen der sogenannten gothischen Schrift. Von Wilhelm Meyer, aus Speyer, Professor in Göttingen. Mit fünf Tafeln. pp. 124. (*Abhandlungen der Königlichen Gesellschaft der Wissenschaften zu Göttingen.* Phil. hist. Klasse. Neue Folge. Band I. Nro. 6.)

Weidmannsche Buchhandlung: Berlin, 1897. 4°.

[Ac. 670.—Cf. pp. 91, 92. and Tafel I, No. 5.]

1898.

274. **Dorsey**, George Amos.—A Bibliography of the Anthropology of Peru. By George A. Dorsey, Acting Curator, Department of Anthropology.— Field Columbian Museum. Publication 23. Anthropological Series. Vol. II. No. 2. [pp. 51–206. Vol. II. Anthropological Series. *Publications of the Field Columbian Museum.*]

Chicago, U.S.A., January 1898. 8°.

[Ac. 1738/6.—A most valuable and exhaustive list, including historical works on Peru, arranged by Authors. There is one curious misprint on p. 121: HEREDES (Homanianos). This entry should be on p. 125, and should read : HOMANN, Johann Baptista.]

1900.

275. **Helps,** *Sir* Arthur, *K.C.B.*—The Spanish Conquest in America, and its relation to the history of Slavery and to the government of Colonies. By Sir Arthur Helps. A new edition. Edited, with an introduction, maps and notes by M. Oppenheim. 4 vols.
John Lane: London and New York, 1900–4. 8°.
[2398. b. 10.] *See* 1855, No. 179.

276. **Patrón,** Pablo.—Origen del Kechua y del Aymará.—Universidad Mayor de San Marcos. Faculdad de Letras.—Discurso de Recepcion del Miembro Honorario Pablo Patrón. pp. 151.
Librería é Imprenta Gil: Lima, 1900. 8°.
[12910. e. 47.]

1901.

277. **Lafone y Quevedo,** Samuel Alexander.—Supuesta Derivación Súmero-Asiria de las Lenguas Kechua y Aymará. Por Samuel A. Lafone Quevedo, M.A. Con una Nota complementaria por Félix F. Outes. (Artículo publicado en los *Anales de la Sociedad Científica Argentina.* Tomo LI. Páginas 123 y siguientes.) pp. 11.
Imprenta y Casa Editora de Coni Hermanos: Buenos Aires, 1901. 8°.
[12902. h. 27. (4).—Ac. 3083.]

278. **Viscarra,** J.—Copacabana de los Incas. Documentos auto-linguisticos é isografiados del Aymáru-Aymára, protógonos de los Pre-americanos. pp. viii. 552.
La Paz, 1901. 8°.
[Not in the British Museum.—Karl W. Hiersemann, Leipzig, *Katalog* 336, No. 1896. 1907.]

1902.

279. **Baessler,** Arthur.—Ancient Peruvian Art. Contributions to the Archæology of the Empire of the Incas. From his collections. By Arthur Baessler. Translated by A. H. Keane. 4 vols.
A. Asher and Co.: Berlin; Dodd, Mead and Co.; New York, 1902–3. fol.
[K. T. C. 114. b. 1.]

280. **Mendiburu,** Manuel de.—Apuntes Históricos del Perú (por el General don Manuel de Mendiburu, Correspondiente de la Real Academia Española), y Noticias Cronológicas del Cuzco. (Gobierno incásico y primer siglo de la Conquista. A.D. 1043–1595.) [By the author of "Anales del Cuzco desde 1600 hasta 1750."] (Apéndice. El Aprendiz de Rico. Poemata en Silva por Espinosa Medrano, el Lunarejo.) 2 pts.
Imprenta del Estado: Lima, 1902. 4°.
[9770. f. 19.]

281. **Santiago de Chile.**—Biblioteca Nacional. Catálogo de la Sección Americana. América en General. pp. 154.
Imprenta Universitaria: Santiago de Chile, 1902. 8°.
[011907. i.]

282. **Stuart,** Maria del Rosario, *Duquesa de Berwick y de Alba.*—Nuevos Autógrafos de Cristóbal Colón y Relaciones de Ultramar. Los publica

la Duquesa de Berwick y de Alba, Condesa de Siruela. [No. 68, p. 69, relates to the Inca Princess, Beatriz Clara Coya.] pp. 294.

Sucesores de Rivadeneyra: Madrid, 1902. fol.

[9551. k. 11.]

1904.

283. **Gutiérrez de Santa Clara**, Pedro.—Historia de las Guerras Civiles del Perú (1544-1548), y de otros sucesos de las Indias. [Quinquenarios.] Por Pedro Gutiérrez de Santa Clara. [Edited by Manuel Serrana y Sanz.] Tom. 1–3. (Colección de Libros y Documentos referentes á la Historia de América. Tom. 2–4.)

Victoriano Suarez: Madrid, 1904-5. 8°.

[9772. df.]

1905.

284. **Enock, C.** Reginald.—C. Reginald Enock's Journeys in Peru. Read... Jan. 9, 1905 by Sir Clements R. Markham, K.C.B., President R. G. S. With Sketch Map of Part of Peru. Showing the Routes of C. R. Enock. 1903-4. (In *The Geographical Journal*. Vol. XXV. pp. 620–633.)

Royal Geographical Society: London, 1905. 8°.

[2058. a. and Ac. 6170.]

285. **Enock, C.** Reginald.—The Ruins of "Huanuco Viejo," or Old Huanuco, with notes on an Expedition to the Upper Marañon. By Reginald Enock. Illustrated. (In *The Geographical Journal*. Vol. XXVI. pp. 153–179. For map: *see* vol. XXV, p. 700.)

Royal Geographical Society: London, 1905. 8°.

[2058. a. and Ac. 6170.]

286. **Soleto Pernia**, Alonso.—Alonso Soleto Pernia. Memoria de lo que han hecho mis padres y yo en busca del Dorado, que ansí se llama esta conquista, y dicen que es el Paytiti. [c. 1650. In the Archivo de Indias.] (pp. 477–483. "Autobiografias y Memorias. Coleccionadas é ilustradas por M. Serrano y Sanz." pp. clxvi, 545.—Nueva Biblioteca de Autores Españoles bajo la direccion del Exmo. Sr. D. Marcelino Menendez y Pelayo.)

Bailly Baillière é Hijos: Madrid, 1905. 8°.

[10632. g. 27.] *See* 1650, No. 108.

1906.

287. **Baessler, Arthur**.—Altperuanische Metallgeräte. Nach seinen Sammlungen von Arthur Baessler. Mit 570 Abbildungen auf 40 Tafeln. pp. vi. 142.

Georg Reimer: Berlin, 1906. fol.

[7709. v. 5.]

288. **Baessler, Arthur**.—Peruanische Mumien. Untersuchungen mit X-Strahlen. Fünfzehn Tafeln nebst erläuterndem Text. Von Arthur Baessler.

Georg Reimer: Berlin, 1906. fol.

[7709. v. 4.]

289. **Sarmiento de Gamboa**, Pedro.—Geschichte des Inkareiches. Von Pedro Sarmiento de Gamboa. (Segunda Parte de la Historia general llamada Índica, la cual por mandado del excelentísimo señor Don Francisco de Toledo, virrey, gobernador y capitán general de los reinos del Pirú y mayordomo de la casa real de Castilla, compuso el capitán Pedro Sarmiento de Gamboa.) [From the 1572 MS. in the Göttingen

University Library. (Cod. MS. hist. 809.)] Herausgegeben von Richard Pietschmann. pp. cxviii. 161. (Abhandlungen der Königlichen Gesellschaft der Wissenschaften zu Göttingen. Philologisch-Historische Klasse. Neue Folge. Band VI. Nro. 4.)
Weidmannsche Buchhandlung: Berlin, 1906. 4°.
[Ac. 670.] *See* 1907, No. 291.

290. **Torres Lanzas**, Pedro.—Relación Descriptiva de los Mapas, Planos, *etc.*, del Virreinato del Perú (Perú y Chile) existentes en el Archivo General de Indias (Sevilla). Por Pedro Torres Lanzas, Jefe de dicho Archivo. pp. 135.
Imp. Henrich y Cᵃ·, en Comandita: Barcelona, 1906. 8°.
[Maps 59. c. 25.]

1907.
291. **Sarmiento de Gamboa**, Pedro.—History of the Incas. By Pedro Sarmiento de Gamboa. [1572.] And The Execution of the Inca Tupac Amaru. By Captain Baltasar de Ocampo. [1610.] Translated and edited, with notes and an introduction, by Sir Clements Markham, K.C.B., President of the Hakluyt Society. [With a map of Central Peru, and of Vilcapampa, and 10 illustrations. Bibliography.]
Printed for the Hakluyt Society: [*University Press*,] *Cambridge*, 1907. 8°.
[Ac. 6172/94.] *See* 1610, No. 80; 1906, No. 289.

ADDENDA.

1890.
292. **Middendorf**, E. W.—Die einheimischen Sprachen Perus. (Bd. 1. Das Runa Simi oder die Keshua-Sprache, wie sie gegenwärtig in der Provinz von Cusco gesprochen wird. Unter Berücksichtigung der früheren Arbeiten nach eigenen Studien dargestellt.—Bd. II. Wörterbuch des Runa Simi oder der Keshua-Sprache.—Bd. III. Ollanta. Ein Drama der Keshua-Sprache. Übersetzt und mit Anmerkungen versehen. Nebst einer Einleitung über die religiösen und staatlichen Einrichtungen der Inkas.—Bd. IV. Dramatische und lyrische Dichtungen der Keshua-Sprache. Gesammelt und übersetzt mit erklärenden Anmerkungen.—Bd. V. Die Aimarà-Sprache. Mit einer Einleitung über die frühere Verbreitung der dieser Sprache redenden Rasse und ihr Verhältnis zu den Inkas.—Bd. VI. Das Muchik oder die Chimu-Sprache. Mit einer Einleitung über die Culturvölker, die gleichzeitig mit den Inkas und Aimaràs in Südamerika lebten, und einem Anhang über die Chibcha-Sprache.) 6 Bde.
F. A. Brockhaus: Leipzig, 1890–92. 8°.
[12910. f. 31.]

1893.
293. **Middendorf**, E. W.—Peru. Beobachtungen und Studien über das Land und seine Bewohner, während eines 25 Jährigen Aufenthalts. Von E. W. Middendorf. Band I. Lima. Mit 21 Textbildern und 32 Tafeln. Band II. Das Küstenland von Peru. Mit 56 Textbildern und 38 Tafeln nach eigenen photographischen Aufnahmen. Band III. Das Hochland von Peru. Mit 79 Textbildern und 93 Tafeln nach eigenen photographischen Aufnahmen sowie einer Karte. 3 Bde.
Robert Oppenheim (Gustav Schmidt): Berlin, 1893–95. 8°.
[010480. h. 1.]

BIBLIOGRAPHY OF PERU.

A.D. 1526—1907.

PART II.
INDEX OF AUTHORS, EDITORS, TRANSLATORS, ETC.

INDEX OF AUTHORS, EDITORS, TRANSLATORS, ETC.

	Year	No.
Archivo de Indias	1650	108
	1829	154
	1865	200
	1867	207
	1872	218
	1874	222
	1905	286
Arias d' Avila, Pedro	1540	19
	1829	154
	1865	201
Arias de Ugarte, Fernando, *Archbishop of Lima*	1607	70
	1608	74
	1842	165
Armendariz, José de, *Marqués de Castel Fuerte, Viceroy of Peru.*	1732	126
	1863	196
Arriaga, Pablo Joseph de, *S.J.*	1621	90
Astete, Miguel de.	1534	9
	1535	12, 13
	1872	217
Atahualpa.	1533	4
	1830	159
	1845	159
	1872	217
Atienza, Juan de, *S.J.*	1594	58
Augustus Frederick, *Duke of Sussex*	1661	111
Austria, Archduke of. *Coat of arms*	1641	103
Auteo, Bartolomé.	1860	189
Avalos y Figueroa, Diego d'	1602	62
Avendaño, Diego de	1668	112
Avendaño, Fernando de.	1648	106
Avila, Francisco de	1608	73
	1873	220
Aymara	1584	48
	1585	49
	1598	59
	1603	63, 64
	1604	67
	1612	82, 83
	1616	87
	1870	211
	1871	215
	1900	276
	1901	277
Baessler, Arthur.	1902	279
	1906	287, 288
Balboa, Miguel Cavello. *See* Cavello Balboa, Miguel.		
Banks, *Sir* Joseph, *Bart.*	1535	11
	1553	27
	1572	44
	1591	56
	1604	66
	1709	121
	1748	132

	Year	No.
Boston Public Library	1847	168
Bouffard, L.	1850	171
Bravo de Sarabia y Sotomayor, Alonso . .	1621	91
Brehm, Reinhold Bernhard	1885	249
British Museum, Add. MSS. 5469 . . .	1625	94
Add. MSS. 17,585 . . .	1610	80
Add. MSS. 25,327 . . .	1631	97
British Museum, Books not in	1538	17
	1549	24
	1557	32
	1586	52
	1603	65
	1633	99
	1648	106
	1668	112
	1677	113, 114
	1747	131
	1785	142
	1793	147
	1847	168
	1858	186
	1865	204
	1895	267
	1901	278
British Museum, Department of MSS. . . .	1875	226
British Museum, Sloane MSS. 3055 . . .	1610	79
Bröé, Samuel de, *Seigneur de Citry et de La Guette* .	1716	123
Buache, Philippe	1744	130
Bueno, Cosme	1763	137, 138
	1863	196
	1872	196
C., S. D. [Samuel de Bröé, *Seigneur de Citry et de La Guette*]	1716	123
Calancha, Antonio de la	1638	101
	1639	102
Calero y Moreira, Jacinto	1791	145
Campbell, John, *LL.D.*	1741	131
	1747	131
Cañete, Marquis de.		
See Hurtado de Mendoza, Garcia, *4th Marquis de Cañete.*		
Cardenas, Bernardino de, *Bishop of Paraguay* . .	1634	100
Cárdenas, Francisco de	1865	200
Cardenas, Gabriel de, *pseud.* i.e. Andrès Gonzalez de Barcia Carballido y Zuñiga	1723	124
Cardona, Enrique de	1591	56
Carrera, Fernando de la	1644	104
Casalbonus, Raphael	1783	141
Casas, Bartolomé de las, *Bishop of Chiapa* . .	1552	25
	1892	258
Castelnau, François de, *Comte*	1850	171
Castilla, Ramon	1865	206
Castilla, Sebastian de	1571	40
Castro y Rossi, Adolfo de	1858	185

	Year	No.
Dávila, Pedrarias.		
See Arias d' Avila, Pedro.		
Desjardins, Antoine Émile Ernest . . .	1858	186
Diaz, Pedro, *S.J.*.	1594	58
Domingo, *de Santo Tomas* . . .	1560	33, 34
	1891	256
Dorsey, George Amos	1898	274
Eder, Franciscus Xavier, *S.J.*	1791	144
Edward VI, *King of England*	1546	20
El Dorado.	1861	194
Encyclopedias	1887	250
English Merchant	1747	131
Enock, C. Reginald	1905	284, 285
Enriquez de Guzman, Luis, *Conde de Alva de Liste y*		
Villaflor, *Viceroy of Peru*	1661	111
Ensenada, Marqués de la.		
See Somodevilla y Bengoechea, Zenón de, *Marqués*		
de la Ensenada.		
Escalona Aguero, Gaspar de	1647	105
Esquilache, Príncipe de.		
See Borja y Acevedo, Francisco de, *Príncipe de Esqui-*		
lache.		
Estete, Miguel de.		
See Astete, Miguel de.		
Ethnological Society of London . . .	1854	178
	1870	211
Falb, Rudolf	1883	245
Ferdinand VI, *King of Spain*	1748	132
	1826	152
Fernández, Diego, *de Palencia*	1571	40
	1863	196
	1876	196
Fernandez de Navarrete, Martin . . .	1829	154
	1851	174
Fernández de Oviedo y Valdés, Gonzalo . .	1526	1
	1533	3
	1534	8, 9
	1535	11
	1547	21
	1830	158
Fernandez de Piedrahita, Lucas, successively *Bishop*		
of Santa Marta and of Panama . . .	1688	115
Field Columbian Museum, Chicago . . .	1898	274
Figueredo, Juan de, *S.J.*	1700	118
	1754	134
Forbes, David, *F.R.S.*	1870	211
Francisca Ñusta, *Inca Princess*	1688	115
Francisco [SOLANO], *Saint*	1630	96
	1677	113, 114
Franciscus, à Victoria	1557	32
	1587	32

	Year	No.
Quichua (*continued*)	1603	65
	1604	67
	1607	70, 71
	1608	74
	1614	85
	1648	106
	1691	117
	1853	177
	1860	189, 191
	1864	199
	1871	216
	1884	247
	1887	251
	1890	292
	1891	256
	1900	276
	1901	277
	1907	291
Quintana, Manuel José	1830	158, 159
Ramirez de Arellano, Feliciano, *Marqués de la Fuensanta del Valle.*	1877	227
	1879	233, 234
	1882	244
	1889	253
	1892	258
Ramos Gavilan, Alonso, *Augustinian* . . .	1621	91
Ranking, John	1827	153
Ravenna, Th.	1538	17
Rayon, José Sancho	1877	227
	1879	233, 234
	1882	244
	1889	253
	1892	258
Real Archivo de Indias	1650	97
	1829	154
	1865	200
	1867	207
	1872	218
	1874	222
	1905	286
Reiss, Wilhelm	1880	241
René-Moreno, Gabriel	1896	270
Ricaut, *Sir* Paul	1688	116
Richelet, Pierre	1737	127
Riveroy Ustariz, Mariano Eduardo de . . .	1851	173
	1853	175
Ross, Thomasina	1847	169
Rouaud y Paz Soldan, Manuel	1865	206
Rousselet, Louis	1890	255
Royal Geographical Society	1871	215
	1905	284, 285
Ruiz de Navamuel, Alvaro	1598	59
Rycaut, *Sir* Paul	1688	116
Salaberry, *Madame* Louise de	1808	150

	Year	No.
Southey, Robert	1763	138
Spain	1534	7
Spain. *Ministerio de Fomento*	1879	235
	1881	243
Squier, Ephraim George	1621	90
	1853	176
	1860	189
	1868	208
	1870	213
	1877	230
Stette, Michael.		
See Astete, Miguel de.		
Stevens, Henry, of Vermont, *F.S.A.* . . .	1534	8
Stevens, Henry Newton, *F.R.G.S.* . . .	1633	98
Stevens, John, *Captain*	1709	121
Stuart, Maria del Rosario, *Duquesa de Berwick y de Alba* .	1902	282
Stübel, Alphons	1880	241
	1892	262
Suarez de Salazar, Juan Bautista . . .	1610	81
Sussex, Duke of.		
See Augustus Frederick, *Duke of Sussex.*		
Sutherland, Duke of	1633	98
Tahuantinsuyu	1885	249
	1895	267
Ternaux-Compans, Henri	1604	67
	1608	74
	1612	83
	1616	86, 87
	1837	161
	1840	162, 163, 164
	1857	184
Thomas, Aquinas, Saint	1607	69
	1729	125
Tiahuanaco	1884	246
	1892	262
Tiraquellus, Andreas	1549	24
	1573	24
Toledo, Francisco de, *Viceroy of Peru* . .	1569	38
	1571	43
	1572	45
	1622	92
	1855	180
	1867	207
	1882	244
	1889	253
	1906	289
	1907	291
Torre Nueva, *Marqués de*	1737	128
Torres, Bernardo de, *Augustinian* . . .	1639	102
Torres de Mendoza, Luis	1867	207
Torres Lanzas, Pedro	1906	290
Torres Rubio, Diego de, *S.J.*	1603	65
	1616	87

	Year	No.
Viscarra, J.	1901	278
Vivien de Saint Martin, Louis	1890	255
West Indies	1534	8
Widenmann, Eduard	1843	166
Wiener, Charles	1874	225
	1880	242
Wilson, Thomas, *D.C.L.*	1581	47
Xéres, Francisco de	1534	9
	1535	12, 13
	1547	21, 22
	1837	161
	1843	166
	1872	217

Yamqui Pachacuti.
See Santa Cruz Pachacuti Yamqui, Juan de.

	Year	No.
Zabalburu, Francisco de	1877	227
	1889	253
Zapata, Antonio, *Cardinal* . . .	1610	81
Zarate, Augustin de	1555	31
	1577	46
	1581	47
	1716	123
	1843	166
Zhaval	Nov. 25, 1534	10
	1700	119
	1850	172
	Sept. 25, 1535	14
Zubieta y Roxas, Bernardo de	1754	134

BIBLIOGRAPHY OF PERU.

A.D. 1526—1907.

PART III.

INDEX OF TITLES

INDEX OF TITLES.

344 BIBLIOGRAPHY

Apuntes Históricos del Perú. 1902.
Mendiburu, Manuel de. 280.

Aqui se contiene una disputa o controversia. 1552.
Casas, Bartolomé de las, *Bishop of Chiapa.* 25.

Arte Breve de la Lengua Aymara. 1603.
Bertonio, Ludovico. 63.

Arte de la Lengua Aymara. 1612. 1879.
Bertonio, Ludovico. 82, 231.

Arte de la Lengua Aymara. 1616.
Torres Rubio, Diego de, *S.J.* 79.

Arte de la Lengua General del Peru, llamada Quichua. 1604.
Quichua. 68.

Arte de la Lengua General del Ynga. 1691.
Melgar, Estevan Sancho de. 117.

Arte de la Lengua Quechua. 1616.
Huerta, Alonzo de. 86.

Arte de la Lengua Quichua. 1619. 1700.
Torres Rubio, Diego de, *S.J.* 88, 118.

Arte de la Lengua Quichua. 1891.
Domingo, *de Santo Tomas.* 256.

Arte de la Lengua Yunga. 1644.
Carrera, Fernando de la. 104.

Arte de Lingua Quiche, ó Utlatica. 1860.
Auteo, Bartolomé. 189.

Arte y Grammatica muy copiosa de la Lengua Aymara. 1603. 1879.
Bertonio, Ludovico. 64, 231.

Arte y Vocabulario de la Lengua Quichua. 1754.
Torres Rubio, Diego de, *S.J.* 123.

Arte y Vocabulario en la lengua general del Peru llamada Quichua. 1586. 1614.
Quichua. 52, 85.

Atlas Geográfico del Perú. 1865.
Paz Soldan, Mariano Felipe. 205.

Atlas Géográphico de la República del Perú. 1869.
Paz Soldan, Mariano Felipe. 210.

Atlas Géographique de la République du Pérou. 1865.
Paz Soldan, Mariano Felipe. 206.

Autobiografias y Memorias. 1905.
Serrano y Sanz, Manuel. 286.

Aviso Historico, Politico, Geographico. 1741.
Alcedo y Herrera, Dionysio de. 129.

Bibliografía Española de Lenguas Indígenas de América. 1892.
Muñoz Manzano, Cipriano, *Conde de la Viñaza.* 261.

A Bibliography of the Anthropology of Peru. 1898.
Dorsey, George Amos. 274.

Biblioteca Hispano-Ultramarina. 1877. 1880.
228, 237, 239.

Biblioteca Marítima Española. 1851.
Fernandez de Navarrete, Martin. 174.

Los Cinco Libros primeros de la Cronica general de España. 1553.
Ocampo, Florian de. 28.

Coleccion de Documentos Inéditos para la Historia de España (1842-95).
1855. 1877. 1889.
Fernandez de Navarrete, Martin, &c. 180, 227, 253.

Coleccion de Documentos Inéditos relativos al descubrimiento conquista y
colonizacion de las posesiones Españolas en América y Oceanía,
sacados, en su mayor parte, del Real Archivo de Indias (1864-83).
1865. 1867. 1872. 1874.
Pacheco, Joaquin Francisco, &c. 200, 207, 218, 222.

Coleccion de Documentos Literarios del Peru. 1863.
Odriozola, Manuel de. 196.

Coleccion de Libros Españoles Raros ó Curiosos. 1879. 1882. 1892.
Ramirez de Orellana, Feliciano, Marqués de Fuensanta del Valle.
233, 234, 244, 258.

Colección de Libros y Documentos referentes á la Historia de América.
1904.
Gutiérrez de Santa Clara, Pedro. 283.

Coleccion de los Mejores Autores Españoles (1845). 1830.
Quintana, Manuel José. 158.

Coleccion de los Viages y Descubrimientos, que hicieron por Mar los
Españoles desde fines del siglo xv. 1829.
Fernandez de Navarrete, Martin. 154.

Coleccion de Obras y Documentos relativos á la Historia Antigua y Moderna
de las Provincias del Rio de La Plata. 1836.
Angelis, Pedro de. 160.

Le Commentaire Royal ou L'Histoire des Yncas. 1633.
Garcilasso de la Vega, el Inca. 98.

Commentarios Reales. 1609. 1723. 1829.
Garcilasso de la Vega, el Inca. 75, 124, 156.

A Concise History of the Spanish America. 1741.
Campbell, John, LL.D. See 1747. 131.

Confessionario para los Curas de Indios. 1585.
Indios. 49.

El Conocimiento de los Tiempos. 1763. 137, 138.

Conquista del Peru. 1535. 1547.
Xéres, Francisco de. 12, 13, 21, 22.

Contributions towards a Grammar and Dictionary of Quichua. 1864.
Markham, Sir Clements Robert, K.C.B., F.R.S. 199.

Copacabana de los Incas. 1901.
Viscarra, J. 278.

Copia delle Lettere del Prefetto della India la nova Spagna detta. 1534.
Peru. 5.

Copy of a Letter…10th November, 1586. 1586. 1896.
Sarmiento de Gamboa, Pedro. 53, 271.

Coronica de las Indias. 1547.
Fernández de Oviedo y Valdés, Gonzalo. 21.

Coronica General de toda España. 1546. 1563.
Beuter, Pedro Antonio. 20, 36.

Coronica Moralizada del Orden de San Augustin en el Peru. 1638. 1639.
Calancha, Antonio de la. 101, 102.

Documents relating to the appointment and administration of Francisco de Toledo. 1569. 1867.
Toledo, Francisco de, *Viceroy of Peru.* 38, 207.

Die Einheimischen Sprachen Perus. 1890.
Middendorf, E. W. 292.

Ensayo Mitológico. 1892.
Lafone y Quevedo, Samuel Alexander. 259.

Ensayo sobre las excelencias y perfeccion del Idioma llamado comunmente Quichua. 1857.
Mossi de Cambiano, Honorio. 183.

Epitome de la Bibliotheca oriental y occidental, &c. 1737.
Leon Pinelo, Antonio de. 128.

Erzehlung des Lebens...des Apostels von Peru...Francisci Solani. 1677.
Kellen, Ludovicus. 114.

Essai sur les Institutions Politiques...de l'Empire des Incas. 1874.
Wiener, Charles. 225.

Essay on the Quichís. 1860.
Squier, Ephraim George. 189.

The Execution of the Inca Tupac Amaru. 1907.
Ocampo, Baltasar de. 291.

Expédition dans les Parties Centrales de l'Amérique du Sud. 1850.
Castelnau, François de, *Comte.* 171.

Expedition of Gonzalo Pizarro to the land of Cinnamon, A.D. 1539–42. 1859.
Garcilasso de la Vega, *el Inca.* 188.

The Expedition of Pedro de Ursua & Lope de Aguirre in search of El Dorado...1560–61. 1861.
Simon, Pedro. 194.

Expeditions into the Valley of the Amazons. 1859.
Markham, *Sir* Clements Robert, *K.C.B., F.R.S.* 188.

Extirpacion de la Idolatria del Piru. 1621.
Arriaga, Pablo Joseph de, *S.J.* 90.

First Part of the Royal Commentaries of the Yncas. 1869.
Garcilasso de la Vega, *el Inca.* 209.

Foreign Countries and British Colonies. 1880.
Markham, *Sir* Clements Robert, *K.C.B., F.R.S.* 240.

Gazofilacio Regio Perubico. 1647.
Escalona Aguero, Gaspar de. 105.

Gazophilatium Regium Perubicum. 1647.
Escalona Aguero, Gaspar de. 105.

Il Gazzettiere Americano. 1763.
American Gazetteer. 136.

General History of the Western Indies. 1859.
Herrera Tordesillas, Antonio de. 188.

The Geographical Journal. 1905.
Enock, C. Reginald. 284, 285.

Geschichte der Entdeckung und Eroberung Peru's. 1843.
Xeres, Francisco de. 166.

Historia del Celebre Santuario de Neustra Señora de Copacabana. 1621.
Ramos Gavilan, Alonso. 91.

Historia del Descubrimiento y Conquista del Peru. 1555. 1577.
Zarate, Augustin de. 31, 46.

La Historia del Mondo Nuovo. 1565. 1572.
Benzoni, Girolamo. 37, 44.

Historia del Nuevo Mundo. 1653. 1890.
Cobo, Bernabé. 109, 254.

Historia del Peru. 1571. 1876.
Fernández, Diego, de Palencia. 40, 196.

Historia del Perú. 1586. 1840.
Cavello Balboa, Miguel. 51, 162.

Historia del Reino de Quito. 1789. 1840.
Velasco, Juan de. 143, 164.

Historia de la Conquista del Nuevo Mundo. 1829.
Garcilasso de la Vega, el Inca. 156.

Historia de las Guerras Civiles del Perú (1544-48). 1904.
Gutiérrez de Santa Clara, Pedro. 283.

Historia General del Perú. [Segunda Parte de los Commentarios Reales.
1609.] 1617. 1723.
Garcilasso de la Vega, el Inca. 77, 124.

Historia general de las Conquistas del Nuevo Reyno de Granada. 1688.
Fernandez de Piedrahita, Lucas, successively Bishop of Santa Marta
and of Panama. 115.

La Historia general de las Indias. 1535.
Fernández de Oviedo y Valdés, Gonzalo. 11.

Historia General de los Hechos de los Castellanos en las Islas i Tierra Firme
del Mar Oceano. 1601.
Herrera Tordesillas, Antonio de. 61.

Historia general llamada Índica. 1572. 1906.
Sarmiento de Gamboa, Pedro. 45, 289.

Historia imperii Peruani. MS. c. 1590.
Valera, Blas. 55.

Historia natural y moral de las Indias. 1590. 1591. 1608. 1792.
Acosta, Joseph de, S.J. 54, 56, 72, 146.

Historical Researches on the Conquest of Peru. 1827.
Ranking, John. 153.

A History of Peru. 1892.
Markham, Sir Clements Robert, K.C.B., F.R.S. 260.

History of the Conquest of Peru. 1847.
Prescott, William Hickling. 168.

History of the Incas. 1907.
Sarmiento de Gamboa, Pedro. 290.

History of the New World. (1572). 1857.
Benzoni. Girolamo. 182.

La hystoria general de las Indias. 1547.
Fernández de Oviedo y Valdés, Gonzalo. 21.

Hystoria o Descripcion del Imperial cibdad de Toledo. 1554.
Alcocer, Pedro de. 29.

Les Incas, ou La Destruction de l'Empire du Pérou. 1777.
Marmontel, Jean François. 140.

Letter of Hernando Pizarro to the Royal Audience of Santo Domingo. 1872.
Markham, *Sir* Clements Robert, *K.C.B.*, *F.R.S.* 217.

Lettera de La nobil Citta. Sept. 25, 1535.
Zhaval. 14.

Lettres du Japon, et de la Chine. 1593.
Jesuits. 57.

Lexicologia Keshua. Uirakocha. 1887.
Villar, Leonardo, *del Cuzco*. 251.

Lexicon o Vocabulario de la lengua general del Peru. 1560.
Domingo, *de Santo Tomas*. 34.

Libro de grandezas y cosas memorables de España. 1548.
Medina, Pedro de. 23.

Libro de la Vida y Milagros de Nuestro Señor Jesu Christo. 1612.
Villegas, Alonso de. 84.

Libro Primo de la Conquista del Peru. 1535.
Xéres, Francisco de. 12, 13.

Libro Ultimo del Summario delle Indie Occidentali. 1534.
West Indies. 8.

Libros Reales de Govierno y Gracia de la Secretaria del Perú. 1625.
Leon Pinelo, Antonio de. 93.

Lima Almanack. 1763. 137.

Lima Fundada, o Conquista del Perú. 1732. 1863.
Peralta Barnuevo Rocha y Benavides, Pedro José de. 126, 196.

The Literature of American Aboriginal Languages. 1858.
Ludewig, Hermann Eduard. 187.

Litteratur der Grammatiken, Lexica, und Wörtersammlungen aller Sprachen
der Erde. 1847.
Vater, Johann Severin. 170.

Mali Galeci sanandi...modi omnes. 1538.
Ravenna, Th. 17.

Manual del Idioma General del Perú. 1889.
Mossi, Miguel Angel. 252.

A Memoir of the Lady Ana de Osorio, Countess of Chinchon, and Vice-
Queen of Peru. 1874.
Markham, *Sir* Clements Robert, *K.C.B.*, *F.R.S.* 223.

Mémoires Historiques sur l'ancien Pérou. 1840.
Montesinos, Fernando de. 163.

Memoirs read before the Anthropological Society of London. 1865.
Bollaert, William. 202.

Memoria de lo que han hecho mis padres y yo en busca del Dorado, que
ansí se llama esta conquista, y dicen que es el Paytiti. 1650. 1905.
Soleto Pernia, Alonso. 108, 286.

Memorial des las Historias del Nuevo Mundo : Piru. 1630.
Salinas y Cordova, Buenaventura de. 96.

Memorial que D. Francisco de Toledo dió al Rey nuestro Señor del estado,
&c. 1571. 1855.
Toledo, Francisco de, *Viceroy of Peru*. 43, 180.

Memorial y Relacion ..de cosas del Reino del Perú. 1634.
Cardenas, Bernardino de, *Bishop of Paraguay*. 100.

Nouvelle Découverte d'un Pays plus grand que l'Europe. 1737.
Hennepin, Louis. 127.

Nouvelles certaines des Isles du Péru. 1534.
Peru. 6.

Nueva Biblioteca de Autores Españoles. 1905.
Menendez y Pelayo, Marcelino. 286.

Nuevo Descubrimiento del Gran Rio de las Amazonas. 1641.
Acuña, Cristoval de. 103.

Nuevos Autógrafos de Cristóbal Colón y Relaciones de Ultramar. 1902.
Stuart, Maria del Rosario, *Duquesa de Berwick y de Alba.* 282.

Obra compuesta por Lucio Marineo Siculo. 1539.
Marineo, Lucio, *Siculo.* 18.

Observations on the Geography and Archæology of Peru. 1870.
Squier, Ephraim George. 213.

Observations on the History of the Incas of Peru. 1854.
Bollaert, William, *F.R.G.S.* 178.

Ollanta. 1871.
Ollanta. 216.

On the Aymara Indians of Bolivia and Peru. 1870.
Forbes. David, *F.R.S.* 211.

On the Geographical Positions of the Tribes, which formed the Empire of the Yncas. 1871.
Markham, *Sir* Clements Robert, *K.C.B., F.R.S.* 215.

Organismus der Khetšua-Sprache. 1884.
Tschudi, Johann Jakob von. 247.

Origen del Kechua y del Aymará. 1900.
Patrón, Pablo. 276.

Origen de los Indios de el Nuevo Mundo e Indias Occidentales. 1607.
1729.
García, Gregorio. 69, 125.

Oviedo de la natural hystoria de las Indias. 1526.
Fernández de Oviedo y Valdés, Gonzalo. 1.

Papeles Varios. 1821.
Tupac Amaru, Juan. 151.

Parte Primera de la chronica del Peru. 1553. 1554.
Cieza de Leon, Pedro de. 27, 30.

Le Pérou avant la conquête espagnole. 1858.
Desjardins, Antoine Emile Ernest. 186.

Pérou et Bolivie. 1880.
Wiener, Charles. 242.

Peru. 1880.
Markham, *Sir* Clements Robert, *K.C.B., F.R.S.* 240.

Peru. Beobachtungen und Studien. 1893.
Middendorf, E. W. 293.

Peru. Incidents of Travel and Exploration in the Land of the Incas. 1877.
Squier, Ephraim George. 230.

Peru. Reiseskizzen aus den Jahren 1838–42. 1846.
Tschudi, Johann Jakob von. 167.

Relacion de lo Acaecido en Perú, &c. 1879.
Hernandez Giron, Francisco. 234.

Relacion de los Fundamentos acerca del notable Daño que resulta de no
guardar á los Indios sus fueros. 1571. 1872.
Ondegardo, Polo de. 42, 218.

Relacion de los sucesos de Pedrarias Dávila. 1540. 1829.
Andagoya, Pascual de. 19, 154.

Relacion de todo lo sucedido en la Provincia del Piru...M.D.X.L.III. 1870.
Peru. 212.

Relación Descriptiva de los Mapas, Planos, etc., del Virreinato del Perú.
1906.
Torres Lanzas, Pedro. 290.

Relacion Historica del Viage á la América Meridional. 1748.
Ulloa, Antonio de. 132.

Relacion Historica de los Sucesos de la Rebellion de José Gabriel Tupac-
Amaru. 1836. 1863.
Tupac Amaru, José Gabrièl. 160, 197.

Relaciones Geográficas de Indias. 1881.
Spain.—Ministerio de Fomento. 243.

Relation Véridique de la Conquête du Pérou et de la Province du Cuzco.
1837.
Xéres, Francisco de. 161.

La Relatione del Viaggio che fece il Signore capitano Ferdinando Picciarro,
etc. 1535.
Astete, Miguel de. 12, 13.

Relectiones Theologicae. 1557. 1587.
Franciscus, à Victoria. 32.

Report by Polo de Ondegardo on the lineage, conquests, edifices, fortresses,
&c., of the Yncas. 1560. 1873.
Ondegardo, Polo de. 35, 220.

Report of Francisco de Xeres. 1872.
Xéres, Francisco de. 217.

Report of Miguel de Astete on the Expedition to Pachacamac. 1872.
Astete, Miguel de. 217.

Report of Pedro Sancho on the partition of the Ransom of Atahualpa. 1872.
Sancho, Pedro. 217.

Reports on the Discovery of Peru. 1872.
Markham, Sir Clements Robert, K.C.B., F.R.S. 217.

Resumen Historico del Origen, y Succession de los Incas. 1748.
Ulloa, Antonio de, Admiral. 132.

Revista del Museo de La Plata. 1892.
Lafone y Quevedo, Samuel Alexander. 259.

Rituale, seu Manuale Peruanum. 1607.
Peruvian Ritual. 71.

The Royal Commentaries of Peru. 1688. 1859. 1869.
Garcilasso de la Vega, el Inca. 116, 188, 209.

R. P. Didaci de Avendaño...Thesaurus Indicus. 1668.
Avendaño, Diego de. 112.

Die Ruinenstaette von Tiahuanaco. 1892.
Stübel, Alphons. 262.

The Ruins of Huanuco Viejo, or Old Huanuco. 1905.
Enock, C. Reginald. 285.

358 BIBLIOGRAPHY

The Travels of Pedro de Cieza de Leon. 1864.
  Cieza de Leon, Pedro. 198.
Las Tres Epocas del Perú o Compendio de su Historia. 1844. 1863.
  1875.
  Córdova y Urrutia, José María. 196.
Tres Relaciones de Antigüedades Peruanas. 1879.
  Jiménez de la Espada, Márcos. 235.
Trübner's Bibliotheca Glottica. 1858.
  Ludewig, Hermann Eduard. 187.
Two Years in Peru. 1873.
  Hutchinson, Thomas Joseph. 219.

Varias Relaciones del Perú y Chile. 1879.
  Cuzco. Hernandez Giron, Francisco. 233, 234.
Ventajas de la Constitucion Española. 1821.
  Tupac Amaru, Juan. 151.
Verdadera Relacion de la Conquista del Peru. 1534. 1547.
  Xéres, Francisco de. 9, 22.
Verzeichniss der Handschriften im Preussischen Staate. 1893. 1894.
  Prussia. 264, 266.
Vidas de Españoles Célebres. 1807. 1830. 1845.
  Quintana, Manuel José. 158, 159.
Vidas de varones ilustres de la Compañia de Jesus de la Provincia del
  Perú. 1631.
  Oliva, Anello, S.J. 97.
La Vie du bien-heureux père Francisco Solano. 1677.
  Courtot, François. 113.
Vocabulario de la Lengua Aymara. 1612. 1879.
  Bertonio, Ludovico. 83, 232.
Vocabulario de la Lengua General de todo el Peru. 1608.
  Gonzalez Holguin, Diego, S.J. 74.
Vocabulario en la Lengua General del Peru, llamada Quichua. 1604.
  Quichua. 68.
Voyage de Humboldt et Bonpland. 1807.
  Humboldt, Friedrich Heinrich Alexander von, Baron. 149.
Voyage Historique de l'Amérique Meridionale. 1752.
  Ulloa, Antonio de, Admiral. 133.
The Voyage of Francisco de Orellana down the river of the Amazons,
  A.D. 1540–41. 1859.
  Herrera Tordesillas, Antonio de. 188.
Voyages, Relations et Mémoires Originaux, pour servir à l'histoire de la
  découverte de l'Amérique. 1837. 1840.
  Ternaux-Compans, Henri. 161–164.

INDEX.

book by Sepulveda, xiii; his Confessor, de Loaysa, 244
Chasquis, Inca couriers, 116
Chauca Rimachi, Don Francisco.
See Rimachi Chaco, Don Francisco
Chauin Cuzco Ayllu, of the lineage óf Ayar Cachi, 46
Checo, Don Diego (Chima Panaca), 1572, 62
Chiapa, 26
Chiapa, bishop of, 5
Chica Ccapac, Sinchi of the Cañaris, conquered by Tupac Inca, 131
Chicha, 30
Chichas, the, 124, 125
Chichima, Francisco, a Pilcosone Indian, 239; heads a negro revolt, 240; his execution, 241
Chihuay Ccapac, death of, 84
Chile, kingdom of, 7, 39; Inca roads from Quito to, 133; invaded by Tupac Inca Yupanqui, 145; Order of our Lady of Mercy first to evangelize, 242; visitation of, by Huayna Ccapac, 159
Chillincay, town, conquered by Yahuar-huaccac, 81
Chima, founder of the Ayllu of Manca Ccapac, 62
Chima chaui, 70
Chima Chaui Pata Yupanqui, remains with Inca Yupanqui, 89: *see also* Apu Chimachaui
Chima Huarhua, Don Juan, 1572, 62
Chima Panaca Ayllu (Manco Ccapac), 62
Chimbo Cisa, sister of Huascar, murdered before his eyes, 186
Chimbo Orma, concubine of Tocay Ccapac, 77; frees Yahuar-huaccac, 77
Chimu, valley of, conquered by Tupac Inca, 131, 137
Chimu Ccapac, Sinchi, captured by Ccapac Yupanqui, 118, 122, 131; his gold and silver house, 137
Chinchay-Cocha, Curaca of, 186
Chinchaycocha, Tomayrica and, *Huaca*, 166
Chinchay-suyu, one of the four divisions of the Inca Empire, 132
Chinchay-suyu, province of, conquered by the army of Pachacuti Inca Yupanqui, 115, &c.; colonists from, transplanted by Pachacuti Inca Yupanqui to Anti-suyu, 120;

expedition of Tupac Inca Yupanqui to, 129, &c.; Huaman Achachi, Governor of, 157; Huayna Ccapac's troops from, 163.
Chinchero, village, 208; Ccapac Huari exiled to, 155; Inca palace still existing at, 153; Tupac Inca Yupanqui dies at, 153
Chincheroca (Sinchi Rocca), 63
Chipana, bracelet, 215
Chiponauas, the, Anti-suyu, 143
Chirao Sucanca, Cuzco, 99
Chiraques, town, conquered by Viracocha Inca, 85
Chirihuanas, eaters of human flesh, 7; subdued by Huayna Ccapac, 159; their rebellion, 165, &c.
Chita, town, 88, 90
Choco, Mama Añahuarqui, of, 107
Chocos-chacona, suburb of Cuzco, 92
Chonay, Doña Elvira, daughter of Cañar Ccapac, spared by Atahualpa, 186
Choyca, town, conquered by Yahuarhuaccac, 80
Chronicle of Peru, The, 1532–50. *See* Cieza de Leon, Pedro de
Chuca-Chucay Pachacuti Coaquiri, a Colla, spreads reports of death of Tupac Inca, and heads a rebellion, 144; his death, 145
Chuccu, Inca head-dress, 101, 208
Chuchi Ccapac, Sinchi of Collao, 111; his murder, 113; the rebellion of his sons, 121–123
Chuco, Inca head-dress, 101, 130, 208
Chucuito, lake, 33
Chucumbi, Martin (Chauin Cuzco Ayllu), 1572, 46
Chucuy Huypa, wife of Huascar Inca, 182, 189; prisoner of Atahualpa, *ib.*
Chumpi-cancha, 58
Chumpivilcas, province of, 232; subdued by Tupac Inca Yupanqui, 145
Chunca curaca, 146
Chuncara, 63
Chunchos, 8; province of the, conquered by Tupac Inca Yupanqui, 143, 144; Juan Alvarez Maldonado, Governor of, 1571, 218
Chuncu-marca, Huayllas, fortress, 131
Chupas, Paullu Tupac Yupanqui with Almagro at the battle of, xviii; Gomez de Tordoya, *id.*, *ib.*
Chupellusca, rock of, Inca Urco killed at, 105

A CATALOG OF SELECTED
DOVER BOOKS
IN ALL FIELDS OF INTEREST

A CATALOG OF SELECTED DOVER
BOOKS IN ALL FIELDS OF INTEREST

CONCERNING THE SPIRITUAL IN ART, Wassily Kandinsky. Pioneering work by father of abstract art. Thoughts on color theory, nature of art. Analysis of earlier masters. 12 illustrations. 80pp. of text. 5⅜ x 8½. 23411-8 Pa. $3.95

ANIMALS: 1,419 Copyright-Free Illustrations of Mammals, Birds, Fish, Insects, etc., Jim Harter (ed.). Clear wood engravings present, in extremely lifelike poses, over 1,000 species of animals. One of the most extensive pictorial sourcebooks of its kind. Captions. Index. 284pp. 9 x 12. 23766-4 Pa. $12.95

CELTIC ART: The Methods of Construction, George Bain. Simple geometric techniques for making Celtic interlacements, spirals, Kells-type initials, animals, humans, etc. Over 500 illustrations. 160pp. 9 x 12. (USO) 22923-8 Pa. $9.95

AN ATLAS OF ANATOMY FOR ARTISTS, Fritz Schider. Most thorough reference work on art anatomy in the world. Hundreds of illustrations, including selections from works by Vesalius, Leonardo, Goya, Ingres, Michelangelo, others. 593 illustrations. 192pp. 7⅛ x 10¼. 20241-0 Pa. $9.95

CELTIC HAND STROKE-BY-STROKE (Irish Half-Uncial from "The Book of Kells"): An Arthur Baker Calligraphy Manual, Arthur Baker. Complete guide to creating each letter of the alphabet in distinctive Celtic manner. Covers hand position, strokes, pens, inks, paper, more. Illustrated. 48pp. 8¼ x 11. 24336-2 Pa. $3.95

EASY ORIGAMI, John Montroll. Charming collection of 32 projects (hat, cup, pelican, piano, swan, many more) specially designed for the novice origami hobbyist. Clearly illustrated easy-to-follow instructions insure that even beginning papercrafters will achieve successful results. 48pp. 8¼ x 11. 27298-2 Pa. $3.50

THE COMPLETE BOOK OF BIRDHOUSE CONSTRUCTION FOR WOOD-WORKERS, Scott D. Campbell. Detailed instructions, illustrations, tables. Also data on bird habitat and instinct patterns. Bibliography. 3 tables. 63 illustrations in 15 figures. 48pp. 5¼ x 8½. 24407-5 Pa. $2.50

BLOOMINGDALE'S ILLUSTRATED 1886 CATALOG: Fashions, Dry Goods and Housewares, Bloomingdale Brothers. Famed merchants' extremely rare catalog depicting about 1,700 products: clothing, housewares, firearms, dry goods, jewelry, more. Invaluable for dating, identifying vintage items. Also, copyright-free graphics for artists, designers. Co-published with Henry Ford Museum & Greenfield Village. 160pp. 8¼ x 11. 25780-0 Pa. $10.95

HISTORIC COSTUME IN PICTURES, Braun & Schneider. Over 1,450 costumed figures in clearly detailed engravings—from dawn of civilization to end of 19th century. Captions. Many folk costumes. 256pp. 8⅜ x 11¾. 23150-X Pa. $12.95

FRANK LLOYD WRIGHT'S HOLLYHOCK HOUSE, Donald Hoffmann. Lavishly illustrated, carefully documented study of one of Wright's most controversial residential designs. Over 120 photographs, floor plans, elevations, etc. Detailed perceptive text by noted Wright scholar. Index. 128pp. 9¼ x 10¾. 27133-1 Pa. $11.95

THE MALE AND FEMALE FIGURE IN MOTION: 60 Classic Photographic Sequences, Eadweard Muybridge. 60 true-action photographs of men and women walking, running, climbing, bending, turning, etc., reproduced from rare 19th-century masterpiece. vi + 121pp. 9 x 12. 24745-7 Pa. $10.95

1001 QUESTIONS ANSWERED ABOUT THE SEASHORE, N. J. Berrill and Jacquelyn Berrill. Queries answered about dolphins, sea snails, sponges, starfish, fishes, shore birds, many others. Covers appearance, breeding, growth, feeding, much more. 305pp. 5¼ x 8¼. 23366-9 Pa. $8.95

GUIDE TO OWL WATCHING IN NORTH AMERICA, Donald S. Heintzelman. Superb guide offers complete data and descriptions of 19 species: barn owl, screech owl, snowy owl, many more. Expert coverage of owl-watching equipment, conservation, migrations and invasions, etc. Guide to observing sites. 84 illustrations. xiii + 193pp. 5⅜ x 8½. 27344-X Pa. $8.95

MEDICINAL AND OTHER USES OF NORTH AMERICAN PLANTS: A Historical Survey with Special Reference to the Eastern Indian Tribes, Charlotte Erichsen-Brown. Chronological historical citations document 500 years of usage of plants, trees, shrubs native to eastern Canada, northeastern U.S. Also complete identifying information. 343 illustrations. 544pp. 6½ x 9¼. 25951-X Pa. $12.95

STORYBOOK MAZES, Dave Phillips. 23 stories and mazes on two-page spreads: Wizard of Oz, Treasure Island, Robin Hood, etc. Solutions. 64pp. 8¼ x 11. 23628-5 Pa. $2.95

NEGRO FOLK MUSIC, U.S.A., Harold Courlander. Noted folklorist's scholarly yet readable analysis of rich and varied musical tradition. Includes authentic versions of over 40 folk songs. Valuable bibliography and discography. xi + 324pp. 5⅜ x 8½. 27350-4 Pa. $9.95

MOVIE-STAR PORTRAITS OF THE FORTIES, John Kobal (ed.). 163 glamor, studio photos of 106 stars of the 1940s: Rita Hayworth, Ava Gardner, Marlon Brando, Clark Gable, many more. 176pp. 8⅜ x 11¼. 23546-7 Pa. $12.95

BENCHLEY LOST AND FOUND, Robert Benchley. Finest humor from early 30s, about pet peeves, child psychologists, post office and others. Mostly unavailable elsewhere. 73 illustrations by Peter Arno and others. 183pp. 5⅜ x 8½. 22410-4 Pa. $6.95

YEKL and THE IMPORTED BRIDEGROOM AND OTHER STORIES OF YIDDISH NEW YORK, Abraham Cahan. Film Hester Street based on Yekl (1896). Novel, other stories among first about Jewish immigrants on N.Y.'s East Side. 240pp. 5⅜ x 8½. 22427-9 Pa. $6.95

SELECTED POEMS, Walt Whitman. Generous sampling from *Leaves of Grass.* Twenty-four poems include "I Hear America Singing," "Song of the Open Road," "I Sing the Body Electric," "When Lilacs Last in the Dooryard Bloom'd," "O Captain! My Captain!"–all reprinted from an authoritative edition. Lists of titles and first lines. 128pp. 5⁵⁄₁₆ x 8¼. 26878-0 Pa. $1.00

THE BEST TALES OF HOFFMANN, E. T. A. Hoffmann. 10 of Hoffmann's most important stories: "Nutcracker and the King of Mice," "The Golden Flowerpot," etc. 458pp. 5⅜ x 8½. 21793-0 Pa. $9.95

FROM FETISH TO GOD IN ANCIENT EGYPT, E. A. Wallis Budge. Rich detailed survey of Egyptian conception of "God" and gods, magic, cult of animals, Osiris, more. Also, superb English translations of hymns and legends. 240 illustrations. 545pp. 5⅜ x 8½. 25803-3 Pa. $13.95

FRENCH STORIES/CONTES FRANÇAIS: A Dual-Language Book, Wallace Fowlie. Ten stories by French masters, Voltaire to Camus: "Micromegas" by Voltaire; "The Atheist's Mass" by Balzac; "Minuet" by de Maupassant; "The Guest" by Camus, six more. Excellent English translations on facing pages. Also French-English vocabulary list, exercises, more. 352pp. 5⅜ x 8½. 26443-2 Pa. $8.95

CHICAGO AT THE TURN OF THE CENTURY IN PHOTOGRAPHS: 122 Historic Views from the Collections of the Chicago Historical Society, Larry A. Viskochil. Rare large-format prints offer detailed views of City Hall, State Street, the Loop, Hull House, Union Station, many other landmarks, circa 1904-1913. Introduction. Captions. Maps. 144pp. 9⅜ x 12¼. 24656-6 Pa. $12.95

OLD BROOKLYN IN EARLY PHOTOGRAPHS, 1865-1929, William Lee Younger. Luna Park, Gravesend race track, construction of Grand Army Plaza, moving of Hotel Brighton, etc. 157 previously unpublished photographs. 165pp. 8⅞ x 11¾. 23587-4 Pa. $13.95

THE MYTHS OF THE NORTH AMERICAN INDIANS, Lewis Spence. Rich anthology of the myths and legends of the Algonquins, Iroquois, Pawnees and Sioux, prefaced by an extensive historical and ethnological commentary. 36 illustrations. 480pp. 5⅜ x 8½. 25967-6 Pa. $8.95

AN ENCYCLOPEDIA OF BATTLES: Accounts of Over 1,560 Battles from 1479 B.C. to the Present, David Eggenberger. Essential details of every major battle in recorded history from the first battle of Megiddo in 1479 B.C. to Grenada in 1984. List of Battle Maps. New Appendix covering the years 1967-1984. Index. 99 illustrations. 544pp. 6½ x 9¼. 24913-1 Pa. $14.95

SAILING ALONE AROUND THE WORLD, Captain Joshua Slocum. First man to sail around the world, alone, in small boat. One of great feats of seamanship told in delightful manner. 67 illustrations. 294pp. 5⅜ x 8½. 20326-3 Pa. $5.95

ANARCHISM AND OTHER ESSAYS, Emma Goldman. Powerful, penetrating, prophetic essays on direct action, role of minorities, prison reform, puritan hypocrisy, violence, etc. 271pp. 5⅜ x 8½. 22484-8 Pa. $6.95

MYTHS OF THE HINDUS AND BUDDHISTS, Ananda K. Coomaraswamy and Sister Nivedita. Great stories of the epics; deeds of Krishna, Shiva, taken from puranas, Vedas, folk tales; etc. 32 illustrations. 400pp. 5⅜ x 8½. 21759-0 Pa. $10.95

BEYOND PSYCHOLOGY, Otto Rank. Fear of death, desire of immortality, nature of sexuality, social organization, creativity, according to Rankian system. 291pp. 5⅜ x 8½. 20485-5 Pa. $8.95

A THEOLOGICO-POLITICAL TREATISE, Benedict Spinoza. Also contains unfinished Political Treatise. Great classic on religious liberty, theory of government on common consent. R. Elwes translation. Total of 421pp. 5⅜ x 8½. 20249-6 Pa. $9.95

EARLY NINETEENTH-CENTURY CRAFTS AND TRADES, Peter Stockham (ed.). Extremely rare 1807 volume describes to youngsters the crafts and trades of the day: brickmaker, weaver, dressmaker, bookbinder, ropemaker, saddler, many more. Quaint prose, charming illustrations for each craft. 20 black-and-white line illustrations. 192pp. 4⅝ x 6.   27293-1 Pa. $4.95

VICTORIAN FASHIONS AND COSTUMES FROM HARPER'S BAZAR, 1867–1898, Stella Blum (ed.). Day costumes, evening wear, sports clothes, shoes, hats, other accessories in over 1,000 detailed engravings. 320pp. 9⅜ x 12¼.
22990-4 Pa. $14.95

GUSTAV STICKLEY, THE CRAFTSMAN, Mary Ann Smith. Superb study surveys broad scope of Stickley's achievement, especially in architecture. Design philosophy, rise and fall of the Craftsman empire, descriptions and floor plans for many Craftsman houses, more. 86 black-and-white halftones. 31 line illustrations. Introduction 208pp. 6½ x 9¼.   27210-9 Pa. $9.95

THE LONG ISLAND RAIL ROAD IN EARLY PHOTOGRAPHS, Ron Ziel. Over 220 rare photos, informative text document origin (1844) and development of rail service on Long Island. Vintage views of early trains, locomotives, stations, passengers, crews, much more. Captions. 8⅞ x 11¾.   26301-0 Pa. $13.95

THE BOOK OF OLD SHIPS: From Egyptian Galleys to Clipper Ships, Henry B. Culver. Superb, authoritative history of sailing vessels, with 80 magnificent line illustrations. Galley, bark, caravel, longship, whaler, many more. Detailed, informative text on each vessel by noted naval historian. Introduction. 256pp. 5⅜ x 8½.
27332-6 Pa. $7.95

TEN BOOKS ON ARCHITECTURE, Vitruvius. The most important book ever written on architecture. Early Roman aesthetics, technology, classical orders, site selection, all other aspects. Morgan translation. 331pp. 5⅜ x 8½. 20645-9 Pa. $8.95

THE HUMAN FIGURE IN MOTION, Eadweard Muybridge. More than 4,500 stopped-action photos, in action series, showing undraped men, women, children jumping, lying down, throwing, sitting, wrestling, carrying, etc. 390pp. 7⅞ x 10⅝.
20204-6 Clothbd. $25.95

TREES OF THE EASTERN AND CENTRAL UNITED STATES AND CANADA, William M. Harlow. Best one-volume guide to 140 trees. Full descriptions, woodlore, range, etc. Over 600 illustrations. Handy size. 288pp. 4½ x 6⅜.
20395-6 Pa. $6.95

SONGS OF WESTERN BIRDS, Dr. Donald J. Borror. Complete song and call repertoire of 60 western species, including flycatchers, juncoes, cactus wrens, many more–includes fully illustrated booklet.   Cassette and manual 99913-0 $8.95

GROWING AND USING HERBS AND SPICES, Milo Miloradovich. Versatile handbook provides all the information needed for cultivation and use of all the herbs and spices available in North America. 4 illustrations. Index. Glossary. 236pp. 5⅜ x 8½.
25058-X Pa. $6.95

BIG BOOK OF MAZES AND LABYRINTHS, Walter Shepherd. 50 mazes and labyrinths in all–classical, solid, ripple, and more–in one great volume. Perfect inexpensive puzzler for clever youngsters. Full solutions. 112pp. 8⅛ x 11.
22951-3 Pa. $4.95

CATALOG OF DOVER BOOKS

PIANO TUNING, J. Cree Fischer. Clearest, best book for beginner, amateur. Simple repairs, raising dropped notes, tuning by easy method of flattened fifths. No previous skills needed. 4 illustrations. 201pp. 5⅜ x 8½.   23267-0 Pa. $6.95

A SOURCE BOOK IN THEATRICAL HISTORY, A. M. Nagler. Contemporary observers on acting, directing, make-up, costuming, stage props, machinery, scene design, from Ancient Greece to Chekhov. 611pp. 5⅜ x 8½.   20515-0 Pa. $12.95

THE COMPLETE NONSENSE OF EDWARD LEAR, Edward Lear. All nonsense limericks, zany alphabets, Owl and Pussycat, songs, nonsense botany, etc., illustrated by Lear. Total of 320pp. 5⅜ x 8½. (USO)   20167-8 Pa. $6.95

VICTORIAN PARLOUR POETRY: An Annotated Anthology, Michael R. Turner. 117 gems by Longfellow, Tennyson, Browning, many lesser-known poets. "The Village Blacksmith," "Curfew Must Not Ring Tonight," "Only a Baby Small," dozens more, often difficult to find elsewhere. Index of poets, titles, first lines. xxiii + 325pp. 5⅜ x 8¼.   27044-0 Pa. $8.95

DUBLINERS, James Joyce. Fifteen stories offer vivid, tightly focused observations of the lives of Dublin's poorer classes. At least one, "The Dead," is considered a masterpiece. Reprinted complete and unabridged from standard edition. 160pp. 5³⁄₁₆ x 8¼.
26870-5 Pa. $1.00

THE HAUNTED MONASTERY and THE CHINESE MAZE MURDERS, Robert van Gulik. Two full novels by van Gulik, set in 7th-century China, continue adventures of Judge Dee and his companions. An evil Taoist monastery, seemingly supernatural events; overgrown topiary maze hides strange crimes. 27 illustrations. 328pp. 5⅜ x 8½.   23502-5 Pa. $8.95

THE BOOK OF THE SACRED MAGIC OF ABRAMELIN THE MAGE, translated by S. MacGregor Mathers. Medieval manuscript of ceremonial magic. Basic document in Aleister Crowley, Golden Dawn groups. 268pp. 5⅜ x 8½.
23211-5 Pa. $8.95

NEW RUSSIAN-ENGLISH AND ENGLISH-RUSSIAN DICTIONARY, M. A. O'Brien. This is a remarkably handy Russian dictionary, containing a surprising amount of information, including over 70,000 entries. 366pp. 4½ x 6¼.
20208-9 Pa. $9.95

HISTORIC HOMES OF THE AMERICAN PRESIDENTS, Second, Revised Edition, Irvin Haas. A traveler's guide to American Presidential homes, most open to the public, depicting and describing homes occupied by every American President from George Washington to George Bush. With visiting hours, admission charges, travel routes. 175 photographs. Index. 160pp. 8¼ x 11.   26751-2 Pa. $11.95

NEW YORK IN THE FORTIES, Andreas Feininger. 162 brilliant photographs by the well-known photographer, formerly with *Life* magazine. Commuters, shoppers, Times Square at night, much else from city at its peak. Captions by John von Hartz. 181pp. 9¼ x 10¾.   23585-8 Pa. $12.95

INDIAN SIGN LANGUAGE, William Tomkins. Over 525 signs developed by Sioux and other tribes. Written instructions and diagrams. Also 290 pictographs. 111pp. 6⅛ x 9¼.   22029-X Pa. $3.95

CATALOG OF DOVER BOOKS

ANATOMY: A Complete Guide for Artists, Joseph Sheppard. A master of figure drawing shows artists how to render human anatomy convincingly. Over 460 illustrations. 224pp. 8⅜ x 11¼. 27279-6 Pa. $10.95

MEDIEVAL CALLIGRAPHY: Its History and Technique, Marc Drogin. Spirited history, comprehensive instruction manual covers 13 styles (ca. 4th century thru 15th). Excellent photographs; directions for duplicating medieval techniques with modern tools. 224pp. 8⅜ x 11¼. 26142-5 Pa. $12.95

DRIED FLOWERS: How to Prepare Them, Sarah Whitlock and Martha Rankin. Complete instructions on how to use silica gel, meal and borax, perlite aggregate, sand and borax, glycerine and water to create attractive permanent flower arrangements. 12 illustrations. 32pp. 5⅜ x 8½. 21802-3 Pa. $1.00

EASY-TO-MAKE BIRD FEEDERS FOR WOODWORKERS, Scott D. Campbell. Detailed, simple-to-use guide for designing, constructing, caring for and using feeders. Text, illustrations for 12 classic and contemporary designs. 96pp. 5⅜ x 8½. 25847-5 Pa. $2.95

SCOTTISH WONDER TALES FROM MYTH AND LEGEND, Donald A. Mackenzie. 16 lively tales tell of giants rumbling down mountainsides, of a magic wand that turns stone pillars into warriors, of gods and goddesses, evil hags, powerful forces and more. 240pp. 5⅜ x 8½. 29677-6 Pa. $6.95

THE HISTORY OF UNDERCLOTHES, C. Willett Cunnington and Phyllis Cunnington. Fascinating, well-documented survey covering six centuries of English undergarments, enhanced with over 100 illustrations: 12th-century laced-up bodice, footed long drawers (1795), 19th-century bustles, 19th-century corsets for men, Victorian "bust improvers," much more. 272pp. 5⅜ x 8¼. 27124-2 Pa. $9.95

ARTS AND CRAFTS FURNITURE: The Complete Brooks Catalog of 1912, Brooks Manufacturing Co. Photos and detailed descriptions of more than 150 now very collectible furniture designs from the Arts and Crafts movement depict davenports, settees, buffets, desks, tables, chairs, bedsteads, dressers and more, all built of solid, quarter-sawed oak. Invaluable for students and enthusiasts of antiques, Americana and the decorative arts. 80pp. 6½ x 9¼. 27471-3 Pa. $8.95

HOW WE INVENTED THE AIRPLANE: An Illustrated History, Orville Wright. Fascinating firsthand account covers early experiments, construction of planes and motors, first flights, much more. Introduction and commentary by Fred C. Kelly. 76 photographs. 96pp. 8¼ x 11. 25662-6 Pa. $8.95

THE ARTS OF THE SAILOR: Knotting, Splicing and Ropework, Hervey Garrett Smith. Indispensable shipboard reference covers tools, basic knots and useful hitches; handsewing and canvas work, more. Over 100 illustrations. Delightful reading for sea lovers. 256pp. 5⅜ x 8½. 26440-8 Pa. $7.95

FRANK LLOYD WRIGHT'S FALLINGWATER: The House and Its History, Second, Revised Edition, Donald Hoffmann. A total revision—both in text and illustrations—of the standard document on Fallingwater, the boldest, most personal architectural statement of Wright's mature years, updated with valuable new material from the recently opened Frank Lloyd Wright Archives. "Fascinating"—*The New York Times*. 116 illustrations. 128pp. 9¼ x 10¾. 27430-6 Pa. $11.95

PHOTOGRAPHIC SKETCHBOOK OF THE CIVIL WAR, Alexander Gardner. 100 photos taken on field during the Civil War. Famous shots of Manassas Harper's Ferry, Lincoln, Richmond, slave pens, etc. 244pp. 10⅝ x 8¼.   22731-6 Pa. $9.95

FIVE ACRES AND INDEPENDENCE, Maurice G. Kains. Great back-to-the-land classic explains basics of self-sufficient farming. The one book to get. 95 illustrations. 397pp. 5⅜ x 8½.   20974-1 Pa. $7.95

SONGS OF EASTERN BIRDS, Dr. Donald J. Borror. Songs and calls of 60 species most common to eastern U.S.: warblers, woodpeckers, flycatchers, thrushes, larks, many more in high-quality recording.   Cassette and manual 99912-2 $9.95

A MODERN HERBAL, Margaret Grieve. Much the fullest, most exact, most useful compilation of herbal material. Gigantic alphabetical encyclopedia, from aconite to zedoary, gives botanical information, medical properties, folklore, economic uses, much else. Indispensable to serious reader. 161 illustrations. 888pp. 6½ x 9¼. 2-vol. set. (USO)   Vol. I: 22798-7 Pa. $9.95
          Vol. II: 22799-5 Pa. $9.95

HIDDEN TREASURE MAZE BOOK, Dave Phillips. Solve 34 challenging mazes accompanied by heroic tales of adventure. Evil dragons, people-eating plants, blood-thirsty giants, many more dangerous adversaries lurk at every twist and turn. 34 mazes, stories, solutions. 48pp. 8¼ x 11.   24566-7 Pa. $2.95

LETTERS OF W. A. MOZART, Wolfgang A. Mozart. Remarkable letters show bawdy wit, humor, imagination, musical insights, contemporary musical world; includes some letters from Leopold Mozart. 276pp. 5⅜ x 8½.   22859-2 Pa. $7.95

BASIC PRINCIPLES OF CLASSICAL BALLET, Agrippina Vaganova. Great Russian theoretician, teacher explains methods for teaching classical ballet. 118 illustrations. 175pp. 5⅜ x 8½.   22036-2 Pa. $5.95

THE JUMPING FROG, Mark Twain. Revenge edition. The original story of The Celebrated Jumping Frog of Calaveras County, a hapless French translation, and Twain's hilarious "retranslation" from the French. 12 illustrations. 66pp. 5⅜ x 8½.   22686-7 Pa. $3.95

BEST REMEMBERED POEMS, Martin Gardner (ed.). The 126 poems in this superb collection of 19th- and 20th-century British and American verse range from Shelley's "To a Skylark" to the impassioned "Renascence" of Edna St. Vincent Millay and to Edward Lear's whimsical "The Owl and the Pussycat." 224pp. 5⅜ x 8½.   27165-X Pa. $4.95

COMPLETE SONNETS, William Shakespeare. Over 150 exquisite poems deal with love, friendship, the tyranny of time, beauty's evanescence, death and other themes in language of remarkable power, precision and beauty. Glossary of archaic terms. 80pp. 5³⁄₁₆ x 8¼.   26686-9 Pa. $1.00

BODIES IN A BOOKSHOP, R. T. Campbell. Challenging mystery of blackmail and murder with ingenious plot and superbly drawn characters. In the best tradition of British suspense fiction. 192pp. 5⅜ x 8½.   24720-1 Pa. $6.95

THE INFLUENCE OF SEA POWER UPON HISTORY, 1660–1783, A. T. Mahan. Influential classic of naval history and tactics still used as text in war colleges. First paperback edition. 4 maps. 24 battle plans. 640pp. 5⅜ x 8½. 25509-3 Pa. $12.95

THE STORY OF THE TITANIC AS TOLD BY ITS SURVIVORS, Jack Winocour (ed.). What it was really like. Panic, despair, shocking inefficiency, and a little heroism. More thrilling than any fictional account. 26 illustrations. 320pp. 5⅜ x 8½. 20610-6 Pa. $8.95

FAIRY AND FOLK TALES OF THE IRISH PEASANTRY, William Butler Yeats (ed.). Treasury of 64 tales from the twilight world of Celtic myth and legend: "The Soul Cages," "The Kildare Pooka," "King O'Toole and his Goose," many more. Introduction and Notes by W. B. Yeats. 352pp. 5⅜ x 8½. 26941-8 Pa. $8.95

BUDDHIST MAHAYANA TEXTS, E. B. Cowell and Others (eds.). Superb, accurate translations of basic documents in Mahayana Buddhism, highly important in history of religions. The Buddha-karita of Asvaghosha, Larger Sukhavativyuha, more. 448pp. 5⅜ x 8½. 25552-2 Pa. $12.95

ONE TWO THREE . . . INFINITY: Facts and Speculations of Science, George Gamow. Great physicist's fascinating, readable overview of contemporary science: number theory, relativity, fourth dimension, entropy, genes, atomic structure, much more. 128 illustrations. Index. 352pp. 5⅜ x 8½. 25664-2 Pa. $8.95

ENGINEERING IN HISTORY, Richard Shelton Kirby, et al. Broad, nontechnical survey of history's major technological advances: birth of Greek science, industrial revolution, electricity and applied science, 20th-century automation, much more. 181 illustrations. ". . . excellent . . ."–*Isis*. Bibliography. vii + 530pp. 5⅜ x 8¼. 26412-2 Pa. $14.95

DALÍ ON MODERN ART: The Cuckolds of Antiquated Modern Art, Salvador Dalí. Influential painter skewers modern art and its practitioners. Outrageous evaluations of Picasso, Cézanne, Turner, more. 15 renderings of paintings discussed. 44 calligraphic decorations by Dalí. 96pp. 5⅜ x 8½. (USO) 29220-7 Pa. $4.95

ANTIQUE PLAYING CARDS: A Pictorial History, Henry René D'Allemagne. Over 900 elaborate, decorative images from rare playing cards (14th–20th centuries): Bacchus, death, dancing dogs, hunting scenes, royal coats of arms, players cheating, much more. 96pp. 9¼ x 12¼. 29265-7 Pa. $11.95

MAKING FURNITURE MASTERPIECES: 30 Projects with Measured Drawings, Franklin H. Gottshall. Step-by-step instructions, illustrations for constructing handsome, useful pieces, among them a Sheraton desk, Chippendale chair, Spanish desk, Queen Anne table and a William and Mary dressing mirror. 224pp. 8⅛ x 11¼. 29338-6 Pa. $13.95

THE FOSSIL BOOK: A Record of Prehistoric Life, Patricia V. Rich et al. Profusely illustrated definitive guide covers everything from single-celled organisms and dinosaurs to birds and mammals and the interplay between climate and man. Over 1,500 illustrations. 760pp. 7½ x 10⅛. 29371-8 Pa. $29.95

Prices subject to change without notice.

Available at your book dealer or write for free catalog to Dept. GI, Dover Publications, Inc., 31 East 2nd St., Mineola, N.Y. 11501. Dover publishes more than 500 books each year on science, elementary and advanced mathematics, biology, music, art, literary history, social sciences and other areas.